KT-455-496

Environmental Law and Ethics

John Alder
Newcastle Law School, University of Newcastle
and
David Wilkinson
School of Law, Keele University

With Chapter 11 contributed by Ilona Cheyne, Newcastle Law School

Law Series editor: Marise Cremona

MACMILLAN

© John Alder and David Wilkinson 1999

All rights reserved. No reproduction, copy or transmission of this publication may be made without written permission.

No paragraph of this publication may be reproduced, copied or transmitted save with written permission or in accordance with the provisions of the Copyright, Designs and Patents Act 1988, or under the terms of any licence permitting limited copying issued by the Copyright Licensing agency, 90 Tottenham Court Road, London, W1P 9HE.

Any person who does any unauthorised act in relation to this publication may be liable to criminal prosecution and civil claims for damages.

The authors have asserted their rights to be identified as the authors of this work in accordance with the Copyright, Designs and Patents Act 1988.

Published by
MACMILLAN PRESS LTD
Houndmills, Basingstoke, Hampshire RG21 6XS
and London
Companies and representatives
throughout the world

ISBN 0-333-67491-X

A catalogue record for this book is available
from the British Library.

This book is printed on paper suitable for recycling
and made from fully managed and sustained forest sources.

Printed and bound in Great Britain by
Creative Print and Design (Wales), Ebbw Vale

10 9   8   7   6   5   4   3   2   1
08 07   06   05   04   03   02   01   00   99

UNIVERSITY OF PLYMOUTH

Item No.   900 450419 - 0

Date   2 6 OCT 2000   B

Class No.   344. 046 ALD

Contl. No.

LIBRARY SERVICES

90 0450419 0

Environmental Law and Ethics

Macmillan Law Masters

Series editor Marise Cremona

Contents

Preface

In recent years there has been a huge increase in interest in general principles of environmental law and in the field of environmental ethics. In its initial stages, environmental law was primarily a pragmatic mix of property law, tort, planning law, public health regulation and other established areas of law applied to environmental problems. As the subject has matured, general principles have emerged and environmental law has taken on a respectable identity of its own. At the same time, environmental ethics has developed from a fringe area of philosophical exotica to a subject of fundamental and practical importance in determining the proper relationship between humans and nature.

This book discusses the main competing perspectives on environmental ethics and attempts to identify some of their legal implications. It is not intended to be a primary environmental law textbook. There are several excellent texts available which perform that function. Rather, this book is meant to complement the standard texts by placing environmental law in its ethical context.

Ethical theories focus upon notions of 'moral status'.Whom or what should we respect as having moral value? Our starting point is to look at what people actually value. Most people accept that human beings have moral status but there is no agreement as to why this should be so. A strong element of our culture is the belief that has profoundly influenced human thought since ancient times, that human beings have superior moral status to the rest of nature and that the rest of nature is a resource which we are free to plunder and treat as a life-support machine.

Some environmentalists argue that humans are rightly the proper focus for morality because morality is based on communication between equals. Others argue that it is arbitrary, if not obnoxious, to confine moral status to human beings. Their difficulty lies in deciding where to draw the line. Diverse criteria, for example rationality, ability to suffer, sense of purpose, life itself and order, are deployed. This extends moral concern ever wider into nature but leads to incoherence and sometimes favours beings with which we have emotional affinity such as attractive or intelligent animals. Different ethical perspectives may be useful in different contexts and there is no overarching guide as to which is the right one.

The most general ethical issue is how far we are entitled to 'harm' nature for our own benefit. There is also the question of whether we owe duties to future generations and of social justice between rich and poor. Poverty leads to environmental degradation and the poor bear a disproportionate share of the costs of environmental protection. How do we balance economic values such as free trade, environmental values and social values – the problem of sustainable development? Different kinds of environmental interest also conflict, for example the culling of animals in the interests of ecological balance against animal rights? Are we entitled to enhance nature by 'improving' natural landscapes or the genetic engineering of species or should we leave nature alone? These are the kinds of questions that we shall examine in this book using the law as our medium.

We do no attempt to suggest any 'right' ethical solution. The law is not a transmission belt for any particular ethical theory. Indeed given the controversial nature of environmental ethics this would be unrealistic. In terms of their legal implications the various ethical perspectives sometimes conflict and sometimes coincide but we hope that any legal decision can be justified by at least one of them. Each of the competing perspectives may be valid on its own terms so that a political choice may have to be made between them. Environmental ethics offers us a tool which helps us to identify common ground or irreconcilable differences.

Furthermore, as the Royal Commission on Environmental Pollution recently pointed out (1998), it is important to distinguish between arguments that are scientific or economic and arguments that are social and political to which we would add ethical arguments. The danger of confusing these types of argument arises particularly in the contexts of risk analysis and economic cost-benefit analysis. Much of English environmental law gives wide discretion to officials the law itself being consistent with a number of ethical perspectives. Questions therefore arise as to how far officials have common ethical values (regulatory culture) and whether the courts play a part in shaping the ethical element of discretionary power law through the law of judicial review.

We have not covered all legal topics in equal depth. We have selected areas of law which we think have particular significance in bringing out ethical dilemmas; within these the treatment of the substantive law varies according to the ethical issues involved. Nevertheless, we have tried to include sufficient legal material to provide a map of the main areas of environmental law. We have concentrated mainly on English law but have included important international and European law principles which are the driving forces of much of UK environmental law.

We do not assume that the typical reader will have any pre-existing knowledge of environmental philosophy and have tried to explain and evaluate the general perspectives offered by the main writers on the subject. We hope the book will be suitable for students of law, environmental studies, political science and philosophy. A substantial bibliography has been provided as an aid to further research. A more selective guide to further reading is provided at the end of each chapter. The references in the text provide detailed sources but are not intended to distract the reader from the flow of the narrative which we hope is self-contained.

The scheme of the book is to start with a general discussion of different perspectives (ethical, economic, political, cultural) followed by a more detailed examination of the main ethical theories. We then move to a discussion of the international, European and UK institutional/policy framework. After a chapter outlining the main legal devices that are available for environmental control including such matters as integrated pollution control and 'market instruments' we single out specific areas of law for more detailed discussion. These are property law, animal rights and nature conservation, waste, and international trade. Waste is given a fuller substantive treatment due to the complexity of the law. We finish the book with a discussion of environmental rights.

We would like to acknowledge the help and assistance of the following, whose patient answers to our queries and willingness to engage in discussions has been of great benefit and encouragement: Ian Dawson, Alf Ellis, Agustin Garcia-Ureta, David Harte, Patsy Healey, Chris Miller, Richard Mullender, Carl Muller, Patricia Park, John Proops, Sandrine Simon. We owe a particular debt of gratitude to Ilona Cheyne for contributing the chapter on international trade law. We would also like to thank Ian Mabbutt and David Milroy for helping to compile the bibliography under Newcastle Law School's student research assistantship scheme.

We have tried to include the law as it stood on 7 October 1998.

JOHN ALDER, DAVID WILKINSON
Newcastle/Keele 7 October 1998

Table of Cases

Table of Legislation

EC Legislation

1 Introduction – Environmental Perspectives

Introduction – Ethical Issues

This chapter will introduce by way of background some basic issues that affect environmental law. We shall firstly outline some general ethical concerns. We shall then briefly introduce the notions of environment and pollution. We shall suggest possible relationships between law and ethics and sketch the evolution of environmental law. Finally we shall try to place the ethical issues against their political, social and economic background. In the following chapter we shall discuss particular ethical theories.

The point of environmental ethics is to understand what it means to act rightly in respect of nature. Environmental ethics help us to deal with clashes between competing interests and values and may help us to identify problems within the law. Environmental ethics may provide tools to identify what factors decision makers should take into account so that these factors can be balanced and choices made. Environmental issues are complex because many different interests collide often against an uncertain factual background including the long-term consequences of human activities in relation to the rest of nature. Environmental issues are particularly difficult for lawyers whose attention is usually focused on short-term human interests defined with relative precision.

Conflicts raised by environmental ethics are of many kinds. Firstly there are conflicts between economic development and conserving resources, which raise problems of social justice. These focus on the question of who should bear the costs of nature conservation. A superficially simple moral principle, that of the 'polluter pays', has been widely accepted but this raises problems of inequity between rich and poor. Environmental degradation is caused both by the rich nations who harness technology, to raise living standards and to entertain themselves, and by the poorer nations who overexploit natural resources in order to survive. The rich can to some extent insulate themselves from environmental damage. What moral right have environmentalists who enjoy the benefits of modern technology to deny the benefits of such technology to others? Why should people, who depend for example on hunting whales, sacrifice their livelihood while others cruelly exploit more common species in factory farms? Should we direct social housing away from the countryside to brownfield urban sites for the benefit of commuters, weekenders and retired people who enjoy a rural life-style, whose income derives from urban sources and whose public services are subsidised by urban dwellers? Should we compensate people who are forced to live near waste disposal sites who lose out because of environmental policies? We may regulate a factory to minimise pollution but the firm might relocate to a cheaper place in order to pollute more efficiently perhaps harming more vulnerable people. Should the misery be shared more equally?

Secondly there are conflicts between the moral and economic values of free trade between countries and environmental protection measures. To what extent is a state entitled to discriminate against imports from countries with lower environmental standards or to disadvantage other countries by giving its own businesses subsidies for environmental purposes? To what extent can the international community accept a common environmental ethic?

Thirdly there is the question of 'intergenerational equity'. Why should we suffer harm now for possible benefits to future generations of whom we know nothing and indeed who only come into existence because of choices we make? Are gains and losses to be discounted because they will occur a long time into the future? If one child's life could be saved immediately by using nuclear power instead of polluting coal power, is this worth more than say a 25% increase in risk of illness to thousands of people arising from nuclear pollution, in 100 years' time?

Fourthly there are conflicts between different kinds of environmental interest, and fifthly conflicts between different non-human species. Should we protect the environment out of concern for human well-being or should we regard ourselves merely as part of a larger natural community which requires us to respect other living things even against our own interests? Human health and amenity might clash with nature conservation, as was the case with the Twyford Down project near Winchester. The purpose of the project is to replace the existing bypass near to the town, which severs the town from its rural hinterland with a new road that was to run through a heathland area of great landscape value and host to rare species. One kind of environmental assessment might concentrate on the environmental benefits of less vehicle pollution and restoring tranquillity to the town. Another kind of assessment based on a different ethic might stress the importance of the heathland as terrain unspoiled by human beings. There may be conflicts between the welfare of individual creatures and the interests of groups such as species. Should we for example exterminate common grey squirrels in order to save the rare species of red squirrel? We like to protect dolphins, leopards and other animals that we admire but must we protect species such as slime mould or maggots, which appear to be no use or attraction to us?

There are few, if any, areas of life to which environmental concerns are irrelevant and environmental issues are usually interrelated. This raises the 'law of unintended consequences' according to which solutions to one problem may create others. For example wind turbines and wave barriers produce renewable energy but might kill birds, destroy habitats, and damage landscapes. Technology used to combat pollution, for example waste recycling, may create its own pollution and certainly uses up energy. The health problems of the third world, for example poor quality water and smoke pollution caused by burning dung for fuel can be alleviated by the kind of modern technology that causes greenhouse gas emissions. We might clean up the beach and in so doing kill millions of creatures some of them rare.

Modern environmental law recognises that the environmental issues of pollution and nature conservation are interrelated. Discussion centres upon three related themes. The first is how far the earth can continue to be used as a receptacle for human waste. The second is how far can the energy resources of the earth last out. The third is that of the value of non-human life and of biological diversity and whether it is desirable to leave natural processes alone. These concerns raise questions about the dominant philosophy of western civilisation of exploiting nature for human benefit and may require us to think about basic legal concepts in a new way.

Why Should We Value Nature?

We may value nature only as an instrument of human welfare for life support, waste disposal and entertainment and some ethical perspectives concentrate on this. At the other extreme it can be argued that we are part of a wider community of all living things and that there is no reason other than selfish 'speciesism' to put our own interests first. Accordingly we must value nature for its own sake irrespective of human interests. Humans are apparently unique in having a moral sense and this imposes grave responsibilities on us to our fellow living beings as self-appointed environmental police.

However, those who claim that we should value nature for its own sake face problems. Nature is indifferent to us and cannot communicate with us. Can nature have 'interests' in any intelligible sense independently of human concerns? If we give animals and natural objects moral interests are we not treating nature as a ventriloquist's dummy attributing to it values that have meaning only in relation to ourselves? Wittgenstein pointed out that if a lion could talk we would not understand him

(*Philosophical Investigations II*, xi, p. 225). We may plausibly assume that it is in the interests of living things to flourish and we can make a reasonable guess as the interests of creatures that seem to have characteristics similar to our own but environmental purists might regard this as 'speciesism' (see Pluhar, 1995). If you were the last survivor of the human race would it be morally acceptable to enjoy yourself by devastating the forest?

This issue is sometimes discussed in terms of three kinds of moral value that can be attributed to nature. Firstly there is 'instrumental' value which comprises the value of nature as a human resource. Instrumentally we might think it right to slaughter fish for our own consumption up to the limits of maximum sustainable yield so as to keep the fish 'stock' replenished. Secondly there is 'existence' value. This means the value, again to humans, of the mere existence of something even if it serves no other purpose, for example a beautiful landscape.(It could possibly be argued that existence value is merely another kind of instrumental value.) Thirdly there is 'intrinsic' or 'inherent' value. This is the more controversial idea at the centre of environmental ethics that nature has value in itself completely independently of human beings even though the very concept of value is, or seems to be a figment of the human mind.

Humans as Part of Nature

How do we distinguish what is 'natural' from our own activities? In nature species are constantly at war with each other and millions of species have come and gone during the history of the earth. Natural processes by definition involve living beings changing their environment and human beings are merely doing so on a larger scale and more quickly than any other creature. There is evidence that, from the start of the human industrial era 200 years ago, other species have disappeared at a faster rate than ever before except in periods of cataclysm and even these do not seem to have caused harm to the earth as a whole (see Kunich, 1991). All living things alter natural processes but humans have done so to such an extent that it is at least possible that we are damaging any natural balance. However, in itself this may not entail any moral conclusions. Conflicts between species are natural and the extinction of species seems to be a permanent and natural feature of life.

We might therefore adopt the position that, as part of nature, we are entitled to pursue our own goals and that nature must take care of itself arguing that in principle our interventions are no different from any other natural events. On this view we can conserve nature only as far as it meets our needs to do so. For example climatic change, global warming and loss of biodiversity *may* threaten human civilisation. Being imprisoned in our human point of view we have no idea of what, if anything, nature is meant to be like. Is it in a state of balance or running down to destruction? Is it good to have many species? Unless we use our own interests as a benchmark how can we ever tell? We do not know whether the proliferation of species is good or bad. Nature is constantly changing, destroying and creating. Humans are part of nature and as predators we are doing what is natural to us. Why should it matter that we are destroying other species unless in doing so we harm ourselves?

On the other hand we might see ourselves as separate from the rest of nature because of our apparently unique capacity for reason and self-awareness. This might entitle us to act as trustees for the interests of other living things and to some extent against our own interests (rather like co-owners of the family home). An extreme version of this would regard human beings as a kind of cancer because of our ability to interfere deliberately with natural processes. It is arguable that our complex, unstable and highly active brains have made the human race a dysfunctional part of nature. On this view, while we might not be required to exterminate ourselves, we would have a duty to minimise the harm we cause.

Balancing Interests – Incommensurables and Uncombinables

Decision makers sometimes have to sacrifice one good for another greater good. The broader our area of environmental concern the more difficult becomes the balancing act. The core environmental objectives have been summarised as:

1   minimising harm to ecosystems and habitats;
2   establishing sustainable patterns of resource use;
3   minimising harm to human health;
4   maximisation of wild space and ecological diversity (Gillroy, 1993, p. 47).

These principles are too general to be applied directly and may conflict with each other. For example forests comprising quick growing conifers are highly sustainable in terms of the timber industry but are not good habitats for wildlife compared with old mixed woodlands.

Conflict between different ethical values is likely to confuse the process of making and interpreting the law. Take for example the question of whether we should protect the elephant as an endangered species. We must line up the interests involved. These include at least the following:

1   the value of living elephants to tourism, hunting and other means of employment and wealth creation;
2   the damage caused by elephants to local farmers;
3   the advantages of the very profitable ivory trade in dead elephants in bringing wealth to a poor country which can be invested in social and environmental projects;
4   the expense of policing any system of conservation, e.g. game wardens and culling;
5   the cruelty of killing individual elephants;
6   the damage caused by elephants to the ecosystem unless the population is controlled;
7   scientific knowledge;
8   conserving the gene pool;
9   human happiness at the existence of the elephant;
10   moral respect for life;
11   uncertainty as to the possible and likely outcomes of our actions;
12   the irreversible nature of our decisions.

A common measure of value would be a useful way to resolve differences between conflicting claims. Is there any common currency in which to compare the issues we outlined in relation to the elephant? Policy makers generally use economic methods that involve cost-benefit analysis. These suppose that the good and bad of interfering with the environment can be expressed in money terms and, of course, commit us to a view of nature that concentrates on human interests. In this context the difference between 'incommensurability' and 'uncombinability' is important and will raise issues throughout the book. In particular the important policy of sustainable development depends on an assumption that environmental good is combinable with other good since sustainable development claims that it is possible to enjoy human economic development and a good environment at the same time and over a long time period.

Incommensurability refers to values. As Isiah Berlin has famously argued (Berlin, 1968, 1990), ethical values are sometimes incommensurable in the sense that each in itself is objectively valid but they cannot logically be reconciled with each other because they are not amenable to ranking on a common scale. In other words there are irreducible conflicts among goods and we have to accept 'tragic choices' in the sense that we can sometimes achieve one goal only at the expense of another. For example, environmental protection and liberal democracy are probably incommensurable and it is arguable that environmental protection and economic values are incommensurable.

Incommensurability does not necessarily mean that moral values are subjective and relative. Berlin argues that there are ethical perspectives each of which is true in its own context but they may be mutually inconsistent because they serve different but equally valid goals. '(T)hough their embodiments in specific forms of life will vary across cultures, ultimate values are objective and universal – as are conflicts among them' (Gray, 1993, p. 66). For example freedom of information cannot be reconciled with a right to privacy although both may be of value. Culling animals to strengthen a rare species is incommensurable with animal rights.

Incommensurability should be distinguished from 'uncombinablity'. Uncombinability is about practical possibilities and applies whether or not interests can be compared on a common scale but where they cannot each be fully satisfied in a single person or group because for example of limited resources (see Raz, 1986; Gray, 1993, p. 301). More of one means less of the other. For example the interests of a factory to boost its production may be uncombinable with the interests of the local neighbours to be free of pollution. Issues of uncombinability may sometimes be expressed in money terms and resolved by techniques of cost-benefit analysis to produce a solution that maximises overall welfare.

There is no necessary connection between incommensurability and uncombinability. For example incommensurable goods might if you are lucky be combined. Liberal democracy might be mobilised towards environmental goods. The rescue of a member of a rare species might happily combine the animal rights and ecocentric ethics and sustainable forestry combines respecting species (but not individual trees) with human well being. On the other hand housing need and the amenities of the countryside for human tourism are commensurable but incombinable. The use of wind turbines as a source of renewable energy is uncombinable with landscape amenity and both incommensurable and uncombinable with wildlife welfare (see *North Devon D.C.* v. *West Coast Wind Farms* [1996] JPL 868).

The wider our ethical concerns the more likely we are to meet incommensurables. For example for how long, if at all, should a power station be shut down so as to rescue a seal that has found its way into the cooling tank? The costs of closing the power station can be calculated in money terms but can the life of the seal? Where we are faced with incommensurables that are also uncombinable the decision maker is forced to make a subjective judgement – a 'tragic choice' that can be justified only by reference to political acceptability. Conversely a court or other decision maker might narrow the focus of a case by excluding moral concerns thus turning the problem into one of incombinables and making it easier to handle (e.g. *R. v. Somerset County Council ex parte Fewings* [1995] 3 All ER 20).

The Meaning of Environment and Related Concepts – Underlying Assumptions

The term 'environment' expresses an assumption that we are in some sense apart from our surroundings. This goes against the grain of some kinds of environmental thinking which stresses that human beings are part of nature and believe that our problems are the result of an arrogant belief that our intelligence entitles us to rule over nature. Indeed it has been suggested that domestic animals and cattle are not part of nature at all in as much as we produce them for our purposes just as we do artefacts such as tables and chairs (see Holmes-Rolston III in Elliot, 1995). Ecology law might be a better label than environmental law.

The environment is usually defined in legislation in open-ended terms to include the natural media of land, air and water. It sometimes includes flora and fauna and the interaction between the natural media and living things and may also include the cultural heritage of the built environment. The Environmental Protection Act 1990 s.1(2) defines the environment as 'all or any of the following media, namely the air, water and land'. Thus living things within the media are not part of the environment but may have interests that are affected by the state of the environment (see also EC Directive 85/337, *The Assessment of the Effect of Certain Public and Private Projects on the Environment*). By contrast, Section 2(1) of the Resource Management Act of New Zealand targets the term environment more precisely as including:

(a) Ecosystems and their constituent parts, including people and communities; and
(b) All natural and physical resources; and
(c) Amenity values; and
(d) The social, economic, aesthetic, and cultural conditions which affect the matters stated in paragraphs (a) to (c) of this definition or which are affected by those matters. 'Natural and physical resources' includes land, water, air, soil, minerals, and energy, all forms of plants and animals (whether native to New Zealand or introduced), and all structures.

It is important to emphasise, as the New Zealand Act does, the interaction between the different elements that make up the environment since the environment is a socially constructed idea that depends upon our purposes. In this sense the environment means the complex of natural objects and forces within which we live and which both limits and supports our development. We are part of the environment and inhabit social and political environments, local and global environments, physical and cultural environments. We also inhabit different environments for different purposes, family environments, work environments, social environments. Each of us gives the environment meaning depending on our particular purposes and beliefs. For example farmers may depict nature in a different way than weekend residents in the countryside, the former but not the latter regarding uncultivated land as waste.

Lawyers encapsulate a similar subjective approach when they talk of the 'curtilage' of a building meaning the ground which is used for the comfortable enjoyment of the building (see *Sinclair-Lockhart's Trustees* v. *Central Land Board*, 1951). Similarly, in the law of Town and Country Planning, the unit to be looked at to see whether planning permission is required is not an objectively determined geographical area but a unit of activity defined by the purposes of the occupier (see *Burdle* v. *Secretary of State*, [1972], 3 All ER 240). On a more general level the environmental policy of the European Union has steadily evolved towards a holistic concept of the environment as being integrated into other policies.

Similarly the concept of pollution is a moral or at least a socially constructed concept. Pollution is often regarded as matter being in the 'wrong' place in excessive quantities. It is highly unlikely that anything in nature is absolutely pure so that what counts for example as water pollution depends upon a social judgement relating to the proper use of the water and is therefore an ethical question. (See *A.G. of New Zealand* v. *Lower Hutt City Corporation* [1964] AC 1469 at 1481; *Young* v. *Bankier Distillary* [1893] AC 691; Caldwell, 1992; Tarlock, 1996.)

The common law seems to define pollution broadly as including any 'sensible' alteration in the quality or quantity of a substance (see *Young* v. *Bankier Distillary* [1893] AC 691). Modern legislation, however, concentrates on the notion of harm. This is usually defined broadly as opening the way to a range of ethical perspectives. For example the Nitrates Directive (91/676 EEC, Art 2(j)) refers to 'hazards to the human health, harm to living resources and to aquatic ecosystems, damage to amenities or interference with other legitimate uses of water'. The Environment Protection Act (EPA) 1990 s.1(2) defines pollution of the environment as 'pollution of the environment due to the release (into any environmental medium) from any process of substances which are capable of causing harm to man or to any other living organisms supported by the environment'. 'Harm' is defined to include 'offence' to any of man's 'senses' (EPA, 1990, s.1(4)). Does this include the aesthetic sense that is offended by the alteration of a favourite landscape? Definitions of harm vary with the context. For example section 78A(4), which applies to contaminated land control, defines harm as 'harm to the health of living organisms or other interference with the ecological system of which they form a part and in the case of man, includes harm to his property'. In the US case of *Babbit* v. *Sweet Homes Chapter of Communities for a Greater Oregon* (1996) 8 JEL 158, the US Supreme Court refused to limit the concept of 'harm' in the Endangered Species Act 1973 to injury to the species itself. The court held that the modification of nature including habitats was the harm that the Act addressed.

Whether something is harmful is therefore not objective but depends upon a value judgement that society would be better off without it. For example pollution caused by vehicle fumes could be seen as a problem or as a necessary price for individual freedom although there are extreme cases, for example pollution which causes children to be born malformed, which would universally be regarded as harm. Similarly there are different ways of evaluating acts done to the environment. A person who damages the environment might be regarded as not doing wrong but as experiencing a technical management or scientific problem. Alternatively environmental damage might be regarded as a crime or a sin. As we shall see, environmental law places wide discretion in the hands of officials so that there is room in these definitions for a wide variety of ethical approaches.

The notion of harm raises problems in relation to liability for damaging non-humans. Traditionally liability in tort relates only to human physical injury or property damage and consequential economic loss. To what extent for example can injury to wildlife or rare species be compensated? If the necessary legal peg is that animals or natural features are in some circumstances the objects of property rights, the measure of damages is unlikely to relate to the true environmental cost. This issue arises at several points in the book notably in connection with the polluter pays principle (Chapter 6), civil liability (Chapter 7) and environmental rights (Chapter 12).

Ethics and the Law

Why should lawyers concern themselves with environmental ethics? The law does not act as a transmission belt for particular ethical theories and there is no necessary connection between ethics and law. On the other hand law and ethics support each other. Ethical standards are a means of criticising the law and revealing its unstated value judgements. Uncertainties and conflicts in the law can often be traced to the absence of common ethical ground. A convincing ethical justification helps to make a law or a court's decision respected. Legal regulation, particularly if it allows negotiation between regulator and regulated may help to shape ethical attitudes. Ethical arguments can be used as ammunition in litigation. Shared ethical values help to co-ordinate the work of different agencies. An important task of the law is to ensure that different points of view get a fair hearing.

It is widely believed that there is no ethical master principle. The natural law theory formed in the pre- Christian world, according to which whatever is natural is right, was kept alive by Catholic morality but by the eighteenth century had been displaced by disputes as to whether morality could be objective at all. Grotius (1583–1645) who is regarded as the founder of modern international law, based his conception of law upon the specifically human capacity to reason and, as he saw it, to form social relationships. He did not accept that moral duties could be owed to non-humans.

The traditional answer to Grotius's point of view is to distinguish between moral agents and moral patients. As far as we know, only rational creatures can be moral agents so as to be aware of morality and make moral judgements. In this sense morality is a purely human creation. There is, however, no logical reason why those to whom we owe duties (moral patients) need to be capable of knowing whether we have broken them or need be members of the moral community themselves. For example it is difficult to deny that we owe moral duties to a newborn baby or even to a psychopath totally incapable of knowing right from wrong.

Whether or not we believe in natural law, it is difficult to deny that a law is likely to command more respect if it has a defensible ethical basis. In this connection the famous debate between Hart (1963) and Devlin (1965) is worth mentioning. Hart, following J.S. Mill, argued that the law should not intervene to enforce morality as such but should intervene only to prevent harm to others. Hart (1961), also argued in favour of a 'minimum content' theory of natural law. This is based upon the human desire to survive and upon our weakness and vulnerability within nature. Such an approach seems to emphasise the interdependence of humans and the rest of nature and could form the basis of an environmental ethic. Devlin regards a common morality as an essential binding force within society and therefore in principle as the law's business. A shared attitude to nature might therefore form the basis of environmental law.

Devlin does not, however, believe that the law has *carte blanche* to enforce all morality. Oppression is morally wrong and it may be oppressive to enforce some moral rules as law. There is a difference between private morality, for example what I feel I ought to do for wildlife and future generations and the possibly lower standards of the law. The law can impose standards of desirable conduct only in so far as they command substantial public acceptance and can be enforced in practice. On the other hand, it might be argued that the law should educate public opinion. An analogy is often drawn between environmental ethics and the ethics of sex and racial discrimination. Just as the law struggled over many years to make these forms of discrimination socially unacceptable so the law should advance to combat discrimination against non-human species.

Many of these points can be illustrated by the debate as to whether foxhunting should be banned (see Brooman and Legge, 1997, p. 297 *et seq*). The 'harm' analysis might draw attention to the suffering of the fox but would balance that against the pleasures of the open-air life, the role hunting is said to play in conservation and the economic harm to rural communities if a ban were in place. Many jobs depend on the hunt. There is also the possibility that if hunting were to be banned farmers might exterminate foxes in even more painful ways. The moral cohesion issue would centre upon whether hunting is essentially sadistic and therefore corrupting or whether love of countryside, and tradition outweigh its murderous aspects. Then the question arises, given the disagreement within society on the matter, whether law or persuasion are the better means of reform. Property rights and civil liberties are at stake. The hunting issue therefore casts light not only upon the role of law but on the conflict between different kinds of environmental value.

Ethical issues are important in the law of judicial review which is frequently used by environmental interests to challenge governmental decisions. In *Council of Civil Service Unions* v. *Minister for the Civil Service* [1984] 3 All ER 935 at 951 Lord Diplock said that a governmental decision was reviewable if among other things it was 'so outrageous in its defiance of.... accepted moral standards that no sensible person who had applied his mind to the question to be decided could have arrived at it'. This is a very stiff test and it is doubtful whether there is currently sufficient public agreement about environmental morality for such an argument to succeed.

It is clear that pollution and other environmental injuries are not widely regarded as absolute wrongs in the sense that for example rape is wrong. In *R.* v. *Somerset County Council ex parte Fewings* [1995] 3 All ER 20 which concerned the Council's decision to ban deer hunting on its land, Simon Brown LJ (at 32) thought that the council was entitled but not bound to take into account ethical arguments about cruelty to animals and, of course, the weight to be given to the ethical arguments is not a matter for the courts. However, in the court below, Laws J. thought that it was improper for a decision-making body to take into account its moral and ethical opinions unless moral concerns were 'part and parcel of the purposes for which the power in question is conferred' [1995] 1 All ER 513 at 526. The power to manage land under which the council was required to act had to be exercised for the 'benefit improvement or development of the area as a whole' and the judges were divided as to whether this included animal welfare. In the end the council's decision was quashed on the ground that it had not applied the statutory test at all. The Court of Appeal therefore did not have to commit itself on the question of what the test meant.

Ethical arguments are used by green interests in lobbying for law reform. As we have seen the green lobby is diverse and not always consistent. However, pressure groups and lawyers do not have to believe the theories that they espouse. From the legal and political point of view the question is not whether ethical theories are 'true' in isolation but whether they fit into a network of shared values and are persuasive and useful to advance a cause. We shall illustrate this in Chapter 11. For instance, concern for the preservation of endangered species is a useful strategy for holding up commercial development for the benefit of people who wish to preserve their life styles. It is therefore in the political interests of opponents of development to endanger as many species as possible rather than helping to make them safe and therefore no longer in need of protective laws. Conversely you may firmly believe in the principle of solidarity with nature but it might be tactically useful to defend the whale out of concern for the future of the whaling industry.

Ethical principles are also important in helping to co-ordinate the activities of the large number of governmental agencies that exercise regulatory powers in respect of the environment. These include the Departments of the Environment, Agriculture, Transport, Health and Trade, the Environment Agency (itself embracing what were previously separate bodies), The European Commission, local authorities, English Nature, The Countryside Commission and various more specialised agencies as well as 'non-governmental organisations' (NGOs) such as Friends of the Earth, Greenpeace, and the RSPB, which advise, lobby, and bring legal actions.

The different agencies, and indeed different professional groups within the agencies develop their own cultures, sometimes called regulatory or interpretative cultures which include the values and assumptions they bring to bear in their day-to-day work. Law is not an exact science and laws might be understood in different ways by, say, local planners than by lawyers. An awareness of underlying ethical values and controversies may help to co-ordinate these different cultures.

Moreover the culture of regulators is affected by the cultures of the different client groups with which they come into contact, for example farmers, traditional and modern, industrialists small and large, environmentalists, householders, judges and magistrates. Each of these groups may offer different or overlapping environmental perspectives there being a continuous struggle to capture or enrol the regulators. It has been argued for example that following the creation of the National Rivers Authority by the Water Act 1989 policy in respect of water pollution became more strongly influenced by ecological interests and public participation than had previously been the case and that this has caused a change in how agricultural pollution is moralised (see Lowe, 1997).

The Evolution of Environmental Law

English environmental law has developed as a series of pragmatic responses to crises or pressure from lobbies. The earliest environmental legislation concentrated on public health aspects of pollution and upon giving remedies to injured individuals and there is still a tendency to compartmentalise environmental issues. The court may have been thinking along these lines in *R.* v. *Secretary of State ex parte Duddridge* [1995] Env LR 151. This case concerned a possible risk of illness due to radiation from high voltage electricity cables which an electricity company proposed to install in north London. It was argued that in deciding whether to give his consent to the installation the Secretary of State should have applied the precautionary principle which requires action to protect the environment even if the harm is not scientifically proven. The court refused to treat the precautionary principle as part of English law saying that the precautionary principle concerned damage to the environment and not risks to human health (see also *R.* v. *Greenwich B.C. ex parte Williams* [1995], *Times*, 29 December for an example of a fragmented approach). Today we take a more holistic approach that recognises that environmental and social problems are interrelated.

In most areas of English law, general principles tend to emerge only at a later stage of development. Environmental law is no exception. Environmental law as a distinct subject was virtually unknown in Britain until the 1970s and general principles are only now beginning to emerge. Environmental worries surfaced at significant periods in economic history, for example in the 1890s, the 1920s, the late 1950s/early 1960s, the 1970s and the late 1980s/early 1990s. In each period there were different concerns.

The earlier periods were primarily concerned with public health and decent housing. A major landmark came with the introduction of general land use control in the form of the Town and Country Planning Act 1947 the main features of which remain today. The Act was not specifically concerned with environmental matters but provides a legal framework within which discretionary powers of control can be used for any purpose relating to land use (*Stringer* v. *Minister of Housing*, 1971). Indeed the concerns of the original legislators were with economic development and resource allocation in a contest of expansion (see Barlow, 1940; Scott, 1942). The introduction of 'green belt' policy in the mid-1950s could be regarded as recognising a distinct environmental interest.

Environmentalism as we understand it developed much earlier in the USA. During the late nineteenth century John Muir pioneered the idea of national parks as wilderness areas to be preserved against human intervention. By contrast, the English National Parks and Access to the Countryside Act of 1949 saw the environment essentially as a human resource. National parks were envisaged as amenity areas for recreation and people live and work within them. In the United Kingdom preservationist concerns were recognised as early as 1907 in the form of a private Act of that year which incorporated the National Trust but there were no significant public controls until after World War II.

The 1960s were at first preoccupied with local issues of participation in land use planning decisions particularly those affecting rural amenities (see, e.g. Town and Country Planning Act 1968). Later in the 1960s and early 1970s came the 'crisis of survival' which introduced a global dimension to environmental concerns. The biologist Rachel Carson's famous book, *Silent Spring*, first published in 1962 was arguably the initial stimulus to the modern environmental movement. *Silent Spring* attacked single-minded technological progress and in particular warned of the dangers of pesticides to many species. Carson represented nature as having an intrinsic value irrespective of human interests but, as we shall see, the question of whether nature has value in its own right is highly controversial.

The Stockholm Declaration of 1972 on the Human Environment marks the first modern attempt at general environmental international policy-making. The tone of Stockholm was firmly human centred emphasising the dependence of 'man' on the environment. During the 1970s apocalyptic fears were voiced of disaster for the human race seen as threatened by technology out of control, overpopulation, and profligate consumption. Reports appeared during this period warning of crisis and paving the way for the creation of general environmental principles such as sustainability and precaution (e.g. The Limits to Growth, Meadows *et al.*, 1974; Blueprint for Survival, *Ecologist*, 1971; see also Meadows, 1992). It was argued that industrial and population growth would inevitably use up the earth's energy resources, that pollution would lead to serious climatic changes and that technological solutions, for example recycling and catalytic converters used up energy and created pollution themselves (Irvine and Ponton, 1988). New moral attitudes about the relationship between human beings and nature were therefore needed. For example Hardin (1968) argued that the only way to safeguard the global commons such as air and water is to abandon some of our existing ethical values in favour of authoritarian regulation including population control: what he calls mutual coercion mutually agreed on.

The 'Global 2000' report in 1982 suggested that, without severe cutbacks in economic development or population, saturation point could be reached at the end of the twenty-first century with severe problems by the year 2000. The 'Global 2000' forecasts are today regarded as exaggerated. Earlier predictions about resource depletion underestimated both potential mineral resources and changing human technologies. The timescale can therefore be indefinitely extended but the basic concerns remain valid.

The significance of the 1970s is that, firstly environmental concerns became international, secondly the interdependence of the different elements of the environment became politically important and thirdly the limits of our scientific knowledge became apparent. We could no longer be confident that technical progress was necessarily good. These concerns were reinforced by the oil crisis of 1973/74, by the Torrey Canyon and Amoco Cadiz oil spills, and the Chernobyl nuclear power station and Bhopal chemical works disasters. Worries about global warming caused by greenhouse gases such as carbon dioxide and damage to the ozone layer also reached the political agenda. Nevertheless from the mid-1970s until the mid-1980s environmental policy in the UK remained sluggish and the law was the result of crisis management or reaction to specific problems and lobbies rather than a concern to develop general principles (see Osborn, 1997). The Control of Pollution Act 1974 was enacted which dealt separately with waste, water pollution and atmospheric pollution. By contrast ambitious and far-reaching legislation was introduced in the USA. This dealt with endangered species (Endangered Species Act 1973), civil liability for pollution (Comprehensive Environmental Compensation and Liability Act 1980 – 'Superfund'), and environmental impact assessment (National Environmental Policy Act 1973).

During the 1980s general political principles emerged. Firstly, the recessions of the 1980s drew attention to links between environmental concerns and social justice. Recent international statements particularly the 'Rio' summit (WCED, 1992) have tried to integrate the concerns of environment, material growth and social justice through the concept of 'sustainable development' (see IUCN, 1980; Brundtland, 1987). The meaning of sustainable development is highly controversial. Its core sentiment seems to be that we should not kill the goose that lays the golden egg and it claims that the three goals of social justice, economic development and environmental protection can be mutually reinforcing. Secondly the precautionary principle was widely accepted according to which we should consider acting in advance to reduce environmental risks even where the scientific evidence is uncertain.

These principles, along with others such as the 'polluter pays' principle and the preventative principle are widely acknowledged in international instruments and are a basis for governmental policies (see HMSO, 1994). Although these principles appear in the Treaty on European Union they do not necessarily have legal force and are probably too vague to be capable of doing so except perhaps in contemporary international law (see *Peralta Case* [1994] ECR 1-3453; McRory, 1996).

Since the late 1970s, a more integrated approach which recognises the interdependence of environmental problems has been developed in international policy and translated into the policy of the EU (see e.g. Nitrates Directive 91/576 EEC; Elworthy, 1998). However, it did not take root in domestic law until the 1990s (see White Paper, This Common Inheritance (1990)). The integrated approach is manifested by the creation of the Environment Agency by the Environment Act 1995 and the concept of integrated pollution control (Environmental Protection Act 1990).

Another factor that is now influencing the law is concern for nature as an end in itself stimulated by the development of green politics during the 1980s. In particular there are signs of a broadening of concern in international law towards valuing nature for its own sake (see Boyle and Anderson, 1996, chapter 4; D'Amato and Chopra, 1991; Emmenegger and Tschentscher, 1994). UK countryside policy has traditionally been concerned with nature as a human amenity, as a sort of art gallery and recreation centre, but there has recently been a move towards environmental protection as an end in itself (see Edwards, 1991; *R.* v. *Secretary of State ex parte RSPB* [1997] JEL 168; Biodiversity: The UK Action Plan, 1993).

English law might briefly be compared with the regime in New Zealand under the Resource Management Act 1991. The Act requires all governmental agencies to pursue a policy of 'sustainable management'. This requires them to manage natural and physical resources so as to 'preserve the life sustaining capacity of air, water, soil and ecosystems', and, except in the case of minerals, to meet the 'reasonably foreseeable needs of future generations' and to avoid, remedy or mitigate any adverse effects on the environment (s.5). The Act also creates a framework for public involvement in decision making. It was a response to conflicting values and priorities between different public agencies and also aimed at bringing greater openness into environmental policy. However, the environmental aims of the Act have to be balanced against social, economic and cultural well being and health and safety, as well as some national concerns including Maori interests.

Science and the Environment

Science and Values

Science cannot tell us what our ethical values should be. By predicting the consequences of our actions science provides a tool to help us put our values (whatever they might be) into practice. The kind of questions which scientists are asked and the interpretation we give to their answers depend on human value judgements as to what counts as a problem and subjective ideas of risk. Within those limits scientific method strives to describe the behaviour of nature and to predict the effects on nature of our interventions.

For example the limits to growth argument relies upon two basic and widely accepted laws of thermodynamics. The first law gives environmentalists a cheerful message in that nothing is used up but merely changes into different forms. Energy is frozen into fuel which is recirculated back into energy. This allows us to think that we might save ourselves by developing ever more sophisticated recycling techniques.

However, the second law of thermodynamics gives a bleaker message. This is the law of entropy according to which, in terms of usable energy, the flow is only one way. Entropy can be regarded as a measure of the capacity of nature to do useful work. Low-entropy energy such as heat dissipates through the economic process and become useless high-entropy energy or pollution. The process is irreversible, the outcome chaos. Conservation does, however, give us a stay of execution. Life temporally stores energy from the sun rather like a battery and uses it to reproduce itself. By conserving life and balancing the needs of different life forms we can stave off our ultimate fate. In the end unless we control ourselves the human population will inevitably exceed the capacity of the earth to support it. The second law raises a problem for those who believe that environmental problems can be solved by technological means in that technology contributes to the entropic process. It also raises problems for the economic view that wealth can increase indefinitely.

Science is also used rhetorically to support our ethical or political beliefs. For example domination of nature perspectives can be buttressed by traditional scientific method which embodies an atomistic, individualistic view of nature as a machine that can be broken down into individual units and so conquered. This leads to the technocratic view of environmental problems that relies on man's inventiveness to find solutions and produce new sources of well being. A technocrat might use science to argue that humans are infinitely resourceful and that nature is resilient and adaptable. This also supports the belief of some economists that wealth is indefinite and, as long as the overall stock of wealth is increasing, the particular form it takes whether environmental or material does not matter as such. At the other extreme the holistic approach sometimes called the 'Gaian' approach after the earth goddess of the ancient Greeks, depicts nature as a self-perpetuating living organism with all its parts dependent on the whole.

It can be argued that our ethical beliefs lead science rather than follow it. We ask the scientists questions that best suit our ethical or political purposes (see Shrader-Frechette, 1994). We usually believe, for whatever reason, that our policies should be consistent with scientific ideas about the way the world works as translated into popular culture. Historically there have always been links between dominant scientific beliefs and dominant political beliefs (see Eckersley, 1992, chapter 3). For example the traditional belief that the environment exists to serve humans was supported by medieval scientific understanding about a natural hierarchy and by the scientific power over nature generated by the industrial revolution. Our attitudes towards foxhunting may influence the scientific theories which we espouse about the balance of nature.

The rhetoric of the green movement relies upon ecology which stresses the interdependence of all living things. Quantum physics can be used to support this view in that it can be interpreted as denying the reality of the individual and presenting the world as a continuous movement of energy within which individuals are temporary knots or whirlpools. Darwin's theory of evolution emphasises the things that human beings have in common with the rest of nature but also provides a banner under which to continue to ransack nature in the form of the 'survival of the fittest', a perversion of Darwinism popularised by Herbert Spencer and later by Sigmund Freud (see Passmore, 1980, p. 23). Darwinism also emphasises the random nature of evolutionary change. According to one version of Darwinism the basic unit of life is the sub-individualistic gene and individuals, species ,biosystems, etc. are essentially byproducts. Ethics in this view are part of the gene's survival pack (see Dawkins, 1989). Darwinism in itself tells us nothing about how we should behave. We can equally resist evolution as go along with it.

A problem with modern ecological and physical science is that they are highly abstract and seem to run counter to our experience. We may be told that individuals are no more than turbulence in an energy flow but there seems to be no practical way of testing the hypothesis. Our experience is that of being separate from nature and that the world is made up of solid particles including ourselves that interact and are prone to collide. Sylvan (1985, p. 17) thinks that the claim of unity between man and nature is illogical. He points out 'Since you and I are both one with the planet and you thin and I fat, you are both fat and thin, old and young and so on' (quoted by Barry, 1993 at 44.). There is an extreme view that science is no more than disguised ideology but if this is so it would be impossible to know since we cannot step outside our human ways of thinking which tell us that there is sometimes a predictable pattern out there in the world.

Scientific Uncertainty and Risk

Environmental issues often depend on scientific evidence but our scientific knowledge may have in-built biases and be too limited to provide a reliable basis for decision making. We do not fully understand how ecosystems or the atmosphere behave or what sort of timescale matters. Ecology is undeveloped and ecologists do not agree on such issues as whether balance or change is natural and whether nature is diversifying or running down (see Elliot, 1995, chapter 12). Environmental consequences tend to be long term and not easily predicted by scientific methods since it may be impracticable or unethical to experiment on ecosystems. Our capacity to monitor nature is limited, we may not be able generalise from evidence about the behaviour of particular species. Modern chaos theory emphasises the uncertainties that arise when we deal with interactions between millions of features when all of them are constantly on the move. For example the evidence of global warming caused by the effect of greenhouse gases on the atmosphere is far from conclusive and the consequences in terms of the possible effects on different communities are unlikely to materialise for at least fifty years. Millions of interacting factors affect climate change and risk assessment based upon analysing one ingredient such as carbon dioxide may be little more than guesswork. The effect of pollution on the ozone layer is better established but still controversial.

Traditional scientific method involves the assumption that a proposition is not true unless it is supported by a consistent pattern of evidence. Similarly, liberal governments may not be prepared to outlaw behaviour unless it is proved to be harmful. The precautionary principle which is an important element of environmental policy requires a different approach to scientific uncertainty one in which we should assume that an activity is harmful even though it has not been proved to be so. The precautionary principle means in essence that decision makers should act to minimise environmental risk even if the scientific evidence is uncertain. This raises problems as to whether it is worth while taking action since unless we know the scientific risk we cannot balance the costs and benefits involved.

A scientist's assessment of a risk may be fundamentally different from that of a non-scientist (see Gillroy, 1993, chapter 6). To a scientist a risk is assessed as the product of the seriousness of the outcome and the likelihood of it happening. To the ordinary person the acceptability of a risk also includes such factors as whether the feared event is dramatic or gruesome and whether it is open or concealed and whether it interferes with some desirable goal. For example we may fear chemical spillage more than flooding even where the latter is more likely to happen and more expensive to alleviate. Different interest groups such as farmers and the medical profession may perceive risks in different ways.

Environmental risk analysis might therefore comprise not only scientific techniques but also social techniques such as mediation and opinion sampling designed to identify the human consequences of uncertainty and recognising that the participants in the process may have different and even irreconcilable values. This means that how we treat scientific data depends on political and social factors. These include our ethical standpoint, our conception of the seriousness of a risk, our attitude to scientists and the extent to which minority or unorthodox opinion gets a hearing. On the other hand, the courts may not be prepared to set aside scientific notions of rationality by permitting, for example planning or pollution control decisions to be influenced by public attitudes towards risk. In *Envirocor* v. *Secretary of State* (1996) 8 JEL 355, a planning inspector refused permission for a waste disposal plant on the basis of a 'worst case' risk scenario wheras scientific risk evaluation produced a lower level of risk. The court quashed his decision for 'irrationality' (see also *Gateshead MBC* v. *Secretary of State* [1994] 1 PLR 85 at 95). On the other hand in *Newport Borough Council* v. *Secretary of State* [1998] JPL 377 the Court of Appeal thought that in principle genuine public fears even without scientific support could justify the refusal of planning permission. In accordance with normal judicial review principles it is for the decision maker to weigh the competing factors. In the *Duddridge* case for example (p. 153) it was held that the Secretary of State was entitled but not bound to apply a scientifically orientated approval to risk assessment.

Politics and the Environment – Technocentrists and Ecocentrists

Law needs to be supported by public opinion. One function of politics is that of influencing public opinion by means of pressure groups as well as political parties. Environmental pressure groups and green political parties influence the law in several ways. They may be consulted as part of the law making or project planning process. In international law, non-governmental organisations (NGOs), have consultative rights under some treaties and conventions, and have been recognised as important actors by the European Commission in its Fifth Action Programme (see Council Resolution 138/1). Pressure groups are increasingly recognised as having *locus standi* to challenge government action in the courts and whether they win or lose they act as a focus for public opinion.

The 'green' political movement has been a prominent political force in Europe since the early 1970s and has attracted increasing interest from philosophers and social scientists most of whom write from a background of the comforts and security of modern technology (see Dobson, 1995). Ecologism draws upon the science of ecology, which dates only from the nineteenth century, and which concerns the interrelationship between living things and their environment. There are also long-established interest groups such as the Council for the Protection of Rural England which were formed to protect the amenity of country dwellers but which may adopt the rhetoric of environmentalism or ecologism to advance their concerns.

There are many diagnoses of the causes of environmental problems. These include overpopulation, technology, consumerism and domination. Solutions are equally diverse. O'Riorden (1981) classifies people who claim to know how to save the environment into 'technocentrists' and 'ecocentrists'. Bear in mind, however, that these are abstract models and that real people may not fall neatly into a category but are free to pick and choose between different ideas. Moreover, as we shall see in Chapter 12, ethical arguments may be cloaks for political agenda.

Technocentrists regard nature as an object to be manipulated. Those at the extreme technocentric wing – 'cornucopists' – believe that, given an unrestrained free market, human technology can solve any problem. They regard economic growth as a good in itself and would rely on improved technology and efficient management to resolve environmental problems.

The methods available to technocentrists include encouraging scientific and technological research into environmental problems, protecting free markets by means of civil liability such as the law of nuisance and influencing the market by means of tax subsidies or pollution pricing to give people incentives to protect the environment. Some technocentrists favour socialist or authoritarian systems and would favour public law 'command and control methods of regulation'. On the whole, technocentrists are 'shallow ecologists' content to work within existing legal concepts and institutions but debating among themselves the proper mix of market forces and state regulation.

Ecocentrists regard nature as a friend. They see nature as a community which includes humans and other living things as part of a larger whole. They draw inspiration from a romantic view of nature and usually recommend small, self-contained communities, low technology, self-sufficiency, and frugal consumption in line with what they regard as natural patterns of behaviour. Ecocentrists tend to distrust the market on the ground that it thinks short term, wastes resources and causes unnecessary consumption. They believe that much of our material consumption is undesirable and that trade and transport cause unnecessary pollution and waste energy. They favour full employment, on the grounds that the unemployed are likely to destroy the countryside and that unemployment is a result of labour-saving but toxic machines. The ecologically correct type of work is informal, small scale and labour intensive, for example manual farming and personal services such as prostitution.

Ecocentrism is not a coherent political theory but a loose group of related ideas. It has been pointed out that there is a larger gap between theory and practice in green politics than is usually the case with political movements (see Vincent, 1992, p. 216). Ecocentrists share the beliefs that nature should be valued for its own sake, that diversity is good, that all aspects of nature are interdependent and that there should be at least a presumption of equality between humans and other natural things. On the other hand they also use arguments about human self-interest. Some ecological groups distrust rationalism and favour mysticism while at the same time accepting scientific hypotheses in favour of ecological balance. There may also be links with fascist and Nazi ideologies which glorify nature (see Vincent, 1992, p. 215). Indeed environmental concerns draw support from both extremes of the political spectrum. The extreme right can rely upon traditional ideas of nature and country life to defend private property and the status quo. The extreme left can draw upon ecocentric ideas of species equality in support of virtually any radical cause.

Deep ecologists favour radical solutions and escape the dilemma of human destructiveness by arguing that humans naturally favour harmony with nature but we have been corrupted by technology. They ask us to re-orientate our relationship with nature by cultivating the belief that harmony with nature enables us to realise our human potential for happiness more fully than does our traditional materialistic culture (see Naess, 1989; Vincent, 1992, chapter 8). Their remedies include setting up new forms of self-sustaining community, based upon a frugal life style and organised in 'bio-regions', a bio-region being the human equivalent of a natural habitat with its own life support network (see Dobson, 1995, p.112). They therefore favour the notion of 'subsidiarity', which is a feature of EC environmental policy. Ecocentrists regard centrist remedies such as the recycling of waste as inadequate and as causing pollution in themselves (e.g. the 'clean' technology of the microchip produces highly toxic waste). They point out that that the scientists and engineers who dominate the regulatory process may be insufficiently objective in that they are being asked to solve problems that were created by their own culture.

Deep ecology has been criticised firstly because it ignores questions of poverty and secondly as degrading environmental concerns by taking them outside rational debate (Barry, 1993). Another problem with deep ecology is that its proponents skate over the many unfriendly aspects of nature and appear to enjoy the simple life style that they advocate. In their case the moral dilemma faced by people who enjoy the amenities of technological development but recognise the environmental risks does not arise.

A less radical ecocentric approach thinks that changes in attitudes can be brought about by middle-class people 'educating' others (see Porritt, 1984, p. 116). The Fifth Action Programme of the European Union (1992) stresses education as a pillar of environmental policy. In this context ecological thinking faces the problem of credibility. Law, at least as it is understood in the common law tradition, is rationalistic. The idea that there is a unity between ourselves and nature is hard to swallow and even harder to use as a law reform platform given the immediate concerns of living standards, health and education. In practice therefore green political arguments often appeal to purely human concerns about the damage which our attitudes to the environment might cause.

Political and Legal Institutions

Dobson (1995, p. 80), following O'Riorden, points to four broad political positions:

1   belief in a global world order through international law (see Palmer, 1992);
2   authoritarian state government;
3   authoritarian small-scale communes;
4   self-reliant co-operative communities modelled on anarchist lines.

To these might be added the 'shallow' position of reliance upon the existing 'liberal' mixture of governmental forms and legal devices.

Hardin (1968) argues that environmental problems are essentially problems of scarcity which call for draconian authoritarian measures. Others argue that ecocentricism is necessarily egalitarian, small scale, democratic and participatory. This is because the interests of the ecosystem are diverse and interdependent (see Eckersley, 1992, chapter 1) because small communities are likely to use less energy and because environmental problems are affected by powerful vested interests both governmental and commercial which are fuelled by economic expansion. Sagoff and also feminist theorists argue that the non-exploitative values associated with environmentalism fit well with liberal democratic ideas of equality and not harming others (see Elliot, 1995). On the other hand, liberal ideas are difficult to reconcile with the sacrifices that environmental protection may require from individuals for the benefit of future generations or animals.

Some commentators suggest a 'many flowers' approach in which each bio-region adopts the form of government most appropriate to its particular environmental needs (Sale, 1984, p. 233) while others (Hardin, 1968) advocate authoritarian controls on the ground that there is no reason to suppose that democratic preferences would favour environmental interests.

There are problems with all these approaches. Authoritarian regimes tend to waste energy, be unstable, and obstruct the flow of information (Dobson, 1995, pp. 83–84). Participatory arrangements create problems for individual freedom in that they encourage conformity and snooping (Dobson, 1995, pp. 117–18). Small -scale arrangements may be unrealistic in that many environmental problems must be tackled on a global scale. It is not obvious that small scattered communities are more environmentally efficient than sometimes concentrations of people (see Dobson, 1995, p. 116 *et seq.*). Moreover small-scale communities must be protected against natural expansionist forces and less favoured groups. This may require authoritarian immigration and trade restrictions and population control.

There seems to be no ideal form of environmental regulation. The Fifth Action Programme of the EC reflects this by recommending a pragmatic mix of command and control and market devices and emphasising the need to incorporate environmental measures into other policies. The concept of 'subsidiarity' is also important. This requires decisions to be taken at a lower level of government unless a higher level is 'better'. Subsidiarity is of general significance in EC law but has been specifically included in the environmental article of the EC Treaty (130R(4)).

In practice, there seems to be a strong correlation between participatory democracy and green politics perhaps because green politics comes from outside established power structures (see Dobson, 1995, chapters 1 and 3). However, participatory government could have the effect of buttressing the status quo. Someone has to organise and regulate the participators. It is not unlikely that the beneficiaries of the process would be those who support the prevailing orthodoxy in that they are less likely to make trouble.

There is also a *de facto* connection between ecocentric beliefs and support for informal co-operative solutions rather than competition on the basis that the aim is 'harmony' with nature. In the legal context mediation might be preferred to the formalised conflict methods of the criminal or civil law. On the other hand mediation and co-operative devices, for example land management agreements, emphasise private interests whereas environmental concerns are public matters.

Finally the eco-activist wing believes that laws can be broken for a higher purpose. Methods include peaceful protest or obstruction that might be condoned by police discretion but which are not protected by English law which gives priority to property rights. For example in *R.* v. *Chief Constable of Devon and Cornwall* (1981), it was held that the police need not remove anti-nuclear protesters from private land. By contrast in *R.* v. *Coventry City Council ex parte Phoenix Aviation* it was held that animal rights protesters had no legal basis for obstructing the transport of veal calves in crates. The difference between the two seems to depend on the exercise of police discretion, a factor which did not arise in *Phoenix*. In both cases the owner of the land chose to give way to the protesters, although in *Phoenix* the owner was a local authority. (What is the relvance of this? See below, p. 71.). Some environmentalists also countenance violent damage to property. The Earth First! movement for example uses the technique of 'monkey wrenching' – sabotage to bulldozers and other machines in order to increase the cost of interference with nature (see Dobson, 1995, p. 145).

Culture and the Environment

The dominant attitude to nature of western civilisation derives from the Christian belief that man has the right and duty to exploit nature. According to this tradition human intellect or the human soul makes us different in kind from other living things and we are entitled and bound to develop our potential as far as we can (see Passmore, 1980, chapter 1). The ecocentric tendency by contrast draws upon the romantic non-rationalist tradition of human culture which claims a spiritual affinity between ourselves and nature. Romanticism, which has its roots in classical antiquity has featured as a counterpoint to the dominant mastery of nature view in English political culture since the late eighteenth century. There are also minority Christian traditions. Firstly there is the idea of stewardship, supported by Chief Justice Hale, according to which our right to exploit nature is qualified by a duty to do so prudently. Secondly there is the doctrine of 'perfectability' according to which man has a duty to improve nature in order to realise the full potential of creation (see Passmore, 1980, chapter 2).

The effect of changing cultural values can be illustrated by comparing grand country houses in different historical settings. From the mid-seventeenth century until the late eighteenth century, their gardens were heavily engineered, artificial and formal. They symbolised man's domination of nature, including the aim of bringing nature to perfection. This was reinforced by the Enlightenment of that period which introduced scientific method and rationality to the culture. From the late eighteenth century by contrast, gardens, for example those designed by Capability Brown became more naturalistic, imitating rather than remodelling nature. In the nineteenth century, as a reaction to the industrial revolution, romantic sentiments of affinity with nature became a powerful literary and cultural movement. An ambivalence about nature can be traced through ideas of town planning from the eighteenth century onwards influenced by a mixture of technological enterprise, concern for health and a romantic love of nature evidenced by the urban gardens and model communities of the Georgian and Victorian periods and the suburban and new town developments of the twentieth century which attempted to blend rural and urban values.

The belief in our natural right to exploit nature and in the power of reason to improve the world have been the driving forces of western civilisation since the enlightenment of the seventeenth and eighteenth centuries. The common law is heavily influenced by enlightenment rationality (see Postema, 1986). Enlightenment thinkers such as Descartes (1596–1650) who placed the human mind outside nature and Bacon (1561–1626) who pioneered the scientific method are among the bogeymen of deep ecologists. Blackstone too regarded man as entitled to exploit nature and gave this as a justification for private property.

The 'regulatory culture' of officials is an important element in law enforcement. For example the attitudes of planners have been said to vary between regarding the environment as a background amenity, treating it as a tradeable commodity and, latterly, treating it as a constraint upon development (Healey, 1994). Romantic attitudes to rural life have also influenced the judiciary, e.g. *New Windsor Corporation* v. *Mellor*, [1975] Ch 380 at 386, *B.R.B.* v. *Glass* [1965] Ch 538 at 557, *Hoveringham Sand and Gravels* v. *Secretary of State* [1975] 1 QB 754 at 760, *Fawcett Properties* v. *Bucks C.C.* [1961] AC636 at 680.

Another cultural concern is the NIMBY (not in my back yard) effect, that is environmental goods can be enjoyed only if other people are kept away from them. Environmental goods are 'positional goods' which lose value as more people acquire them. For example if you have access to the mountain as well as myself the mountain will be eroded more quickly. Garrett Hardin (1974) famously suggested that if we wish to save the environment we would have to rethink some basic ethical values. Social justice for example might have to be abandoned in favour of only allowing the strongest aboard 'lifeboat earth'. Hardin thought that overpopulation was the cause of environmental problems and recommended that environmental assets should be rationed by creating private property rights in them and, where that is not possible, by means of draconian state controls. Aid should not, according to Hardin, be given to poorer peoples since this might lead to even greater consumption of environmental assets.

Vincent (1992, p. 212) suggests that environmental concern, tends to follow in the wake of periods of economic expansion and that 'once material needs have been satisfied for a certain sector of society... people begin to express concern about the "costs" of prosperity and also about the "natural" surroundings which they now have the leisure and time to enjoy'. This link between environmental concern and economic expansion is not clear-cut. It could be argued for example that lawyers look most actively for environmental business at times of recession when other commercial work is falling away. Vincent goes on to suggest, however, that 'those who express ecological anxieties are often members of social classes on the periphery of industrialisation, usually in the professional services section of the community (academics, teachers, artists, actors, clergy, social worker, and so on)'. He adds that 'the central ironic paradox here, of course, is that is that economic growth with its consequential environmental effects (which are deplored by ecologists) has facilitated expansion of an affluent educated service sector which has in turn developed the capacity to enjoy the environment which is being disrupted by such growth'.

Related to the NIMBY tendency is a tendency to favour species that are relatively similar to us or are attractive or useful to us and so fit into our culture. This tendency plays a large part in nature conservation law.

Another important cultural influence is our attitude to the countryside and agriculture which is ambiguous and provides a good illustration of how the way we depict the environment depends upon our particular interests. On the one hand farming can be regarded as an industry responsible for pollution and devastation of the natural countryside, regarding nature purely as a resource. On the other hand farming is associated with the contrast between the urban and the rural that since the industrial revolution has influenced public attitudes. For example in the current debate about rural housing agricultural land is sometimes described as 'virgin' countryside. Farmers themselves appear to be ambivalent sometimes regarding nature as a force to be overcome, sometimes treating themselves as stewards of nature which is depicted as self-renewing. From this perspective conservationists and statutory agencies are regarded as representing urban values (Burgess, 1993).

Until the late 1980s farming was less strongly regulated than other polluting activities and pollution was regarded as a necessary side-effect.

Agricultural and forestry uses are still outside planning controls, nature conservation relies on incentives and agreements rather than command and control powers and, until the Water Act 1989, farmers could raise a defence of 'good agricultural practice' to prosecutions for water pollution. However, during the late 1980s, when the effect of farm pollution upon water quality became a serious problem there was a change in the political culture. This resulted in special agricultural privileges being eroded and in new controls in the form of agricultural waste regulations (Control of Pollution (Silage, Slurry and Fuel Oil) Regulations 1991, SI 1991 no 324). This change of policy was partly generated by European Community requirements (see Elworthy, 1997, chapter 9) but may also have been influenced by a shift in the cultural perception of agriculture from being part of nature towards being an industry. The romantic attitude to nature of the non-agricultural workers also be relevant. Since World War II there has been a marked tendency for people without any interest in farming as a means of livelihood to live in the countryside because they conceive rural life as 'natural' but are not prepared to tolerate its unpleasant features. Farmers can therefore be separated from the rural environment and stereotyped as a category of greedy business interests (see Lowe, 1997).

Finally there is the question of whether pollution and other environmental violations are regarded as real crimes or merely as technical regulatory matters. This particularly affects enforcement. There is a strong tradition in England even in relation to pollution control of using voluntary methods such as negotiation and compromise rather than criminal penalties as enforcement tools. One result of this is to place regulators in a relatively close working relationship with those they regulate. However, in recent years there has been a trend towards a more legalistic approach to pollution regulation (see Lowe, 1997).

Valuing Environmental Interests – The Economic Perspective

The economic perspective is concerned with the efficient use of resources in the sense that we should maximise the overall benefit from our use of resources by allocating costs and benefits in a rational way to produce the solution that brings about the maximum possible net benefit. The economic approach has been influential as an apparently objective attempt to guide policy and in particular to provide a measuring rod to settle disputes about 'uncombinables' (see above and Pearce *et al.*, 1989; Winpenny, 1991; Brundtland, 1987).

The dominant economic approach in the UK depends on certain ethical and political assumptions. It relies firstly on the notion of the free market. Its units of value are the actual preferences of individuals measured by willingness to pay – 'consumer sovereignty'. It assumes that the individual self-interested person, the rational wealth maximiser, is in the best position to make rational choices about gains and losses and that the overall good is best served if a tradable object ends up in the hands of whoever values it most as measured by willingness to pay. The price mechanism is supposed to carry the information concerning the worth of a given action. The economic approach rests on the ethical assumptions that individual freedom, equality and self-interest in maximising wealth are good (but not necessarily the only good). It regards nature as a means of human welfare and is not concerned with the distribution of wealth between rich and poor ('Kalder–Hicks' efficiency) but treats a transaction as efficient if at least one person is better off and no one is worse off in the sense that the loser can in principle be compensated from the winner's profit. In other words, the economic approach will protect the environment only where this is less lucrative than exploiting it.

The economic approach to environmental policy faces three related problems. Firstly there is the problem of externalities. There is an externality where a person passes the costs of an activity on to third parties that are uncompensated, for example where a factory dumps its pollution into the local river. Economics assumes that the person who causes an action is usually in the best position to assess its costs and benefits so that costs should where possible be 'internalised' i.e. absorbed by the causer. The polluter pays principle expresses this idea which may require legal intervention in that we are motivated by a desire to maximise our individual benefit but that, left to ourselves, we would not be sufficiently altruistic to avoid putting costs on to others. Civil liability in tort is an attempt to deal with externalities of this kind. In effect the court is fixing retrospectively a price for the pollution. On the other hand in economic terms it might be more cost-effective for the victim or the public to pay, for example by giving subsidies to polluters or by householders boiling polluted water rather than requiring the factory to install expensive purification plant. Thus economics may collide with other ideas of fairness and justice.

Secondly environmental goods cannot easily be reduced to private property which can be packaged and sold on the market so that there is a motive to conserve them. Environmental goods such as air, wildlife and natural beauty have traditionally been regarded as free and in unlimited supply. We have therefore exploited them with a clear conscience. This creates the 'free rider' problem whereby people can benefit from the activities of others without paying their fair share. For example I am a free rider on the efforts of environmental pressure groups that help to conserve the countryside on behalf of the public.

Thirdly there is the problem of information. Environmental concerns relate to the long-term future of the world and supposedly include the interests of future generations and from some perspectives those of animals and other living things. None of these categories can enter the market in any meaningful sense so as to express their preferences through the price mechanism. The economic approach is therefore human centred and includes nature only in as far as nature can contribute to human wealth (see Posner, 1981, chapters 3 and 4). Another informational problem relates to causation and proof. The consequences of pollution are often diffused over a wide area and over a long period of time and may be caused by a combination of the independent actions of many different people. It is therefore difficult to discover who should be considered as in the market.

The law can be used to combat these problems either by rejecting market solutions in favour of other forms of regulation such as punishing those who harm nature or by making up rules which manipulate market behaviour in favour of the law's goals, for example by imposing pollution taxes or charges or allowing pollution permits to be traded. Indeed markets necessarily presuppose law in that only the law can create and guarantee the property rights that are the subject of market transactions. Economists often recommend 'market mechanisms', sometimes called 'economic instruments', as a way of dealing with environmental problems because they internalise costs while giving the appearance of individual choice. Civil liability in the form of compensation also manipulates market behaviour. However, civil liability creates its own inefficiencies which direct market mechanisms avoid. These include the delay and expense of legal actions. coupled with the principle of limited liability, this allows a polluting firm to make a profit, spend it and escape liability by winding up.

Behind these problems is the more fundamental issue of incommensurability, that is how to compare the value of environmental goods which cannot be traded and therefore have no market value, with goods which have a money price. We can partly value some environmental goods in money terms, for example the opportunity costs of cleaning up a beach meaning the loss of whatever else could be bought with the money spent on the clean-up, but this does not capture the value of the beach itself. How do we compare the environmental benefits to a country town of a new bypass, with the loss of a rare species due to the bypass destroying its habitat? There is no room within the economic approach for concerns about the intrinsic value of nature for its own sake since economic evaluation depends on human preferences. At best economics can only attempt to quantify the 'existence value' of an environmental good to human beings. Related to this is the problem that economists would disperse with the 'non-valuable' parts of nature, although because all of nature is interdependent, this might have unforseeable side-effects (see Gillepsie, 1997, p. 47).

An important policy tool is the technique of cost-benefit analysis. Cost-benefit analysis attempts to identify and to express in the common measure of money the advantages and disadvantages of a given proposal such as building a road through a nature reserve and balancing these against the cost of measures to protect the environment. This must be distinguised from cost-effectiveness analysis which asks how much it would cost to achieve a given level of environmental protection. Not all environmental goods can, of course, actually be bought and sold, for example a rare species, but restoration or replacement costs could be put into the equation. Economic analysis also attempts to put a value on environmental goods through the idea of a 'shadow market', for example by asking a sample of people how much hypothetically they would pay to secure a beautiful landscape or a rare species or conversely how much they would want to be paid to forgo them (contingent relative valuation). One obvious difficulty with this is providing the sample with sufficient information. There is a huge literature upon this subject which is beyond the scope of this book (see Pearce *et al.*, 1989).

Cost-benefit analysis is built into the law. Section 39 of the Environment Act 1995 imposes a general duty upon the Environment Agency in exercising any of its powers 'unless and to the extent that it is unreasonable to do so in view of the nature or purpose of the power or in the circumstances of the particular case, take into account the likely costs and benefits of the exercise or non-exercise of the power or its exercise in the manner in question'. The EPA also imposes the requirements of BATNEEC (Best Available Technique Not Entailing Excessive Costs) in connection with integrated pollution control and genetic engineering. Environmental impact assessment requires only that environmental information be taken into account and is therefore ethically more versatile than cost-benefit requirements.

It is often argued that economic analysis has limited relevance in the environmental context (see Sagoff, 1988; Gillroy, 1993, chapters 1 and 2). Economists are sometimes accused of confusing preferences with values and of destroying values such as respect for nature by subjecting them to a money analysis. Even if these values can be expressed as money it is said that to do so takes away the very reason why we have such values. It is argued that the moral essence of the environment is that it should not be traded and that many people would regard it as meaningless or repulsive to express for example sympathy for a dolphin or delight in a landscape in terms of a price. We can use economic methods to identify the costs and some of the benefits of tourism in a national park but not the satisfaction someone might get from knowing that a wilderness exists but that he will never visit. Sagoff (1988) argues that the economic approach treats us as consumers and ignores our roles as citizens, roles in which, according to Sagoff, we value the environment more than our self-interest. However, Keat (1994) suggests that Sagoff's contrast between consumers and citizens is false. Consumerism is also a community value which as citizens we are concerned to advance. Many of our legal institutions, notably that of private property embody consumerist values. Both consumerism and environmentalism are legitimate public goals albeit incommensurable.

It is also argued that classical economics is biased in favour of growth and industrialisation and that we might be tempted to ignore things that cannot be measured or to bias our calculation in order to advance a political agenda or to reflect unconscious moral assumptions. In particular the costs of protecting the environment are easier to evaluate than the benefits of so doing (Vincent, 1992, p. 229; Tribe, 1974.) It is also said that if we express value in terms of willingness to pay, the interests of the rich will count more than those of the poor. Poor people are unlikely to be able to put the environment at the top of their shopping list.

Perhaps these accusations against economists are unfair. Economists do not necessarily deny that there may be moral values other than wealth maximisation including non-anthropocentric concerns or that some values are morally debased if reduced to money. They claim only that the environment is not free and that it may be helpful to measure as many costs and benefits as possible. An economist is concerned to identify the advantages and disadvantages of policy decisions in terms of human preferences and not to claim that economic analysis is the best route to justice (see Calabresi and Melamed, 1972 but compare Posner, 1981). In this context money as one aspect of the decision-making process is often a useful measure and is a way of expressing what other goods we might have to sacrifice in order for example to pay for an environmental clean up.

There is an analogy here with human rights law. We would not kill or torture a human being on the basis of a cost-benefit analysis alone. On the other hand we do not regard human life as absolutely sacrosanct. For example we limit the amount of public money which we are prepared to spend on road safety. We lawfully kill in self-defence and the defence of others and even possibly of property (*R.* v. *Hussey*, 1924). A cost-benefit approach is therefore relevant as a contribution to solving a problem but must be weighed against other concerns on some other basis. Precisely what that other basis should be is the great-unsolved mystery.

Summary

1. This chapter explains the need for the study of environmental law to be underpinned by an understanding of ethics, science and politics. Without these the appropriateness of particular forms of regulation cannot be assessed. There is a need to move beyond the study of technical details to consider the purposes of and justification for environmental protection. Philosophical theories concerning environmental protection can help in the formulation of new laws, analysis of existing laws and the resolution of conflicts in environmental issues. Ethical assumptions lie behind political and economic policies.

2. Concepts of environment, harm and pollution are related to our purposes rather than being scientifically determined.

3. We explained that environmental ethics concern the interests of future generations and how far we owe moral obligations to nature independently of our own human welfare. We outlined some broad approaches to environmental values. These include approaches based upon human interests – anthropocentric approaches, approaches based upon the welfare of non-human creatures and ecocentric approaches based upon the well-being of collective entities such as ecosystems.

4. We suggested that ethical theories relate to law in five main ways, as tools of persuasion, as means of integration and dispute resolution, as critical standards, as standards for judicial review, and as value judgements implicit in legal rules and decisions.

5. We outlined the development of the law which since the nineteenth century has broadened from concentrating upon public health and amenities towards wider concerns which emphasise the holistic aspects of the environment. English law has traditionally taken a fragmented approach to environmental protection but influenced especially by international law may be gradually broadening its concerns from exclusive preoccupation with narrow human interests to a broad ecocentric perspective.

6. We tried to relate the concerns of environmental ethics to scientific concerns emphasising the uncertainties of science mean that scientific evaluations depend upon political and ethical.

7. We outlined the different kinds of green politics which correspond broadly to the different ethical perspective and emphasised that in practice ethical arguments may be used pragmatically as a tool of persuasion. Green politics does not offer a coherent approach to questions of legal and political structures.

8. We suggested that scientific, ethical and legal attitudes are conditioned by our cultural practices giving illustration relating to NIMBYism and the ambivalent position of agriculture. Ecological principles can be translated into action in many different ways and ethical ideas are used pragmatically and not always consistently.

9. We looked at economic approaches to the environment emphasising the traditional concerns of economics in seeking efficient market solutions and pointed out the individualistic human-centred basis of the economic

approach. We mentioned the problems associated with dealing with the external costs of our activities. We also drew attention to the problem of how to value environmental interests which are not capable of being traded on the market.

Further Reading

Ball, S. and Bell, S. (1997) *Environmental Law: The Law and Policy Relating to the Protection of the Environment*, 4th edn, chapter 1 (London: Blackstone Press).

Cooper, D.E. and Palmer, J.A. (eds) (1992) *The Environment in Question: Ethics and Global Issues*, chapters 10, 12 and 17 (London: Routledge).

Des Jardins, J.R. (1997) *Environmental Ethics: An Introduction to Environmental Philosophy*, 2nd edn, chapters 1 and 3 (Belmont, CA: Wadsworth).

Dobson, A. (1995) *Green Political Thought*, 2nd edn, chapter 1 (London: Routledge).

Dobson, A. and Lucardie, P. (eds) (1993) *The Politics of Nature: Explorations in Green Political Theory*, chapters 1 and 2 (London: Routledge).

Elworthy, S. and Holder, J. (1997) *Environmental Protection, Text and Materials*, chapters 1, 2, 6, 7 and 8 (London: Butterworths).

Garner, R. (1994) Wildlife Conservation and the Moral Status of Animals. *Environmental Politics*, 3, 114–29

Gillroy J.M. (ed.) (1993) *Environmental Risk, Fundamental Values and Political Choices*, chapters 1, 2, 3 and 6 (Boulder, Colorado, Westview Press).

Lowe, P., Clark, J., Seymour, S. and Ward, N. (1997) *Moralising the Environment*, chapters 1, 7 and 8 (London: UCL Press).

Malcolm, R. (1994) *A Guidebook to Environmental Law*, chapters 1 and 10 (London: Sweet and Maxwell).

Passmore, J. (1980) *Man's Responsibility for Nature: Ecological Problems and Western Tradition*, 2nd edn, chapters 1, 2 and 3 (London: Duckworth).

Pearce, D. (ed.) (1991) *Blueprint 2, Greening the World Economy*, chapters 1 and 3 (London: Earthscan).

Sagoff, M. (1988) *The Economy of the Earth: Philosophy, Law and Economics* (Cambridge: Cambridge University Press).

Simmons, I.G. (1993) *Interpreting Nature: Cultural Constructions of the Environment* (London: Routledge).

Workshop

1. What is an environmental issue and what is special about environmental law?

2.   To what extent is the environment 'culturally constructed'?

3.   Population growth is thought by many to be the principal cause of environmental degradation. To what extent should the law be involved with keeping populations at a sustainable level?

4.   Explain the concepts of existence value, intrinsic value and instrumental value.

5.   Explain the significance of the concepts of incommensurability and uncombinability in environmental policy and give your own examples of each.

6.   Sleepville Council owns a site that it proposes to set aside as a nature reserve in which wildlife, both indigenous and imported, can roam free without any form of human interference. Quickbuck, the Chair of the local house owners' association who is worried about the effect of the proposal on local house prices, wishes to challenge the proposal at a public inquiry. Advise the counsil how it should defend its proposal and what kinds of issues arise. Advise Quickbuck how to put his case to avoid being accused of NIMBYism.

7.   Argue the case for and against permitting the ivory trade.

8.   A factory on which the livelihood of thousands of people depends is polluting the local neighbourhood. Its owners have done all they can to alleviate the problem. What is the best ethical solution? Is the approach taken in *St Helens Smelting Co* v. *Tipping* (1865) 11 HLC 642 a good one? Compare *Boomer* v. *Atlantic Cement Co.* 257 NE 2d 870.

9.   What is the relationship between environmental law and environmental ethics? Should, for example, people be entitled to expect that legal decisions should be grounded on ethical principles?

10.   What problems arise out of the relationship between science and environmental policy?

2 The Main Ethical Approaches

Introduction – Normative and Descriptive Ethics

In this chapter we shall briefly introduce some broad ethical approaches and then discuss the main kinds of environmental ethic. Themes introduced in this chapter will reappear in various guises in later chapters. In Chapters 5 and 6 we shall introduce some general environmental principles such as sustainable development and the precautionary principle. These have ethical roots, which are linked to political and economic concerns, thus providing bridges between ethics and the law.

The term ethics has different meanings. Its root – the Greek *êthikos* – means simply a person's set dispositions to behave in one way or another. The term is still used in this descriptive sense to mean the set of values or views actually held by some individual or group (in our context, about the environment). The process of identifying and analysing existing values or norms is referred to as descriptive ethics. Descriptive ethics can be useful because it can reveal new perspectives on the human/nature relationship which can challenge us to identify limitations in our own views (see Rodman, 1983). Lawyers would use descriptive ethics to search for the assumptions implicit in the language of the legal sources.

In modern times the words 'ethics' and 'morals' are more frequently used in a prescriptive sense, to tell us what we should do and to provide arguments to justify this. These sets of prescriptions and the process by which they are derived are referred to as normative ethics. Prescriptions given by normative ethics are generally taken to include, expressly or implicitly, terms such as 'should', 'ought', 'right', 'good' or their opposites. Examples include the statements 'killing whales is wrong', 'we should not allow companies to contaminate land', 'it is right to recycle waste whenever possible', 'one should respect nature'. Normative ethics is fundamental to legal argument and law reform. In a sense though normative and descriptive ethics cannot be separated. The way that we usually reason morally is to start with existing widely accepted moral assumptions and apply them to new problems.

Approaches to Normative Ethics

How can ethical theories be constructed? In order to answer that question it is necessary to give a brief outline of the main kinds of ethical thought. Ethical theories can be classified in many ways but it is common to divide them into three groups: consequentialist or instrumental ethics, deontological ethics and virtue ethics.

Consequentialist Ethics – Utilitarianism

Consequentialist ethics identify outcomes or goals which rational agents ought to try to attain. Actions are 'right' to the extent that they produce the specified consequences and 'wrong' to the extent that they do not. The best-known consequentialist ethic is utilitarianism. In its simplest form – that elaborated by Jeremy Bentham – an ethical act is one which increases 'utility'; utility being equivalent to pleasure (happiness) or absence of pain. 'Nature has placed mankind under the governance of two sovereign masters, pleasure and pain. It is for them alone to point out what we ought to do' (1789, para. 1).

> 'An action then may be said to be conformable to the principle of utility, or, for shortness sake, to utility (meaning with respect to the community at large) when the tendency it has to augment the happiness of the community is greater than any it has to diminish it' (1789, para. 3).

Utilitarianism is the dominant ethic underlying public law methods of environmental regulation. These typically confer discretionary powers upon officials to issue permits and prosecute defaulters on the basis of balancing the competing interests involved – costs and benefits – in the light of prescribed objectives such as sustainable development, itself partly a utilitarian concept (see below). Despite its influence on twentieth-century policy, especially through its 'daughter' discipline, economics, utilitarianism has been subject to criticism (see Smart and Williams, 1973; Simmonds, 1986). One obvious difficulty is the weighting of happiness and pain consequent upon any proposed act. It is not clear that these are opposites. One can be happy and in pain. Indeed at least one ecocentrist has argued that pain is ecologically desirable as a carrier of messages about the environment (see Elliot, 1995, chapter 2).

Neither is it clear that any one person's happiness or pain can be compared to another's, for reported levels of happiness are not susceptible to objective confirmation. This problem becomes especially difficult if we try to bring non-humans into the equation. If animals can feel pain then they should be included in any utilitarian calculation but because they cannot express their interests there is no common measure that we can bring to bear.

The problem of balancing the interests of the human species against those of other parts of nature is an intractable one that pervades the whole of our subject. For example, Bentham's disciple John Stuart Mill believed that the 'higher pleasures to be derived from intellectual stimulation, poetry, etc. were to count for more than the "lower" pleasures that we seem to share with animals. It is better to be Socrates dissatisfied than a pig satisfied' (Mill, 1861, p. 260). Bentham, however, recognised that in principle utilitarianism could apply to future generations and to animals (see Bentham, 1789, chapter cvii, para. 4).

Modern liberal versions of utilitarianism substitute preferences and sometimes the paternalistic notion of 'interests' for happiness. The life of an animal may be less valuable than that of a human in terms of its relative capacity for happiness, but in relation to the preferences or interests of the animal it is equally important. How can we therefore decide whether for example we should experiment on animals in order to save human life? Modern economic approaches attempt to measure preferences objectively through the medium of money or by using sampling techniques. These may be valuable ideas within the human context of economic and social policy but are difficult to apply to environmental issues.

Utilitarianism also runs up against the 'sensation machine' scenario which environmentalists are fond of raising. If a machine could be invented that gives its user permanent and continuous happy experiences indistinguishable from the best features of the real world would this be as morally right as a good environment? The expected answer is no although no clear reason is offered for this.

Objections to utilitarianism are often factual rather than principled (see Carr, 1992) focusing for example upon the practical difficulties of ascribing interests to animals and future generations. How can we predict the consequences of our actions? Human affairs are filled with unintended consequences. Environmental interests are particularly problematic because the consequences of interfering with the environment may be very long term and difficult to predict because of scientific uncertainty. The precautionary principle (see below) tries to meet this problem.

A fundamental moral concern is that utilitarianism can lead to repugnant conclusions. Some critics have argued that since all that utilitianism requires is the maximisation of happiness or the satisfaction of the most possible preferences, there can be no fixed moral rules: 'right' is whatever creates the largest amount of happiness or satisfies the most preferences. In a community of sadists public torture of innocent children would constitute a morally laudable act. Even in 'normal' communities it follows also that one person's happiness or well being must be sacrificed if the total gain in happiness is more than he would lose. A few rural dwellers would rightly lose their homes, landscape and peace and quiet in return for the mild advantages obtained by millions of users of a new airport runway. We might rightly make animals suffer for entertainment and financial gain or destroy rare specimens of species in the interests of commercial well being.

Finally utilitarianism has been condemned as treating individuals merely as units of pleasure and not as valuable in themselves. Suppose for example there is an overpopulated country in which the standard of living is ten times lower than a neighbouring country where the population is ten times lower. The total happiness seems to be the same. What would a utilitarian recommend in relation to population policy?

Utilitarianism has been influential in environmental thinking in connection with animal rights but more generally in relation to traditional human-centred approaches that assume that we protect the environment in the interests of human welfare. If we believe this then we are committed to an instrumental view of the rest of nature. The further we move from a human-centred perspective the more artificial does utilitarianism appear. Pinchot (1910), one of the pioneers of nature conservation, claimed that conservation is founded upon 'the greatest good of the greatest number over the longest period of time'. This illustrates another fundamental problem with utilitarianism that is echoed in the fashionable idea of sustainable development, namely that it is impossible to achieve these three goals at the same time. They are *incombinable*. Some other principle independent of utilitarianism must therefore be brought in to decide whether size of good or length of time or number comes first.

Deontological Ethics

Deontological (duty) ethics avoids the problems of utilitarianism by defining morality not in terms of consequences or outcomes, but in terms of rights and duties. The basic idea is that moral entities are valued for their own sake as ends in themselves (intrinsic value) and that these ends may prevail over the general public welfare. Environmentalists often rely on the idea that nature has intrinsic value when confronted by examples of obnoxious or useless natural objects. A duty to protect the environment may, for instance, be found in the Judaeo-Christian doctrine of stewardship. Sir Matthew Hale notably considered that 'the End of Man's Creation was that he should be [God's] Viceroy...Steward, Vicillus, Bailiff, or Farmer of this goodly farm of the lower world'. Attfield

(1983) concludes that biblical teachings reveal a positive obligation to care for nature and a prescription 'not to subvert its integrity by subordinating it ruthlessly to [human] purposes'.

Stewardship has been promoted in support of the government's environmental policy as 'a moral duty to look after our planet and to hand it on in good order to future generations' (see White Paper, 'This Common Inheritance', 1992, para. 1.14). Stewardship can be used to claim that individuals have moral obligations in respect of consumer and investor decisions, or to adopt simpler life styles.

The best-known duty-based ethic is that developed by the Prussian philosopher Immanuel Kant. Kant aimed to demonstrate that ethics could be based on rational thought (rather than divine inspiration or intuition). In order to do this he considered it necessary that ethical principles must be those capable of being followed by all agents at all times. This led Kant to one formulation of his famous 'categorical imperative': 'Act only on the maxim through which you can at the same time will it to be a universal law'. Kant also held that ethical acts must be such as to treat other persons with respect since other persons are equal to the actor in their claim to autonomy. This is expressed in another formulation of his categorical imperative: to 'treat humanity on your own person or in the person of any other never simply as a means but always at the same time as an end'. This requires not that we never treat others instrumentally but that we should never fail to treat them at the same time with the respect that is due to a human individual.

Although Kant's ideas have had considerable influence on Western political and ethical thought they have not gone unchallenged. Some critics maintain that Kant's categorical imperative is empty or purely formal. Quite trivial acts could be universally willed and performed without treating others as means. Others have observed that it is impossible to determine whether an act could be universally willed unless one first has regard to the consequences (indeed Kant himself often argued from the consequences of allegedly immoral acts).

A premise of Kantian ethics is that morality makes sense only within a rational community. Morality depends upon the mutual acceptance of rights and obligations by equal and rational individuals. A variation of this is the belief that morality makes sense only between beings who can communicate with each other. Value, on this view, arises out of respect for other people's claims and wishes. If this is so then the premise that we owe duties to nature which is the basis of much environmental theory is flawed. Kant himself thought that we should not be cruel to animals but only because it might encourage us to be cruel to people, an idea which has influenced the English law of charities (see *Re Wedgwood* [1915] 1 Ch 113 at 122).

Modern liberal theories of justice are based on the idea of a social contract in which equal and rationally autonomous beings agree to give up some of their freedom in return for the protection of their important interests expressed in terms of rights and duties. The details of what must be surrendered vary and, of course, it is common ground that no such contract could ever have been made. Nevertheless, even though it is merely a convenient metaphor, the idea of social contract embodies the essential Kantian morality of equal respect for individuals and seems to tie environmental ethics to the interests of human beings.

The social contract idea is of limited value in the environmental sphere. Not only is it limited to human beings but it is widely accepted that we owe a duty to future generations not to despoil the environment which they will inherit. Even in theory the social contract cannot apply to future people. There must therefore be a more basic idea, not only to cover future people, but also to explain why we should enter into a social contract at all. The most widely accepted concept is that all people are equal and deserve equal respect whatever their position in space and time. As we shall see later this raises further problems.

It can be argued that both Kantian ethics and the related social contract theory are not as such wrong but tell only part of the story. These theories were invented in the historical and cultural conditions of the late eighteenth and early nineteenth centuries 'enlightenment' when human reason and individualism use primary values. There is no reason therefore why ideas of justice should in all contexts be based upon rationality or social contract, however plausible these ideas may be between human beings. Justice in its most general sense is concerned with what is due to an entity and there seems to be no reason why duties in this sense should not be owed to non-rational beings. We saw in Chapter 1 that a distinction can be made between moral agents and moral patients. Duties are widely accepted as owing to human beings who are incapable of reason. Some environmentalists extend moral concern not only to living things but even to inanimate objects such as rock formations and would label Kantianism 'species chauvinism' (see Elliot, 1995, chapters v and vi).

Virtue Ethics

Virtue ethics contrasts with both consequentialist and deontological ethics and may help to resolve clashes between the other approaches. Rather than focusing on the right act, or the act that produces the happiest outcomes, virtue ethics focuses on the individual and his or her attitude. The outcomes of our actions are less important than that we have the right attitude and that we do things for the right reasons. Thus virtue ethics might help to resolve disputes arising from the incommensurable aspects of instrumental and deontological ethics.

Virtue ethics seek to identify and explain morally praiseworthy personal characteristics and to answer questions such as 'what is the life worth living?' or 'what kind of person should I be?'. A strength of virtue ethics is its ability to account for supererogatory acts: acts which are praiseworthy but not morally obligatory, for example acts 'beyond the call of duty'. The foundation of virtue ethics is Aristotle's, *Nicomacean Ethics*. Aristotle suggested that personality should be developed around the concept of 'the mean', that is be neither too bold nor too timid, neither too kind nor too hard. Most general virtue ethics can be interpreted in this way. Aristotle's advice to act in accordance with the 'mean' could, in an environmental context, be interpreted as indicating the need to temper exploitation with sufficient attention to resource conservation and to have an attitude of respect for living things.

Virtue ethics imply the need for proper respect for the environment and consideration of the environmental implications of our activities. 'Process Rights' such as environmental impact assessment and access to environmental information are therefore generated by virtue ethics. Virtue ethics would allow us to harm animals for right purposes but not to harm them as an end in itself or beyond what is necessary for socially accepted purposes (proportionality). In environmental debate virtue ethics could therefore serve as an escape route in that, as long as we have a respectful attitude towards nature we can cut down that forest after all.

There are also specific environmental virtues and vices. Hill and Passmore, for example argue that a person who engages in wanton environmental destruction is lacking in essential human qualities of humility, self-acceptance and aesthetic appreciation. The claim that there are specific environmental virtues and vices is also made in some variants of ecofeminism ('the position that there are important connections – historical, experiential, symbolic, theoretical – between the domination of women and the domination of nature, an understanding of which is crucial to both feminism and environmental ethics', Warren, 1990). So-called 'cultural ecofeminists' argue that traditional ethics have been abstract, rational and rule-based – all masculine patterns of thought – and suggest the possibility of re-interpreting human-nature relations based on specific 'women's ways' of understanding the world. Feminine attributes such as caring, trust, responsibility and love are posited as providing a better basis for environmental policies than rule-based abstract principles. Inculcating virtue is beyond the reach of the law although the educational objectives of the Fifth Action Plan of the Commission of the European Communities (1992) make a contribution.

The Application of the Three Perspectives

The three perspectives, utilitarian, deontological and virtue are not self-contained rivals competing for exclusive control. Utilitarianism depends upon at least one deontological principle: namely that happiness or fulfilling preferences are good in themselves. Otherwise we would be stuck in a logical circle. Similarly, giving people intrinsic value could be justified as being important for happiness so that 'rights' are part of the utilitarian calculus. Virtue ethics provides procedural devices that ensure that we at least consider the relevant issues in good faith. The three approaches might be used together to solve a practical problem or each might be useful for different kinds of problem. For example, environmentalists sometimes explain why we should give intrinsic rights to nature on the utilitarian basis that this device might help to stave off ecological disaster for the human race (see Elliot, 1995, pp. 127–8).

Courts may draw on any of these approaches. For example in *Boomer* v. *Atlantic Cement Co*, 257 NE 2d 870 (1970), the Court of Appeals of New York adopted a utilitarian approach by refusing to grant an injunction against a factory that polluted neighbouring residents on the ground that to close the factory would have severe economic consequences for the local community. By contrast in the English case of *Pride of Derby Angling Co* v. *Derby Corporation* [1953] Ch 149, the Court of Appeal granted an injunction to protect the property rights of a fishing club against river pollution by the Corporation whose sewage treatment plant was not able to cope with the city's expanding population. The interests involved were not balanced and the court adopted a deontological approach which gave absolute priority to property rights. In *National Anti-Vivisection Society* v. *IRC* [1948] AC 31, the House of Lords refused to recognise that animals have 'rights' by adopting a utilitarian perspective on the question whether the society could have charitable status holding that the benefit to human medicine from vivisection outweighed any (human) benefit from protecting animals.

We can examine how the three types of theory might be applied to the example of the proposed development of a wetlands site which would threaten a population of wading birds, an endangered species (see also O'Connor, 1994). Arguing in a consequentialist mode the would-be developers might point to the economic and social benefits that would result from the proposed changes. These would have to be weighed against the 'cost' of loss of happiness to people and possibly to the birds from the destruction of habitat, loss of aquatic ecosystem, etc. and also against the possible loss of the species in terms of biodiversity, scientific knowledge and uncertainty of consequences. A net loss or gain would be calculated. Of course, calculations of this kind are notoriously difficult to make but are held by some to be theoretically possible (Winpenny, 1991).

The decision to allow or reject the project might also be examined from the deontological perspective of 'rights' or 'duties'. Environmentalists might assert that, regardless of the potential net human welfare, a duty exists to avoid harming members of the endangered species, the species itself and/or the wetland as a habitat. A version of these claims based on the alleged infringement of the moral rights of those entities could be advanced. The developers might invoke virtue ethics by replying that people have a right to comment on the planning procedure and to expect their views to be fairly taken into account. The decision might be considered 'wrong' because it failed to protect an endangered species or 'right' because it conformed to values of legal process.

In terms of virtue ethics we might also characterise the developers as morally deficient in countenancing the destruction of a wetland. Alternatively it could be said that the disruptive tactics of protesters display vicious personalities or that the method of assessment is biased.

This example illustrates that moral values may be incommensurable. How do we decide which of these approaches is 'right' and how do we balance them against each other? The virtue approach helps by insisting upon 'due process'. The legal expression of the due process approach is the requirement for access to environmental information and an environmental impact assessment before a development project is authorised by the state.

Provided that all relevant interests get a fair hearing and show tolerance to each other's views and provided that illegitimate arguments are excluded, the outcome must be left to political judgement. We can disagree with it from our personal ethical standpoint but cannot condemn it as wrong from the standpoint of the community.

Normative Ethics – Some Criticisms

Amorality

First there is rejection of ethics out of hand: the amoral stance. Given a choice between a life spent ethically and a life pursuing self-interest it is not clear that ethical reasons alone would convince the amoral person to embrace ethics; *ex hypothesi* that person is not (yet) moved by ethical argument (MacIntyre, 1985). This impasse could be met by persuading the amoral person that self-interest is part of ethics, that we accept constraints on our behaviour in order to survive in a hostile world. Saints aside, the desire to satisfy one's own interests may be part of any practical morality (Mackie, 1977; Rand, 1964). Alternatively, and perhaps rather desperately, the objection could be pushed aside as being irrational, for it is not clear whether any argument could persuade a truly amoral person to become ethical because such a person is likely to be a psychopath (Williams, 1972)

Dominance

Secondly it has often been said that normative ethics are no more than subterfuge: attempts by interest groups to dominate others. Neitzche, for example, regarded most of what passes today for ethics as masquerade, attempts by the weak to assert their 'will to power' against the strong by surreptitious and ignoble means. Marx also rejected morality – even working class morality as an ideological tool by which classes retain their economic and social roles in the mode of production (Wood, 1991).

Subjectivism

This is the famous 'is/ought' distinction forcibly argued by the Scottish enlightenment philosopher David Hume (1711–1776) whose philosophy centred upon the limits of reason. However honestly and genuinely held, an ethical value can never be objectively true in the same sense that a factual statement about the world can be true. Whatever we say about what nature is like, nothing follows logically from this about how we should behave. There is an unbridgeable logical gulf between the 'is' and the 'ought'. Factual statements such as scientific propositions are 'true' in the sense that they can be confirmed by experience – they have power to predict but are always open to being disproved by an experience which does not fit. This can never be said of an ethical statement.

Hume believed that morality is determined by sentiment responding to social practices and interests, and that there are no external moral 'facts' to be discovered through reason:

> 'take any action allowed to be vicious: wilful murder for instance. Examine in all its lights and see if you can find that matter of fact or real existence which you call vice... you can never find it till you turn your reflexion into your own breast and find there a sentiment of disapprobation which rises in you towards this action. Here is a matter of fact but it is the object of feeling not reason.'

The is/ought problem creates a difficulty for all ethical theories but especially so for environmentalists who rely on the belief that nature is 'good'. Animal rights theorists rely on the capacity of animals to suffer or upon the purposeful nature of some animals but in themselves these facts carry no moral message. Ecocentric theories rely on ecological and biological insights concerning the interdependence and the complexity of nature and upon the functions of the human being within nature. According to the is/ought distinction, none of these can lead to any moral conclusion. Scientific hypotheses such as those of ecology are methods of achieving our goals but cannot determine what those goals should be. It is only once we agree upon a fundamental ethical assumption, for example that 'nature is good', that we can start to reason in the ethical mode.

Two variations of subjectivism have been influential in modern ethical debate. The first, 'relativism', claims that the concepts of 'right 'and 'good' are given by cultural norms that vary geographically and over time. Mackie (1997) for example maintains that societies necessarily create their own ethics and that these possess no objective reality. For a relativist the rightness or wrongness of, for example, killing whales depends on the cultural values of the observer which in turn are related to economic self-interest. If the observer comes from the Inuit society in which whale killing is prized the killing of whales is good. From the perspective of English middle-class culture it may be wrong to kill whales.

Relativism raises serious problems for environmental law. Environmental problems do not respect human boundaries, cultural or geographical, but are sometimes global for example climate change and loss of species. International regulation is therefore important in the form of measures protecting the global commons such as the high seas. The relativist perspective implies opt outs protecting local cultures and opens up the danger that measures to protect the environment will be seen as excuses for cultural imperialism.

Opponents of relativism point out that the existence of widely divergent moral views does not make them right nor does it exclude the possibility that there might be a single right answer to an ethical problem. Abhorrence of murder may be less than universal but murder may, nevertheless, be immoral. Opponents also point out that tolerance of the views of others – the supposed corollary of relativism – has no theoretical basis in relativism itself (Williams, 1972): relativist 'ethics' of intolerance are as 'correct' as those which demand the greatest regard for the views of others: there are, therefore, no rational grounds for opposing the morality of the most aggressive societies. An alternative response to the scepticism engendered by relativism is 'so what?': the possibility of more than one 'right' morality that does not make it wrong for one to propagate an ethic of universal and non-discretionary application (Waldron, 1984).

Whatever its problems, relativism is imbedded in the principle of sustainable development promulgated by the Rio Declaration (UNCED, 1992). Rio emphasised the right of different cultures to pursue environmental and economic goals in their own ways.

A more extreme form of subjectivism is *emotivism*: the view that moral statements are merely expressions of emotion or attitude. More complex versions of emotivism add that expressions of attitude are usually coupled with an appeal to the hearer to adopt a similar emotion or attitude (Stevenson, 1945; Ayer, 1950). Thus 'killing whales is wrong' is, on this account, equivalent to 'I disapprove of whale killing; I desire that you disapprove too'. Responses to emotivism include outright denial (Bambrough, 1979); the claim that while ethical utterances may be used in this way, this is not what they mean (MacIntyre, 1985); and the objection that emotivism is impossible to apply in real life (Williams, 1972).

From the above we can see – and it is important to bear in mind – that normative ethics, of which environmental ethics forms but a part, does not have a settled over-arching theory – a *meta ethic*. The function, status and justification of ethics are matters that philosophers of meta ethics still fiercely debate. We shall proceed on the basis that normative ethics has survived the general onslaught and turn to an examination of environmental ethics in more detail.

The Varieties of Environmental Ethics

The range of perspectives on environmental ethics is diverse. It can broadly be divided into two main schools of thought. The most basic division is between 'anthropocentric' theorists who rely upon traditional values based on human well being or human rights and non-anthropocentrists who claim that natural objects have value irrespective of human concerns (intrinsic value). There are many shades of opinion within and between these groups. They are best regarded as parts of a spectrum shading into each other and do not necessarily point to different practical legal solutions. We shall classify them according to how far into non-human nature they award moral value.

A further distinction can be made between individualistic approaches and collective approaches. According to the individualistic approach which is most clearly represented by the animal rights movement there is no morally legitimate distinction between human individuals and other creatures at least those who are capable of experiencing harm and suffering. Therefore any attempt to prefer our own interests to those of other creatures, except for very strong reasons such as self-defence, is wrong. According to this view all sensate creatures are equal and attempts to defend human privileges, for example to kill animals for non-essential cultural reasons such as cosmetics, food, clothing and sport are akin to racism ('speciesism'). The ecocentric or collective approach values groups such as species or ecosystems and treats the individual as morally considerable only in relation to the group.

The main justification for anthropocentrism is to argue that we are intrinsically more valuable than animals because we have a greater capacity for richness of experience and therefore to be harmed. However, this defence backfires in that it implies that less favoured human beings, such as the mentally handicapped are proportionately less valuable. On the other hand, non-anthropocentric perspectives may well face the same problem since whatever quality they use on which to hang moral value, for example capacity to suffer, some humans have it to a greater extent than others. It is also contrary to the is/ought distinction . Why should intelligence be of greater moral value than, say, the ability to fly? It is true that the enterprise of making moral judgements requires intelligence but it does not follow that moral duties are owed only to intelligent beings. Are we to accept for example that we owe no moral duties to brain damaged persons?

The main strategy of non-anthropocentric thinkers is 'extensionism', that is to fix on some human characteristic that is widely accepted as morally important and show that the same characteristic applies also to non-humans so that any attempt to limit morality to humans is revealed as selfish speciesism. Unfortunately there is no agreement as to what characteristics should be fixed on. Some concentrate on desires, others on capacity to suffer, others on an apparent purpose such as an acorn growing into an oak, others on organisation so as to bring in non-living things such as stalactites or even collective entities such as ecosystems. Thus the scope of environmental ethics ranges from those who prioritise animals that appear to be relatively intelligent such as dolphins through animals that appear to have a sense of purpose and well being and animals that appear to feel pain to all living things (biocentric ethics) and even all natural things living or otherwise.

Ecocentric enthusiasts prefer groups such as species or ecosystems to individuals. They seek analogies in collective human concepts such as communities or cities. Ecocentric theory draws on the moral tradition most well-known through the writings of the eighteenth-century philosopher Jean-Jacques Rousseau (1712–1778) that human beings are communal animals whose true nature can be realised only as part of a wider community of mutual support and co-operation. From this perspective the role of law is to support the realisation of the community the scope of which should include the non-human world. This can be contrasted with liberal traditions which regards people as autonomous individuals who need to be protected from each other or which regards 'social solidarity' as a support system for individuals.

Some thinkers such as Rodman argue that we cannot make progress in environmental ethics unless we avoid treating nature as an extension of ourselves and try to rethink our relationship with nature so as to value it on its own terms. However, we are prisoners of our human mind-set and cannot control the categories in which we think so that we inevitably project ourselves on to nature. Thus it is sometimes argued that the whole non-anthropocentric enterprise is futile and that environmental ethics should be based on a belief that *human* happiness and survival is best achieved by co-operating with nature rather than by exploiting it (see Passmore, 1980). Our human nature creates a trap for non-anthropocentric ethics in that in practice it is difficult to avoid tipping the scales in favour of qualities that are attractive or familiar to us.

Anthropocentric Perspectives

Traditional Anthropocentrism

The fundamental anthropocentric assumption is that only human beings can have direct moral value and that we can value other natural things only in relation to human purposes and goals. Morality is said by some to involve a reciprocal relationship based on communication between rational beings. Others derive morality from religious beliefs, all of which share the feature of regarding themselves as especially important. Animals are not kind to us so why should we be kind to them? There is also an indirect form of anthropocentrism which argues that, while we may owe moral duties to the rest of nature, we have a particular social and biological bond with our own species that justifies us giving ourselves special favours and putting moral duties to humans on a higher plane. Even proponents of animal rights may accept this argument. It also generates the belief that a non-human species has an especially strong claim to moral concern (albeit not as strong as that of real humans), if the species shares features which are prominent in humans such as intelligence, ability to communicate, adaptability, and a communitarian way of life. Much effort has gone into attempts to identify such characteristics in for example dolphins and chimpanzees. However, this line of thought might be regarded as misconceived and repugnant in as much as it suggests that living things are entitled to respect only as honorary human beings.

There are different versions of anthropocentrism. At one end is traditional conservationism pioneered by Gilbert Pinchot (1910) for whom nature is a resource to be conserved to meet human welfare. The view of humans as masters of nature is popular with policy makers and is the orthodoxy against which other views must compete. For example James Watt, a former US Interior Secretary, said that 'nature is for humans not for animals or aesthetics' (Pluhar, 1983, p. 50). A recent report from scientists in the USA estimated the total value of 'ecosystem services' as £20 trillion per annum (see *The Independent*, 15 May 1997). Ecosystem services include general life support such as climate and perhaps natural beauty, absorbing human waste – the sink function, and supplying energy and raw materials. Natural resources might be renewable such as trees and fish or finite such as fossil fuel. Biodiversity is important to us as a gene pool of resources for the future. The preservation of habitats such as wetlands and hedgerows supports biodiversity and has amenity and entertainment value.

The anthropocentric view of nature, which can be traced back at least as far as the philosophy of the Stoics (Passmore, 1980; Hargrove, 1989), received an influential theoretical embodiment in Aristotle's teleological theory of nature. Aristotle believed that everything in nature fulfils a purpose and that the ultimate purpose of nature is the satisfaction of human needs:

'Plants exist for the sake of animals... all other animals exist for the sake of man, tame animals for the use he can make of them as well as for the food they provide; and, as for wild animals, most though not all of these can be used for food and are useful in other ways; clothing and tools can be made out of them. If we are right in believing that nature makes nothing without some end in view, nothing to no purpose, it must be that nature has made all things for the sake of man.'

Medieval Christian doctrine reinforced the same view on the basis that our rationality and immortal souls gave us the right to exploit nature and our fall from grace gave us the necessity to do so. For this reason God said to Noah: 'As the green herbs, I have delivered all flesh to you.' The central Christian philosopher of this period, Thomas Aquinas, perpetuated the outlook that nature exists merely to satisfy human needs in his combination of theology and Aristotelian teleology.

Science historian Lynn White traces the 'historical roots of our ecological crisis' to the attitude of nature domination engendered by Judaeo-Christian religion (White, 1967). Specifically White claims that the religious doctrine of man's creation in the image of God implied human transcendence over nature, thereby sweeping away the protection for nature that paganism, with its sacred groves and streams, had provided. Passmore (1980, p. 20), while critical of White's theology, agrees that 'Christianity encouraged certain special attitudes to nature: that it exists primarily as a resource rather than as something to be contemplated with enjoyment, that man has a right to use it as he will, that it is not sacred, that man's relationships with it are not governed by moral principles.'

Related to the idea of nature as resource is a strand of Christian thinking that requires us to try to improve nature in order to bring it to perfection (Passmore, 1980, pp. 32–40). The combination of scientific rationality technology and the profit motive which was introduced by the eighteenth-century enlightenment reinforced that which Christianity had already sanctioned and was given practical expression in the industrial revolution which epitomised humanity's domination of nature. Among the philosophers who have influenced western thought Descartes (1596–1650) thought that animals were like machines without consciousness and Hegel (1770–1831) considered nature to be totally lacking in virtue in its untransformed state, and only worthy of admiration when converted into some form of garden or farm. Hobbes (1588–1679) and Locke(1632–1704) thought that only human beings have value and that, by desiring, we project our values onto a worthless world. From a non-Christian standpoint Marxism also regards nature as of value only as a human instrument.

Francis Bacon, a seventeenth-century founder of modern scientific method and a common lawyer, thought that the justification for science was the transformation of nature by reason, 'the empire of man over things' and the re-creation of the Garden of Eden (Passmore, 1975). Bacon also thought that English common law was the rule of reason. Grotius (1583–1645), one of the founders of international law, thought that only humans could have rights.

It is important to note this affinity between anthropocentrism and the law. After the seventeenth-century enlightenment, science and technology were seen as the keys to progress. The individualistic and rationalist temper of the common law was in harmony with this. According to the Christian tradition we not only have a right to exploit nature but we may have a duty to do so. The nineteenth-century common law took up this theme which still influences the law of property (see Chapter 8).

Historically, then, there is little doubt that domination, exploitation and 'perfection' of nature can be traced to attitudes fundamental to our culture. Despite great changes in popular outlook that have occurred alongside – or as a result of – the emergence of the environmental movement, the purely anthropocentric view of nature remains pre-eminent. Economics, in particular, as the inheritor of utilitarian thought, continues to promulgate the view that nature is a manipulable object, to be used so as to maximise the 'harvest' or 'yield': a 'composite asset that provides a variety of 'services' (Tientenburg, 1992). Exploitation of nature, at least within sustainable limits, is for some the very essence of virtue (Simon, 1981).

Enlightened Anthropocentrism

Not all anthropocentric ethics have been despotic or exploitative. In what follows we review some 'enlightened anthropocentric' ethics which begin to express the relationship between environmental protection and non-material human concerns. Enlightened anthropocentrism is possibly a kind of virtue ethics. It emphasises that we are part of nature and that in our own interests we should respect nature for its existence as well as a resource. Passmore (1980) argues that familiar and established ethical principles can be turned to purposes of environmental preservation motivated for example by our comparison for fellow creatures, our aesthetic appreciation of natural beauty or a psychological need for contact with nature, our fear of the unknown leading to the prudent precautionary principle and our dislike of waste and vandalism. In particular we should have reverence for other forms of life and value diversity. This does not require us to put the interests of other species before our own but does require us to give a strong reason for overriding other life. These sentiments are underpinned by the realisation that nature is independent of us and that, while we need nature, nature is indifferent to us. Passmore also argues that reforms are likely to be more successful if they follow the grain of existing values and traditions.

Utilitarianism, as we have seen, claims that the object of morality is to maximise human happiness or minimise pain. It is possible to construct an 'enlightened' environmental ethic on this basis alone. Clearly human happiness requires, as a minimum, the maintenance of an environmental life support system (Narveson, 1983). Moving beyond bare existence, human happiness turns out to be dependent on medicinal, economic, aesthetic and other instrumental values possessed by nature. The utilitarian John Stuart Mill in his 'Principles of Political Economy' (1904) recognised the value of contact with wild nature in developing the more intellectual or virtuous kinds of happiness:

> 'A world from which solitude is extirpated, is a very poor ideal. Solitude, in the sense of being often alone, is essential to any depth of meditation or of character; and solitude in the presence of natural beauty and grandeur, is the cradle of thoughts and inspirations which are not only good for the individual, but which society could ill do without. Nor is there much satisfaction in contemplating the world with nothing left to the spontaneous activity of nature; with every rood of land brought into cultivation, which is capable of growing food for human beings; every flowery waste or natural pasture ploughed up, all quadrupeds or birds which are not domesticated for man's use exterminated as his rivals for food, every hedgerow or superfluous tree rooted out, and scarcely a place left where a wild shrub or flower could grow without being eradicated as a weed in the name of improved agriculture'.

Concern for aesthetic value in nature is also reflected in G. E. Moore's 'ideal utilitarianism'. Moore proposes that the ethical consists of maximising not happiness but, rather, the 'good'; good being an irreducible non-natural property (i.e. one that cannot be further analysed as composed of other properties such as happiness). Beauty is among the most important forms of good; there exists, therefore, a moral obligation to act in such a way as to make the world beautiful. Eugene Hargrove has argued that this principle extends to the preservation of natural beauty in the environment; and that because everything in nature is beautiful (although some things more so than others) all of nature is worthy of protection (Hargrove, 1988).

Enlightened anthropocentrists argue that in practice all important environmental problems can be dealt with in such ways. This has the advantages of going with the grain of our culture and recognising that the notion of nature having interests other than those which humans impose on it is implausible. They suggest, however, that we are sufficiently similar to the rest of nature for what is good for us is also to be good for nature. The enlightened anthropocentric approach has influenced domestic conservation law, and is reflected in several international instruments which stress nature's aesthetic value (e.g. CITES 12 ILM (1973) 1088; World Charter for Nature, 22 ILM (1983) 455).

Notwithstanding the above arguments, even enlightened anthropocentric thinking tends to privilege things that are useful or attractive to ourselves such as elephants or lakes (see Chapter 11 and Gillepsie, 1997). Enlightened anthropocentrism also depends on a gamble that, when it comes to law making, our human needs to relate to nature outweigh other more immediate needs. The 'goods' that environmentalists seek may be remote, speculative or intangible, e.g. the well being of future generations or the survival of a species. The evil that these objectives entail on the other hand may be immediate and concrete, restrictions on using cars for example or 'green' taxes.

An illustration of the difference between the two versions of anthropocentrism and how ethical assumptions may affect legal reasoning can be found in the decision of the Court of Appeal in *R.* v. *Somerset County Council ex parte Fewings* [1995] 3 All ER 20. The case concerned whether the Council could lawfully ban deer hunting on its land under s.120(1)b of the Local Government Act 1972. The Act required that any decision about the management of the land had to relate to the 'benefit, improvement or development' of the area as a whole. The three judges approached the question in different ways. Lord Bingham M. R. held that the ban was invalid because the authority had not considered the particular statutory provisions in question but left open the question whether, had they done so, the cruelty factor would have been relevant. Swinton Thomas L. J. agreeing with the outcome seemed to take the narrow anthropocentric line that the moral interests of animals did not fall within the Act at all. Nor would preservation fall within the concept of benefit to the area. Simon Brown L. J. (dissenting) held that the cruelty issue was relevant not because of the interests of the deer as such but because 'human well being for many will depend on their satisfaction as to animal welfare', a characteristic 'enlightened anthropocentric' stance.

Extended Anthropocentricism: Concern for Future Generations

In a well-developed literature almost all the concepts and theories of ethics have been applied to future generations. The importance of extending anthropocentric ethics to future generations is widely accepted but, without a reasoned view of why we should take such persons into account, no environmental law can be expected to make such allowances, or be criticised for failure to do so.

The principle is often called intergenerational equity. This captures the idea that a balance based on fairness must be struck between our own interests and those of our descendants. Intergenerational equity is supportable on utilitarian grounds in that maximising welfare should be indifferent to time. Less convincingly there could be a deontological case if we can owe duties to an abstract class of hypothetical people. One perhaps impossibly demanding version of this is to say that we must leave to our descendants an environment in no worse condition than the one we enjoy, including the options made possible by a diverse resource base (Weiss, 1989). Another and ambivalent version is associated with the notion of sustainable development, that we must meet our needs without compromising the ability of future generations to meet their own needs (Brundtland, 1987).

The case is far from clear. It is arguably wrong to deprive people of benefits now in favour of speculation about the future particularly as the very notion of future people who have rights now is to say the least obscure and is unlikely to have political appeal. There are also practical problems. We do not know whether they will want or need our help. We do not know precisely what we should save for the future or whom the required sacrifices should fall on. There are enormous difficulties associated with future benefits and in trying to guess the future so that there is a risk of wasting our efforts at the expense of real people with real problems. It is also argued that morality is a matter of give and take – 'what have future generations done for us?' (see Gillespie, 1997, p. 117). We shall discuss these matters in Chapter 5 because intergenerational equity forms the cornerstone of the policy of sustainable development.

Non-Anthropocentric Individualism

So far we have examined some ethics that justify environmental protection as simply an extension of concern for humans – either living or potential. In these ethics only humans are accepted as morally considerable.

There are, however, many ethics that accept that we can meaningfully speak of the moral considerability of animals, plants, etc. These ethics consequently postulate direct duties to, or rights of, the environment. They make a crucial jump beyond the standpoint that duties can be owed only to rational beings. This raises considerable problems.

Animal Welfare

The most important deontological argument for animals is that developed by Tom Regan. Regan maintains that human ethics are properly based on rights (not utility) because, in his view, this is the only way to deal with 'marginal cases' such as humans with severe mental enfeeblement (see also Pluhar, 1995). Regan makes the uncontroversial claim that the content of human rights includes, as a minimum, a right to life. This, he says, is based on the possession of inherent value; and in order to have inherent value one must be the *'subject of a life'*. To be a subject of a life is to have: 'beliefs and desires; perception, memory, and a sense of the future including their own future; an emotional life together with feelings of pleasure and pain; preferences and welfare interests; the ability to initiate action in pursuit of their desires and goals; a psychophysical identity over time; and an individual welfare in the sense that their experiential life fares well or ill for them, independently of their utility for others' (Regan, 1983, p. 243). While admitting the difficulty of this classification Regan claims that all mentally normal mammals of a year or more in age are 'subjects of a life', therefore possessors of inherent value and a moral right to life.

Regan's conclusions are controversial. Some have denied that it makes any sense at all to speak of animals possessing rights, on the basis that rights are generated by consent and are by their very nature limited to human beings or at least to beings with linguistic abilities (Francis and Norman, 1978) or self-awareness (Watson, 1979). From a utilitarian standpoint Frey (1980) argues that the autonomy and richness of experience of the human being usually gives humans greater value than animals and justifies using animals (and also some humans) for purposes such as medical experimentation.

Environmentalists also criticise Regan but have taken a different tack, emphasising their belief that respecting the rights of individual sentient animals is unlikely to provide a proper basis for the protection of lower animals, plants and, crucially, rare species. Regan would value the life of a horse more than those of the last pair of grass snakes. Moreover the protection of individual animals such as deer might cause damage to the ecosystem as well as to human interests where the deer population expands beyond the carrying capacity of its habitat. Others have been concerned that the moral valuation of just the 'higher' animals is a form of 'speciesism'. Animal rights are, after all, achieved by identifying certain characteristics that animals share with humans – characteristics that are unlikely to provide any grounds for protecting a river, a stand of trees or an untouched wilderness. If taken to its logical conclusion an ethic that valued animals on the basis of existence of 'higher faculties' might, once the planet becomes somewhat fuller, imply a policy of elimination of 'lower animals', until all that remains are humans and grain-bearing plants (Auxter, 1980). The same ethic would also down-grade humans who lack some of the favoured attributes such as the severely mentally handicapped, the very young and the very old.

There are also utilitarian approaches to animal welfare. Jeremy Ben-tham who was an ardent supporter of the campaign for animal rights, concluded that 'The day may come when the rest of animal creation may acquire those rights which never could have been withheld from them but by the hand of tyranny... a full-grown horse or dog is beyond comparison a more rational as well as more conversable than an infant of one day, or a week or even a month old. But suppose the case were otherwise, what would it avail? The question is not can they reason? Nor, can they talk? But can they suffer? Why should the law refuse protection to any sensitive being? The time will come when humanity will extend its mantle over everything that breathes...' (Bentham, 1789, chapter 17, para. 4).

The concern with animal welfare on utilitarian grounds has been extended by Peter Singer whose book *Animal Liberation* (1995b) did much to highlight the arguably cruel practices of factory farming. Singer argues that the exclusion of animals from moral consideration is 'speci-esism': arbitrary discrimination on a par with discrimination on grounds of race or gender. According to Singer a fundamental principle of moral theory is that all moral interests should be given equal consideration. All creatures with capacity to suffer have a moral interest – at least an interest in not suffering. The conclusion is that (at least) serious animal suffering should not be allowed merely for human convenience.

Critics of the animal welfare ethic have presented a number of chal-lenges to that position. There is, for some, the question of whether animals (or all animals) can feel pain. Descartes, for one, thought otherwise. Furthermore, since Singer's animal liberation ethic is based on an extended utilitarianism, standard criticisms of utilitarianism are applicable. In particular critics have pointed out that if human satisfac-tion from killing and eating animals is great enough then factory farming must be allowed to continue.

There is also the problem of comparing and balancing interests: Singer admits that some human interests may outweigh those of other sentient animals on the basis that humans have a greater capacity for suffering. But how are these interests to be balanced? Can, for instance, the human interest in preventing a serious illness justify experimentation on rats? Moreover, Singer's argument implies that some animals may have a greater value than some humans where the human capacity to suffer is less, for example in the case of an unconscious person or perhaps a very young baby (Singer, 1995a). These issues will be discussed in Chapter 12.

The utilitarian approach is also vulnerable to the 'replaceability argument' which applies equally to humans and animals (see Pluhar, 1995, p. 185). There seems to be no utilitarian objection to killing creatures if we can do so painlessly and replacing them with equal or better substitutes. Ecological perspectives would also support this.

Respect for Nature/Reverence for Life (biocentric ethics)

There have been several attempts to construct an ethic that deals with broader range of natural entities than those animals at the centre of animal rights arguments. One of the earliest 'whole nature' ethics is that of Nobel Prize winner, Albert Schweitzer (1875–1965). This ethic remains individualistic but extends to all living things.

Schweitzer rejected all previous ethics as either pessimistic (hence futile) or morally empty. His own view was that ethical thought and action was encapsulated in the attitude of 'reverence for life'. The basis of reverence for life is mystical, and can be reached only by transcending rational thought since 'all valuable conviction is non-rational and has an emotional character, because it cannot be derived from knowledge of the world but arises out of the thinking experience of our will-to-live'. The content of Schweitzer's reverence for life ethic is demanding:

> 'A man is truly ethical only when he obeys the compulsion to help all life which he is able to assist and shrinks from injuring anything that lives. He does not ask how far this or that life deserves one's sympathy as being valuable, nor, and beyond that, whether and to what degree it is capable of feeling. Life as such is sacred to him. He tears no leaf from a tree, plucks no flower, and takes care to crush no insect. If in summer he is working by lamplight, he prefers to keep the window shut and breath stuffy atmosphere rather than see one insect after another fall with singed wings upon his table. If he walks upon the road after a shower and sees an earth worm which has strayed onto it, he bethinks himself that it must get dried up in the sun, if it does not return soon enough to ground in which it can burrow, so he lifts it from the deadly stone surface, and puts it on the grass. If he comes across an insect which has fallen into a puddle he stops a moment in order to hold out a leaf or a stalk on which it can save itself.'

In situations which necessitate a trade between human interests and respect for life Schweitzer maintains that we should drop the 'pretence' that compromise is itself ethical and, instead, acknowledge that our actions imply a debt to nature. This outlook implies an abandonment of utilitarianism and its goal of happiness maximisation, for we are never free to go beyond that which is absolutely necessary for human life. Given its high demands and mystical basis Schweitzerism has not been widely accepted. At best it seems to be a virtue ethics ideal without carrying policy or legal implications. However, it could be linked with the legal doctrine of proportionality which requires us not to cause more harm than is necessary to achieve a socially approved purpose.

A similar but non-mystical view to that of Schweitzer has been proposed by Paul Taylor (1986). Taylor believes that all living organisms – whether plants or animals – are moral subjects because they have 'inherent worth'. The basis for possessing inherent worth is that individual plants and animals have a good of their own, for example a tree grows to maturity without being an instrument of another being – they are 'the teleological centres of a life'; that is they generate their own purpose even if they are not aware of it (e.g. a tree) – 'it is possible for us imaginatively to look at the world from their standpoint, to make judgments about what would be a good or bad thing to happen to them, and to treat them in such a way as to help or hinder them in their struggle to survive.'

Recognising that, because of the 'is/ought' distinction, this observation cannot itself show why we ought to respect plants and animals, Taylor adds a normative argument based on 'species egalitarianism' an acknowledgement that, on the basis of the centre of a life idea, all species including humans are logically equal. Taylor maintains that this leads naturally to the attitude of respect for nature which in turn leads to a number of duties towards all natural organisms. These are:

(i) the duty of 'non-maleficence' (a duty not to do harm to any entity in the natural environment which has a good of its own);
(ii) the duty of non-interference(a 'hands-off' policy in relation to biotic communities);
(iii) the duty of fidelity (a duty not to deceive for example by trapping or to break trust that a wild animal has had to place in us in a situation of our making);
(iv) the principle of 'restitutive justice' (a duty to compensate a moral subject where the subject has been wronged by the moral agent).

Conflicts between these duties and duties to other humans are to be resolved by reference to a number of priority rules broadly in the manner developed by constitutional lawyers in applying principles of human rights. Firstly, according to Taylor all rights of others can be overridden in defence of basic interests, life and apparently health but only as a last resort. In other cases conflicts must be resolved according to principles of proportionality, minimum wrong, distributive justice and restitutive justice.

Proportionality governs conflicts between human non-basic interests and the basic interests of non-humans. We should not prefer human non-basic interests to the basic interests of others. It is therefore crucial to know what a basic interest is. It is easy to say that we should not kill animals to make fur coats but are we entitled to kill wildlife to make a farm which produces essential foods more productive? Is hunting permissible as a way to protect agricultural land?

The minimum wrong principle allows us to prefer 'important' non-basic human interests to the interests of others 'so long as so doing involves fewer wrongs than other alternatives' (1986, pp. 281–4). Taylor gives the example of the cultural, aesthetic, intellectual, legal, political and economic systems 'needed for a community's steady advance towards a high level of civilised life'. On this basis the equality principle seems to have become an ordinary utilitarian approach although Taylor denies this on the basis that the individual being is not just a container of value but is valuable in itself. Nevertheless, according to Taylor, we can remove a community of wild dogs in order to build a library. The minimum wrong principle might also justify razing a forest to build a highway and performing experiments upon animals. However, in all cases the wrong must be a last resort. There must for example be no better site for the library.

Distributive justice appears to apply to basic interests other than life or health and requires that burdens between us and other living things be shared equally although the minimum wrong and proportionality principles seem to override this.

Restitutive (corrective) justice is a last resort and requires compensation to be made in respect of damage that cannot be justified under the other principles but, given Taylor's individualistic approach, it is not clear how compensation would work. Taylor recommends dealing with the wild-dog problem (above) either by relocating the dogs or doing something for other dogs. Similarly Stone (1972) suggests that damage to trees can be remedied by providing replacements or even by substituting some other environmental asset such as a lake. The relocation method is used in the human context in relation to the compulsory acquisition of land but the notion that we can compensate for the deliberate killing of one human by benefiting another has little in its favour. Providing a replacement or some other environmental asset achieves human instrumental goals but has nothing to do with respect for the individual. This kind of compensation makes greater sense from the ecocentric perspective according to which we value the forest but not the individual tree as such.

Critics of Taylor's theory have pointed out a number of apparent weaknesses in his approach (see Des Jardins, 1997). First, Taylor's grounds for claiming that all living plant and animals have inherent worth is said to be too broad: even such things as tractors and computers could be construed as having a 'good of their own' in the same way as plants grown by human beings. Indeed Taylor gives no objective reason for his starting point that all centres of a life have inherent worth.

Secondly, Taylor's priority principles are human centred. Non-essential but socially valuable human needs override the essential needs of other species. Taylor seems to be saying little more than we should not assume that human interests should always come first or that, yes, all species are equal but they need not be treated the same and can be treated according to how *we* value their needs against our own.

Thirdly, Taylor's ethic has no place for species or other 'wholes'. The last pair of blue whales is, for Taylor, no more important than a common dandelion.

Nevertheless, Taylor's views mark a coherent and well-reasoned extension of ethics beyond the narrow concern for sentient animals of the animal rights movement. At the same time Taylor's somewhat legalistic, adversarial approach exposes the difficulties faced by those who want to extend environmental law beyond human concerns. Taylor's approach is perhaps best regarded as an example of virtue ethics, providing us with a process for decision making rather than direct guidance as to outcomes.

Nature as Art – the Aesthetic Approach

Some writers go further along the individualistic road by giving moral value to non-living natural objects such as rocks. Elliot (1995) makes what is essentially an aesthetic argument for saying natural objects have intrinsic value (as opposed to 'existence value' to human beings) by drawing an analogy with works of art (see also Hargrove, 1987, 1989; Nash, 1977). The aesthetic value of natural objects lies in the fact that they are natural. This leads to the conservationist issue of whether we should restore or even improve upon nature as a remedy for interfering with it for example by landscaping a worked mine – the plastic trees problem. It also raises the problem that we might discriminate against the ugly. Elliot points out that in practice rather than relying on this aesthetic argument conservationists are more likely to succeed by pointing to inadequacies in restoration schemes.

Moreover Elliot's position seems to be anthropocentric albeit of the enlightened variety. It can be argued that faked nature is akin to a faked work of art but does it make sense to speak of a work of art has having any kind of value except its value to the human observer?

Ecocentric Perspectives

A new dimension comes in with the *ecocentric* or '*holistic*' approach. This is based upon the assumption that all life is interdependent and that human beings are parts of a wider whole. There is nothing especially surprising about ecocentrism as such, once we accept the possibility of non-anthropocentric values there is a parallel between ecocentric theories and theories of human political philosophy such as those of Hegel and Rousseau that submerge in the individual in the community and deny that the individual in isolation is fully human. Ecocentrists value 'systems' such as species which form a biological life line or ecosystems or indeed the whole biotic community including its relationship with non-living colleagues such as rocks and water. Individuals are valued according to the part they play within the larger entity. Endangered or rare species are therefore of particular value but only if they contribute to the well being of the community as a whole. There is some support for ecocentrism within the Christian tradition. Aquinas argues that 'in every case except man God cares nothing for the benefit of the individual but does watch over the species as a whole' (Passmore, 1980, p. 117).

There are different kinds and degrees of ecocentrism. Taken to extremes ecocentrism is bad news for the human race in as much as we are unsavoury members of the ecological community. Edward Albee (see Des Jardins, 1997) for example would apparently prefer to kill a human being rather than a rattlesnake because the latter is a rare species. Garrett Hardin (1969) would not rescue people trapped in the wilderness on the ground that the human race is not an endangered species. Should we introduce population controls or encourage euthanasia in the interests of the balance of nature?

In practical terms ecocentric ethics are not always at odds with anthropocentrism or with individualistic approaches. Ecocentrism and individualism are therefore incommensurable but not necessarily uncombinable. There are many self-serving and individualistic reasons why we should protect ecosystems and encourage biodiversity. They include scientific knowledge, recreation, aesthetic enjoyment, education, a resource base in the gene pool and fear of the unknown consequences of irreversible loss. An extreme version of holism, the 'Gaia' hypothesis pioneered by the eminent scientist James Lovelock, treats the earth as if it was a single self-sustaining organism, the parts of which sustain each other in equilibrium – 'Gaia'. According to one version, Gaia is indifferent to the human race and if we damage the environment she will eliminate us just as millions of other species have been eliminated in the past and some other mechanism will fulfil our role (Lovelock, 1986). The Gaia hypothesis therefore suggests that our reason for precautions must be our own self-interest. Darwinian theorists such as Dawkins reject Gaia arguing that nature's driving force is the random self-replication of indivudual genes. From this view, morality lies in human will and is unrelated to any particular state of nature. Lovelock also suggests that the key to Gaia's homeostasis lies in lowly micro-organisms rather than the larger and more attractive creatures that are typically the concern of environmental law.

The Land Ethic

The 'father' of ecocentrism is usually acknowledged to be the American game manager and writer Aldo Leopold (1887–1948). Leopold propounded what he described as a 'land ethic' which he believed could take in the whole biotic community. According to Leopold 'a thing is right when it tends to preserve the integrity, stability, and beauty of the biotic community. It is wrong when it tends otherwise' (Leopold, 1949, p. 262).

Leopold's view matched, in philosophical terms, the science of ecology in which ecosystems are understood as complex integrated and interactive units. It does not necessarily favour rare or more diverse ecosystems over common or simpler, since it implies only that the three values (integrity, stability and beauty) be preserved in whatever natural ecosystems there are. It does, however, form a basis for protecting 'wholes' such as species and habitats that previous ethics had ignored.

Criticisms of the land ethic are twofold. First, it is said to violate the is/ought distinction. The fact that an action preserves the integrity, etc. of an ecosystem is not in itself a reason why we ought to do that act. One response to this difficulty is offered by Baird Callicot. Callicot maintains that the connection between ecology and ethics is indirect, and takes the form of an attitude of reverence, respect or love which arises in a person who pays attention to the details of nature and thus 'invests' in nature. Nature study begets nature valuation which in turn provides a sufficient reason to act so as preserve the land (Callicott, 1989). However, Callicot's argument seems to confuse normative with descriptive ethics. The fact that I invest in nature may make nature of value to me but is of no moral weight to anyone else. One might as well argue that Nazi atrocities acquire moral value by study.

A second criticism of the land ethic is that it posits moral value only in 'wholes'. One version of this attack argues that such alleged 'wholes' exist only in the human imagination. Species and ecosystems are no more than collections of individuals sharing common features designated by humans or interacting in certain ways and, therefore, it is illogical to try to preserve them except as life support mechanisms for individuals. Communities are not, in this view, organisms (Tansley, 1935). It is also suggested that the land ethic implies that individual plants and animals – perhaps even humans – may be sacrificed for the greater good. Indeed, Aldo Leopold's own lifelong love of hunting demonstrated his willingness to kill individuals when this had no overall effect on the ecosystem. The land ethic has been described by Tom Regan as 'environmental fascism' and by Marti Kheel as 'totalitarianism' (Kheel, 1985).

One response to the fascism charge is to reply that preservation of the 'whole' is not the only, or most important, objective. Individuals matter too (Marietta, 1988). As with a human community, the good of individuals and of groups within the community must be balanced against the good of the community as a whole or the public interest a process familiar to the law of human rights. This line of argument raises once more the general problem of incommensurability, i.e. how we can balance interests that cannot be directly compared against a common measure (see Chapter 12 and above).

Holmes Rolston III attempts to justify putting the group first. Rolston argues that each organism has a good of its own but that inherent value or worth in nature is located at the group level.

> 'Value is something dynamic to the specific form of life. The species is a bigger event than the individual with its interests or sentience. Events can be good for the well being of the species, considered collectively, although they are harmful if considered as distributed to individuals. When a wolf is tearing up an elk, the individual elk is in distress, but *Cervus Canadensis* is in no distress. The species is being improved, shown by the fact that wolves will subsequently find elk harder to catch' (Rolston, 1994).

Deep Ecology

'*Deep*' ecocentrists, such as Arne Naess (1973), for whom the writer William Golding coined the term, try to synthesise the anthropocentric and ecocentric viewpoints by telling us to re-orientate how we perceive nature and to cultivate a mental 'state of being' in harmony with nature which should lead to an environmentally friendly life style. Deep ecologists suggest that if we understood our 'true nature' we would distrust the rationalistic thinking that encourages us to separate ourselves from nature, abandon material wealth in favour of the pleasures of living close to nature and regard nature as an extension of ourselves. We should cultivate direct, hands-on, sensuous, experiences of natural objects (see Dobson, 1995, chapter 2; Fox, 1990).

Eco-anarchists such as Bookchin (see Des Jardins, 1993, chapter 11) emphasise human concerns and believe that our environmental problems are concerned with the domination of some human beings over others that is a feature of most legal and political institutions. They recommend small democratic units of government in which everyone has an equal voice. They share some common ground with deep ecology.

Deep ecology is sometimes linked with the idealisation of primitive communities drawing comfort from assumptions that they live in 'harmony with nature' because of uniform philosophical beliefs rather than because their life styles are determined by technological limitations. Evidence is mixed as to whether primitive peoples within the techniques available to them follow much the same rapacious practices as ourselves (see Elliot, 1995, chapter viii).

Other obvious problems with deep ecology are as follows:

1   In as much as it depends on subjective experience my relationship with my car could equally create an attitude of affinity and extension of myself.
2   If deep ecologists want everyone to experience wilderness directly then the wilderness would cease to be wild. ✳
3   Rejecting particular kinds of reasoning such as economic reasoning does not require us to reject reason altogether. Without reason deep ecologists would be unable to pursue their arguments since there would be no way of preferring anything to anything else.

Barry (1993) believes that '(a)t both the pragmatic and theoretical levels deep ecology seems to have been responsible for more harm than good, creating a major ideological schism within green political theory and hampering its political effectiveness'.

Justifying Ecocentrism

The main theoretical difficulty at the root of ecocentrism is how to justify giving value to natural phenomena. As we have seen, the 'is/ought' distinction prevents us from maintaining that what is natural is automatically right. As Macdonald (1984) puts it, '(N)ature provides no standards or ideals... Standards are determined by human choice, not set by nature independently of man. Natural events cannot tell us what to do until we have made certain decisions, when knowledge of natural fact will enable the most efficient means to be chosen to carry out those decisions. Natural events have no value, and human beings as natural existants have no value either whether on account of intelligence or having two feet.'

Interdependence

First there is the assertion that all life forms are interdependent, we are one life form among many and that if life is 'good' we must value all its features including its interdependence. An extreme version of the inter-dependence theory is to deny that individuals are real. Individuals could be regarded as communities of cells, or, in accordance with modern theories of quantum physics, as transitory phenomena in an energy flow. It is argued that our understanding of scientific data is not objective but conditioned by our human perceptions, emotions and purposes (see Capra, 1997; Callicot, 1989; Eckersley, 1992, chapter 3). The merits of this debate about the nature of reality are well beyond our scope and we referred earlier to the practical problems of translating this view of the world into political or legal principles.

Spiritual Harmony

This seems to mean that spiritually nature is an extension of ourselves so that if we value ourselves we must value the whole of nature (see Naess, 1989; Fox, 1984; Elliot, 1995, chapter viii). The spiritual harmony rationale has found judicial support in the dissenting speech of Douglas J. in *Sierra Club* v. *Morton*, 405 US 727,1972. The case concerned a proposal to develop a Disneyland resort in the Sequoia National Park in California. The majority of the US Supreme Court denied standing to the Sierra Club, a long-established conservation group, to challenge the proposal on the ground that the members of the club were not directly affected by it. Douglas J., an ardent conservationist, allowed standing on the basis that the club's members had a 'meaningful' or ' intimate' relationship with nature and were 'its legitimate spokesmen' able to speak for its values (see Gray, 1994, p. 192). Although the Sierra Club lost the legal battle, the development did not take place, thus illustrating the use of litigation as a means of mobilising political forces.

In as much as the spiritual harmony approach is openly non-rational it is difficult to comment upon except as a report of the protagonist's own feelings. People who feel harmony with nature have legitimate interests but this does not mean that their claims are morally superior to those of the many people who would have welcomed the Disneyland in the park. The spiritual harmony approach is anthropocentric and does not give us an independent reason for valuing nature. It is akin to the enlightened anthropocentric approach which relies upon ideas of beauty and 'integrity' maintaining that nature is there to be admired as a kind of interactive work of art (see Austin, 1985). Along the same lines is the virtue ethics view that people who value nature are somehow nicer people (see Hill, 1983).

Extensionism

Ecocentrics adopt an extensionist approach by comparing ecosystems with states, cities, companies and other abstractions to which we undoubtedly give moral standing and which the law treats as persons. However, this analogy seems to break down. We do not value companies as ends in themselves but only as tools. The complex network of rules that create and drive a company ultimately boils down to rules benefiting or penalising individuals. We certainly treat of a company as an entity and speak of the individual's interests giving way to the general good but these are no more than shorthand for aggregating individual goods.

The main problem with extensionism is how to justify the initial choice of what counts as good. For example do we value people because of their intellect or because they are vulnerable to suffering? As we have seen in this chapter our initial choice determines how far into nature our moral concern extends. This problem of finding a starting point is common to all ethical theories. It can perhaps be met by pointing to assumptions that are widely shared (see Wenz, 1988), although this might, in some socities support, for example slavery or cannibalism.

Fictionism

A fourth approach is to admit that the idea of giving moral status or rights to ecosystems is no more than a convenient fiction but is a useful way of drawing attention to the environmental problems that face us helping to ensure that environmental interests get a hearing. Fictions are a well-known device in legal and political thought. Traditional liberal theory bases the notion of society and justice upon the idea of a 'social contract' under which free and equal people knowingly agree to give up some of their freedom for the general good (see Rawls, 1972). Nobody suggests that there ever was or could be such a contract. The social contract is no more than a convenient myth to give us a reason for accepting authority.

In the same way, but by using a different myth, we can try to protect animals, species and ecosystems. The social contract theory was invented for a particular human purpose, that of justifying the political power of the state on an assumption of human rationality, and that there is no reason why the social contract fiction should provide a general model of justice nor that value is linked only to reason. For example Rawls (1972,

p. 312) said that animals could not be included in his theory of justice but went on to suggest that harm to nature is nevertheless 'a great evil' and that 'a theory of the world and our place in it' should be developed. The fiction approach will be discussed in connection with environmental rights in Chapter 12.

The fiction device avoids a problem shared by the other non-anthropocentric strategies both individualist and ecocentric namely that it is impossible to detach ourselves from our human perspective. The idea that 'nature', which simply *'is'* in a sense utterly unknowable to us, can have interests other than those we invent for it is said by Sagoff and others to be meaningless. Nature makes no claims and has no interests except those which human beings attribute to it. We can assign value to nature just as we can pretend that a piece of plastic is a person but in doing so we are expressing only our human preferences. Sagoff (1974, pp. 220–4) points out that when we are attributing interests to nature, how do we know that nature's interests are environmental? A mountain's interests might lie in being covered by a ski resort. A tree's interest might be served best if it were the only tree in a car park rather than hidden from the sun in a dank forest. The argument is not that we can give nature only such values as benefit ourselves, which is patently untrue. It is that we can give nature only the kind of values as we have and that there is no reason to think that these are relevant to nature.

The usual answer to this line of argument is to claim that, because we have many features in common with other living things, we can make a reasonable guess as to what is in their interests. We are doing the best we can and so virtue ethics at least is satisfied. It is also said that human interference with nature is so large, so deliberate and so rapid as to be dangerous by any standards. According to Sagoff (1980), although millions of species have been wiped out during the earth's history, half of the known extinction's of the last 2000 years have taken place during the most recent sixty years. Our genetic makeup has given us the power to reason and to make moral judgements. Natural selection has therefore cast us in the roles of arch-criminal, police force, judge and executioner rolled into one.

Summary

1.   This chapter reviews the main groups of environmental ethics and outlines some general problems. General theories of ethics can broadly be divided into *consequentalist* theories which focus on achieving well being, and *deontological* theories which are concerned with rights and duties, and virtue ethics which concern our attitudes. These approaches may conflict as where governmental policies aimed at the good of the

community clash with individual property rights but may complement each other.

2. Difficulties with ethical principles include the 'subjectivist' is/ought distinction. This creates a problem for environmental arguments which claim that nature has intrinsic value. We stressed that scientific and factual statements cannot in themselves tell us how we should behave although science may be used to support value discovered in other ways.

3. There are a variety of environmental ethics, differing both in their substantive content and the range of entities to which they are addressed. They can be classified on a scale according to how closely they relate to human concerns ranging from narrow or traditional anthropocentric concerns through broad or 'enlightened' anthropocentrism, then to individual animal rights theories to biocentric theories which embrace all living things, ending up with 'ecocentric theories' which value groups or systems such as, forests, habitats, ecosystems or the whole planet rather than individuals. The practical consequences of the different theories are not always different and depend on the reasoning which is used to justify the theory.

4. A general problem with attempts to create a non-anthropocentric ethic is that we cannot know what is good or bad about nature except in relation to human ideas about good or bad. Nature has no interests other than those we define for it and impose on it. We are law maker, judge and executioner as well as being a self-interested protagonist in competition with other beings for survival.

5. Intergenerational equity claims that we should conserve the environment for the benefit of our descendants. The policy of sustainable development reflects the same principle. Intergenerational equity is discussed in Chapter 5.

6. Individualist animal rights theories are a step towards valuing nature. The different approaches rely on different human characteristics and extend these to animals, with different outcomes depending on the favoured characteristic. Regan, from a deontological position, gives greater weight to the 'higher' qualities such as self-awareness. Taylor favours life itself. Singer, a utilitarian, relies on the capacity to suffer. Animal rights arguments may involve treating some humans worse than some animals and also making the innocent suffer. Their individualistic nature puts them in conflict with environmentalism.

7. Taylor's biocentric approach attempts to give equal value to all living things but is again individualistic and tends to privilege human concerns. It raises serious problems about how to settle conflicts between different kinds of being which are at the heart of environmental law. Elliot's aesthetic approach provides a reason for valuing both living and non-living nature and raises the conservationist problem of whether we should fake nature. This will be discussed in Chapter 9.

8. Ecocentric theories look at living things as parts of systems or members of communities. The ecocentric approach of Aldo Leopold's land ethic

is the basis of environmental preservation. According to this approach, the overall well being of the ecosystem is the measure of what is right or wrong. This cuts across the other approaches, for example by condoning acts of cruelty to individuals. It addresses the problem of how we compensate nature for the damage we do to it, but raises the same problem of balancing different interests, in this case between the biotic community and individuals and groups within the community. There is no agreement as to how to justify ecocentrism and attempts to do so either violate the is/ought distinction or rely on human interests.

9. The most sensible approach is possibly to be honest and recognise that our ethics can only be human centred and that the concept of nature's rights is no more than a fiction although as such it may still be very useful. Many anthropocentric values are capable of being elaborated in ways which benefit environmental protection, although these may ultimately result only in the protection of aspects of the environment that are considered important for human well being.

Further Reading

Cooper, D.E. and Palmer, J.A. (eds) (1992) *The Environment in Question: Ethics and Global Issues*, chapter 1 (London: Routledge).

Des Jardins, J.R. (1997) *Environmental Ethics: An Introduction to Environmental Philosophy*, 2nd edn, chapters 2, 7, 8, 9 and 10 (Belmont, CA: Wadsworth).

Dobson, A. (1995) Green Political Thought, 2nd edn, chapter 2 (London: Routledge).

Eckersley, R. (1992) Environmentalism and Political Theory: Toward an Ecocentric Approach, chapters 1, 2 and 3 (London: UCL Press).

Elliot, R. (ed.) (1995) Environmental Ethics, chapters II, VI, VIII, XI and XIII (Oxford: Oxford University Press).

Gillespie, A (1997) *International Environment Law Policy and Ethics* (Oxford: Clarendon Press).

Leopold, A. (1949) A Sand County Almanac; and Sketches Here and There, (New York: Oxford University Press).

Passmore, J. (1980) *Man's Responsibility for Nature: Ecological Problems and Western Tradition*, 2nd edn, chapters 1, 2 and 7 (London: Duckworth).

Regan, T. (1981) The Nature and Possibility of an Environmental Ethic. *Environmental Ethics*, **3**, 19–34.

Regan, T. (1983) *The Case for Animal Rights* (London: Routledge & Kegan Paul).

Rodman, J. (1977) The Liberation of Nature? *Inquiry*, **20**, 83–145.

Singer, P. (1995b) *Animal Liberation*, 2nd edn, (London: Cape).

Taylor, P.W. (1986) *Respect for Nature: A Theory of Environmental Ethics* (Princeton, NJ: Princeton University Press).

Workshop

1. Is it morally right to (i) cull individual animals in order to 'manage' the environment? (ii) to perform experiments on living animals in order to find a cure for asthma and if so under what conditions? (iii) to hunt foxes and catch fish for sport?

2. You are the managing director of a development company proposing to build a holiday park in a wilderness that contains unique specimens of flora and many deer. Outline the ethical arguments for and against the proposal, from the perspectives of Singer, Regan, Taylor and Leopold. If the proposal went ahead, how you would deal with the flora and deer?

3. An oil spill has damaged a beautiful stretch of coastline which is host to a number of endangered species as well as to common species of seals and seabirds that are attractive to visitors. The local community depends on tourism. The cleaning up operations will restore the beach to a pristine state cleaner than it was before the spill, will save many seals and birds but will destroy several rare species of insects and lowly marine life. What course of action would you advise and what ethical principles would you draw upon?

4. Compare the cases of *R.* v. *Somerset County Council ex parte Fewings* with *R.* v. *Coventry City Council ex parte Phoenix Aviation* (see also p. 26). Could the court have used an animal rights perspective in *Phoenix*?

5. 'Elephants are important because we enjoy seeing them'. Why should we value an endangered species?

6. Is a genuine non-anthropocentric ethic possible?

7. Are human beings entitled to prey on other species?

8. To what extent are animal rights ethics compatible with the land ethic?

9. Are there absolute environmental rights which we should never violate?

10. Do you agree that the enlightened anthropocentric perspective provides a strong enough ethical basis for environmental policy? Is it possible to be anthropocentric without being 'speciesist'?

11. What are the ethical justifications for the ecocentric approach to environmental ethics?

12. Discuss the ethical implications of a planning permission to turn a woodland nature reserve into a rubbish dump on condition that the trees were removed and reinstated in a nature reserve in another part of the district. The only other possible site for the rubbish dump would be near a hospital specialising in the treatment of babies under six weeks old.

3 Institutional Arrangements for Environmental Law

Introduction

Environmental problems are increasingly recognised as a field in which global and regional responses are as important as local initiatives: pollution has little respect for national boundaries, animals migrate, international trade connects cause and effect in diverse national territories, etc. In this chapter we examine the role of institutions directly in the formation of environmental law, and indirectly as constituents of the world system in which environmental law is embedded. Only when institutional structures are strong and supportive of environmental law can we expect to find it operating effectively in the prevention of environmental degradation. In this chapter institutions include not only fixed bodies with clearly defined functions, but also defining moments in world environmental policies, such as major environmental conferences and conventions.

Institutions are important as originators of environmental law and also as applicators of the law. In both capacities they are vehicles for the introduction of ethical values. Crucial to this is the question of which bodies have rights to be consulted as part of the decision-making process. The originating function of institutions can be clearly observed at the international level through the example of the United Nations; the applicatory function is exemplified by the role of the Environment Agency and other regulatory bodies at UK national level. Application of environmental law depends on the availability of resources and funding mechanisms. The lack of adequate resources can reduce an otherwise strong regime to the status of 'paper tiger'. On the other hand funding that is directed towards projects that have negative environmental consequences can undermine the efforts of funding for environmentally benign development.

The policies and laws promulgated by international institutions have ethical implications in relation to the treatment of the environment. An important way in which theories of environmental ethics can be brought to bear on institutional policies is through access by environmental non-governmental organisations (NGOs) to institutional processes. NGOs have observer status as participants in the proceedings of many international institutions and also provide monitoring and scientific information to international bodies, notably in relation to the CITES Convention on Trade in Endangered Species (see Birnie, 1992, pp. 76, 477). There is also the device of the conference of the parties. This is a forum created under several international treaties, which permits representatives from the parties to the treaty to review its operation, to set policy objectives and sometimes to alter the treaty itself. An outstanding example is that of the International Whaling Commission which, as we have seen, has gradually changed the emphasis of whale conservation policy away from resource management towards what is claimed to be the intrinsic value of the whale.

International Institutions

The range of international institutions dealing with environmental protection is vast, ranging from small non-governmental organisations, through important single issue bodies such as the International Whaling Commission, through to the largest intergovernmental institutions for international political co-operation such as the United Nations – the focus of this chapter.

The United Nations

The United Nations (UN) organisation was forged in 1945 from the failure of the League of Nations to prevent the Second World War. The UN consists, formally, of a number of principal bodies ('organs'). These are the General Assembly; the Security Council; the Economic and Social Council; the Secretariat; the Trusteeship Council; and the International Court of Justice. It also has a number of specialist agencies, the activities of which have significant environmental dimensions, including the Food and Agriculture Organisation (FAO), the International Maritime Organisation (IMO), the World Health Organisation (WHO), the World Meteorological Organisation (WMO), the International Atomic Energy Agency (IAEA) and the World Bank.

At the time of the UN's formation there was little understanding of the growing global environmental crisis; consequently none of the UN's principal organs were specifically empowered to promulgate environmental policies or legislation. Nevertheless, many of the UN organs and specialist agencies have exerted a significant effect on the evolution of international environmental law, especially by guiding and overseeing the creation of new conventions.

The UN has exerted a significant effect on the evolution of international environmental law both through catalysing and guiding the development of new legal instruments, especially through the UN Environment

Programme (UNEP), and through the creation of 'soft law' instruments such as declarations and recommendations.

The United Nations General Assembly and The Economic Commission for Europe

Of the principal organs listed in the UN Charter, those that have played the most significant roles in the field of environmental protection have been the UN General Assembly (UNGA) and the Economic Commission for Europe (ECE).

UNGA resolutions, such as UNGA Resolution 37/7 adopting a World Charter for Nature, create influential soft law. Often UNGA resolutions contain principles which are later substantively embodied in the 'hard law' of conventions (Fitzpatrick, 1996). For example, the notion that various unowned aspects of the environment ('the commons') should form part of the 'common heritage of mankind' originated in UNGA Resolution 2749 which declared that 'The sea-bed and ocean floor, and the subsoil thereof, beyond the limits of national jurisdiction ... are the common heritage of mankind'. UNGA has also been instrumental in catalysing legal responses to climate change: after adopting Resolution 43/53 which declared the climate to be a 'common concern of mankind' and urged its protection as a matter of priority on governments and other institutions, UNGA established itself as the de facto international co-ordinator in this area: establishing an intergovernmental process for negotiation of a climate change convention; setting 1992 as the target for the conclusion of this convention; and providing institutional and financial support for the negotiating process.

UNGA comprises all the member states. It is therefore dominated by the interests of numerous small developing countries. All members have an equal vote. UNGA continues to be active as a central focus of legal policy for the international environment. Agenda 21 – one of the principal outcomes of the United Nations Conference on the Environment and Development (UNCED) held at Rio de Janeiro in 1992 – confirms UNGA as the principal policy-making and appraisal organ on matters relating to the follow up of the UNCED.

The UN has five regional economic commissions which report to the General Assembly through the Economic and Social Council (ECOSOC). The Economic Commission for Europe has been influential in certain areas of environmental law having overseen negotiation of both the 1979 Geneva Convention on Long-Range Transboundary Air Pollution and the 1991 Convention on Environmental Impact Assessment in a Transboundary Context, and having prepared the Draft Charter on Environmental Rights and Obligations (ECE, 1990).

The United Nations Environment Programme

The United Nations Environment Programme (UNEP) was an outcome of the 1972 Stockholm Convention on the Human Environment. UNEP was formally established by UNGA Resolution 2997 in order to 'promote international co-operation in the field of the environment and to recommend, as appropriate, policies to this end; [and] to provide general policy guidance for the direction and co-ordination of environmental programmes within the United Nations system'. Although it lacks a founding treaty or charter, UNEP nevertheless exists as a semi-autonomous structure within the UN system, consisting of a governing council of 58 members elected by and responsible to the UN General Assembly, serviced by a small secretariat based in Nairobi and with offices in Geneva.

UNEP is expressly authorised by its founding resolution to act on the UN's general authority to develop international environmental law. Its approach to this task has generally been to accumulate and analyse scientific data, then to prepare a draft convention for consideration by governments, special interest groups and NGOs. Following achievement of consensus on the basic features of the draft convention, a conference is convened at which the draft convention, with suitable revision is adopted. A notable feature of this approach, as evidenced by the Vienna Convention for the Protection of the Ozone Layer and the subsequent Montreal Protocol on Substances that Deplete the Ozone Layer, is that UNEP conventions tend to be of a 'framework' nature – setting basic principles – leaving many of the detailed and substantive elements to be set by protocols agreed at a later date. This strategy increases the likelihood of political acceptance of the instrument under discussion (Nanda, 1995).

UNEP's environmental programme initially lacked direction from the Governing Council but was revised in 1982 and thereafter took a more systematic approach to the promulgation of environmental law in the form of the 'Programme for the Development and Periodic Review of Environmental Law' (the 'Montevideo Programme'). The Montevideo Programme aimed at facilitating, both within and without the UN, the conclusion of international legal agreements, the development of international principles and guidelines, and the provision of assistance for construction of national environmental legislation in developing countries. The UNEP's regional seas conventions (UNEP, 1990; Sand, 1988) and other important instruments were adopted under the Montevideo Programme, including:

— the 1978 Guidelines on the use of shared natural resources;

— the 1979 Bonn Convention on the Conservation of Migratory Species;
— the 1982 World Charter for Nature;
— the 1985 Vienna Convention for the Protection of the Ozone Layer;
— the Montreal Protocol to the Vienna Convention (as amended);
— the 1987 Guidelines on Environmental Impact Assessment;
— the 1989 Basle Convention on the Control of Transboundary Movements of Hazardous Wastes and their Disposal; and
— the 1992 Convention on Biological Diversity.

UNEP provides secretariat services to other important environmental conventions: the 1979 Bonn Convention on the Conservation of Migratory Species of Wild Animals and the Convention on Conservation of Migratory Species (CITES).

In addition to catalysing and servicing international environmental law UNEP provides information and monitoring services under its Earthwatch programme. This includes the Global Environmental Monitoring System (GEMS) and the International Referral System for Sources of Environmental Information (INFOTERRA). GEMS aids national governments in the acquisition, analysis and dissemination of environmental information, as well as undertaking long-term environmental monitoring. INFOTERRA is a decentralised information system operating through a world-wide network of national environmental institutions designated and supported by their governments as national focal points (INFOTERRA, 1997). The programme is co-ordinated by a programme activity centre at UNEP headquarters in Nairobi and now covers over 8,400 registered sources in over 76 countries (Nanda, 1995, p. 639).

UNEP has also established, in Geneva, an International Register of Potentially Toxic Chemicals (IRPTC) which collects and processes information on the properties of hazardous chemicals, and disseminates this information via a global network for information exchange. The information service includes data profiles of chemical substances, databases of international regulations for controlling chemicals and recommended methods for handling/disposing of hazardous wastes, and a query-response service.

The UNEP environmental law programme has suffered from weaknesses. In particular it has constantly been affected by severe financial constraints. It is funded partly from a specialised Environment Fund and partly from the UN overall budget. The Environment Fund, which is serviced by voluntary contributions only, has often not met even basic UNEP projected expenditures. Allocations from the overall UN budget have been badly affected by the chronic economic crisis affecting that organisation caused by unpaid dues (Taylor, 1995, chapter 7). Fortunately there is some evidence that these financial constraints are easing (Momtaz, 1996).

A further problem is lack of executive power. As Palmer notes '[UNEP] can push states, probe their policies and plead with them; it cannot coerce them' (1992, p. 261). Although this may be advantageous in persuading states to be open, rather than defensive, it results in poor ratification and weak implementation of many of the measures concerned. Birnie and Boyle write, 'few of the conventions ... are subscribed to by all the states concerned in the problem addressed or, if they are, are not fully and effectively implemented by them. There remains a huge task to be performed by this small secretariat' (1992, p. 51).

Despite these hurdles UNEP's activities in promoting environmental law are generally agreed to have been successful. It has facilitated the conclusion of many new legal institutions in the form of conventions, secretariats, conferences of the parties, etc., and discharged credibly its assessment functions under the Earthwatch programme (Thacher, 1992). It has also aided the position of developing states both through practical assistance in strengthening national legislation and, more generally, by promoting their cause at the international level (Momtaz, 1996, p. 270). UNEP is set to retain a central role in international environmental policy making. In 1987, the World Commission on Environment and Development (WCED) recommended extending its catalytic role as part of refocusing all UN agencies to the challenge of sustainable development.

More recently Agenda 21, following on from UNCED (below), has identified the specific areas in which UNEP should, in the future, focus its activities, including further development of international environmental law, in particular conventions and guidelines, promotion of its implementation, and co-ordinating functions arising from an increasing number of international legal agreements, *inter alia*, the functioning of the secretariats of the conventions, taking into account the need for the most efficient use of resources, including possible co-location of secretariats established in the future.

UNEP has responded to this mandate by elaborating a Long-Term Programme for the Development and Periodic Review of Environmental Law for the 1990s (Montevideo II), which anticipates legal action in 18 targeted areas including importantly, 'concepts and principles which may be applicable to the formation and development of international law in the field of environment and sustainable development'. The second limb of this new mandate appears to imply expansion of UNEP's co-ordination function. To this end UNEP has already begun holding co-ordination meetings between the secretariats of a number of environmental conventions (Timoshenko and Berman, 1996).

The United Nations Development Programme

The United Nations Development Programme (UNDP) was established in 1965 by UNGA Resolution 2029 with the principal objective of assisting developing countries to develop their own abilities and skills, thereby meeting their own needs. Since its inception UNDP has promoted a number of initiatives with positive human-environmental dimensions such as reducing malaria, restoring water quality and soil fertility, and promoting environmentally benign farm management practices (Timoshenko and Berman, 1996).

UNDP's role in development projects is mainly that of facilitator, co-ordinator and provider of technical assistance. It performs these task in a number of ways: by directing funds to other UN specialised agencies; by project execution through its own Office of Project Services or by direct execution by the recipient country government (Von Molkte, 1992). Through its system of resident representatives UNDP provides the UN organisation as a whole with a unique system of permanent links with host governments. Because of the advantage that derives from its world-wide web of connections UNDP co-operation is normally specified in the execution of other UN development initiatives (for example, the GEF discussed below).

UNDP has focused, in its drive to assist developing countries, on the objectives of giving priority to the poor, creating employment, advancing the status of women, and regenerating the environment. The most effective means of achieving these ends have been capacity building; development management; grass-roots development; promoting access to technology; and promoting financial and technical co-operation between developing countries.

In 1990 UNDP adopted a plan to incorporate environmental concerns into its other development activities consisting of five initiatives:

— institutional adjustments at its headquarters;
— promotion of environmental awareness of UNDP staff through, *inter alia*, funding for workshops on environment and sustainable development and improved co-operation between field staff and non-governmental organisations;
— establishment of a 'Sustainable Development Network' at the country level;
— formulation of Environmental Management Guidelines (EMG) to provide systematic integration of the environmental dimension into UNDP programmes and project design;
— introduction of EMG to field offices through 'bottom-up' training.

The Sustainable Development Network provides information on sustainable development to decision makers and exists to 'foster interlinkages and informed dialogue between governmental, non-governmental, grass roots and entrepreneurial organizations and institutions which could benefit and/or contribute to economic development that is sustainable and environmentally sound' (Timeshenko and Berman, 1996, p. 47). In 1993, in order to reflect the recognition in Chapter 37 of Agenda 21 that achievement of sustainable development is dependent on prior institutional capacity, UNDP launched an initiative titled Capacity 21. Capacity 21 is designed to compliment UNDP's existing strengths in technical assistance and capacity building, it consists of a 'catalytic fund' to be used for projects which assist developing countries to integrate environmental dimensions into developmental policies and to create a national body of sustainable development expertise.

The Commission on Sustainable Development

The Commission on Sustainable Development (CSD) was formally created by UN Resolution 47/191 as a functional commission of the UN Economic and Social Council (ECOSOC) to ensure the effective follow up of the [Rio] Conference including, specifically, examination of the progress of the implementation of Agenda 21 at the national, regional and international levels.

At the UNCED developed states opposed the creation of a new institution to oversee the conference outcomes on the grounds that existing UN institutions were competent to deal with the environmental and developmental issues arising from the Rio Declaration and Agenda 21. Less developed states pointed out, however, that existing institutions had been unsuccessful in dealing with the sustainability/development nexus, and that existing institutional arrangements were insufficiently geographically representative (Mensah, 1996). Agenda 21 concluded the debate by calling for, *inter alia*, the creation of a new high-level Commission on Sustainable Development.

The CSD is composed of representatives of 53 states elected by the ECOSOC' with due regard to equitable geographical representation'. This arrangement provides less developed states with a fairer bargaining position *vis-à-vis* developed states. Less than a quarter of the representatives are from developed states (Roddick, 1994, p. 504) and the dominance of developed states is weakened by the decision not to allow the European Community voting rights in its participation in the CSD (Mensah, 1996, p. 51).

The CSD is required to meet once a year for a period of two to three weeks. It may meet in any location but has so far restricted its venue to

New York. At its first session in June 1993 the CSD adopted a multi-year programme of work, taking a differentiated approach to 'clusters' of the chapters of Agenda 21: some clusters were identified as necessitating a multi-annual consideration, others were to be looked at just once (Mensah, 1996, p. 34).

The second CSD session in 1994 examined cross-sectoral issues (trade, environment and sustainable development, consumption patterns and major groups) and sectoral issues (health, human settlements, freshwater resources, toxic chemicals, and hazardous, solid and radioactive wastes). The CSD's second session was notable for a perceived decrease in the urgency of action since UNCED, in part brought about by more cautious prognosis on climate change, in part by concerns of developed nations about their own economic position (Roddick, 1994). The second session also highlighted the failure of states to provide funds necessary for implementation of the Agenda 21, including the failure of many developed countries to meet the 0.7% of GNP target for overseas development aid agreed to in Chapter 33 of Agenda 21.

The CSD's third session in 1995 focused on the second tranche of issues indicated in its multi-year thematic programme of work: planning and management of land resources; deforestation; desertification and drought; sustainable mountain development; sustainable agriculture and rural development; conservation of biological diversity; and environmentally sound management of biotechnology. The third CSD session also established an *ad hoc* Intergovernmental Panel on Forests empowered to promote multi-disciplinary action consistent with the UNCED Authoritative Statement of Forest Principles (Doran, 1996). At its fourth session the CSD focused on the atmosphere, and the oceans and seas, thus completing its review of all the chapters of Agenda 21 in the context of its first multi-year thematic programme of work.

Opinions on the contribution of the CSD to combating global environmental problems vary. According to the CSD itself it 'has established itself as a key intergovernmental forum for follow-up to UNCED and implementation of the Rio commitments' (UN, 1996, chapter II, para. 5). However, the CSD has suffered from some difficulties. CSD sessions in general have been dominated by governmental representatives, with too few NGO and local authority participants. There have been problems in obtaining the national reports envisaged in Resolution 47/191 due to disagreements about 'the use of sustainability indicators', which less developed states fear may be used as a form of 'conditionality' management tool (Roddick, 1994). The CSD has also had little success in persuading states to commit sufficient resources to fund the sustainable development commitments and has appeared to be unable – or unwilling – to push national governments to make progress for fear of loss of political or financial support (Schmidt, 1997).

The Global Environmental Facility

The Global Environmental Facility (GEF) was originally formed in 1991 for a 'pilot phase' of three years in response to proposals from WCED for the creation of a mechanism to finance conservation projects and provide resources for environmentally sound development in developing countries. It is now of importance as the principal funding mechanism for the Climate Change Convention and the Biodiversity Convention agreed at UNCED.

In its Pilot Phase the GEF consisted of around $1 billion held in a Global Environmental Trust fund (GET) to fund projects undertaken by developing countries in response to four key global environmental problems: climate change; protection of biodiversity; protection of the ozone layer and protection of international waters. Grant criteria included the requirement that potential projects should benefit the world at large and not be supported by existing development assistance or environmental programmes. The Pilot Phase GEF introduced, for the first time, a formal mechanism for institutional co-operation on environmental problems between the Bretton Woods and UN systems. This consisted of a tripartite arrangement between UNEP, the UN Development Programme (UNDP) and the World Bank. UNEP was given responsibility for strategic planning of the GEF in the global context, UNDP charged with ensuring the complimentarity between environmental and developmental concerns, organising technical assistance and institution building. The World Bank was given the dominant role as administrator of the trust fund administrator and placed in charge of project identification, appraisal and supervision with participation of UNDP and UNEP.

The pilot phase GEF was a mixed success. Disagreements arose concerning the GEF's mandate and strategy, its governance arrangements, and opportunities for NGO participation (Fairman, 1996). Projects were proposed and approved hastily ahead of full elaboration of project criteria, resulting in failure to meet the GEF objectives. A perception arose that, in some cases, GEF projects were simply added on to existing World Bank projects either as a kind of 'window dressing' or as a 'bait' to induce governments to accept World Bank loans that they might not otherwise accept (Gupta, 1995). The GEF's narrow focus on global environmental problems was criticised on the grounds that global environmental problems are inextricably linked to local environmental degradation. The GEF was seen to be institutionally weakened by the dominant position afforded to the World Bank with its poor environmental record. NGOs further asserted that GEF projects lacked transparency, accountability and afforded insufficient opportunities for participation by NGOs and local communities (Sjöberg, 1996; Fairman, 1996).

The GEF was reformed and reconstituted as a permanent financial institution by an agreement in March 1994. The 1994 agreement retains the special link between Bretton Woods and UN institutions created in the Pilot Phase and addresses many of the criticisms discussed above, but the GEF is now functionally independent from the World Bank (Anderson, 1994). Universal participation is now provided through a new Assembly, in which all participating countries meet at least every three years to review GEF policies. Operational policies and programmes are the responsibility of a new Council which meets at least biannually. Membership of the Council has been devised to maintain an equilibrium of power between developed and developing state. Decisions in the Council are normally to be on the basis of consensus or, if that cannot be reached, by voting by a double majority system (60% of the votes of all participating countries and votes representing 60% of contributions to the fund).

As a result of parallel negotiations beginning in 1993, GEF participants meeting in 1994 agreed to replace the GEF with a new Global Environment Trust Fund of approximately $2 billion. The largest donations to this fund, all of which are over and above those made through ordinary development aid channels, were made by the USA (SDR 307m), Germany (SDR 171m), France (SDR 102m) and the UK (SDR 96m). The provisions of the 1992 Climate Change and Biodiversity Conventions, and the 1994 agreement, specify the GEF as the interim structure for the implementation of the financial provisions of those conventions. The GEF also holds and manages funds, under the Montreal Protocol to the Vienna Convention for the Protection of the Ozone Layer, for projects to assist developing states acquire technologies to reduce reliance on CFCs and other ozone depleting substances.

The revised GEF is an improvement over the Pilot Phase GEF. However, it has not been immune from criticism. The double voting system, which gives an effective veto to the more developed countries based on 'one dollar-one vote' is said to be inherently democratic. There is also said to be a lack of clarity over the relationship between the GEF and the Climate Change and Biodiversity Conventions; despite textual elaboration of this relationship in the 1994 Agreement it appears that there is doubt over the actual power relationship between the participants of the GEF and the parties to the conferences (Jordan, 1994; Gupta, 1995, p. 31).

The World Bank

Environmental law always has an economic and developmental aspect. The substantive policies of environmental legislation requires funds to be put into effect and may, on occasion, be in tension with developmental policies. Consequently, legal attempts to protect the environment in developing countries have to be understood within the context of development agency projects which may have significant environmentally advantageous or damaging consequences.

With a portfolio of around $150 billion and over 1900 projects the International Bank for Reconstruction and Development (IRBD), or 'World Bank' as it is commonly known, is the largest and most influential development agency in the developing world. The impetus for the bank derived from Keynes' ideas for global economic stability through elimination of trade surpluses and proposals during the Second World War for a European Reconstruction Fund. This fund never materialised since, by the end of the War, European reconstruction was already catered for by the Marshall Plan and the large US loan to the UK (Singer, 1995). By this time development in poorer countries had assumed a higher priority. Against this background world leaders met in the New Hampshire town of Bretton Woods in 1944 to attempt to create a new economic order, consisting of four 'pillars': the IBRD, the International Monetary Fund (IMF), an International Trade Organisation (ITO) and a 'soft aid' programme linked directly to the UN.

Legally the World Bank is a UN specialist institution responsible to UNGA through ECOSOC. In reality, however, all the 'Bretton Woods' institutions operate at arms length from the political forum of the UN. This, in part, is due to a 1947 agreement negotiated between the IRBD and the UN which affords the bank the status of an 'independent international institution' (Werksman, 1996). Furthermore, as a supposedly non-political institution, the bank's Articles of Association forbid it from taking into account political or other non-economic influences or considerations when making loans.

The bank's environmental record is generally accepted to be poor (Schwartzman, 1986). Critics point out that the World Bank projects create additional pressure to exploit natural resources by targeting development with potential to generate foreign exchange for repayments and, cumulatively, by exacerbating poverty through increasing overall national debt (Onimode, 1989). Furthermore, although the bank has funded projects of an environmental nature since the 1960s (e.g. water sanitation, erosion control, wildlife management), its critics contend that the benefit of these projects is insignificant in comparison with the environmental damage caused by the bank's regular developmental projects. Examples of IRBD funded development projects with negative environmental and human impacts include forced resettlement of 1.8 million people in Indonesia, massive programmes of highway construction in forested areas of Brazil and associated resettlements of indigenous Amerindian peoples; and tropical forest destruction in Guinea (Horta, 1996b, p. 141).

The bank has responded to criticisms of its record on the environment by introducing Environmental Guidelines to govern the procedure of the banks project cycle, a central environment department, and regional environmental units for the bank's operational regions (Horta, 1996b). In 1989 it introduced an Operational Directive on Environmental Assessment which requires preliminary assessment of the environmental consequences of all projects and further assessment where significant effects are likely. Unfortunately these measures proved insufficient in raising the IRBD's environmental record (Rich, 1990). In 1992 an internal bank report concluded that 37.5% of World Bank projects were unsatisfactorily implemented (Wapenhans, 1992). In 1994 the bank agreed to a US Treasury suggestion to create an Inspection Panel to oversee the bank's performance in implementation of environmental projects. Whether the inspection panel alone will restore credibility to the bank's environmental record remains to be seen. Critics maintain that despite these changes there is still a 'loan approval' culture in the bank which focuses attention primarily on meeting lending targets and rapid approval of loans, reducing issues of environmental and social sustainability to a largely rhetorical level (Horta, 1996b).

Non-Governmental Organisations and International Institutions

Non-governmental organisations (NGOs) have played an influential role in shaping the policies and laws promulgated by international institutions. One kind of NGOs is what Haas refers to as an epistemic community, i.e. 'a network of professionals with recognised expertise and competence in a particular domain and an authoritative claim to policy-relevant knowledge within that domain or issue-area' (Haas, 1993). In epistemic community theory scientific knowledge becomes public knowledge, and in turn influences political/legal outcomes. Kamarotos, for example, argues that scientific oriented NGOs, such as the International Council of Scientific Unions have, by engendering close relations with UN agencies, exerted influence on the environmental policies. Peterson has similarly demonstrated the influence of the cetologist epistemic community in the international management of whaling. A further example of the influence of epistemic communities is the influence of the wider scientific community in the evolution of a legal regime for ozone protection (see Haas, 1993).

A more familiar kind of NGO is the environmental pressure group (EPG). EPGs exert influence on international institutions both directly and indirectly. Direct pressure is most easily brought to bear when pressure groups are given observer status at meetings of the institution in question. Over 400 NGOs, for instance, participated in the 1972 United Nations Conference on the Human Environment. Major environmental conventions, such as the International Convention for the Regulation of Whaling (ICRW) and the Convention for the Protection of Endangered Species (CITES), often provide expressly for NGO observer status. This status allows EPGs a forum to advance arguments for environmental protection which are often based on ethical premises and the notion of 'rights' of individual animals or other aspects of the environment. This ethical orientation, on occasion, brings EPGs into conflict with the epistemic community, whose concern is more usually directed towards sustaining aspects of the environment that have human-centred benefits. This clash of ethical ideologies can be seen most clearly in the conflict between the epistemic community and EPGs in relation to whaling: the former leaning towards 'sustainable' harvesting strategies, the latter committed to a total ban on whaling on humane or 'rights' grounds.

Some international institutions have formal arrangements for NGO participation and involvement. Article 71 of the United Nations Charter, for example, charges ECOSOC with establishing formal consultative arrangements with NGOs. The presence of formal requirements to consult does not, however, necessarily empower NGOs *vis-à-vis* the UN. Not all NGOs are granted formal consultative status. Furthermore, ECOSOC policy on NGO consultation has allowed NGOs only a passive role in ECOSOC and, by creating a hierarchy of NGOs, has placed the NGO community in a 'supplicant' position.

The indirect influence of EPGs on international institutions comes about as the end product of domestic political pressure on states to take international action to secure environmental protection. Greenpeace and Friends of the Earth, for instance, have been very successful in lobbying national governments to ratify international treaties for wildlife conservation. National EPGs also serve to create large and vocal constituencies of concerned citizens who monitor the international policies of national governments. EPGs are also frequently involved in monitoring the implementation, at a national level, of international environmental legislation.

EPGs have maximised their influence on global and regional institutions through strategic organisation of their efforts. This has been achieved, internationally, through the Environment Centre Liaison International (ECLI): a body which aims to facilitate co-operation between NGOs and to build links between NGOs and governments and other institutions concerned with environmental policies.

European Institutions

The principal institutions providing the context to European environmental law are the Council of Europe, the Organisation for Economic Co-operation and Development (OECD) and the European Union.

The Council of Europe

The Council of Europe (COE) was founded in 1949 with the purpose of fostering political co-operation at a European level. The COE has two major organs: the Committee of Ministers and the Parliamentary Assembly. The Committee of Ministers is an executive body composed of the member states' foreign affairs ministers. Decision making in the Committee requires unanimity on most matters which means that any country can veto a decision. The Parliamentary Assembly is a deliberative body comprising members appointed by the member states' national parliaments. Its role is purely consultative. The COE also has a secretariat, based in Strasbourg, consisting of around 1000 civil servants, headed by a Secretary General elected for five years from a list of candidates proposed by the Committee of Ministers. Unlike the European Union, the COE is a pan-European body comprising, currently, 32 members covering the whole of western Europe. Recent entrants include Slovakia and Romania. Special guest status has been conferred on some states from the former USSR, such as Moldova, Russia and the Ukraine.

The COE has been active in areas of environmental information, nature conservation, and environmental liability. In 1967 the COE set up the European Information Centre for Nature Conservation which has published periodical inventories of plant and animal species threatened with extinction in Europe as well as a detailed European Vegetation Map providing information on about 100 'fundamental vegetation units'.

Two major legal instruments expressly designed for environmental protection have been developed by the COE. The first is the 1979 Convention on the Conservation of Wildlife and Natural Habitats in Europe (the Berne Convention). This bestows legal protection on around 400 animal and 119 plant species that are rare or threatened with extinction, and was the model for the European Communities Habitats Directive. The second is the Convention on Civil Liability for Damage

Resulting from Activities Dangerous to the Environment (Council of Europe, 1993). Additionally, the COE's European Convention for the Protection of Human Rights and Fundamental Freedoms (ECHR) has been used, with limited success, to assert a human right to a decent environment.

The ECHR has been incorporated into UK law by the Labour government (Human Rights Act 1995) but does not override statutory provisions that are necessarily inconsistent with the convention.

The COE has also concluded a number of conventions dealing with the transportation, breeding and slaughter of animals as well as the use of animals in experimentation. These include the European Convention for the Protection of Animals during International Transport and the European Convention for the Protection of Animals kept for Farming Purposes, the European Convention for the Protection of Animals for Slaughter, the European Convention for the Protection of Vertebrate Animals used for Experimental and other Scientific Purposes and the European Convention for the Protection of Pet Animals. These are important legal mechanisms for the implementation of animal welfare and rights policies (see Chapter 9).

The European Union

The European Union (EU) differs from all other international and European institutions in that it is a supranational organisation in which its members have given up part of their national sovereignty in order to form a cohesive political unit. The EU has legislative powers and is the principal institution for the formation of European level environmental legislation.

The origins of the EU can be traced to the Schulmman plan, in 1950, for a Franco-German coal and steel community which would rationalise coal and steel production and bind Germany, which was still perceived as a potential threat, into an economic and political union of European states (Borchardt, 1995). This developed, in 1952, into the European Coal and Steel Community (ECSC). After the failure in 1954 to achieve a European Defence Community replacing national armies with one European Army, attention returned to the development of economic integration. This process resulted in the conclusion, in 1957, of treaties establishing the European Atomic Energy Community (Euratom) and the European Economic Community (EEC).

In 1957 the EEC consisted of six founder states: France, Germany, Belgium, Italy, Luxembourg and the Netherlands. Since then it has undergone considerable incremental expansion. In 1972 treaties of accession of Denmark, Ireland and the United Kingdom were ratified by the parliaments of those states. In the same year Norway failed to ratify a treaty of accession after an unfavourable referendum: an outcome repeated in 1994. In 1981 Greece became a member of the EEC. In 1982 Greenland, which had joined in 1972 through Denmark, withdrew from the community. 1986 marked growth of the EEC through the addition of Spain and Portugal. The collapse of the Berlin Wall in 1990 effectively enlarged the EEC by inclusion of the former German Democratic Republic. Austria, Finland and Sweden become members of the European Union in 1995 bringing it to a total of 368 million people and 15 member states. Accession negotiations have started with six other countries (Poland, Hungary, the Czech Republic, Estonia, Slovenia, Cyprus) and in the case of five other countries (Bulgaria, Romania, Slovakia, Latvia, Lithuania) negotiations will start when these states fulfil certain political and economic requirements.

Although the preamble of the EEC Treaty recalled the determination of the parties to 'lay the foundations of an ever closer union amongst the peoples of Europe' the principal task of the EEC was economic not political: 'to promote ... a harmonious development of economic activities, a continuous and balanced expansion, an accelerated raising of the standard of living ...' (Article 2). Progress on political integration during the 1970s included the setting up in 1970 of European Political Co-operation (EPC) for foreign policy co-ordination and the European Monetary System (EMS) in 1979. Further work in the 1980s resulted in the conclusion, in 1987, of the Single European Act (SEA). The SEA amended and added to the treaties establishing the Communities, creating a legal framework for achieving a single market by 1992 and closer policy co-operation on, *inter alia*, the environment.

At a political level the single market project added impetus to the larger project of European integration. Two intergovernmental conferences followed and resulted in the Treaty on European Union (TEU), signed by member states in Maastricht in 1992. Amendments to the TEU and the EC Treaty were decided upon in a Treaty agreed in Amsterdam in June 1997 (the Amsterdam Treaty) which reforms EU institutions in readiness for enlargement.

The TEU changed the title of the EEC to the 'European Community' (deletion of 'economic') and created a new European Union consisting of three 'pillars':

1   The Three European Communities (EC, Euratom and ECSC)
2   A Common Foreign and Security Policy
3   Co-operation in the Fields of Justice and Home Affairs

By this means the EEC was transformed into the EC which now lies at the heart of the EU. All three original communities (EC, Euratom and ECSC) still exist and are still governed by the law of their respective treaties as amended.

The Objectives of the EC are spelt out in Article 2 EC Treaty (as modified by the Amsterdam Treaty): establishing a common market and an economic and monetary union and by implementing the common policies or activities referred to in Articles 3 and 4, to promote throughout the Community a harmonious and balanced development of economic activities, a high level of employment and of social protection, equality between men and women, sustainable and non-inflationary growth, a high degree of competitiveness and convergence of economic performance, a high level of protection and improvement of the quality of the environment, the raising of the standard of living and quality of life, and economic and social cohesion and solidarity among Member States. It is noteworthy that the environment seems to be treated as an object in its own right separate from the idea of sustainable development.

The main institutions responsible for development and application of EU environmental law are:

— the Council of the European Union;
— the European Commission;
— the European Parliament;
— the European Court of Justice.

These institutions are supported by the European Environment Agency, the European Investment Bank, the European Central bank and the European Monetary Institute.

The Council of the European Union

The Council of the European Union is the main decision-making institution of the EU. It meets periodically to discuss selected topics and, when in session, comprises one minister from each member state (Article 146 EC Treaty). The identity of the Council thus varies according to the topic under discussion: environment ministers meet to discuss environmental affairs; transport ministers meet to discuss transport matters and so on. Member states take it in turn to hold the Presidency of the Council which enables them to set the agenda. The Presidency rotates every six months.

The Council is charged, by Article 145 EC Treaty, with the task of ensuring co-ordination of the general economic policies of the member states, with the power to take decisions, and with the power to confer powers for the implementation of Council Rules on the Commission. Decisions in the Council may be made in three ways: by simple majority, by qualified majority or by unanimity. Members states have differential voting strength, designed to reflect their varying population levels, ranging from ten votes each for the UK, Germany, Italy and France down to two votes for Luxembourg. The Council votes by simple majority unless the Treaty provides otherwise (Article 148(2) EC Treaty) but decisions relating to proposals for environmental matters are generally taken by qualified majority. A qualified majority is presently 62 votes out of 87.

The European Commission

The European Commission is composed of a college of 20 commissioners nominated by the members states for a five-year period. Commissioners are assisted by cabinets and collectively headed by a President. At the beginning of each term the President allocates policy portfolios to each commissioner. The Commission's day-to-day work is carried out by civil servants organised into units known as 'Directorate Generals'. Directorate Generals responsible for policies and legislation affecting the environment include DG XI (environment, nuclear safety and civil protection), DG VI (agriculture) and DG XIV (fisheries).

The Commission has three functions: initiator of legislation; guardian of the Treaties; and executive (Art 155 EC Treaty). EU legislation is generally generated by an initial proposal from the Commission which, after consideration by the European Parliament, is adopted by the Council. Legislative proposals are published in the *Official Journal of the European Communities*. In the field of environmental law the Commission's proposals are derived both from its own medium or long-term goals for legislation, set out in the form of Action Programmes, and in part by developments in national legislation which often prompt a need for co-ordinating measures at the Community level. The relationship between national parliaments and the EU will be strengthened by a Protocol to the 1997 Amsterdam Treaty which will provide for a six-week period between the tabling of any legislative proposal by the Commission and the placing of that decision before the Council for decision, thus enabling proper consideration of that proposal in national parliaments.

As guardian of the treaties it is the Commission's task to ensure that EU law is properly implemented. If EU law is not properly implemented in any member state, Article 169 EC Treaty provides a formal mechanism for enforcement which may result in the offending state being brought before the European Court of Justice.

The European Parliament

The European Parliament is a consultative and advisory body consisting of 626 MEPs directly elected for a period of five years. Formally the functions of the Parliament are: to scrutinise legislation (especially through the influential Environment, Public Health and Consumer Committee); in some cases, to act in concert with the Council in passing legislation; and to exercise control over the EU budget. Informally the Parliament sees itself as the champion of citizen rights.

Depending on the provisions of the EC Treaty the Parliament may be involved in the passing of legislation through one of three procedures: the consultative procedure, the co-operation procedure or the co-decision procedure. For most legislative proposals involving environmental affairs the co-operation procedure is specified. This procedure allows Parliament to improve proposed legislation by amendment following two readings in Parliament. The co-decision procedure applies to a minority of environmental legislation, including the production of Action Programmes on the Environment – effectively medium term plans for legislation. The co-decision procedure gives Parliament an effective veto on proposed legislation. The Amsterdam Treaty when it comes into force, will apply co-decision to almost all legislative proposals for which qualified majority voting is currently specified, including proposals under Article 130s for environmental legislation.

The European Court of Justice

The European Court of Justice (ECJ) exists to hear disputes relating to European Union law and to ensure that EU law is applied (Art 164 EC Treaty). The Court has 13 judges appointed by the member states for terms of six years. Six advocate generals advise the Court in the form of detailed argument in open court.

Since 1988 cases have been divided between the ECJ and a new Court of First Instance. The Court of First Instance is restricted in the type of case that it can hear and only rarely hears cases involving environmental issues. The ECJ hears actions brought by the Commission, under Article 169 EC Treaty, where member states are alleged to have failed to properly implemented Community law. Member states may also challenge the legality of each other's laws or actions under Article 170: this procedure is rarely used it but was evoked, in an environmental context, when France successfully challenged the UK's fishery conservation measures (Case 141/78 *France* v. *United Kingdom* [179] ECR 2923). The court also provides opinions on the interpretation of Community law when asked to do so by member states under Article 177 EC Treaty.

Courts of last resort i.e. courts against whose decisions there is no judicial remedy in national law (e.g. House of Lords in the UK) are obliged to refer cases involving genuine disputes; all other courts have a discretion to do so.

The decision of the Court is binding on EU member states. Until the modifications to the EC Treaty under the Maastricht Treaty came into effect the Court's powers in cases of a proved infringement of EU law were weak: consisting only of a power to make a pronouncement on the non-compliance of a member state. The Maastricht Treaty addresses this by providing the Court with the power to impose monetary penalties on member states that fail to comply with its judgements. This power has not yet been used. It has been argued that in general terms the Court has been ready to support environmental arguments and to give them greater weight in some cases than economic interests (*R* v. *Secretary of State for the Environment ex parte RSPB* (1997) 9 JEL 168; Sands, 1996).

The European Environment Agency

The European Environment Agency (EEA) was established by Regulation (EEC) 1210/90, which entered into force on 30 October 1993. Regulation 1210/90 established, alongside the EEA, a European Environment Information and Observation Network (EIONET) with the purpose of providing the European Union and member countries with objective, reliable and comparable information on the environment. The key tasks of the Agency are to:

— establish and co-ordinate the EIONET;
— provide the EU and member states with information for framing and implementing environment policies;
— encourage harmonisation of measurement methods and help ensure data comparability;
— record and assess data and provide assessment criteria;
— ensure dissemination of information including publication of a report on the state of the environment every three years, expert reports and environmental monographs;
— stimulate application of forecasting techniques and preventative measures;
— stimulate further development of methods for assessing environmental costs and exchange of experience on Best Available Technologies (BAT) between countries.

These tasks have been organised into a multi-annual work programmes of 93 projects covering the period 1994–99. The criticism of the role of the EEA is that, at present, it has no direct policing or enforcement powers

Other EU Institutions

In addition to those discussed above the EU has a number of other institutions. The Council, which is temporary and periodic, is assisted by a permanent body, the Committee of Permanent Representatives (COREPER). COREPER's work allows the Council agendas to be divided into two parts: those issues on which a unanimous view has been reached within COREPER, which can be agreed without discussion, and those on which such a view has not been achieved. The Economic and Social Committee (ECOSOC) and, since the Maastricht Treaty, the Committee of the Regions, exist to fulfil a purely consultative role, representing a broad range of social and regional interests. The EC Treaty provides for formal consultation of these bodies on certain matters. ECOSOC issues opinions that carry the informal authority of representing a broad cross-section of the Union's social and economic life. The European Court of Auditors is responsible for auditing the revenue and expenditure of the Community and all bodies set up by the Community.

European economic institutions include the European Investment Bank (EIB), the European Bank for Reconstruction and Development (ERBD) and the European Monetary Institute (EMI). The EIB has a lending portfolio of over 20 billion ECU, making it the world's largest lending institution. Its main function is to make long-term loans for capital investment to promote the EU's balanced economic development and integration. The ERBD was the first international organisation to be created after the end of the East-West conflict in Europe. It was formed in 1991, on a French initiative, with capital of 10 billion ECU, to finance projects aimed towards the redevelopment of Eastern Europe. The EMI, created in 1994, is responsible for guiding EU monetary union. Specifically its tasks are: to help achieve the conditions necessary for the last stage of monetary union, especially the convergence of the main macroeconomic indicators; to make preparations for the European System of Central Banks (ESCB) and the initiation of a single monetary policy and a single currency.

NGOs in European Institutions

NGOs have exerted considerable pressure on European institutions but have not been as influential as in the global arena. In Europe Environmental Pressure Groups (EPGs) have formed a liaison and umbrella group known as the European Environmental Bureau (EEB). The goal of the EEB is to co-ordinate the input of European EPGs in the formation of EU policy on the environment. The EEB has over 100 NGO members.

Despite the existence and actions of the EEB, Kramer (1992) asserts that EPGs have been relatively isolated in terms of the formation of EU environmental policy. Kramer estimates that from between 2000 and 3000 pressure groups are active in the EU but few have a permanent presence in Brussels. EEB and other EPGs attempt to influence Council decisions by sending memoranda to the presidency of the Council. The Commission has set up several advisory committees, including several with environmental remits. It does not organise consultations with EPGs in any formal way but prefers to approach selected EPGs in relation to particular proposals for legislation. The most extensive and direct access by EPGs occurs in relation to the European Parliament. EPGs are often invited to address public hearings on environmental matters held by the Environment and Animal Welfare committees of the European Parliament.

United Kingdom Institutions

Responsibility for law and policy on environmental issues in the UK is divided between many bodies and organisations: parliament, central government departments, environmental regulatory agencies, other specialist regulators and local authorities.

Parliament

All primary legislation, including environmental law, in the UK is made by the Queen in Parliament. In practice, however, much detailed environmental legislation including water and atmospheric quality standards, exemptions from planning controls and clean up liability for contaminated land is made by the executive under powers delegated by Act of Parliament. European law is usually implemented by means of delegated legislation, notably environmental assessment requirements, access to information rights and habitat protection.

The stimulus for new environmental legislation may come from a variety of sources. Sometimes, as in the Deposit of Poisonous Wastes Act 1972, the need for new law may be highlighted by an event which captures media attention (in this case the hazard to children of exposure to toxic waste). Ongoing review of UK environmental legislation is undertaken by the Royal Commission on Environmental Pollution (RCEP) a permanent institution with its own secretariat set up in 1970. RCEP reports, while not universally followed by governments of the day, have nevertheless been influential in determining the content and direction of UK environmental law. RCEP reports have been especially influential in promoting the characteristics of openness and transparency in environmental administration.

The content of environmental legislation is also influenced by parliamentary select committees. The House of Commons Environment Committee has been especially influential in reviewing existing legislation, making proposals for new law, and in scrutinising the content of specific legislative proposals.

Historically, environmental legislation has often been catalysed by the issue-promoting activities of environmental non-governmental organisations. Some of the UK's earliest measures, such as the Sea Birds Preservation Act 1869 and the Wild Birds Preservation Act 1876, arose as direct responses to the campaigning of conservation groups. Today it is common for the more 'respectable' environmental NGOs, such as Friends of the Earth and the World Wide Fund for Nature, to be consulted about the content of proposed environmental legislation. Environmental NGOs may still occasionally directly stimulate new environmental law through the private members' Bill procedure, as occurred in the case of the Home Energy Conservation Act 1995. More frequently, environmental NGOs provide, through their campaigning and direct action, the general background and tone out of which the perception of the need for new environmental legislation arises.

The most important stimulus for UK environmental legislation is European Union environmental law. The constant flow of environmental Directives from the EU sets an agenda to which the UK parliament must respond. One effect of European influence has been to erode the traditional English penchant for administrative discretion in favour of fixed rules and a culture of rights.

Central Government Departments

The Department of the Environment (DoE) originated in 1972 in response to the need to provide a focus to environmental policy in the wake of the Stockholm Conference on the Environment. In June 1997 it merged with the Department of Transport to become the Department of the Environment, Transport and the Regions (DETR). DETR has prime responsibility for development of UK environmental policy (including countryside and wildlife law, radioactive substances, toxic substances, water and waste and oversight of the Environment Agency). These policies find their expression in subsequent environmental legislation and in Guidance Notes and Circulars which are intended to assist both regulators and regulatees. The DETR is responsible for planning matters (including appeals and planning inquiries) and, since the June

1997 merger, all matters relating to national transport policy, including the controversial matter of the siting of new road projects.

The Secretary of State for the Environment, who is responsible to parliament for the activities of the DETR, has quasi-legislative and arbitrational responsibilities in relation to the completion and application of environmental legislation. These include, importantly, the promulgation of regulations which add detail to environmental legislation (which is often only framework in style). The Secretary of State also issues directions to bodies such as the Environment Agency; exercises discretionary powers such as designation of Special Areas of Conservation under the habitats Directive, and determines appeals against the decisions of environmental regulators such as the Environment Agency.

There are a number of other central government departments with important roles in relation to the environment. Generally all governments departments operate a policy that environmental considerations should be taken into account in the development of their policies and programmes of action. Some departments, however, have more direct environmental responsibilities.

The Ministry of Agriculture, Fisheries and Food (MAFF) has responsibilities including matters of implementation of EU fisheries and agricultural policies, farm support schemes, control of animal and plant diseases and the regulation of pesticides. In the past MAFF has been criticised for preferring the interests of farmers to those of the environment. Now, under section 17 of the Agriculture Act 1986, the agriculture ministers have a responsibility to seek to balance agricultural interests with the wider economic and social needs of rural areas and the needs of conservation and recreation.

The Department of Trade and Industry (DTI) makes policy with significant effects on industrial practices, with necessarily significant environmental effects. The DTI, for example, issues licenses for the extraction of oil from the deep sea bed. The Secretary of State for Trade and Industry has responsibilities in relation to electricity supply in England and Wales under section 3 of the Electricity Act 1989 and Wales and is responsible for the promotion and control of atomic energy under the Atomic Energy Act 1946.

The Treasury controls the funding available to all other governmental departments. It is possible, therefore, to view the Treasury as being the most important department in terms of overall effectiveness of environmental law. Although taxes and other economic instruments are increasingly used to supplement the traditional 'command and control' style of regulation, and large fines are increasingly imposed on transgressors of environmental law, funds raised in this way are not usually directed back to the institutions which raise them. Consequently treasury funding still provides the means and sets the limits to action by most other governmental environmental institutions.

Environmental Regulators

The United Kingdom now has two specialised integrated environmental regulators: the Environment Agency and the Scottish Environmental Protection Agency (SEPA). The Environment Agency is a product of amalgamation of three agencies with responsibilities for pollution control and conservation in England and Wales: the National Rivers Authority (NRA), Her Majesty's Inspectorate of Pollution (HMIP) and local authority Waste Regulation Authorities (WRAs). The NRA, which was created in 1989 in parallel with the privatisation of the former water authorities, had responsibilities for the regulation of water pollution, water resources, flood defence and (salmon, trout, freshwater and eel) fisheries. The principal roles of HMIP, which was created in 1987 by amalgamation of the Industrial Air Pollution Inspectorate and the Radiochemical, Hazardous Waste and Water Inspectorates of the DoE, were the application of Integrated Pollution Control under the Environmental Protection Act (EPA) 1990 and authorisation of radioactive emissions. Local authorities were designated as WRAs under EPA 1990 in order to separate the regulation of waste disposal from its strategic and operational aspects.

The government recognised that this fragmented regulatory framework was disadvantageous to industry and could hinder the identification of the 'best practicable environmental option', and could permit differing regulatory styles in relation to different operations. The tasks of NRA, HMIP and the WRAs were, in consequence, passed to the Environment Agency when the Environment Act 1995 came into force in April 1996.

The Environment Agency is created, by section 1(1) of the Environment Act 1995, as a body corporate, i.e. a body independent of any central government department (unlike the former HMIP). The legal composition of the Agency is eight to fifteen members: three appointed by the Minister of Agriculture Fisheries and Food, the remainder by the Secretary of State. Operationally the Agency is organised on a regional basis, closely following the catchment basin areas of the old assisted by regional advisory committees and a Welsh advisory committee.

The principal aim of the Agency, as laid down in section 4 of the 1995 Act, is:

'(subject to and in accordance with the provisions of [the] Act or any other enactment and taking into account any likely costs) in discharging its functions so as to protect or enhance the environment, taken as a whole, as to make the contribution towards attaining the objective of achieving sustainable development ....'

The general functions of the Agency in relation to pollution include exercising its powers for the purpose of preventing or minimising the effects of pollution of the environment (section 5(1)); compiling information relating to pollution (section 5(2)); carrying out assessments of the effects of pollution on the environment and preparing reports identifying options for preventing, minimising, or remedying or mitigating the effects and the costs and benefits of such options (section 5(3)).

In respect of water the Agency has a duty, so far as it considers it desirable, to promote the conservation and enhancement of the natural beauty and amenity of inland and coastal waters and of land associated with such waters, the conservation of water dependent flora and fauna, and the recreational use of such land and waters (section 6(1)). The Agency also has a duty to take such action as it may from time to time consider necessary, in accordance with directions issued by the Secretary of State, to be either necessary or expedient to conserve, redistribute or generally augment water resources in England and Wales (section 6(2)).

The Agency has a duty when formulating or considering proposals to take into account conservation concerns and also the economic and social well being of local communities in rural areas (section 7). It has consultative duties with respect to sites of special scientific interest (section 8). While the language of these provisions stresses human interests it would arguably be open to the Agency to adopt a non-anthropocentric approach. One of the more contentious features of the legislation establishing the Environment Agency is the entirely new requirement, contained in Section 39, to have regard to costs and benefits when exercising any of its powers. Although this duty does not apply if, or to the extent that it is unreasonable in view of the nature or purpose of the power and the circumstances of the particular case, it is considered by some to be a backdoor mechanism for the introduction of narrowly conceived cost-benefit analysis into environmental decision making. Could for example the Agency lawfully promote a policy of restricting an industrial process that turns out cheap products in order to protect a rare plant species?

Despite the rhetoric of integration, the Agency's environmental functions are far from comprehensive. It has only consultative powers in relation to land-based conservation and planning. Some pollution control powers including drinking water quality, statutory nuisances, air pollution assigned by order to local authorities, most contaminated land cases, and environmental health are outside its remit.

SEPA was created under the Environment Act 1995 to provide a unified environmental regulatory agency for Scotland similar to the

Environment Agency. SEPA is not, however, a direct Scottish equivalent of the Environment Agency. In Scotland, river purification boards (RPBs), which prior to SEPA were responsible for the regulation of water pollution, did not have the broader environmental responsibilities of their Anglo-Welsh counterpart, the NRA. Consequentially, the SEPA, which has assumed the powers of the RPBs, has somewhat narrower powers in relation to water. SEPA's functions are, in one other respect, broader than the Environment Agency, it also has responsibility for regulation of air pollution from processes not covered by the scheme for Integrated Pollution Control contained in Part I of EPA 1990.

In Northern Ireland there is no independent environmental regulatory agency. Instead environmental legislation is administered centrally by the Department of the Environment (Northern Ireland). Since 1996 this government department has delegated operational tasks, such as water and sewerage delivery, to a number of units within the department known as 'next steps agencies' which have separate budgets and directors. Thus, at a time when in Great Britain environmental regulation has increasingly been concentrated into fewer larger agencies, the process in Northern Ireland has been one of fragmentation (Turner and Morrow, 1997).

As we have seen the environmental agencies do not provide a fully integrated approach to environmental protection and English law has no mechanism for co-ordinating the activities of the different environmental bodies comparable for example with New Zealand's Resource Management Act 1991.

Conservation Bodies

Conservation in Britain was originally administered by a single Nature Conservancy Council (NCC). In 1991, under provisions of the Environmental Protection Act 1990, the NCC was divided into three regional Nature Conservancy Councils (NCCs) for England, Wales and Scotland. Co-ordination between the three regional NCCs takes place through a Joint Nature Conservation Committee.

In England responsibility for conservation is now divided between three bodies. The regional NCC, English Nature, is responsible for conservation of wildlife including the identification of Sites of Special Scientific Interest under the Wildlife and Countryside Act 1981. The Countryside Commission is responsible for promoting beauty and amenity including, among other things, the preparation of plans for long-distance routes (e.g. the Pennine Way) under sections 51–55 of the National Parks and Access to the Countryside Act 1949 and the designation of Areas of Outstanding Natural Beauty. The conservation of ancient monuments and buildings is dealt with by English Heritage.

In Wales and Scotland conservation and amenity functions are combined into unitary bodies: the Countryside Council for Wales (CCW) and Scottish Natural Heritage. In Northern Ireland conservation is the responsibility of the Department of the Environment (Northern Ireland).

Local Authorities

Local authorities in the UK have a number of responsibilities for the administration of environmental law. In Britain (but not Northern Ireland) they are charged with administration of the development control system under the Town and Country Planning Act 1990 and other related legislation. Local authorities have further environmental responsibilities including (in England and Wales) regulation of air pollution for processes not coming within integrated pollution control under part I of the EPA 1990; investigation and control of statutory nuisances under Part III of EPA 1990; application, where adopted, of the provisions of the Noise Act 1996; control of emissions of dark smoke under the Clean Air Act 1993; and oversight of the storage of hazardous substances under the Planning (Hazardous Substances) Act 1990.

Water and Sewerage Undertakers, OFWAT and the Drinking Water Inspectorate

The operational aspects of water supply and sewerage in England and Wales are provided by a number of private companies, created from the privatisation of the water industry that took place under the 1989 Water Act. Water companies hold licences to supply and charge for water and sewerage services under the provisions of the Water Industry Act (WIA) 1991. They are regulated by the Office of Water Services (OFWAT).

OFWAT, although not ostensibly an environmental regulator, has a pivotal role in aquatic environmental protection due to the knock-on consequences of its functions as economic regulator of water and sewerage companies. Water and sewerage undertakers are, under the terms of the WIA 1991, restricted to increasing water and sewerage charges to customers in line with inflation plus amounts determined by the head of OFWAT, the Director General of Water Services. These price increase limits restrict the amount of capital investment that water companies can, or – being profit-oriented bodies – are willing, to make. This is important as capital investment is usually necessary to achieve improvements in water quality. The Environment Agency theoretically has an unfettered discretion to seek improvements in the quality of discharges to the aquatic environment through a tightening of the conditions of water companies' discharge consents. However, in practice the Agency is limited, in the scope or rate of improvement of the aquatic environment it can request, to those improvements which can be paid for from the charge increases allowed by OFWAT. Thus, OFWAT, in conjunction with this is in the position of effectively determining the rate of improvement of aquatic environmental quality. OFWAT, after consultation with the Secretary of State for the Environment, has thus far chosen to err on the side of customer protection by limiting the rate of increase of water charges to very nearly just the amount required to pay for infrastructure improvements which will allow the UK to meet the standards of EC water legislation.

Drinking water quality is monitored for conformity with the standards prescribed by the European Community's Drinking Water Directive by the Drinking Water Inspectorate. This independent quality regulator was not absorbed into the Environment Agency on the ground that drinking water quality can be considered as a public health issue rather than an environmental matter.

Summary

1. The formation and application of environmental law depends on the existence of a strong and effective institutional framework.
2. At the international level the United Nations has occupied a central role as a catalyst of environmental law and policy. This has been achieved through the adoption of UN General Assembly resolutions, the oversight of development of new environmental law, and through the direct activity of UN programmes such as UNEP and UNDP. The UN has also given impetus to the development of international environmental law through the hosting of two key conferences: the 1972 Stockholm Conference on the Human Environment and the 1992 Rio Conference on the Environment and Development.
3. Funding mechanisms for the application of international environmental law are poorly developed. The Global Environmental Facility and the World Bank have, however, both provided novel mechanisms, over and above national government funding, for achieving the desired objectives specified in recent environmental conventions.
4. European institutions for environmental law include the Council of Europe and the European Union. The Council of Europe has promulgated several pan-European environmental conventions as well as animal welfare treaties and the European Convention of Human Rights. The pre-eminent European institution for the development of environmental law is the European Union. The European Union has grown out of the European Economic Community to a powerful quasi-federal structure consisting of 15 states. The obligations of European Union legislation are, in most cases, the principal factor in the development of national level environmental law.

5.　In the UK environmental law is influenced, in its formation, by many bodies including RCEP, the House of Commons Select Committee on the Environment, pressure groups and environmental NGOs. The application and administration of environmental law falls to a variety of bodies. In England and Wales the principal bodies in relation to pollution controls and conservation are the Environment Agency and English Nature, respectively.

Further Reading

Birnie, P.W. and Boyle, A.E. (1992) *International Law and the Environment*, chapter 2 (Oxford: Clarendon Press).

Cameron, J. and Mackenzie, R. (1996) Access to Environmental Justice and Procedural Rights in International Institutions. In Boyle, A.E. and M.R. Anderson (eds) (1996) *Human Rights Approaches to Environmental Protection* (Oxford: Clarendon Press).

Hession, M. and Macrory, R., Maastricht and the Environmental Policy of the Community. In D.M. O'Keefe and P.M. Twomey (eds) (1994) *Legal Issues of the Maastricht Treaty*.

Malcolm, R. (1994) *A Guidebook to Environmental Law*, chapter 3 (London: Sweet and Maxwell).

McEldowney, J.F. and McEldowney, S. (1997) *Environment and the Law: An Introduction for Environmental Scientists and Lawyers* (Harlow, Essex: Longman).

Somsen, H. (ed.) (1996) *Protecting the European Environment, Enforcing EC Environmental Law*, chapter 3 (London: Blackstone Press).

Werksman, J.D. (1996) *Greening Environmental Institutions* (London: Earthscan).

Workshop

1.　Consider the institutions that influence the formation of environmental law at the international level. Do those institutions that have been most successful in the advancement of international environmental law share any common features?
2.　Discuss the evolution of the European Union. What features of this institution make it particularly important as a source of environmental law? What characteristics of the European Union hinder efforts to ensure proper application environmental law?
3.　Given the diverse range of bodies that are involved in the administration of environmental law at the UK national level, what arguments are there for further integration of conservation and pollution bodies?
4.　What role should NGOs play in the overall institutional framework?

4 The International Development of Environmental Values

In this chapter we outline the general framework which international law and European law provides in relation to domestic environmental law. Particular aspects of both international and European law will reappear in later chapters. Environmental law has a strong international dimension. Pollution is no respecter of national boundaries. Both pollution and deforestation increase the carbon dioxide in the atmosphere thereby contributing to global warming. The international community shares the resources of the high seas. The interests of biological diversity do not depend upon where species happen to reside and many species migrate between countries. Some landscapes are of international importance. International law also has to address the problem of social justice: the benefits of exploiting nature and the costs of protecting the environment do not fall equally between the rich and the poor. These factors mean that the traditional principle of state independence has limited application to environmental matters.

International Law

International law is based on the principle of state sovereignty over its internal affairs. International law is binding on individual states in relation to trans-boundary issues, for example atmospheric pollution, or events outside the jurisdiction of individual states such as conservation of wildlife in the high seas. Problems such as wildlife conservation within state boundaries can be linked to international law concerns by treaty or through concepts such as the need to preserve the diversity of the world's resources. Environmental problems such as pollution and resource depletion can be linked to broad international concerns through the concept of social justice between rich and poor nations.

Environmental policy therefore rests on vague and to some extent conflicting international values. In order to attract support, international instruments must strike a careful balance between competing concerns at the expense of diluting environmental objectives. This can be illustrated by the 'Rio' Declaration (1992) (see below).

International law may also involve hidden political agendas. For example, political concerns in relation to financial interests can be presented as environmental concerns. On the other hand the agreed goals of trade policy could be distorted by moral crusades (see chapter 10 and Nolkaemper, 1996).

International Law and Domestic Law

There is a two-way relationship between international law and domestic law. In one direction international law filters down to domestic law. International law has no enforcement mechanisms other than voluntary co-operation between states and must therefore be implemented through domestic law. In the other direction the principles of international law are generated by the consent and practices of the states, members of the international community.

In some jurisdictions, international law is automatically part of domestic law and may be incorporated in the Constitution (e.g. Constitutions of Greece and Germany, see Kiss and Shelton, 1993, chapter 1). In English law the general principles of customary international law are part of the common law but give way to legislation and are no more than persuasive authority even within the common law. International treaties can alter the existing law only if they are enacted by statute.

Statute may transpose international law into domestic law in three main ways. Firstly, treaties may be enacted by statute as in the case of the legislation which implemented various international conventions relating to liability for oil pollution damage (Merchant Shipping (Oil Pollution) Act, 1971, Merchant Shipping Act, 1988, Schedule 4, Merchant Shipping (Salvage and Pollution) Act, 1994). Secondly, international law may be implemented by means of discretionary administrative powers, for example to grant pollution permits or to give planning permission. For example, section 7(2) of the Environmental Protection Act, 1990 requires the authority enforcing integrated pollution control to impose such conditions 'as it considers appropriate' for the purpose, inter alia, of complying 'with any directions by the Secretary of State given for the implementation of any obligations of the United Kingdom under ... international law relating to environmental protection'. This imposes wide powers which can be balanced against other statutory objectives. Thirdly, the objectives of a treaty can be introduced into domestic law as modifications to existing legal machinery. This was the case with the Berne Convention on Habitats which ultimately fed through to the UK conservation legislation (see Chapter 9).

Unless a statute is specifically enacted to give effect to a treaty, the English courts do not feel themselves bound to interpret the law in line with international obligations. There is a sound political reason for this. From the point of view of domestic law, treaties are merely agreements made by the executive and it would be a serious infringement of the rule of law if courts were required to obey the executive (see *Brind* v. *Secretary of State for theHome Dept* [1981] 1 AC 696. Even in the case of implementing legislation, the courts have sometimes preferred the strict language of the legislation and even executive discretion rather than the intention of the treaty (e.g. *R* v. *Poole Borough Council ex parte Beebee*: [1991] JPL 643, *R* v. *Swale Borough Council ex parte RSPB* [1991] 1 PLR 6 – environmental impact assessment).

Values generated within domestic law may, in their turn, influence international law. The three primary sources of international law are treaties, custom and 'the general principles of law recognised by civilised nations' (Statute of the International Court of Justice Art. 38(1)). All three in different ways depend upon the consent and practices of individual countries and mutually reinforce each other. Non-governmental organisations (NGOs) both international and national such as environmental pressure groups, often take part in the proceedings of international law making and supervisory bodies thus providing a mechanism for feeding domestic ethical values into the law-making process (see Boyle and Anderson, 1996, chapter 7). However, it is the normal practice that a national NGO must be accredited by its parent state with the danger that the more radical viewpoints will be excluded.

Sources of International Law

The basic source of international law is the consent of equal sovereign states thus providing an example of enlightenment social contract ethics. Consent manifests itself in two main ways: custom and treaty. 'General principles' of law form a third more controversial manifestation.

Customary law depends upon the practice of states in their international affairs coupled with evidence that the practice is regarded as binding (*opinio juris*). Custom and treaty may overlap in that a treaty entered into by many states may be used as evidence of an underlying custom thus binding even those states that were not parties to the treaty. Treaties may also build upon customary law by developing custom in more detail and providing regulatory machinery. This has been the case, for example, with the law of atmospheric pollution which builds upon a rather crude and uncertain customary principle that a state must not cause harm outside its boundaries and must warn other states of potential dangers (see *Trail Smelter Arbitration* 33 AJIL (1939) 182).

It has been suggested that the much recited 'duty to future generations' is an emerging principle of customary law although participatory machinery is conspicuously lacking (see Weiss, 1984). Other environmental principles which are becoming widely accepted so as possibly to acquire the status of customary law are the precautionary principle and the polluter pays principle (see McIntyre, 1997; Shannuganthan, 1997). If this is so then despite cases such as *Duddridge* (p. 153) these concepts might be argued in common law contexts.

The International Court of Justice has dealt with relatively few environmental cases although it now has an Environmental Chamber which might stimulate the development of the law. In the *Nuclear Tests Case* ICJ Rep (1974) 457 (*New Zealand* v. *France*) the International Court of Justice gave legal effect to a press statement by the French government to cease atmospheric testing of nuclear weapons in the Pacific pending the decision of the Court on the substantive issues. In the *Nuclear Tests Case*, 1995 (Communiqué No. 95/29), where France was accused of breaking this undertaking, three dissenting judges took the view that the concept of sustainable development and the precautionary principle were a recognised part of international customary law. The French government could therefore be required to carry out an environmental impact assessment in relation to a proposal to carry out nuclear tests in the Pacific. The majority did not confront this issue but rejected New Zealand's claim on the narrow ground that the tests concerned were not strictly atmospheric.

The significance of general principles of law as a source of international law is controversial. According to one view, general principles of law are derived from common understandings of justice held in the world community (see Birnie and Boyle, 1992, p. 21 *et seq*). On this basis, general principles of law could be derived from theoretical reasoning about environmental values and supported by grandiose declarations such as Stockholm and Rio without necessarily having to be found in state practice. However, there is a narrower understanding of general principles of law which limits the concept to principles of legal process commonly applied in national courts such as the right to be heard and good faith. On the whole the International Court of Justice has taken a cautious approach to general principles of law. It has used the doctrine mainly as a source of equity in cases where it has a discretion and as reinforcing outcomes derived from other sources (see *Diversion of Waters from the Meuse Case*, 1937).

The formal sources of international law each have their strengths and weaknesses but it has been said that none of them are powerful enough to tackle the environmental problems that face the world thus echoing Garrett Hardin's call for a voluntary acceptance of centralised authority (see Palmer, 1992). Treaties have the advantage of flexibility and detail and can include administrative and regulatory machinery. For example, treaties often include compliance mechanisms in the form of monitoring arrangements, financial incentives, arbitration, the fixing of quotas etc.

On the other hand a treaty may be deliberately couched in vague or ambiguous language in order to satisfy a wide range of political opinion and it may be difficult to establish sufficient common ground between nations to produce workable enforcement provisions. Moreover, a signatory to a treaty may opt out of aspects of the treaty that clash with its self-interest.

Custom and general principles may reflect strong and widely held social values but the development of customary law is slow and haphazard and the outcome may be uncertain and open ended. For example it is problematic whether custom with its slow and uncertain evolution is capable of meeting the threats of greenhouse gases and the ozone layer. The customary law of atmospheric pollution has been reinforced by important treaties (Vienna Convention for the Protection of the Ozone Layer 1985, Montreal Protocol 1990) and features in the influential Rio Declaration (UNCED, 1992).

The weaknesses of the formal sources of law and the controversial nature of environmental values have led international environmental law to rely heavily on 'soft law'. Soft law consists of principles that are not capable of direct application but carry authority either because they embody shared values or because they emanate from a respected official source. Perhaps the closest domestic analogy is to be found in the maxims of equity such as the principle that 'he who comes to equity must come with clean hands'. Resolutions of the UN General Assembly such as the Stockholm and Rio Declarations and the World Charter for Nature are probably soft law, as are the influential documents used by UNEP. Soft law is less binding than a formal treaty or a customary rule but has more authority than a policy statement such as the Brundtland Report (WCED, 1987). It can provide a framework for the making of more specific and binding rules. The sustainable development concept and the precautionary principle are perhaps soft law.

From one perspective soft law might be regarded as a feeble evasion. Some writers deny that the concept of soft law makes sense arguing that there is no halfway house between binding law and policy guidance (see Birnie and Boyle, 1992, p. 26). On the other hand soft law has political advantages (see Palmer, 1992). Environmental values are controversial and the international community includes many different cultural, economic, social and religious attitudes. States are more likely to agree to soft law embodying a value around which they can unite than to a binding treaty. Soft law can draw attention to ethical issues and express fundamental ethical values around which opinion can crystallise while leaving states the freedom to implement these in their own way. Soft law can also provide a catalyst for the later development of hard law principles (e.g. Helsinki Declarations on the Protection of the Ozone Layer, 1990).

Concepts of International Environmental Law

International law has produced three kinds of environmental concept. Firstly, there are concepts which are intended to justify the direct intervention of the international community in environmental matters. Secondly, there are expressions of substantive environmental values which can be adopted by states through their own laws. Thirdly, there are procedural values which can also be adopted by states. Substantive and procedural value will be discussed in particular contexts. In this section we will briefly discuss justification concepts. However, it must constantly be borne in mind that international principles particularly those of an ethical character are typically vague and open ended so as to be capable of many different interpretations within different cultures.

1. *Common property* Common property comprises the 'resources' of territory outside the jurisdiction of individual states, mainly the high seas such as fish and whales and requires that these be equitably distributed and that states should not interfere ?????? with the rights of others, perhaps extending to pollution. Customary law originally assumed that living resources were inexhaustible and was concerned only to ensure that states had equal access to these resources. The law was therefore narrowly anthropocentric. The emphasis of modern law has shifted, at least to conservation (*Icelandic Fisheries Cases* ICJ Rep (1974) 104) and possibly to the ecocentric preservation of marine life for its own sake (see below).

2. *Shared resources* This controversial concept refers to international watercourses. The general principle is analogous to that regulating the use of waterways within domestic law requiring an equitable division between the competing purposes of different users of the water (*Lac Lanoux Arbitration* 24 ILR (1957) 101).

3. *Common heritage* This doubtful concept means non-living resources in areas outside state jurisdiction such as the sea bed (Birnie and Boyle, 1992, p. 120). Common heritage differs from common property in that it claims that the mineral resources of the sea bed are for the benefit of all, not only for those who extract them (UNCLOS, 1982, Arts. 36, 37). Common heritage has not generally been applied to living resources (but see World Heritage Convention 1992 which applies to important landscapes and habitats).

4. *Common concern* The doctrines of common property, shared resources and common heritage extend to pollution control and ecological protection as incidental to the conservation of the resource. The doctrine of common concern is broader. It is not confined to exploitable resources but could include any environmental feature

which is of importance to the international community. The scope of the common concern doctrine is, therefore, uncertain and controversial. The climate and the atmosphere may be treated as matters of common concern so that activities within national boundaries such as pollution and deforestation fall within international jurisdiction (Birnie and Boyle, 1992, p. 390). The atmosphere consists of fluctuating and moving material that cannot be confined within national boundaries but because it also falls within national boundaries, cannot be regarded as common property either. The concept of common concern overlaps with the customary law principle of transboundary harm but is different in that, if a matter is of common concern, a state does not have to show that it has been directly injured in order to enforce the law. It is possible that any state might have standing to bring proceedings in an international tribunal under the doctrine of *erga omnes* (see *Barcelona Traction Case* ICJ Rep (1970) 4, but c.f. *Nuclear Tests* cases, 1974, International Law Commission, Draft Articles on State Responsibility Art. 19).

The protection of birds and migratory species might also be matters of common concern. The Biodiversity Convention 1992 describes biodiversity as a matter of common concern but the protection of individual animals and animal rights has not been given general status. There are, however, regional conventions within Europe protecting animals used for human purposes against suffering (Birnie and Boyle, 1992, pp. 424–5). Widely accepted conventions such as CITES, the International Convention for the Regulation of Whaling 1946 and the Antarctic Convention 1980 declare the importance of conservation of wildlife and marine resources and emphasise the need for international co-operation. This is similar to the doctrine of common concern, so that there may be a general custom at least in favour of nature conservation. However, it is not clear whether this is anthropocentric or ecocentric.

Environmental Interests and Values in International Law

The general policies and principles that give some shape to environmental law have been promoted through international instruments notably the Stockholm Declaration (1972) and the Rio Declaration (1992) (see below). These principles which have been applied also at European level include sustainable development, the preventative principle, the precautionary principle and the polluter pays principle. They will be discussed in the following chapters.

There is no coherent system of international environmental law. The law comprises a patchwork of concepts and rules developed in response to particular problems. Unlike the case for example with international trade law there are no central policy-making, dispute resolution or enforcement bodies. Environmental values are therefore at something of a disadvantage in that in the context of, say, international trade disputes they play the role of outsiders trying to override established systems.

The substantive principles of international environmental law feed into domestic law and will be discussed in particular contexts. Neither international law nor domestic law has produced a coherent concept of what is meant by environmental harm or damage or environmental rights. Should a polluter compensate only physical harm to human health or property or should purely economic loss be included (see e.g. *Merlin* v. *British Nuclear Fuels* [1990] 2 QB 557). There is also the question whether harm to non -human entities or ecosystems should be compensated and what form the compensation should take. This again raises the question of whether or not the law is anthropocentric. Another uncertain area is that of human rights. Does human rights law include a right to a decent environment? Such a right has been included in several state constitutions but at the international level has been recognised only as an arguable aspect of other rights contained in instruments such as the European Convention on Human Rights, for example, the right of life (see Chapter 12).

It is often argued that procedural rights such as participation are a fruitful technique for environmental protection and the Rio Declaration emphasises public participation in government decisions affecting the environment (see p. 382). As we have seen the ecocentric tendency claims that environmental protection is necessarily connected with participatory values but this claim is controversial. International law has promoted a range of participatory techniques which have filtered into domestic law and will be discussed in context. They include access to environmental information, and environmental impact assessment (see e.g. UNEP Goals and Principles of Environmental Impact Assessment, 1987; World Charter for Nature, 1982, Art. 11(b)(c); Biodiversity Convention, 1992, Art. 14; Rio Declaration, 1992, Principle 17, Principle 22).

Trade Restrictions

Another important relationship between international law and environmental law which has ethical implications concerns the possibility of conflict between the values of free trade and those of environmental protection. Environmental regulation or market incentives such as subsidies may be used as pretexts for trade protection and self-interest cloaked in the guise of ethical arguments (see Nolkaemper, 1996). To what extent can environmental measures taken by individual countries be justified in the light of the international community's concern to protect freedom of trade which it manifests through international bodies and dispute resolution mechanisms such as the World Trade Organisation?

The GATT Art XX allows environmental factors to moderate the concerns of free trade, this is closely followed by the EC Treaty which enables trade restrictions to be justified 'for the protection of health and life of humans, animals or plants' provided that there is no arbitrary discrimination or a 'disguised restriction on trade between member states'. The European Court has also developed the concept of mandatory overrides which include environmental concerns and polices the overrides strictly. For example in the 'Danish Bottles' case (*Commission v. Denmark*, Case 302-86 [1988] ECR 4607), Danish laws requiring drink cans and bottles to be returned for recycling were upheld but additional requirements restricting the size and shape of bottles were not. The Court took the approach that the restriction must be 'proportionate' in the sense of not going beyond what is necessary to achieve a legitimate objective in this case environmental protection.

There is a particular overlap between trade concerns and waste management problems. For example the disposal of waste could be regarded as a matter of international free trade (see e.g. *Commission v. Belgium*, Case C-2/90 [1992] 1 ECR 4431 (*Wallonian Waste* case)). When can a state ban imports of hazardous waste for environmental reasons? To what extent should developing countries be protected against the dumping of waste on their territories by other states? (See Basel Convention on the Control of Transboundry Movements of Hazardous Waste and their Disposal, 1989 29 ILM 649.)

The problems arising out of conflicts between international trade and environmental interests will be discussed further in Chapter 1.

The Key International Instruments

At international level explicit statements of ethical positions are usually couched at a very general level and emerge when laws are made rather than when they are applied to particular cases. Moreover ethical statements may be confined to preambles rather than to operative language. At the level of decision making in particular cases, ethical discussion is less likely to be explicit and ethical attitudes may be revealed only as implicit assumptions. Even where ethical arguments are expressly made they may be produced as rhetorical devices to mask a political or economic agenda. In Chapter 11 we shall discuss an example of ethics in action in international law. Here we shall outline some landmark international instruments.

The 1972 United Nations Declaration on the Human Environment

The 1972 Stockholm Conference on the Human Environment was convened by UNGA in response to a growing realisation of the limited nature of earth's resources. The formal outcomes of this, the first truly global environmental conference, were:

— an Action Plan for environmental policy;
— an Environment Fund;
— a new UN Environment Programme (UNEP); and
— a Declaration on the Human Environment.

The Action Plan consisted of 106 recommendations organised into three main areas: a global environmental assessment programme (Earthwatch); environmental management activities; and international measures to support national and international assessment and management.

The Declaration contained 26 principles. Two proclaimed 'rights' including, importantly, Principle 1 ('Man has the fundamental right to freedom, equality and adequate conditions of life, in an environment of a quality that permits a life of dignity and well-being, and he bears a solemn responsibility to protect and improve the environment for present and future generations') and Principle 21 ('States have, in accordance with the Charter of the United Nations and the principles of international law, the sovereign right to exploit their own resources pursuant to their own environmental policies, and the responsibility to ensure that activities within their jurisdiction or control do not cause damage to the environment of other States or of areas beyond the limits of national jurisdiction'). These principles appear to conflict and are strongly anthropocentric. Other principles concern pollution (Principles 6 and 7); the conservation of resources (Principles 2–5), developmental issues (Principles 8–15); demographic policies (Principle 16); scientific research and development (Principle 20); state responsibility for the environment (Principle 22); applicability of values (Principle 23); and nuclear weapons (Principle 26).

The Declaration is not regarded as legally binding, although some of its provisions may have acquired this character through incorporation into customary law (Sohn, 1973). The Declaration has, however, been highly influential as 'soft law': it is cited in the preamble material of many environmental conventions and agreements, and many of its principles have been given effect through later 'hard' instruments of environmental law. Most of the Declaration's principles were updated and reformulated from the outcomes of the 1992 UN Conference on the Environment and Development (see below).

The United Nations 'Rio' Declaration on Environment and Development (UNCED)

During the late 1980s a combination of factors elevated global concern for the environment including increased acceptance, especially by developing states, of the link between poverty and environmental degradation; environmental disasters such as the Bhopal gas explosion and the Chernobyl nuclear accident; and the publication of key environmental reports such as the World Commission on Environment and Development's 'Our Common Future'. In December 1988 the UNGA responded to this increased concern by resolving to hold a Conference on Environment and Development (UNCED) in 1992.

UNCED was based around the concept of 'sustainable development'. Sustainable development probably derives from the concept of 'eco-development' launched by UNEP in 1973 (Timoshenko and Berman, 1996). It achieved prominence with the publication of the World Conservation Strategy (IUCN, 1980) and grew considerably in status as a result of the influential 'Brundtland Report' (WCED, 1987). Although the concept is contentious (see below) many commentators accept the definition of sustainable development provided by the Brundtland Report: 'development that meets the needs of the present generation without compromising the ability of future generations to meet their own needs' (WCED, 1987, p. 8). The central feature of Brundtland enthusiastically taken up by at UNCED is the belief that economic growth and environmental protection are compatible so that policies in favour of free trade which are intended to increase economic growth can be pursued along with environmental regulation.

Sustainable development is central to the five outcomes of UNCED: the Rio Declaration; the Framework Convention on Climate Change; the Convention on Biological Diversity; Agenda 21; and the non-legally binding Forest Management Principles. The Rio Declaration was originally hoped to be an 'Earth Charter' with the moral and political authority equivalent to that of the Universal Declaration of Human Rights. The Declaration which emerged from UNCED is, unfortunately, much weaker, merely modifying the 1972 Stockholm Declaration on the Human Environment.

Agenda 21 is a comprehensive programme of action to achieve global sustainable development. Titles include Agriculture, Biotechnology, Business, Consumption Patterns, Children, Combating Poverty, Conservation, Biodiversity, Decision Making, Deforestation, Desertification and Drought, Education, Financial Resources, Freshwater Resources, Hazardous Wastes – Management, Human Health, Human Settlement, Indigenous Cultures, Local Authorities, Non-Governmental Organisations, Atmosphere, Oceans, Radioactive Wastes, Farmers, Science, Technology, Solid Wastes, Sustainability, Sustainable Development, Technology Transfer, Toxic Chemicals, Trade Unions, and Women.

Chapter 33 of Agenda 21 requires states to

> 'reaffirm their commitments to reach the accepted United Nations target of 0.7 per cent of GNP for ODA and, to the extent that they have not yet achieved that target, agree to augment their aid programmes in order to reach that target as soon as possible and to ensure prompt and effective implementation of Agenda 21.'

Key themes of the Rio Declaration which might be difficult to reconcile are the principles of 'common but differentiated responsibilities' (Principle 7) and state sovereignty (Principle 2). 'Common but differentiated responsibility' recognises the need for all states to 'co-operate in a spirit of global partnership to conserve, protect and restore the health and integrity of the Earth's ecosystem' while at the same time acknowledging the special responsibility of developed states 'in view of the pressures their societies place on the global environment and of the technologies and financial resources they command'. State sovereignty is enshrined in Principle 2 which asserts the 'sovereign' right of states to exploit their own resources pursuant to their own environmental and developmental policies. On the other hand Principle 12 requires states to co-operate in supporting free trade and economic growth and not to use environmental measures in a discriminatory way or as disguised trade restrictions. In particular 'unilateral actions to deal with environmental challenges outside the jurisdiction of the importing state should be avoided . Environmental measures addressing transboundary or global environmental problems should as far as possible be based on an international consensus'. (See also Principle 5, co-operation to eradicate poverty; Principle 6, special needs of developing countries; Principle 11, environmental policies may vary between countries because of economic and social costs; Principle 22, the identity, culture and interests of indigenous people and their communities and 'other local communities' should be respected.)

The 27 principles of the Declaration can therefore be regarded either as a delicate balance between developmental and environmental interests (Nanda, 1995) or, because of their emphasis on development and sovereignty, as a retrograde step in econcentirc terms.

The Framework Convention on Climate Change has the objective of 'stabilisation of greenhouse gas concentrations in the atmosphere at a level that would prevent dangerous anthropogenic interference with the climate system' (Article 2) . Guided by a number of principles (Article 3), the parties to the convention agree, among other things, to develop national inventories of anthropogenic emissions and sinks of greenhouse gases, to develop regional programmes to mitigate climate change, to promote and co-operate in transfer of technology to combat climate change, and to aim to return anthropogenic emissions of carbon dioxide and other greenhouse gases not controlled by the Montreal Protocol to their 1990 levels by the year 2000.

The Biodiversity Convention has the twin objectives of 'conservation of biodiversity and the sustainable use of its components' and 'the fair and equitable sharing of the benefits arising out of the utilisation of genetic resources'. The convention confirms the traditional assumption that conservation of natural resources is best achieved through assertion of state sovereignty over those resources. To this end states are placed under a number of requirements in relation to conservation and sustainable use (Articles 6–9) including, *inter alia*, national identification and monitoring of biological diversity; environmental impact assessment, and in-situ and ex-situ conservation measures.

Although states are to 'endeavour to create conditions to facilitate access to genetic resources' (Article 15) the Convention does not create any right of access to such resources but, rather, confirms the right of sovereign states to determine such access. This access is envisaged to be dependent on a sharing by developed states 'in a fair and equitable way' of the benefits arising from such access and exploitation (Article 15.7), on the provision of technologies (Article 16) and on the provision of 'new and additional' financial resources (Article 21). As Boyle (1994) notes, the success of the convention is likely to depend heavily on the practical outcome of these anticipated benefits. The USA refused to sign the Convention due to objections to these provisions and provisions relating to intellectual property rights and the role of the GEF.

The Broadening of International Law

It has been argued that, since the Second World War, the concerns of international law have gradually widened from the narrowly anthropocentric through intergenerational equity towards an ecocentric perspective but not yet reaching the holistic, deep ecology stage (Birnie and Boyle, 1992, pp. 211–13; Boyle and Anderson, 1996, chapter 3; Emmenegger and Tschentscher, 1994). This line of argument should be considered cautiously. The international instruments are not consistent, non-anthropocentric sentiments are often preambular rather than contained in the substance of the treaty or in executive instruments. Ethical arguments are frequently used at the policy-making stage but might be a cloak for other concerns and in any case are less frequently used at the implementation stage. In Chapter 10 we shall discuss a particular example.

The dominant international policy of sustainable development is expressly anthropocentric (e.g. RIO Principle 1: 'human beings are at the centre of concerns for sustainable development') (see also Stockhom, 1992). On the other hand there is evidence for the evolutionary argument in the history of the international regulation of whaling (see D'Amato and Chopra, 1991). Originally the purpose of regulation was to protect the whaling industry. Under the 1946 Convention for the Regulation of Whaling this broadened out to embrace the interests of future generations. Emmeneger and Tschentscher (1994) argue that by showing concern for the interests of future generations, international law took a decisive step forward since, in their view, concern for future generations cannot be explained in terms either of utilitarianism or human rights. The influence of non-whaling nations subsequently increased leading from 1986 to a moratorium on the hunting of the larger species of whale. The purpose of the moratorium was ostensibly to benefit the species for their own sake.

References to future generations have become commonplace in international conservation instruments. Examples include the Whaling Convention, 1946, preamble; CITES, 1972, preamble; Biological Diversity Convention, 1992, preamble; Berne Convention on European Wildlife and Natural Habitats, 1979, preamble Art. 2; Bonn Convention the Conservation of Migratory Species of Wild Animals, 1979, preamble; Stockholm, 1972, Principles 2 and 6; UNCED, 1992, Principle 3. However, these references are confined to general expressions of approval and there is no enforcement provision. Weiss (1990, p. 198) recommends that the collective rights of future generations could be represented by an official such as a guardian.

There is evidence that international law is taking a broad view of the meaning of harm for the purpose of compensation arrangements, including in particular restoration costs to the national environment (see Birnie and Boye, 1992, p. 100). The *Trail Smelter* (p. 105) was compared to property damage but the relevant law was US law.

Some international instruments assert that nature has intrinsic value separate from human interests (e.g. Biological Diversity Convention, 1992, preamble; World Charter for Nature: 1982; Berne Convention on the Conservation of European Wildlife and Natural Habitats, 1979). On the other hand the Ramsar Convention on Wetlands of International Importance which has considerable influence on European and domestic policy is anthropocentric in tone. It regards man and the environment as separate but interdependent and justifies protecting wetlands on the ground that 'wetlands constitute a resource of great economic, cultural, scientific and recreational value, the loss of which would be irreparable'.

Ramsar illustrates a problem with attempts to promote a biocentric agenda. It may be difficult to distinguish genuinely ecocentric concerns from a broad 'enlightened' concern with human interests. If we include aesthetic appreciation, prudence and fear among the human interests we are concerned to protect, it is difficult to conceive of any interest that could be respected exclusively upon non-anthropocentric grounds (see Glennon, 1990; Huffman, 1992; Elder, 1984). The position is complicated because it is not clear whether the strategy is to believe that nature really does have value (and possibly rights) for its own sake or whether the concept of the intrinsic value of nature is a device intended to stress the importance of environmental concerns to people and to focus legal machinery. For example the World Charter for Nature lurches in different directions and features all three tendencies – anthropocentric, biocentric and ecocentric. It proclaims that 'man is a part of nature and life depends on the uninterrupted functioning of natural systems which ensure the supply of energy and nutrients' and that 'living in harmony with nature gives the best opportunities for the development of his creativity and for rest and recreation'. It also asserts that 'every form of life is unique, warranting respect regardless of its worth to man, and to accord other organisms such recognition, man must be guided by a moral code of action'. This suggests an individualistic philosophy. However, the Charter also takes an ecocentric stance. It states 'The genetic viability on the earth shall not be compromised, the population levels of all life forms wild and domesticated must be at least sufficient for their survival' and 'special protection shall be given to unique areas, to representative samples of all the different types of ecosystems and to the habitats of rare or endangered species'. There is then a shift to the narrower anthropocentric mode. 'Ecosystems and organisms ... that are utilised by man, shall be managed to achieve and maintain optimum sustainable productivity'.

The emphasis of international conservation treaties is upon rare or endangered species. This is consistent with an ecocentric perspective. The Whaling Convention illustrates the difficulty of determining how far anthropocentric, biocentric or ecocentric values influence events. The ban on whaling can be rationalised on all three grounds. Anthropocentrists point to the fact that human beings have traditionally admired and respected great whales. Whales are also regarded as like us in being relatively sociable and intelligent. From the biocentric perspective it could be argued that essential human interests are not at stake and that important human interests in scientific research are catered for by granting exemptions under the treaty. Finally, an ecocentrist might point to the fact that large whales are an endangered species and support an ecosystem of their own in terms of other creatures that depend on them.

International law is not strong on individualistic biocentric values. There are no universal animal rights instruments. There are some regional instruments but these concern the well being of animals that are either used as human resources or are closely associated with us as pets (see Birnie and Boyle, 1992, p. 424; European Conservation for the Protection of Pet Animals, 1987).

International pollution law sends out a mixed message. For example, UNCLOS Part XII which deals with marine pollution is concerned with non-human as well as human affairs while the 1992 Helsinki Convention in the Transboundary Effects of Industrial Accidents and the 1972 Convention for the Protection of Marine Pollution by Dumping are anthropocentric. Pollution treaties commonly separate humans from other interests by claiming to protect 'human health and the environment' (e.g. Vienna Ozone Convention, 1985 and Montreal Protocol, 1987; Geneva Convention on Long-Range Transboundary Air Pollution, 1979; Basel Convention on the Control of Hazardous Waste, 1989).

Taken as a whole, the international instruments reflect the uncertainty and incoherence of environmental philosophy and politics. There is attention upon the ecocentric concerns of biodiversity and habitat protection but the law is most developed in relation to the relatively straightforward problems of pollution where human interests are most obvious or where we are dealing with species close to us as in the case of the 1946 Whaling Convention and other instruments which have been introduced to protect creatures that human beings find attractive or interesting. Another aspect of this is to reason anthropomorphically from human characteristics so as to justify favouring the members of certain species as honorary human beings. Hence there is considerable attention to questions such as whether whales or apes can communicate. Such reasoning applied to human groups would be widely regarded as obnoxious. Again this illustrates the fundamental problem that environmental ethics lacks coherent foundations.

We are also faced with the problem of weighing competing interests. Should we, for example, conserve a species such as a midge that is inconvenient but not life threatening to human beings? Emmeneger and Tschentscher (1994, p. 585) take the familiar approach based upon whether the so-called right holder has characteristics similar to humans, e.g. the intellectual and social capacities of whales and elephants. They also rely upon the difference between survival interests and less serious interests in a way reminiscent of Taylor's biocentrism.

Emmeneger and Tschentscher also distinguish between ecocentric and biocentric approaches. They argue that the more individualistic biocentric approach is likely to represent the present state of international law partly because there has only been a gradual extension from anthropocentrism and partly because international law reflects the market-orientated adversarial attitudes of the majority of states. They regard biocentrism as consistent with competition between diverse entities even to the extent of extinguishing species provided that the rules of the game are fair. By contrast they regard harmony as essential to the ecocentric approach and, therefore, treat competition as destructive. However, it is questionable whether harmony is an ingredient of ecocentrism. Ecological science has not told us whether stability or change is natural. The notion of harmony in itself is an entirely human construction. Moreover, competition may be a natural device for sustaining ecosystems. Aldo Leopold's land ethic does not outlaw hunting and Leopold stresses that we can use nature as a resource just as can other members of the land community (Leopold, 1949).

The European Union

The mechanics of the European Union and its relationship with English law are discussed in many student texts. We shall concentrate on the European Union as a means of creating and transmitting general environmental principles. We shall deal with particular European laws and their enforcement in later chapters as the context requires.

The law made by the Communities of the European Union, and particularly by the European Community forms a transmission belt between international law and domestic law. The European Community is committed to complying with international environmental policies and has acknowledged, in particular, the Rio Declaration and the instruments made under it which promote the aims of sustainable development and biodiversity (see Council Resolution (138/1) 1993). The European Community can be a party to international environmental treaties (Art. 130R(5) EC).

Unlike other international bodies the European Union penetrates deeply into domestic legal systems. Its constitutional basis lies in a series of treaties, founded upon the Treaty of Rome (1958) which have been transposed into English law by the European Communities Act, 1972 as amended. The main treaty from an environmental perspective is the European Community Treaty. There is, of course, nothing unusual in treaties being implemented by domestic legislation but the European treaties are unique in three respects. Firstly, they delegate powers to administrative bodies (the European Commission and the Council of Ministers) and to the European Court of Justice to make laws which are directly binding in member states. Secondly, European law so made is intended to take priority over domestic law (*Costa* v._*ENEL*, 1964). Thirdly, European law can be enforced by and against individuals and national remedies must be effective to enforce EC rights (Art. 5 EC).

As Shaw has remarked (1996, p. 17) the European Court of Justice has consistently distanced itself from 'ordinary' international law 'arguing that by accession to the EU the member states have transferred sovereign rights to the Community, creating an autonomous legal system in which the subjects are not just states but also individuals'. Article 5 EC is particularly important in the environmental context since it creates a general obligation to conform to the objectives of the European Union not just to the specific law. 'Member states shall take all appropriate measures, whether general or particular to ensure fulfilment of the obligations arising out of this treaty or resulting from action taken by the institutions of the Community. They shall facilitate the achievement of the Community's tasks. They shall abstain from any measure which could jeopardise the attainment of the objectives of this treaty.'

Until the Treaty of Rome was modified by the Single European Act of 1986 and the Treaty of European Union (Maastricht Treaty) 1992, the legal basis of the Community's environmental activities was doubtful. The purpose of the Community was primarily to advance the economic interests of its members but after the Stockholm Conference of 1972, the Community actively developed an environmental policy. According to the Paris Summit of 1972, this was originally justified, somewhat vaguely, on the basis that economic development was not an end in itself but a means of advancing the well being of the citizens of the community an anthropocentric sentiment that also informs the notion of sustainable development. The Single European Act, 1996 modified the original Treaty to make environmental protection an explicit objective both in its own right and as a component of the Community's other policies (Art. 130 EC).

Article 130r, (now Art. 174 after the Treaty of Amsterdam), includes the following objectives: 'to preserve, protect and improve the quality of the environment, to contribute towards protecting human health, to ensure a prudent and rational utilisation of natural resources, to promote measures at international level to deal with regional or worldwide environmental problems'. A high level of protection is required. Article 174 is wide enough to embrace non- economic environmental concerns thus providing a possible base for non-anthropocentric ethical arguments. This will be discussed in the chapter on nature conservation.

However, a more anthropocentric approach seems to pervade the new Art. 6 introduced by the Treaty of Amsterdam in 1998. This requires environmental protection to be integrated into the definition and implementation of Community policies and activities in particular with a view to promoting sustainable development. Article 2 which sets out the broad objectives of the European Union includes that of promoting 'economic and social progress which is balanced and sustainable'.

Before these specific environmental provisions were introduced, environmental policy was implemented under two provisions of the EC treaty. The first, Art. 100 (now Art 95), deals with the common market. Under Art. 95, environmental measures to a 'high level of protection' should be harmonised between the member states in the interests of fair competition. This indirect method of pursuing environmental goals was supplemented by Art. 235 which permits measures not authorised elsewhere if 'action by the Community should prove necessary to attain in the course of the operation of the common market'. Article 235 has been applied broadly by the European Court of Justice. For example, the Wild Birds Directive 79/409 was made under Art. 235 on the dubious basis that the conservation of wild birds is necessary for the harmonious development of economic activities (see Freestone, 1991).

The environmental powers now embodied in Art. 174 presumably mean that Art. 235 can no longer be relied upon for environmental purposes. However, there is still an overlap with Art. 95. After the Treaty of Amsterdam this seems to be of limited practical importance since in both cases the co-decision procedure usually applies. This involves qualified majority voting, gives the European Parliament a veto, and requires consultation with the Committee of the Regions (Art. 251, formerly Art. 189b). Town and country planning measures, fiscal measures and energy policy are not subject to this procedure but require unanimity in the Council and Parliament has no veto. A remaining difference between Art. 174 and Art. 95 is that under Art. 174 a state can keep or introduce more stringent protective measures of its own provided that they are compatible with the treaty and are notified to the Commission. Under Art. 95 a state can maintain existing requirements for the protection of the environment subject to notifying the Commission (Art. 95(4)) but can introduce new national provisions only where they are based on new scientific evidence to deal with a problem specific to that state, again subject to notifying the Commission (Art. 95(5)).

Measures, the main purpose of which is to protect the environment must now be promoted under Art. 174. In the 'Titanium Dioxide' case, *Commission* v. *Council* [1991] 3 LMELR 164 the ECJ suggested that, where the impact of a measure affects the single market, the measure can be promoted under either what was then Art. 130 or Art. 100A.

However, the Court has subsequently used the test of whether the main purpose of the measure, usually a directive, is the protection of the environment (see *Commission* v. *Council* [1993] ECR1-939). If so Art. 174 must be used.

Article 174 is broadly drawn. In principle, it could include the full range of environmental ethical values in that it specifically separates the goals of environmental protection from those of protecting human health and conserving resources. Article 174 repeats the general environmental principles that have become a familiar feature of international instruments, namely, the preventative principle, the 'rectification at source' principle, the polluter pays principle and the precautionary principle. All these provisions are consistent with the range of ethical perspectives. Article 174 opens the way to non-anthropocentric ethical concerns by allowing member states to take provisional measures for non-economic environmental reasons, subject to a Community inspection procedure. On the other hand in preparing its policy the community must take into account 'the potential costs and benefits of action or lack of action'.

There are certain limitations upon the exercise of discretion by EU bodies. One is the principle of proportionality, that the measure must be suitable and necessary for achieving the object sought. Another is the principle of non-discrimination which prevents the unequal treatment of economic sectors or products of a member state unless the unequal treatment can be objectively justified by reference to an overriding policy, including environmental policy (see p. 111). Thirdly, the principle of 'subsidiarity' requires that the EC shall take action 'only if and so far as the objectives of the proposed actions cannot be sufficiently achieved by the Member States and can, therefore, by reason of the scale or effects of the proposed action be better achieved by the Community' (Art. 3B).

European Environmental Policy

The European Court of Justice has recognised that environmental protection is one of the Community's 'essential objects' (see Kramer, 1992, p. 9). As we have seen there is no agreement between governments as to what kind of environmental ethic should be followed. European policy reflects this. There has been some broadening of concern but the emphasis remains anthropocentric. The Community has produced five successive Action Programmes on the Environment in 1973, 1977, 1983, 1987 and currently 1992. The Fifth Action Programme (OJC 138/5) is intended to cover the period until the year 2000.

The first two Action Programmes concentrated upon remedying and preventing pollution. Programmes 3 and 4 introduced procedural measures including environmental impact assessment and access to environmental information thus opening up the process to a broader range of ethical perspectives. The current Fifth Action programme 'Towards Sustainability: 1993' reflects the international preoccupation with sustainable development. A central concern is that of 'shared responsibilities'. Reliance is placed upon changing the voluntary behaviour of individuals and companies as well as upon direct state regulation. Market mechanisms such as pollution charges, voluntary agreements and tradable permits are in favour. There is also an integrated approach to pollution control across the environmental media and emphasis is placed upon the activities that generate problems – industry, tourism etc. – rather than dealing with environmental impacts in isolation. The programme also stresses the importance of 'education in the development of environmental awareness', and access to information. These concerns provide the framework for a wide-ranging ethical debate.

Nothing in the Fifth Action Programme suggests that its concerns are anything other than human although particular Directives, for example the Nitrates Directive (91/576 EEC), do go beyond human interests. The Fifth Action Programme's approach to the protection of nature remains anthropocentric even though it claims to take a broad approach. It refers to 'mankind's fundamental desire to live in harmony with nature and to enjoy and derive pleasure from it ... the overall maintenance of the ecological balance, ... a genetic bank which is essential to medical, biological, agricultural and other scientific progress' (ibid, p. 44). Similarly the 'priceless' aspects of the environment are defined apparently by reference to human entertainment; 'the last giant panda or elephant, the singing of birds, aspects of cultural heritage'.

The Action Plan relies upon the economic valuation approach which attempts to identify the costs and benefits both of action and inaction (Art. 130 r (3)). However, it also recognises that 'unlike business which uses money as a common unit of measurement, there is no "numeraire" for environmental variables. This means it is difficult to weigh up true opportunity costs of improving one environmental variable against another ... because all environmental variables interlink, environmental policy requires an integrated or holistic approach' (p. 96).

European Law and Domestic Law

European Community law penetrates into domestic law in four ways. Firstly, member states are bound to implement the requirements of European Community law through their own legal mechanisms. In the case of the UK, this normally means by statute or subordinate legislation. In some cases, however, the UK has implemented European requirements through the discretionary practices of officials, e.g. pollution control agencies, under the guidance of government circulars. This could result in conflict with the European Court of Justice. One of the basic values of European law is the principle of legality according to which 'there must be a clear, specific legal framework relevant to the subject matter of a directive so that individuals are in a position to know their rights in order to rely upon them where appropriate' (*Commission* v. *Germany* [1991] ECR 1-825, air quality directives). Modern environmental legislation reflects this for example in relation to pollution standards.

EC law is heavily influenced by civil law culture under which broadly drafted codes containing general principles are applied by the courts with the aim of giving effect to their purposes. English law by contrast takes a more pragmatic, utilitarian approach which favours administrative discretion. For example in *R.* v. *Secretary of State for the Environment ex parte Friends of the Earth* [1995] Env LR 11, it was held that the Secretary of State had adequately implemented the European Drinking Water Directive (778/80 EEC), by taking undertakings from the water company concerned rather than use his legal powers of enforcement even though the undertakings fell short of an absolute obligation to comply. Similarly, in *R.* v. *Poole Borough Council ex parte Beebee* [1991] JPL 643 it was held that, provided the environmental issue – in that case the preservation of a habitat for rare lizards – was drawn to the council's attention, the council could grant planning permission for housing development without holding a formal environmental assessment as required by EC law (85/337 EEC). This ignores one of the main purposes of environmental assessment, that of public participation.

Secondly, some EC instruments are automatically enforceable in domestic law (Chapter 12). The English courts have accepted that where there is a conflict between an enforceable Community law and a domestic law, the former prevails (*R.* v. *Secretary of State for Transport ex parte Factortame* [1991] 1 AC 603), and to this extent our traditional doctrine of parliamentary supremacy has been modified. European law also requires that domestic law should provide effective remedies.

Thirdly under the doctrine of 'indirect effect', domestic law must be interpreted in line with European law even perhaps where the domestic law predates the relevant European law (see *Marleasing SA* v. *La Commercial Internacional de Alimentacion SA* [1990] ECR 1-135).

Fourthly under the principle in *Francovich* v. *Italy* [1991] ECR 1-5357 an individual may obtain compensation from a state for damage suffered due to the state's failure to implement a European law or possibly due to a defective implementation. This raises the difficult question of what counts as environmental damage.

Summary

1. The bulk of our statutory environmental law is either a direct enactment of European requirements or is heavily influenced by European law and policy. International law's influence is less direct but equally important. International law is not binding upon English courts directly but feeds into the law by influencing legislation and through European law.

2. The sources of international law include custom, treaties and general principles of law recognised by civilised communities. There is a distinction between 'hard law' and the disputed notion of 'soft law' which consists of emerging principles that have not crystallised into enforceable rules. The precautionary principle, intergenerational equity, and sustainability are emerging ideas the status of which is unclear.

3. International law has developed concepts which allow it to regulate areas outside the territories of states (common property) and also to concern itself with internal matters (common concern and common heritage).

4. International human rights may also include environmental interests but the scope of these is not clear. Process rights such as access to information are of considerable importance.

5. International law has broadened its concerns from narrowly anthropocentric to ecocentric but not in a coherent way.

6. Environmental concerns are a basic purpose of the European Union but fall within different parts of the treaty which may have different consequences.

7. Where European measures are transposed into UK legislation there is a tension between the rule-based approach of European law and English law's liking for administrative discretion.

8. EC environmental law remains predominantly anthropocentric but is extending towards broader concerns.

Further Reading

Birnie, P.W. and Boyle, A.E. (1992) *International Law and the Environment*, chapters 1, 3 and 5 (Oxford: Clarendon Press).

D'Amato, A. and Chopra, S.K. (1991) Whales: Their Emerging Right to Life. *American Journal of International Law*, **85**, 21-62.

Elworthy, S. and Holder, J. (1997) *Environmental Protection, Text and Materials*, chapter 5 (London: Butterworths), pp. 123–32, 165–211.

Emmenegger, S. and Tschentscher, A. (1994) Taking Nature's Rights Seriously: The Long Way to Biocentricism in Environmental Law. *Georgetown International Environmental Law Review*, **6**, 545–92.

Gillespie, A (1997) *International Environment Law Policy and Ethics*,(Oxford: Clarendon Press).

Glennon, M.J. (1990) Has International Law Failed the Elephant? *American Journal of International Law*, **84**, 1–43.

Holder, J. (ed.) (1997) *The Impact of EC Law on the United Kingdom* (Chichester: John Wiley and Sons).

Kiss, A. and Shelton, D. (1993) *Manual of European Environmental Law* (Cambridge: Grotius Publications).

Malcolm, R. (1994) *A Guidebook to Environmental Law* (London: Sweet and Maxwell), pp. 52–65.

Muller, C. *Environmental Perspective: Limited Perspective*, chapter 2.

Sands, P.H. (ed.) (1993) *Greening International Law* (London: Earthscan).

Somsen, H. (ed.) (1996) *Protecting the European Environment, Enforcing EC Environmental Law*, chapters 1, 2, 4 and 10 (London: Blackstone Press).

Sunkin, M., Ong, D. and Wight, R.(1998) *Sourcebook on Environmental Law* (London: Cavendish), pp.1–21.

Workshop

1. Are the traditional sources of international law adequate vehicles for developing environmental values?
2. Explain the significance of the concepts of common property, common concern, and common heritage in relation to nature conservation.
3. To what extent has international law adopted a non-anthropocentric environmental perspective and what forces may have brought this about?
4. Suppose you were asked to argue the *Duddridge* case before the House of Lords. Outline possible arguments to persuade their lordships that the lower courts were wrong.
5. To what extent does the Rio Declaration embody coherent environmental values?
6. What distinctive contribution has the European Union made to the development of environmental values?

5 Environmental Policies – Sustainable Development

Sustainable development is a term that has come to pervade environmental policy discussion. However, its meaning and value are hotly contested. At one end of the spectrum sustainable development is regarded as an empty platitude intended to provide a formula acceptable to most ethical and political points of view. At the other extreme sustainable development is regarded as a useful policy guide although no one believes that the concept is capable of being directly applied in law. In this chapter we shall discuss possible meanings of sustainable development, attempt to relate the concept to the law, and draw attention to some of its main criticisms. Sustainable development is closely related to the precautionary principle that is discussed in Chapter 6. It is a strongly anthropocentric concept.

The Meaning of Sustainable Development

The word sustainable means either 'worthy of support' or 'capable of keeping going indefinitely'. Neither has any special connection with the environment. The first is merely an expression of approval, the second carries no ethical meaning, in that keeping something going is not necessarily good, for example Nazi concentration camps. Sustainable development takes on meaning only if we know what 'development' means. As a description 'development' means progress towards a goal. It is, therefore, a value-laden concept. For example one meaning of 'development' is economic growth expressed in terms of money as gross domestic product (GDP). This does not cater for non-financial environmental values such as health or natural beauty. Indeed GDP rates measures to overcome environmental damage as benefits rather than costs.

The most influential version of sustainable development and the one adopted by the UK government (DoE, 1994b, p. 27), is that provided by the Brundtland Commission in its report, 'Our Common Future' (WCED, 1987). Brundtland defines sustainable development as:

> 'development that meets the needs of the present generation without compromising the ability of future generations to meet their own needs.'

Brundtland's contribution is to define development broadly as the achievement of human welfare or meeting human needs rather than the narrow meaning of economic growth and to suggest that the interests of growth, environmental protection and social justice are combinable and can be harmonised. Brundtland (1987, p. 53) treats 'development' and 'need' as compendium terms to include all aspects of human welfare as well as the protection of natural beauty, thus allowing the proponents of economic growth and those of the environment to share the same platform and requiring environmental costs and benefits to be included in planning and project evaluations.

However, when sustainable development is applied as a policy tool it is easy to blur the difference between the two senses of development and questions arise as to whether the components of sustainable development are commensurable or combinable. Some interests emphasise development in the narrow sense others the wider sense. In this connection it should be remembered that Brundtland and the Rio Convention were influenced by the conflicting claims of the underdeveloped nations and the developed nations as to what should be sustained.

The interests of the two groups are likely to collide on the questions of the weight to be given to economic growth, who should pay for environmental protection and biodiversity. They have different needs and different attitudes to the environment. The developed nations, having achieved high standards of material well being look to the environment for health, convenience and entertainment. They stress firstly long-term global survival, for example the concerns of ozone depletion and global warming and secondly the scientific and amenity values of nature as a source of rare species and beautiful landscapes. The poor stress immediate survival problems such as water pollution, the cost of energy and soil degradation.

The poorer nations can claim that it would not be equitable to require them to reduce pollution until their living standards are raised to the levels of those of the rich nations whose wealth has been generated by pollution. Hence an important element of Rio is the concept of 'common but differentiated State responsibility', which distributes the burden of environmental protection according to equitable principles and ability to pay.

There have been other attempts to define or at least encapsulate the elusive notion of sustainable development (see Pearce, 1989). The IUCN, for example (see Ginther, 1995), presents a version that avoids endorsing economic growth, namely that sustainable development means achieving a quality of life (or standard of living) which can be maintained for many generations because it is socially desirable. It fulfils peoples' cultural, material and spiritual needs in equitable ways, and is economically viable, with costs not exceeding income. It is also ecologically sustainable, maintaining the long-term viability of supporting ecosystems.

Ethical Basis of Sustainable Development

Sustainable development could fall within all three ethical approaches. It might be regarded as a deontological principle in as much as it seems to imply that future generations have inherent rights which require us to postpone our own enjoyment. Similarly in its concern for social justice sustainable development is deontological in character. Its problem here is that it proclaims positive rights to environmental quality whereas the law is generally more comfortable with the idea of negative rights not to be interfered with. Moreover sustainable development does not give absolute rights to any particular assets to our descendants. It does not therefore necessarily support a preservationist ethic.

A utilitarian approach would aim at maximising welfare including the supposed welfare of future generations but not would not seek to meet the needs of any particular interest group. For example from a utilitarian perspective the uncertainties of the future might persuade us that the maximum possible welfare lies in our exploiting the environment as much as possible. Brown-Weiss (1989) proposes the trust as the best model. If we pursue this legal analogy a 'planetary trust' would create limited rights in an unspecified class of beneficiaries but only to the effect that the trustees, that is ourselves, carry out their duties in good faith. It may be that this concept places sustainable development in the virtue ethics camp.

It is not universally accepted that we owe duties to future generations at all. It is also arguable that, even if we do owe duties to the future, our duties to the present will usually outweigh any duty to the future. We could also say that by maximising present welfare in the broad enlightened anthropocentric style we automatically fulfil our duty to our descendants.

Strong and Weak Sustainability

Distinctions can be made between 'strong' and 'weak' sustainability. According to strong sustainability we should leave future generations the same environmental resources as we ourselves inherited. This is strictly impossible since resources such as oil are non-renewable and the loss of species or landscape is irreversible. Weak sustainability means that distributive justice between generations requires each generation to pass onto the next generation an equivalent or better *total* stock of overall resources – including infrastructure, knowledge and technological capacity – than it inherited. An extreme version of this idea is that all human assets are interchangeable. We can therefore do what we like including degrading the natural environment provided that we substitute man-made capital or leave a fund to an equivalent value so that the total level of consumption remains the same (see Pearce *et al.*, 1989, pp. 3–4, 43 *et seq.*; Beckerman, 1994). A problem here is that of incommensurability. Is there a common scale to weigh the value of the landscape we devastate now against that of the improved road we pass to our descendants and why should we assume that they agree with our valuation? Perhaps, in virtue ethics style, we should be content with being sure that we are doing our best such as it is. An intermediate position is that we must leave our successors the same options that are available to us. For example if we use up oil we must provide alternative energy sources which are at least as good.

Deontological Approach

From a deontological perspective it can be argued that we owe duties to or in respect of future persons. We may owe a duty to God to preserve the environment in a relatively unharmed condition for the benefit of those who will come after us. However, teachings are ambivalent on the question of intergenerational equity ('sufficient unto the day is the evil thereof', Matthew, 6:34).

Secular duties may also exist based on the principle of equality. In imposing a test of potential universalisation ('can I will this rule for all?') Kant's categorical imperative implicitly requires future persons be taken into account. Kant himself noted that, 'Human nature is such that it cannot be indifferent even to the most remote epoch which may eventually affect our species, so long as this epoch can be expected with certainty'. The actions of the present generation – pollution of the earth and loss of species and habitat – may be less than terminally destructive for the global ecosystem in our own time, but catastrophic if continued for generation after generation. Since such cumulatively destructive exploitation cannot be willed as a universal maxim – universal, that is, across generations – it seems that Kantian ethics imply a duty to avoid such actions.

An interesting duty-based argument concerning future generations is advanced by Richard and Val Routley (1978) in their consideration of the ethics of nuclear waste. The Routleys invite us to consider the immorality of dispatching a consignment of highly toxic explosive gas on a bus containing innocent people that must make a long journey over hazardous terrain. They maintain that generation and storage of nuclear waste is morally similar, as it will present a grave hazard to unknown people in the future. They conclude, on the grounds of this supposed similarity, that such action cannot be considered ethical and that, regardless of the cost we must avoid the generation of nuclear waste.

Duty-based theories do not necessarily create corresponding 'rights' in those who benefit from the performance of a duty. A duty might be enforceable only by the state through the criminal law. Whether there should be environmental rights as such will be discussed later. All duty-based theories face the formidable problem of knowing what the content of the duty is. Are our successors entitled to a minimum ecological standard to meet their 'needs' or to the same standards that we inherited or to particular features such as the elephant? When do the rights of present generations override duties to the future? What of different kinds of future interest? In ordinary legal discourse a claimant puts forward his own interest which the other side attempts to deny. As with animals and natural objects we are in the fortunate position in respect of the claims of the future of being advocates for both sides.

Although not strictly a 'duty-based' ethic, Rawls' Theory of Justice has been considered by some to provide an adequate basis for concern for future generations. Rawls' basic idea is that 'justice' consists of all those principles for organising social institutions that would be agreed to by representative persons behind a 'veil of ignorance' in which they lack any knowledge about the particular station in life that they will occupy. The participants in this 'original position' know that they will be born into the same generation, but not which generation this will be. In these circumstances, Rawls argues, the principles agreed to would be, first, that 'each person is to have an equal right to the most extensive basic liberty compatible with a similar liberty for others' and, second, that 'social and economic inequalities are to be arranged is that they are both (a) reasonably expected to be to everyone's advantage and (b) attached to offices and positions open to all.'

Passmore (1980, pp. 88–89) argues that our duty to future generations is a limited one based on the present benefit of love for our immediate posterity – our children and grandchildren . The duty is based upon doing what we can to make the world a better place *now,* since this will automatically benefit the generation immediately following to whom the same duty will apply. Similarly Rawls assumes that persons in the original position would be concerned, as an aspect of their own welfare, with the welfare of the descendants of their family lines. However, this is not sufficient to explain why we should try to stave off problems such as global warning which may not materialise for many years or why we should plant trees or improve landscapes that will not be enjoyed by our immediate successors.

Utilitarian Approach

Utilitarianism also has a hard job justifying sustainable development. It is clear that in utilitarian theory the happiness of future persons is of no less concern, *per se*, than the happiness of those currently alive but future generations are at a particular disadvantage with utilitarianism because the value of future interests may be discounted, i.e. reduced because enjoyment is postponed (see Pearce *et al.*, 1989). Thus the exploitation of non-renewable resources such as coal, perhaps even species, may be indicated on the grounds that the certain gains in welfare from the consumption of such resources now are to be preferred to the uncertainty of the future. For example we do not know whether coal will have any value in 200 years time or when our rate of consumption will overtake economies made by improved production methods. Efforts taken now to preserve rare species or conserve energy resources may all be pointless if, in the future, people lose interest in nature and develop safe alternative energies. Of course, this argument is subject to the objection that certain key needs and desires of future persons (e.g. a clean and safe environment) can be identified now and are unlikely to change.

Thus the further away in time that a benefit is enjoyed the less value it has. Utilitarianism may, therefore, require that development be made non-sustainable if this will maximise happiness. Wenz (1988, p. 244) argues that at a discount rate of 5% one life today is worth four lives in 28.8 years and in 489.6 years would be worth more than 16 billion lives. Arguably, however, the practice of discounting should not be applied to future people at all but is relevant only to the postponement of pleasure that could be enjoyed now. On the other hand without discounting a utilitarian approach is faced with the likelihood that future people will outnumber ourselves by many orders of magnitude making it necessary always to prefer their interests to our own. It has been suggested that the well-established conservationist notion of maximum sustainable yield gives better results than discounting (Williams in Elliot, 1995).

Similar difficulties arise from the ambiguity of the maxim 'maximise happiness'. Should this be total happiness or average happiness? Maximisation of total happiness require raising population levels to the greatest number of humans that the global ecosystem can tolerate long term; for a vast number of moderately happy people will outweigh, in the hedonistic calculus, a smaller number of very happy people. Maximising average happiness, on the other hand, may require prohibition of reproduction unless the children born will increase average happiness. By implication more affluent countries should arguably be given reproductive priority, since children born into affluent conditions are likely to have the longest lives and the greatest satisfaction of life opportunities.

It could be argued from a virtue ethics standpoint that we should respect future generations out of gratitude to our predecessors for making our existence possible. The virtue ethics perspective also raises the question whether we should be paternalistic towards our successors or whether our duty to them is about not foreclosing options. Should we for example as Stone suggests (1996, p. 77) invest resources in creating well-secured waste disposal sites that future people would not be tempted to invade?

Parfit's Paradox

There are a number of general obstacles faced by all future generation ethics. Perhaps the most important of these is the view known as 'Parfit's paradox' (Parfit, 1976). This holds that whatever we do now destroys the interests of future persons since any action we take to protect the environment will inevitably result in different persons being born. We therefore destroy a class of persons who would have wanted to live even if in reduced circumstances. This is the same kind of moral wrong as to turn a family out of bad housing accommodation in order to do it up for someone who will pay a higher rent.

This argument makes two assumptions: first, that personal identities are genetically and biologically constituted (rather than, as Plato believed, embodiments of pre-existing souls) and, secondly, that all present actions have causal properties radiating outwards without end. According to modern chaos theory the chain of events that result in the conception of any future person extends backwards and is linked to all actions taken now. Even a fractional delay in the conception of a future person (for example by using a car with a catalytic converter) has the paradoxical result that any action taken to preserve the rights of future persons would be counterproductive in an ultimate sense. 'How can we owe a duty to future persons if the very act of discharging that duty wipes out the very individuals to whom we allegedly owe that duty?' (D'Amato, 1990, p. 190). It is arguably better to act selfishly for the benefit of existing people rather than destroy a life.

A possible answer to this concern is to reject the necessity for particular persons as objects of the duty. In the law of negligence duties are owed to an abstract class, for example road users. English law is familiar with the notion of a contingent interest in an unborn person, for example a will made by a person who at the time was childless leaves property to 'the first of my grandchildren to reach 21'. In other words intergenerational equity is a group right similar to a public right or charitable trust where the duty is to the public represented by the state rather than to individuals (see below and Weiss, 1990, p. 198). Another approach found in the law of restrictive covenants is to attach an environmental benefit

to the land itself so that anyone with an interest in the land can enforce
it and the covenant will permanently run with the land. On the other
hand the point of Parfit's paradox is not just that the beneficiaries are
not ascertained but that our attempts to help them end up by destroying
them. In this respect it seems to make no difference whether the beneficiaries are individuals or an abstract class which comes into existence
at the expense of the deliberate destruction of another class comprising
those who would have lived albeit in a worse environment.

Policy Implications of Sustainable Development

The Brundtland version of sustainable development has four interrelated policy elements.

1. It merges the three problems of environmental protection, economic growth and the relief of poverty on the basis that they are
   inseparable as both causes and consequences of environmental
   problems (see UNCED, 1991). The poorer nations are forced to
   exploit natural resources intensively in order to survive and the poor
   are less able to protect themselves against environmental damage.
   According to Brundtland, economic growth can combat environmental problems in that the wealth generated by growth can be
   spent on research and environmental technology as well as alleviat-
   ing poverty. Environmentalism might also help to combat poverty
   by creating employment in labour intensive jobs such as tourism in
   wildlife reserves and sustainable agriculture that rely upon human
   rather than energy profligate and polluting technological inputs.
   Energy saving helps the poor most because the poor spend a higher
   proportion of their income on energy. In Brundtland's view therefore, by giving priority to social justice and selecting environmentally
   friendly forms of growth, we can alleviate all three problems at once.
   Indeed some economists argue that economic growth does not
   increase pollution. Other areas also raise the question whether what
   appear to be competing goals can be harmonised or whether we
   have to accept that gains to the environment entail losses elsewhere.
   For example can wealth be maximised through environmentally
   friendly international trade? (See Schoenbaum, 1997.)
   The integrated approach also recognises that solving one environmental problem may create others – the law of unintended consequences. For example harnessing wind power by means of wind
   turbines erected in the countryside saves energy but might damage
   landscapes, destroy jobs and kill birds. If we reduce fishing we may
   increase the pressure on land resources by cutting down forests in
   order to grow other forms of food. Nuclear energy reduces acid rain

caused by burning coal but contributes to global warming and so on. Where we cannot replenish resources, Brundtland argues that we should spin out resources as long as possible while using the proceeds of growth to develop alternatives.

Brundtland recognised that there are limits to growth, for example, some resources can never be replaced, but regarded these limits as flexible and capable of being stretched indefinitely by technological developments and conservation practices such as recycling, optimum sustainable yield of renewable resources and energy efficiency.

2. Sustainable development is based upon intergenerational equity and, therefore, looks to the long term although there is no agreement as to how long. The precautionary principle with its existence on 'cost-effective' measures might help to provide time horizons by discounting remote consequences on the basis that the present cost of protective measures outweighs the future benefit. Far from protecting the future, the precautionary principle with its cost-effectiveness qualification sometimes works to justify present consumption.

3. Brundtland requires that decision making should be based upon methods of cost-benefit analysis that include a proper weighting being given to environmental costs and benefits. This is implemented through environmental impact assessment. We noted in Chapter 1 the considerable problems inherent in trying to value environmental goods.

4. Brundtland requires that there be public participation in governmental decision-making processes affecting the environment and, therefore, public access to environmental information. According to Brundtland (1987, p. 65) sustainable development 'needs community knowledge and support which entail greater public participation in the decisions that affect the environment. This is best secured by decentralising the management of resources upon which local communities depend and giving those communities an effective say over the use of those resources. It will also require promoting citizens' initiatives, empowering peoples' organisation, and strengthening local democracy. Environmental impact assessment and public access to information are important and environmental objects must be built into taxation, investment, technology choice and foreign trade decisions.'

Cooper and Palmer (1992, p. 182–3) suggest that the following substantive policies are entailed by sustainable development:

— slow population growth
— reduce poverty, inequality and third world debt

— make agriculture sustainable, for example, by relying upon energy efficient natural processes
— protect forests and habitats
— protect freshwater quality
— increase energy efficiency
— develop renewable sources of energy
— limit air pollutants, notably greenhouse gasses
— reduce waste generation and increase recycling
— protect the ozone layer
— protect ocean and coastal resources
— shift military spending to sustainable development.

These objectives are sometimes uncombinable. For example sustainable forestry might mean sacrificing species diversity.

Legal Implementation

Among the Rio principles the following have particular legal importance.

1. A human 'entitlement' to a 'healthy and productive life in harmony with nature' (Principle 1).
2. State sovereignty. Subject to avoiding damage outside their jurisdiction, states have a right to exploit their resources (Principle 2). (This negative right clashes with the positive right in Principle 1.)
3. A 'right' to development (Principle 3). Is this stronger than the 'entitlement' mentioned in Principle 1?
4. Intergenerational equity including environmental needs (Principle 3).
5. Public participation, access to information and effective access to judicial and administrative proceedings (Principle 10).
6. 'States shall enact effective environmental legislation' the content varying with the 'environmental and development' context (Principle 11).
7. National and international law shall be developed regarding liability and compensation for pollution and 'other environmental damage' (Principle 13).
8. 'The precautionary approach shall be widely applied by States according to their capabilities. Where there are threats of serious or irreversible damage, lack of full scientific certainty shall not be used as a reason for postponing cost-effective measures to prevent environmental degradation' (Principle 15).
9. The polluter pays principle applied through economic instruments but without distorting international trade and investment (Principle 16).

10. Environmental impact assessment for 'proposed activities' that are likely to have a significant adverse impact on the environment and are subject to a decision of a competent, national authority (Principle 17).

Sustainable development is probably too broad a concept to be binding as customary international law and at best has the status of soft law. The main international instruments which incorporate sustainable development values are the Fifth Action Programme of the EC, 'Towards Sustainability', and the Rio Declaration. The Amsterdam Treaty has made sustainable development an express environmental goal of the EC (EC Treaty Art 6). Rio was followed by Agenda 21 and two important framework conventions (Biodiversity, 1992; Climate, 1992) both of which are couched in general terms leaving states to apply them in their own ways. Agenda 21 is a non-legally binding action plan based upon sectors (atmosphere, water, etc.), issues (poverty, health, etc.) and machinery such as dispute resolution.

The notion of future generations has been incorporated into other treaties including the London Ocean Dumping Convention 1972, the CITES Convention 1973 and the World Cultural and Natural Heritage Convention 1972.

Some jurisdictions have attempted to incorporate sustainable development principles directly into their domestic law (see Boer in Ginther, 1995). The guiding principle of the Resource Management Act 1991 (New Zealand) is that of 'sustainable management' which requires an integrated approach to the environmental media, requires cost-benefit analysis, and provides for a range of economic instruments (see Richardson, 1998). A statutory definition of sustainable development is illustrated by the State Policies and Projects Act, 1993 of Tasmania. The schedule to the Act defines sustainable development as follows: sustainable development means managing the use, development and protection of natural and physical resources in a way or at a rate which enables people and communities to provide for their social, economic and cultural well being and for their health and safety while:

a. sustaining the potential of national and physical resources to meet the reasonably foreseeable needs of future generations: and
b. safeguarding the life-supporting capacity of air, water, soil and ecosystems: and
c. avoiding, remedying or integrating any adverse effects of activities on the environment.

Implementation in the UK

The creation of the Environmental Agency by the Environment Act 1995 and the introduction of integrated pollution control by the Environmental Protection Act 1990 are examples of the sustainable development ethos. The UK approach emphasises the following (DoE, 1994):

1. Environmental costs and benefits must be taken into account in making public decisions.
2. A weak version of the precautionary approach (see below).
3. The carrying capacity of ecosystems and habitats as life support for humans must be safeguarded.
4. The measuring of human wealth must allow for national environmental capital. This raises the question of whether it is possible to compare market and non-market factors (see above).
5. The needs of future generations must be balanced against the advantages of economic developments on a case-by-case basis. Renewable resources must be conserved and non-renewables used at a rate that considers the needs of future generations.
6. The polluter pays principle but also the 'user pays' principle. The consumer should ultimately bear the cost of pollution so as to reduce demand.
7. Better information about environmental matters. The government's policy statements emphasise scientific studies as opposed to public access to information.
8. Reliance upon economic and market instruments with direct regulation as a last resort (see DoE, 1993).
9. Environmental assessment techniques.
10. Cost-benefit analyses to include environmental factors. Risk assessment techniques must begin with the best available science and give 'proper weight to uncertainties in the science'.

True to its traditional reliance upon executive discretion, English law has incorporated the concept of sustainable development indirectly by requiring public bodies to take account of sustainable development in their decision-making processes (HMSO, 1990; DoE, 1994b). For example, guidance issued by the DoE to development control authorities incorporates sustainability policies notably in relation to the green belt, mining, agriculture, transport and housing (Millichap, 1993; Tromans, 1996). International policy instruments such as Agenda 21 could obtain legal status as policy presumptions by being incorporated into development plans made under the Town and Country Planning Act 1990 (s.54A).

The Environment Agency has as its 'principle aim…. in discharging its functions so as to protect and enhance the environment, taken as a whole, to make the contribution towards the object of achieving sustainable development which ministers consider appropriate' (EA, 1995, s.4(1),(3)). In relation to functions of the Agency *other than pollution control* it seems that, subject to any specific statutory requirements, ministers when making proposals must put sustainable development first (EA, 1995, s.7(1)(ii)).

This less than wholehearted commitment is supplemented by a general requirement to have regard to costs and benefits unless it would be unreasonable to do so (*ibid*, s.39) and is subject to guidance issued by ministers. It does not include a definition of sustainable development. However, in accordance with the dicta of the House of Lords in *Pepper* v. *Hart* [1993] 1 ALL ER 42, the courts are likely to rely upon the Brundtland definition which has been adopted by the statutory guidance (DoE, 1996, p. 11).

The current statutory guidance (DoE, 1995a) requires the Environment Agency to take an holistic approach to environmental protection which integrates different methods of regulation. It requires a long-term approach in the interests of intergenerational equity and incorporates international obligations relating to the atmosphere and biodiversity. It requires the Agency to work in partnership with the bodies that it regulates to achieve improved technologies and management techniques and with other public bodies in developing policies. A voluntary approach is stressed. The Agency is charged with providing advice and information on its work and also on good environmental practice. The overall approach of the guidance is human centred reflecting the 'enlightened anthropocentric' perspective. Natural environmental capital is treated as an aspect of the quality of life and the aim of sustainable development is said to be to enhance total wealth including natural environmental capital (*ibid*, p.12).

The integrated approach featured to some extent in UK legislation before the concept of sustainable development was formulated although its potential has not been litigated. Section 11 of the Countryside Act 1965 requires all public bodies to take the natural beauty and amenity of the countryside into account when exercising any relevant statutory powers. The EC Environmental Impact Assessment Directive was adopted in 1985.

The English legislation's commitment to sustainable development emphasises developmental concerns rather than those of environmental protection (see Jewell and Steele, 1996 to which this section is indebted). The standard of pollution control required under the integrated pollution control system of the EPA 1990 is geared to the concept of BAT-

NEEC (best available technique not entailing excessive costs). BAT-NEEC prevents the environmental agency from prioritising environmental protection over the concerns of development.

Moreover the Environmental Agency is not wholly integrated. It exercises control over most but not all areas of pollution and has few powers in relation to nature conservation where its role is largely consultative. Other agencies notably local authorities in relation to land use planning have overlapping powers. Local authorities are concerned with development interests as well as environmental protection so that conflicts may arise. Even in relation to pollution, integration is far from complete. Local authorities are responsible for contaminated land except in the case of 'special sites' for which the Agency takes over responsibility (EPA 1990 s.78C). Local authorities are also responsible for certain atmospheric emissions (Clean Air Act 1993; EPA 1990 ss.6–8). The Environment Agency is not concerned with vehicle emissions, which are the largest single source of greenhouse gases. The different policy and ethical perspectives which different bodies bring to the exercise of their powers may therefore create problems.

In relation to its pollution control powers, the duty of the Environment Agency in respect of nature conservation is limited to taking conservation factors into account. In relation to its other functions, however, mainly river management, the Agency has the stronger duty to further conservation goals (EA 1995 s.7(1)). Policy guidance places emphasis on the pollution licensing functions of the Agency in relation to the interests of business and upon the desirability of a voluntary approach. This reflects the integrated approach inherent in the idea of sustainable development but exploits the ambivalence of the concept (DoE, 1995).

The law relating to contaminated land (EA 1995 s.57 inserting Part IIA into EPA 1990) also illustrates a prodevelopment interpretation of sustainable development.

Problems with Sustainable Development

There is a large literature analysing and criticising the concept of sustainable development. Opinions range from rejecting the concept as meaningless or a cloak for self-interest to enthusiastic endorsement as a moral lodestar (e.g. Reed, 1995; Redclift, 1992; Dobson, 1995, chapter 3; Malanczuk in Ginther, 1995; Jacobo, 1989; Beckerman, 1994).

Despite the difficulties of defining sustainable development, the main policy and moral elements of the concept are reasonably clear. These are its long-term time perspectives and its attempt to merge environmental considerations with growth and social justice concerns. Much of the criticism stems from the tension between the idea of sustainability and that of development. This tension is likely to affect law making and the exercise of discretionary powers so that judicial intervention would be limited. The main criticisms are as follows:

1. *Sustainable development is a contradiction in terms,* in that growth and environmental protection are enemies. Because the earth has finite resources, it is impossible to achieve growth, social justice and environmental benefits simultaneously. According to this view it is impossible for the poorest nations to raise their living standards to the level of the richest. It is also morally obnoxious for wealthy environmentalists cushioned by affluence bestowed on them as a result of pollution to suggest that the poor should accept lower living standards than themselves. Poverty can therefore be reduced and the environment improved only if the rich accept lower living standards. This is consistent with the 'deep' ecology ethic (see Dobson, 1995, chapter 3; IUCN, 1991, p. 10). Similarly the goals of free trade cannot be harmonised with those of environmental protection. One must be at the expense of the other so that compromise is called for. For example the GATT Article XX which came into force long before the idea of sustainable development was formulated allows trade restrictions on environmental grounds provided that they do not provide a means of 'arbitrary or unjust discrimination...or a disguised restriction on international trade'.

2. *The concept of 'need' has no ethical basis.* Apart from bare survival what is a 'need'? The needs of the urban rich, who can insulate themselves from much environmental degradation and who regard environmental assets such as the countryside as entertainment, are different from the needs of the rural poor, who may need to despoil the environment in order to survive. It has also been argued that in practice need means demands and that the concept of sustainable development has regressed to one of sustainable growth with the emphasis on growth (see Jewell and Steele, 1996).

3. *Sustainable development penalises the poor.* Brundtland claims that economic growth both alleviates poverty and can be used to solve environmental problems, for example by investing in clean technology or environmentally friendly jobs. However, it is objected that the root cause both of poverty and environmental problems is economic growth which is generated by exploiting the poor in a world of finite resources (see Redclift, 1992). A certain amount of environmental benefit comes from developing clean technology but this is expensive and in our present state of knowledge is unlikely to improve third world living standards as quickly and to the same extent as dirty technology such as the car industry.

4. *Sustainable development is narrowly anthropocentric* treating the environment solely as a support system for human beings. Much of

the language of Rio reflects this. The same is true of the UK government's policy statement 'Sustainable Development: The UK Strategy' (DoE, 1994b) and the Fifth Action Programme of the EU. Conservation concepts, notably that of 'maximum sustainable yield' are imbued with anthropocentrism.

5. *Environmental protection might require restrictions upon personal freedom* which make it incompatible with the goal of overall human welfare. Authoritarian solutions are recommended as relatively speedy, coherent, and strong in situations of scarcity. Democracy is favoured for its capacity to generate and disseminate information, its sensitivity to a wide range of interests and its moral legitimacy in underpinning hard choices (Paehlke, 1995; Dobson, 1995, pp. 80, 117).

6. *The problem of intergenerational equity.* This has several facets, some of which were discussed earlier. The following practical issues arise:

   i Whose future interest are we expected to benefit and which present or indeed future people should bear the costs? Should we for example cut back on public health spending, thus helping the environment by reducing the number of people in the immediate future in favour of research into alternative energy which will not be translated into practical measures for many years? Is it preferable to husband a resource to ensure that each generation has the same access to it or is it more cost-effective to build a new set of machines to exploit the resource, operate it at a harvest level above maximum sustainable yield until the machines are worn out or the resource on the brink of exhaustion and then build up the resource again thereby denying the next generation the resource in the interest of *their* successors? (See Williams in Elliot, 1995.)

   ii Strong sustainability (above) requires us to choose the kind of world that our descendants will inhabit thus imposing our own values on our descendants. As in the case of Bills of Rights which try to bind lawmakers, it is arguably an affront to human dignity for us to place the dead hand of our values upon our descendants. We might be tempted for example to enact laws which forbid our descendants from burning down the forest which we have sacrificed ourselves to bequeath to them. It is worth noting that English law is reluctant to impose 'dead hand' restrictions upon the rights of future generations (e.g *Re Brown* [1954] Ch 39 and see the rule against perpetuities).

   iii Weak sustainability is said to have the liberal advantage of leaving our descendants with freedom of lifestyle choice (Stone, 1996, p. 112). However, even in the case of weak sustainability we still have to choose which assets should represent the hypothetical total wealth. Relative values constantly change as technology and human interests change. Without a reliable common denominator of value communicated to us by our descendants how do we know whether our descendants would have any use for tin or prefer a motorway or a rare snail?

iv. Present interests are worth more than future interests. This relates to what we said earlier about discounting the future. For example a future forest worth £1,000,000 in 100 years might be worth only £1000 today and so its interests are easily overridden.

Stone (1996, p. 72) suggests some narrower goals that might make sense of our obligation to the future. One might be to ensure that the costs on our descendants of our activities are compensated by those who create them, for example by investing pollution taxes in long-term environmental projects. Another is to take special precautions against known irreversible or long-term calamities – 'long fuse' risks – or safeguarding special assets such as valuable landscapes. Our current conservation law to some extent embodies this policy. Another is to leave our descendants with governmental structures that enable them to respond to environmental problems, for example by reforming the common agricultural policy of the EU to discourage wasteful production.

7. *The distribution of costs and benefits between rich and poor.* Rawls' savings principle would include clean air, water, land biodiversity and energy but participants in the original position would only agree to patterns of use of natural resources that guarantee justice both within and between generations. Sustainable solutions do not benefit or harm us all equally. Saving the whale puts pressure on other food supplies. Whose present consumption should be sacrificed? Saving elephants creates a few jobs in tourism and security and adds value to the leisure of the wealthy but might reduce the quality of life for thousands of people including farmers threatened by a proliferation of elephants. The costs of environmental measures may fall disproportionately on the poor in terms of loss of jobs and high land costs.

8. *It is impossible to provide an objective evaluation of environmental policy.* There is no common measure of value by which we can compare different types of asset because environmental goods have no market value. This criticism can partly be met by emphasising the 'process' aspect of sustainable development which requires us to take both environmental and economic factors into account but which leaves the outcome to political judgement or public opinion. Concepts such as 'precaution' help to weigh the different components of the decision.

Conclusion

In defence of the vagueness and inconsistencies of sustainable development, it could be argued that the concept is an example of 'virtue ethics' rather than a recipe for particular outcomes. As with ideas such as justice and the rule of law, sustainable development is a moral rallying point that can be applied in many different ways. In essence sustainable development is a reminder to take long-term environmental considerations into account across the whole range of policies in an open and accountable way.

The English law of judicial review is capable of policing this. Judicial review can require government decision makers to take all relevant factors into account but, unless the governing legislation imposes a clear duty, cannot impose any particular outcome (see *Tesco Stores plc* v. *Secretary of State* [1995] 2 ALL ER 636.) For example if there had been a general presumption of sustainable development, the notorious case of *Bromley L.B.* v. *Secretary of State* [1982] 1 ALL ER 129 might have been argued and decided differently. The House of Lords decided that a decision by the Greater London Council to subsidise public transport in their area for environmental reasons was unlawful, because the governing legislation required public transport to be run 'economically'. According to some of their lordships, this required a financial cost-benefit analysis that did not include non-financial environmental benefits.

Summary

1. The concept of sustainable development is an attempt to produce an internationally accepted formula that embraces the competing interests of economic development and environmental protection. Its proponents claim that these can at least sometimes be harmonised while its detractors regard the concept as self-contradictory or empty.

2. Although the term has been defined in many different ways the version put forward by the Brundtland Commission has been widely accepted and adopted in international policy including the policy of the UK. Brundtland's version relates intergenerational equity to the integration of environmental, economic and social policies, and to public participation in decision making.

3. There are 'strong' and 'weak' versions of sustainability. These centre on the question whether we must leave environmental capital to our successors or whether capital is interchangeable. Once more the problem of valuing incommensurables raised in Chapter 1 is presented.

4. Sustainable development raises several other problems including its anthropocentric nature, its internal contradictions and its relationship with social justice within as well as between generations.

Further Reading

'Agora' (1990) What does Our Generation Owe to the Next? *American Journal of International Law*, **84**, 190.

Des Jardins, J.R. (1997) *Environmental Ethics: An Introduction to Environmental Philosophy*, 2nd edn, chapter 4 (Belmont, CA: Wadsworth).

Dobson, A. (1995) *Green Political Thought*, 2nd edn, chapter 3 (London: Routledge).

Elworthy, S. and Holder, J. (1997) *Environmental Protection, Text and Materials* (London: Butterworths), pp. 132–53.

Ginther, K and Denters, E. (eds) (1995) *Sustainable Development and Good Governance* (Amsterdam: Kluwer).

Jewell, T. and Steele, J. (1996) UK Regulatory Reform and the Pursuit of Sustainable Development. *Journal of Environmental Law*, **8**, 283.

Passmore, J. (1980) *Man's Responsibility for Nature: Ecological Problems and Western Tradition*, 2nd edn, chapter 4 (London: Duckworth).

Pearce, D., Markandya, A., Barbier, E.B. (1989) *Blueprint for a Green Economy*, chapters 2 and 6 (London: Earthscan).

Shannuganthan, P. and Warren, L.M (1997) Status of Sustainable Development as a Norm of International Law, *Journal of Environmental Law*, **9**, 221.

Workshop

1. Is it possible to define sustainable development as a practical legal concept?
2. Explain the differences between 'strong' and 'weak' sustainability. What ethical problems are posed in relation to future generations?
3. What rights do future generations have to inherit an environment that is diverse and ecologically healthy?
4. 'Sustainable development manages to be both vacuous and contradictory. The concept is therefore incapable of providing legal or ethical guidance.' Discuss.
5. Is sustainable development an instrumental, a deontological or a virtue ethics concept?
6. Suppose that you are a local planning officer in a rural district that includes several valuable wildlife and landscape sites and also some villages dominated by wealthy commuters one of whom chairs the local planning committee. Your district also has many homeless people and a chronic shortage of jobs. You are asked by the local planning committee to outline the extent to which the council would be obliged to pursue policies of sustainable development and to make suggestions as to how it might draw up a plan for the district embodying such policies.

6 Environmental Principles

In this chapter we examine the role and content of general *principles* in environmental law. We shall limit our attention to the following principles which inform much of environmental law:

— the precautionary and preventative principles;
— the polluter pays principle (PPP).

What are Principles?

A principle, according to the *Oxford English Dictionary* is 'a source of action' or 'a general law or rule adopted or professed as a guide to action'. Principles are useful as general guides for the development of specific rules, and have a normative character in novel situations. Principles for environmental protection are sometimes treated as principles of *policy*, social, economic or other. In some contexts principles and policy must be distinguished. The idea of principles can be associated, as in the writings of Ronald Dworkin, with the deontological values of rights and duties. This can be contrasted with policies which are instrumental in character and refer to community goals. For example the precautionary principle is sometimes called the precautionary 'approach'. Many ethical issues present themselves as conflicts between principles and policies. From this perspective the so-called environmental principles have features of both principle and policy in the Dworkinian sense, This may be one reason why they are often said to be incoherent. In any event, whether such principles can properly be described as *legal* principles depends upon the existence of a sufficiently close nexus between the body of policy concerned and some associated body of law. The required nexus can arise in a number of ways.

If the law in a given area corresponds closely to practices that follow, logically, from a policy principle, then we may say that such a principle has become a *legally substantiated principle*. For example, UK government policy in relation to property transactions has, since the early twentieth century, been concerned with promoting the transferability of land. The Law of Property Act 1925 and associated legislation promotes and corresponds very closely to this objective. In some cases legally substantiated principles come about as a result of primary legal rules which require subsequent or subordinate legislation to be fashioned so as to follow the principles in question. In 1986 the Single European Act amended the Treaty of Rome by, among other things, inclusion of a new chapter on environmental policy. This was again amended by the Maastricht Treaty in 1992 so that Article 130R(2) of the Treaty now states that, 'community policy on the environment shall aim at a high level of protection taking into account the diversity of situations in the various regions of the community. It shall be based on the precautionary principle and on the principles that preventative action should be taken, that environmental damage should as priority be rectified at source and that the polluter should pay.'

Because all future community environmental policy must take these principles into account there is good reason to believe that community environmental law, which is adopted to implement this environmental policy, will substantiate these principles. Nevertheless principles such as the precautionary principle are not legally enforceable in their own right (see *Re Peralta* C-379/92 (1994), ECJ, *Duddridge* case (p. 153)).

There is an alternative sense in which principles may be described as legal principles. In some cases principles while falling short of being detailed rules, bind ministers, public authorities and others who fall within their ambit. In these cases we can refer to such principles as binding legal principles. There is, for example, a well-known principle of English administrative law that public bodies and ministers must, when exercising discretion, act within the powers that they have been granted, implicitly or explicitly by Parliament. To do otherwise is to act *ultra vires*. In order to avoid acting *ultra vires* public bodies must exercise their discretion reasonably (see *Associated Picture Houses Ltd.* v. *Wednesbury Corporation* [1948] 1 KN 223). Decisions so outrageous of logic or of accepted moral standards that no sensible person could have reached it them are unreasonable (*Council of Civil Service Unions* v. *Minister for the Civil Service* [1985] AC 734, per Lord Diplock). This reasoning could, presumably, apply to decisions of public bodies which are totally contrary to accepted environmental ethics or morality.

Decisions should also only be taken on the basis of relevant considerations, and then only to serve legitimate ends. It could be argued for example that a decision-maker must take into account the ethical values of animal welfare. However, as the law stands it appears that ethical values are relevant only if they are authorised by the particular legislation (see *R.* v. *Somerset County Council ex parte Fewings* [1995] 3 All ER 20).

Policy principles may also be included in substantive law as *guiding principles* i.e. as guides to the interpretation of statutes or the development of common law rules. In relation to statutory interpretation the decision in *Pepper* v. *Hart* [1993] 1 All ER 42 is important. This established that where the meaning of legislation is unclear the courts may refer to the debates of parliament, recorded in *Hansard*, to determine the intention of parliament. Most environmental legislation will be intended to implement one or more of the basic principles of environmental policy to which the UK is committed, and it is likely that this fact will emerge during parliamentary debates. As a result courts may need to refer to principles of environmental policy in determining the precise meaning or application of environmental legislation.

In relation to the development of law, the courts frequently find themselves faced with the question of whether existing propositions should be extended to novel situations. In determining such matters the courts often search for some underlying principle for that area of law. In recent years UK courts have shown a general reluctance to develop new areas of law in relation to matters which they consider are the proper domain of parliament, to be developed through legislation. In *Cambridge Water Company* v. *Eastern Counties Leather* [1994] 2 AC 264 the House of Lords drew back from a logical extension of the rule in *Rylands* v. *Fletcher* (1868) LR 3 HL 330 and rules affecting continuing nuisance to historical contamination of groundwater, in part because of a reluctance to undertake 'judicial legislation'.

Problems with Principles

Principles are sometimes criticised for their vague and indeterminate nature. Bodansky (1991, p. 5), for example, argues in relation to the precautionary principle (see below) that is 'too vague to serve as a regulatory standard because it does not specify how much caution should be taken'. The answer to this is that principles are, by definition, general guides to action: they do not and are not intended to provide specific rules of behaviour or precise technical standards. Generality is their great strength: they indicate certain *types* of response and contra-indicate others. It is, therefore, unprofitable to examine either legal or policy principles for concrete solutions to particular problems. As Cameron answers to the charge of 'vagueness': 'The precautionary principle is a general principle. To say so says nothing about its legal effect. At the international level it is not intended to be a command and control-type regulatory standard this does not in any way deny its general effect as a general principle'.

Some jurisdictions have incorporated general environmental principles into their law. For example, in New South Wales, which has a special environmental court, the Protection of the Environment Administration Act 1991 includes 'the precautionary principle', 'intergenerational equity', the 'conservation of biological diversity and ecological integrity' and 'the improved valuation and pricing of environmental resources' (see also State Policies and Projects Act 1993 (Tasmania), Resource Management Act 1991, New Zealand). These principles are applied by the courts when scrutinising governmental action although, as in the UK, where competing factors have to be balanced, as they usually do, the courts defer to the executive (see e.g. *Friends of Hinchinbrook Society* v. *Minister for the Environment* (1997) 142 ALR 632).

The Precautionary and Preventative Principles

It is now common to find assertions that environmental policy should be based on the precautionary principle. Indeed the precautionary principle is closely linked to the concept of sustainable development. Although, as we shall see there is uncertainty as to its meaning, the precautionary principle can be loosely described as a reflection of the adage 'better safe than sorry', i.e. that precautions should be taken to protect human health and the environment even in the absence of clear evidence of harm and/or causal linkage with some activity or proposed activity, and despite the indisputable costs of taking such a conservative approach. The precautionary principle has been described as 'a statement of common sense ... applied by decision-makers in appropriate circumstances prior to the principle being spelt out ... directed towards the prevention of serious or irreversible harm to the environment in situations of scientific uncertainty ... that where uncertainty or ignorance exists concerning the nature or scope of environmental harm. Decision-makers should be cautious (*Leatch* v. *Director-General National Parks – Wildlife Services and Shoalhaven City Council* (1993), Land and Environment Court of New South Wales 1993 NSW LR p.29).

The precautionary principle should be distinguished from the preventative principle. The preventative principle has a longer history and is more widely accepted. It requires that environmental damage should where possible be prevented in advance rather than put right or compensated after the event. It does not concern itself with assessing costs and benefits as such but lays down preventative strategies that must be followed. The preventative principle can be illustrated by the waste management regime introduced by the Environmental Protection Act 1990 which imposes a detailed licensing and registration regime on those who handle waste. The preventative principle complements the precautionary principle in requiring protective measures to be based on high scientific standards although sometimes modified by cost concerns. For example the (due diligence) defence in waste management law (below, p. 279) (see London Convention for the Prevention of Marine Pollution by Dumping of Waste and Other Matter (1972), Basel Convention on the Control of Transboundary Movements of Hazardous Wastes and their Disposal (1989)).

The Precautionary Principle and Environmental Ethics

Questions arise as to whether the precautionary principle is informed or underpinned by any particular theory of environmental ethics. The answer to this, we suggest, is no. The precautionary does not tell us what we should take precautions against and what must be sacrificed in the process. In other words the precautionary principle is consistent with any of the ethical perspectives. Even the most technocentric anthropocentrist would hesitate to take a serious risk. Precautionary action will, if successful, be of great value to future as well as present generations. Consequently the precautionary principle may, in part, be based on principles of intergenerational equity which, of course, are derived from anthropocentric environmental ethics. But it is also true that protecting the basic conditions of environmental viability through a policy of prior care is compatible with biocentric and ecocentric environmental ethics. All that changes here is the *object* of moral concern for which precautionary action is considered necessary.

Attfield and Williams (1994b) concludes that the precautionary principle has no inherent ethical basis but is derivative from other principles concerning justice, welfare and rights. They also find the principle to be qualified, rather than absolute, because the principle may need to be compromised against other principles. The only aspect of the precautionary principle which appears to carry a distinctive relationship to theories of ethics is the last – the need for those who cause most environmental damage to pay the most for future precautions. This would appear to be a matter of intergenerational or intragenerational equity, similar to the English law doctrine of mutual benefits and burdens ('he who takes the benefit must share the burden', *E.R. Ives Investment Ltd* v. *High* [1967] 2 QB 379). But this might be outweighed by the widely accepted legal principle against retrospective liability.

The Legal Status of the Precautionary Principle

The precautionary principle is now a pervasive feature of international environmental policy. For example, Principle 15 of the 1992 Rio Declaration on Environment and Development states that:

> 'In order to protect the environment, the precautionary approach shall be widely applied by states according to their capabilities. Where there are threats of serious or irreversible damage, lack of full scientific

certainty shall not be used as a reason for postponing cost-effective measures to prevent environmental degradation.'

The precautionary principle is now found in several international law/policy instruments:

— the 1982 World Charter for Nature states that activities 'likely to pose a significant adverse risk to nature' should not proceed where 'potential adverse effects are not fully understood';
— the 1984 Bremen Ministerial Declaration of the [first] International Conference on the Protection of the North Sea provides that states 'must not wait for proof of harmful effects before taking action';
— the 1987 London Ministerial Declaration of the Second International Conference on the Protection of the North Sea states that 'in order to protect the North Sea from possibly damaging effects of the most dangerous substances, a precautionary approach is necessary which may require action to control inputs of such substances even before a causal link has been established by absolutely clear scientific evidence';
— Article 2 of the 1992 Paris Convention for the Protection of the Marine Environment of the Northeast Atlantic (the 'OSPAR' Convention) requires that preventative measures be taken where there are 'reasonable grounds for concern ... even where there is no conclusive evidence of a causal relationship between inputs and their alleged effects'.

According to the preamble to the 1992 Convention on Biological Diversity, '... where there is a threat of significant reduction or loss of biological diversity, lack of full scientific certainty should not be used as a reason for postponing measures to avoid or minimise such a threat'.

On the other hand the Basel Convention on Trade in Hazardous Wastes and Substances (1989) while adopting a preventative approach does not expressly include precautionary concepts. (See also the Bergen Ministerial Declaration adopted by the Economic Commission for Europe (ECE); the Montreal Protocol on Substances that Deplete the Ozone Layer; the 1992 United Nations Framework Convention on Climate Change; Article 3(3) of the 1992 UN Framework Convention on Climate Change.)

A number of writers contend that the precautionary principle is sufficiently widely accepted to be or is emerging as, a principle of customary international law (Cameron and Aboucher, 1991; Bodansky, 1991; Gundling, 1990; McIntyre and Mosedale, 1997). A problem with this view is that the precautionary principle is more a general approach or aim rather than calling for any particular course of conduct. In particular there is no shared understanding of what the precautionary principle requires in relation to the level of uncertainty.

At a European level the precautionary principle was added into the EC Treaty by the 1992 Maastricht Treaty: Article 174 EC treaty now requires that 'Community policy on the environment shall aim at a high level of protection taking into account the diversity of situations in the various regions of the Community ... [and] ... shall be based on the precautionary principle'.

The strength of this requirement is somewhat diluted by a parallel duty, imposed by Article 174, to take account in the preparation of environment policy of:

— available scientific and technical data;
— environmental conditions in the various regions of the Community;
— the potential benefits and costs of action or lack of action;
— the economic and social development of the Community as a whole and the balanced development of its region.

However, the precautionary principle has been realised in many European directives, for example on environmental impact assessment (below, see 97/1 EC), The Nitrates Directive provides a good illustration of how the precautionary principle, favouring as it does a loose approach to the question of causation might conflict with the polluter pays principle. The directive requires the designation of 'nitrate vulnerable zones' (NVZ) in order to combat pollution in conditions of scientific uncertainty (91/576 EEC, SI 1996 no. 888). Designation puts severe restrictions upon farming activities and a farmer might fall within a NVZ even though some of the pollution might be caused from outside the designated zone (see *R.* v. *Secretary of State for the Environment ex parte Standley* (1998) 10 JEL 93, Elworthy, *ibid* 103).

The UK White Paper on environmental policy, 'This Common Inheritance' (HMSO, 1990), makes several references, implicit and explicit, to the precautionary principle. Having set out that the general approach of UK environmental policy is based on stewardship (para 1.14) the Paper goes on to state, in paragraph 1.15: 'First, we must base our policies on fact not fantasy, and use the best evidence and analysis available. Second, given the environmental risks, we must act responsibly and be prepared to take precautionary action where it is justified.'

Expanding on the notion of precautionary action, the report adds, in paragraph 1.18: 'That does not mean we must sit back until we have 100% evidence about everything. Where the state of our planet is at stake, the risks can be so high and the costs of corrective action so great, that prevention is better and cheaper than cure. We must analyse the possible benefits and costs both of action and inaction. Where there are significant risks of damage to the environment, the government will be prepared to take precautionary action to limit the use of dangerous materials or the spread of potentially dangerous pollutants, even where scientific knowledge is not conclusive, if the balance of likely costs and benefits justifies it. The precautionary principle applies particularly where there are good grounds for judging either that action taken promptly at comparatively low costs may avoid more costly damage later, or that irreversible effects may follow if action is delayed.'

The legal status of the precautionary principle in UK law was examined in *R* v. *Secretary of State for Trade and Industry, ex parte Duddridge and Others* [1994] ELR 1. Three children sought judicial review of the Secretary of State's decision not to make regulations limiting electromagnetic radiation from a high voltage cable which the National Grid Company was proposing to lay close to their homes. The applicants based their case, in part, on the argument that the precautionary principle was a binding legal principle of UK law and EC law and that by not making the regulations limiting electromagnetic emissions the Secretary of State had breached that principle. Smith J., however, held that as the UK had accepted the precautionary principle voluntarily and then as a principle of policy only, it is entitled to set the threshold for action at any level. In relation to EC law, Smith J. held that although the principle is incorporated into what was then Article 130(R) of the EC Treaty this amounts to no more than a guide to the formulation of EC policy relating to the environment.

Nevertheless the precautionary principle is of considerable significance in influencing statute law and its interpretation and also the exercise of discretionary powers. We shall meet examples throughout the book. Particularly noteworthy are the concepts of BATNEEC and BPEO and the Secretary of State's power under s.92 of the Water Resources Act 1991 to make regulations regarding precautions to be taken against water pollution. It is this power that, during the 1980s, enabled the Secretary of State to bring agricultural pollution within the realm of environmental protection contrary to the cultural perception of farming as part of nature (see Control of Pollution (Silage, Slurry and Agricultural Fuel Oil) Regulations 1991 (S.I. 1991 no 324)).

In other common law jurisdictions the precautionary principle has also remained at the level of 'guiding principle'. In *Leatch* v. *Director-General National Parks – Wildlife Services and Shoalhaven City Council* (Land and Environment Court of New South Wales, 1993 NSW LR 29) the applicant made a statutory appeal against a licence granted by the Director General to permit the council to 'take' endangered species in connection with a proposed road development by the council. The applicant argued that once the precautionary principle had been raised in a public submission the Director General was bound to take that principle into account in determining whether to issue a licence under the 1974 Act. Stein J. observed that although adoption of a cautious approach' was 'clearly consistent with the subject matter, scope and purpose of the Act' the 1974 Act contained no express provision obliging consideration of the precautionary principle.

In the New Zealand case of *McIntyre* v. *Christchurch City Council* [1996] NZRMA 289 the applicant sought amendment of a council consent for construction of a radiocommunications transmitter in a residential area, limiting the power output of the transmitter, on the basis that the radiation emitted by the proposed facility would be potentially harmful to health and that the New Zealand Resource Management Act contains a precautionary policy. The Tribunal held merely that 'there may be resource consent applications in which a consent authority may consider it relevant and reasonably necessary to have regard to the precautionary principle' and that, in such cases, 'a consent authority may allow its discretionary judgement to grant or refuse consent to be influenced by the precautionary principle to the extent consistent with the statutory purpose of promoting the sustainable management of natural and physical resources and with judicial exercise of that discretion'.

The Scope of the Precautionary Principle

There is a spectrum of precautionary possibilities ranging from 'strong' precaution to 'weak' precaution (O'Riorden, 1995). The strong version requires us to refrain from action that might cause serious or irreversible environmental damage whatever the cost and is therefore consistent with non-anthropocentric perspectives. Weak precaution (the version espoused by the UK) requires only that we should take precautionary measures where the balance of costs and benefits justifies doing so. This is more consistent with an anthropocentric stance. Weak precaution means that we can harm nature as long as we are net gainers from so doing. A further problem with weak precaution is that, because of scientific uncertainty, it may not be possible to know whether costs outweigh benefits or what might be the consequences of our actions. A cost-benefit analysis would have to include a weighting for uncertainty and also a weighting to allow the effect on future generations to be ranked fairly against present costs and benefits. The chosen time scale is therefore crucial but it is difficult to see how this might be selected without bias in favour of such knowledge as we do have which is likely to favour our own short-term interests.

In order to determine the scope of the precautionary principle it is useful to look back to its origins. It is generally agreed that the precautionary principle is derived from German administrative law in the 1970s, specifically the notion of *Vorsorgeprinzip* (Boehmer-Christiansen, 1994). This roughly translates into English as 'prior worry or care'. According to O'Riordan and Cameron (1994) *Vorsorgeprinzip* comprises the following approaches:

1. preventative anticipation – a willingness to take action in advance of scientific proof of evidence of the need for action;
2. safeguarding of ecological space or room for manoeuvre by not approaching, much less breaching, margins of tolerance;
3. cost-effectiveness of margins of error – effectively introducing a bias to conventional cost-benefit analysis to allow for ignorance;
4. duty of care or onus of proof on those who advocate change;
5. promoting the cause of intrinsic natural rights – recognising the pressing need to allow natural process to function so as to maintain essential support for life on earth;
6. paying for ecological debt – those who have in the past caused a large ecological burden should pay the greatest burden of future precautions.

These aspects are considered below, except for (5), which is considered in Chapter 12 and (6) which is dealt with as part of the polluter pays principle (below).

Action Ahead of Scientific Uncertainty

A central theme of the precautionary principle is the need to take action to protect the environment *ahead of full scientific certainty* of environmental damage.

An early example of this aspect of the precautionary principle is the response in international law to the problem of ozone depletion which was detected in Antarctica in the 1970s which may be affected by the discharge of chlorofluorocarbons (CFCs) into the atmosphere. CFCs are used in a wide range of applications including use as a refrigeration gas, making expanded plastics, as aerosol propellants and in certain medical applications. The characteristic feature of CFCs, which makes then suitable for these uses, is their inertness and stability, i.e. their lack of reactiveness with other substances and their propensity to avoid degradation. Ozone exists both in the stratosphere and at low levels. At low levels ozone has a very destructive effect, being harmful to plant and animal life, human health and an aggressive oxidiser of materials. But at high levels ozone is beneficial, filtering deadly ultraviolet radiation from the sun. In humans, exposure to ultra-violet light correlates with levels of skin cancer. Without the ozone layer most terrestrial life on earth would cease to exist. Of equal concern is the possibility that increases in ultra-violet radiation may affect marine phytoplankton and zooplankton.

This could, according to Gaian theory, result in the margins of tolerance for the earth organism being breached with a resultant collapse of all life on earth.

In 1985, concerned by the possible loss of ozone, and consequential increases in cancer and other harmful effects, the international community adopted the Vienna Convention on Protection of the Ozone Layer. This convention provided for a progressive phase out in the production and use of CFCs and other ozone-depleting substances. The range of substances affected and the timetable for phase out were elaborated in a protocol to the Convention (the 'Montreal Protocol') with subsequent amendments. The European Community signed the Montreal Protocol in September 1987 and reflected its obligations in Community law through Regulation 3322/88. Even as this transpositive legislation was being formulated it was becoming evident that the terms of the Montreal Protocol would not, alone, be sufficient to curb the problem. Accordingly amendments were made to the Protocol by a meeting of the parties to the convention in Copenhagen in 1992, agreeing to phase out CFCs completely by 1996; four years ahead of the date originally set by the Protocol. Amendments to the Protocol also extended the range of substances to which the Protocol applies and introduced requirements in relation to recycling of CFCs. The EC adopted further measures requiring the phase out of production and use of non-essential uses of CFCs by 1995.

The Vienna Convention, the Montreal Protocol and subsequent amendments and transpositive laws together comprise a good example of legal action taken ahead of full scientific certainty. When negotiations for the Convention began in the early 1980s the CFC theory of ozone depletion had gained some scientific respectability but was not accepted as 'proven'. As it became clear that ozone loss presents serious and possibly irreversible consequences, which affects the arctic as well as the Antarctic atmosphere, so the willingness of the international community to tackle this problem galvanised. The subsequent rapid amendments to the Montreal Protocol demonstrate the ability of the international community to take swift cautionary measures when faced with risks of serious but unknown magnitude.

European Community environmental law contains other elements reflecting the need to act on environmental problems ahead of full scientific certainty. Most EC environmental directives do not make any explicit reference to the precautionary principle – not least because the principle was only inserted into the Treaty in 1992 by the Maastricht Treaty. Nevertheless, several environmental directives are implicitly premised on the need for action ahead of full scientific certainty. Directive 76/403 requires strict control of disposal of PCBs and PCTs despite these being only 'widely recognised' to be harmful; Directive 78/176 regulates waste from the titanium dioxide industry even though such waste is, according to the directive's preamble, merely 'liable' to be harmful to human health.

On the other hand, a strong interpretation of the precautionary principle may do 'too much' because protective action itself carries environmental risk. As Bodansky (1991) stresses, the choice is never between environmental risk and safety but between different types and magnitudes of risk. With the benefit of hindsight it sometimes transpires that supposedly precautionary action carried risks greater than those avoided, e.g.:

— specification of tall chimneys for gaseous emissions, in order to satisfy the test of 'best practicable means' under the 1956 Air Pollution Act, reduced local air pollution but exacerbated long-range acid rain pollution;

— Greenpeace's direct action to prevent the sinking of the Brent Spar oil storage tank in the Atlantic Ocean in 1996 probably increased overall environmental risks since, as Shell pointed out, dismantling and disposal of such structures on land involves environmental risks to terrestrial ecosystems which are arguably greater than those created in relation to the marine environment from the proposed dumping;

— it has been suggested that the banning of organochlorine pesticides such as DDT – after Rachael Carson's book, *The Silent Spring*, exposed their bioaccumulation and biomagnification in higher animals – resulted in a switch to organophosphate pesticides with a concomitant increase in risk to human health and environment due to their higher toxicity (Cross, 1996);

— generation of energy from conventional rather than nuclear power plants may increase overall environmental risk (burning of coal and oil contributes more to global warming, creates higher mortality and disease from mining and shipping, and emits more radioactivity than routine use of nuclear fuels) (Cross, 1996);

— the policy of removing old asbestos from buildings releases more asbestos into the air than would be present were such 'precautionary' action not taken (Cross, 1996);

— attainment of 'Polished Earth' standards during the remediation of contaminated land under the American 'Superfund' legislation probably increases risks due to exposure and release of toxic substances.

Environmental Impact Assessment

The requirement, explicit in the precautionary principle, that action be taken ahead of full scientific certainty in relation to perceived environmental threats requires knowledge of the existence of such threats. Since any human activity may potentially have diverse and far-reaching environmental consequences some form of systematic investigation and assessment of likely environmental effects of a given proposed course of action is required. This function is termed 'environmental impact assessment' or simply 'environmental assessment'.

In EC law the requirement to carry out environmental assessments is imposed by Directive 85/337/EEC (the assessment of the effects of certain public and private projects on the environment). Directive 85/337/EEC has been amended by Council Directive 97/11/EC which makes express reference to the precautionary and preventative principles and introduces changes which must be given legal effect in each member state's national laws by March 1999. The objective of the Environmental Impact Assessment (EIA) Directive is to ensure that information about likely environmental consequences is gathered and taken into account in the process of issuing project authorisations in order to prevent or minimise pollution or environmental damage. However, there is no requirement as to what the relevant standard of proof or what action should be taken so that at best EIA is an example of weak precaution. Article 3 of the Directive, as amended, merely requires that EIA shall identify, describe and assess direct and indirect effects of such projects on human beings, fauna and flora, soil, water, air, climate and the landscape, interactions between the above; and material assets and the cultural heritage.

Environmental assessment also has the object of providing a vehicle for public participation in environmental decision making which is an independent component of sustainable development. The English courts' treatment of the requirement to carry out an EIA seems to overlook this participatory function. In *R.* v. *Poole B.C. ex parte Beebee* [1991] JPL 643 Schiemann J. took the view that it did not matter that the local authority had failed to carry out a formal EIA provided that there was some evidence that the environmental concerns of the site had been drawn to its attention.

The Directive requires environmental impact assessment for certain categories of projects, which are likely to have significant environmental impacts. These are listed in two Annexes to the Directive. EIA is required to be carried out prior to authorisation of all Annex I projects. Annex I of the amended Directive consists of 21 classes of projects (new additions to Annex I by virtue of 97/11/EC are italicised):

— crude oil refineries;
— thermal power stations;
— radioactive waste reprocessing or storage plants;

— iron and steel smelting works;
— asbestos manufacturing plants;
— integrated chemical installations;
— construction of long distance railway lines and airports and express ways;
— large inland waterways and ports;
— *hazardous waste disposal or incineration installations*;
— large installations for the disposal of non-hazardous waste;
— high volume ground-water abstraction or recharge schemes;
— high volume water resource transfer schemes;
— high capacity waste water treatment plants;
— commerical extraction of petroleum or natural gas in large quantities;
— construction of large dams or other large water retention installations;
— long, large diameter oil, gas or chemical pipelines;
— large poultry or pig rearing units;
— pulp production units and large paper or board production units;
— large-scale quarries, open-cast mining or peat extraction works;
— construction of long, high voltage electrical power lines;
— high capacity petroleum, petrochemical or chemical storage plants.

EIA is only required for Annex II projects where member states determine the characteristics of the project so required. Defence projects and projects given consent through an act of national legislation are excluded from the requirement of assessment. Member states may also, in exceptional circumstances, exempt a specific project in whole or in part from the obligations of the Directive (Article 2(3)) except where such a project is likely to have transboundary effects (Article 7).

Member states are free to determine which Annex II projects require assessment either on a case-by-case basis or by reference to thresholds or criteria. In either case member states must take into account the criteria for selection listed in Annex III to the Directive. These comprise three sets of considerations: characteristics of projects, location of projects; and the characteristics of the potential impact. The characteristics of projects include, for example, the question of cumulation with other projects. The location of projects includes consideration of whether the project will affect areas designated as protected areas under the Wild Birds Directive 79/409/EEC and the Species and Habitats Directive 92/43/EC.

The process of EIA consists of three stages. In the first stage the developer is required, by Article 5 of the Directive, to submit an Environmental Statement (ES) including an outline of the main alternatives studied by the developer and an indication of the main reasons for his choice, taking into account the environmental effects.

More detailed guidance as to the type of information which should be included in the ES is prescribed by Annex IV to the Directive. Despite this guidance there is no formal 'scoping' mechanism for determining the scope of the considerations which should be included in the EIA process or the range of alternatives that should be considered (Alder, 1993; Sheate, 1997).

The second stage of EIA consists of consultation in respect of the ES provided by the developer. Article 6 of the Directive requires that the ES be made available to the public and that the public concerned be given an opportunity to express their opinion on it. Since in practice it has been shown that the public are often better at providing environmental information than developers this is an important feature (Alder, 1993). As amended by 97/11/EC the Directive also requires the competent authority to consult environmental authorities on the information provided by the developer.

The third stage of EIA is the requirement that, in the development consent process, the ES and the result of consultation should be taken into account. No particular weight has to be given to the assessment. Consent can therefore be granted even where significant and possibly irreversible environmental damage will occur. In this respect the Directive can be subject to the criticism that it falls far short of the requirements of the precautionary principle (or the precautionary principle itself can be criticised on the grounds that it provides no clear guidance to action).

In the UK the Directive has been given effect principally by requiring EIA as a prerequisite to the grant of planning permission as required under the Town and Country Planning Act 1990. Projects which are required to be subjected to environmental assessment being listed in the Town and Country Planning (Assessment of Environmental Effects) Regulations 1988 (SI 1988/1199 as amended). In relation to projects which do not fall within the system of town and country planning, and for which consequently no planning permission is required, the requirement for EIA is imposed through specific regulations (e.g. regulations requiring EIA for trunk roads and motorways; power stations and overhead power lines; afforestation projects; and land drainage improvement schemes).

The Directive affords considerable discretion to member states in determining which Annex II projects should be subject to EIA. In UK law this is principally left as a matter for the local authorities who operate the development control system. In this matter, however, local authorities are subject to advice given by the government through circular 15/88. This sets out general criteria applicable to all projects, as well as indicative criteria/thresholds specific to certain classes of projects, to be taken into account in the determination of whether EIA is required. The general criteria are:

1. whether the project is of more than local significance in terms of its size and physical scale;
2. the sensitivity of the location of the development;
3. the polluting effect of the development and whether or not it is likely to give rise to complex or adverse effects.

The specific criteria/thresholds in circular 15/88 are intended to be indicative only (i.e. not absolute and mandatory). This flexibility creates some problems. There is some evidence that the application of these criteria varies considerably between authorities. The thresholds, being size related, could theoretically allow for EIA to be circumvented by developers proposing more but smaller projects (e.g. two small pig-rearing units rather than one large pig-rearing unit). This concern arose and was addressed by the courts in *R. v. Swale Borough Council, ex parte Royal Society for the Protection of Birds* ([1991] JPL 39) in which the applicants challenged a grant of planning permission which had been made without any EIA for the reclamation of the Medway mudflats. The applicants contended, among other things, that the project was either a trading port (hence an Annex I project) or part of a larger scheme which would have significant environmental effects (hence requiring EIA as an Annex II project). Simon Brown J. held that the question whether or not the development was of a category covered by either Annex was to be answered strictly in relation to the development applied for, and not in any development contemplated beyond that. But in relation to the further question of whether the development 'would be likely to have significant effects on the environment' one should ask whether the proposed development was, in reality, an integral part of a more substantial development. Were any other approach taken, he argued, developers could defeat the object of the Directive by piecemeal development proposals. The inclusion of 'cumulation with other projects', in the selection criteria in Annex III of amended Directive, goes some way to addressing this concern.

There is no requirement in the Directive as amended, or in the UK regulations, for developers to apply prior to making an application for planning permission for a determination of whether EIA is required. Any such pre-application determinations of the need for EIA are voluntary. This has the effect of reducing the opportunity for public involvement in the EIA process – the first opportunity for public comment is usually when the developer's ES is received by the competent authority at the time of the application for planning permission. It also creates a pressure for developers to submit environmental assessments in cases where no EIA is required, in order to avoid the risk of costly delays to a project. This weakness is redressed to a limited extend by the requirement, in Article 4 of the amended directive, that the competent authority must make public any determination of whether an Annex II project requires EIA. Regulation 5 of the UK regulations permits, but does not require, pre-application determination by local authorities of the necessity (or otherwise) of EIA in the case of Annex II projects.

Safeguarding of Ecological Space

Insofar as it reflects the *Vorsorgeprinzip* the precautionary principle is said to require the safeguarding of ecological space or room for manoeuvre by not approaching, much less breaching, margins of tolerance. This is an aspect of the precautionary principle which has been taken up in several treaties for conservation of marine flora and fauna.

The United Nations Convention on the Law of the Sea (UNCLOS) 1982 has provided a framework for the elaboration of detailed fisheries regimes. Control over stocks of fish that move across or 'straddle' boundaries between the Exclusive Economic Zone and the high seas has been provided for through the 1995 Straddling Stocks Agreement negotiated under UNCLOS. The thrust of the Agreement is to safeguard fish stocks which straddle the boundaries of the Exclusive Economic Zone and the high seas by keeping fishing effort for these stocks *well below* the maximum sustainable yield. Article 6 and Annex II of the Agreement apply the precautionary principle by requiring the establishment of 'reference points'. When reference points are approached they must not be exceeded, and exploited stocks must then be monitored in more detail. If natural events render stocks more susceptible then temporary emergency measures must be taken.

A similar response can be seen in the moratorium on killing of large whales agreed under the International Convention for the Regulation of Whaling. During the evolution of the regime under the ICRW various systems had been applied for determining Total Allowable Catches (TACs). All of these proved inadequate for the conservation of whales mainly because of three factors: scientific uncertainty concerning the population levels of whales; uncertainty over the numbers of whales that could be safely harvested without affecting long-term species viability; and political unwillingness to follow the advice of the scientific community in setting TACs. The moratorium, or zero quota, adopted by the IWC in 1980 provided a precautionary answer to these problems in so far as cessation of whaling provided certainty that population levels would not be taken any closer to, or could recover to, ecological boundaries.

One difficulty with the concept of safeguarding ecological space is the uncertainty, perhaps unknowability, of the location of margins of tolerance. A policy response to this weakness has been to require the carrying out of risk assessment, as a strategy for ascertaining, in the case of any given project, whether ecological damage is likely to be caused. Legal examples of prerequisite risk assessment include the legal regime governing authorisation of operational discharges from nuclear power plants and nuclear fuel reprocessing plants. Risk assessment of ecological safety is also a central theme in the regime governing the authorisation of releases of genetically modified organisms. In European law genetically modified organisms are governed by Directive 90/219/EEC on the Deliberate Release into the Environment of Genetically Modified Organisms (GMOs) and the Directive 90/219/EEC on the Contained Use of Genetically Modified Organisms. The 'Contained Use' Directive sets out common protective measures for contained use of GMOs, including prior risk assessment based on a list of criteria listed in the Directive. The 'Deliberate Release' Directive deals with marketing of products containing GMOs and the deliberate release of GMOs into the environment. In the latter case the release must be authorised by a competent authority. Applications for release must be accompanied by a risk assessment in relation to human health and the environment.

In the UK the requirements of the GMO Directives are transposed through sections 106–127 of the Environmental Protection Act (EPA) 1990 and through regulations issued under that Act. Control over GMOs varies according to whether they are intended for 'contained use' or 'deliberate release'. The former are governed by the Genetically Modified Organisms (Contained Use) Regulations SI 1992/321, as amended; the latter by the Genetically Modified Organisms (Deliberate Release) Regulations SI 1992/3280, as amended. Section 108 EPA 1990 requires prior risk assessment by all those who would import, acquire, keep, release or market GMOs. Section 109 imposes further obligations to continue to assess the risk and, if necessary, to cease or not proceed with the intended actions if it appears that, despite any additional precautions, there is a consequential risk of damage. Similar risk assessment prior to consent is required in relation to the deliberate release of GMOs.

The technique of setting environmental standards by reference to identifiable 'safety margins' has been utilised in US environmental law since the 1970s (Bodansky, 1994). For example the 1970 Clean Air Act required regulators to set standards for emissions of hazardous pollutants with an 'ample margin of safety'. (This provision, in practice, had the opposite effect since the US Environmental Protection Agency, which viewed this measure as unreasonably strict, delayed designation of substances as 'hazardous'.)

Shifting the Burden of Proof

Another technique for implementing the precautionary principle is to alter the usual rule that those who oppose some environmentally harmful activity have the burden of proving, with a high degree of certainty, its harmful nature. This shift can be achieved in one of two ways: first, by reversing the burden of proof; second, by altering the standard of proof, so that it is no longer necessary to have conclusive proof of the harmfulness of the proposed activity to justify regulatory controls.

There are a number of examples of each approach in environmental law and related areas of law. Statutes which reduce the standard of proof that triggers environmental action are now quite commonplace. For example in UK law, section 78A.2 of the Environment Act 1990 defines contaminated land as:

> 'any land which appears to the local authority in whose area it is situated to be in such a condition, by reason of substances in, on or under the land, that
> (a) significant harm is being caused *or there is a significant possibility of such harm being caused* or
> (b) pollution of controlled waters is being, *or is likely to be*, caused (emphasis added).

Examples of reversal of the burden of proof are increasingly common in pollution legislation:

— The Commission of the Convention for the Prevention of Marine Pollution by Dumping from Ships and Aircraft 1972 (the Oslo Convention) adopted a Prior Justification Procedure whereby certain substances may only be dumped at sea if there are no practicable alternatives on land and if it has been shown, with an acceptable margin of certainty, that they do not cause harm to the marine environment (Freestone, 1991).
— The Convention on the Protection of the Marine Environment of the Baltic Sea Area (the Helsinki Convention) prohibits dumping at sea and covers any substances which are *liable* to create harmful effects.
— The 1992 Convention on Protection of the Environment of the Northeast Atlantic (the OSPAR convention), which replaces the Oslo Convention and the Paris Convention for the Prevention of Marine Pollution from Land-based Sources, provides that those parties which wish to retain the option of dumping low and intermediate level radioactive waste at sea (UK and France) must report to the OSPAR Commission on 'progress in establishing alternative

land-based options and on the results of scientific studies which show that any potential dumping operations would not result in hazards to human health, harm to living resources or marine organisms, damage to amenities or interference with other legitimate uses of the sea'.

— The United States Federal Water Pollution Control Act Amendments demonstrate burden of proof, shifting by their *presumption* that discharges of pollution are harmful in water and that such discharges require reduction (Bodansky, 1994).

— Article 4(1) of the EC Plant Protection Products Directive requires member states to ensure that a plant protection product (i.e. a pesticide) is not authorised unless it satisfies criteria including the requirement that it is established that it has no harmful effect on human or animal health, on groundwater, and no unacceptable influence on the environment, having particular regard to its fate and distribution in the environment, particularly contamination of water including drinking water and groundwater and its impact on non-target species.

— Section 25 of the Environmental Protection Act 1990 puts the burden of proof on the accused to show that he has complied with BATNEEC (see below and EPA, 1990, s.81(7)).

— A related device is to take a broad view of causation by regarding action that contributes to pollution as a cause of the pollution even if it is not the operative cause or is one of a number of possible causes (see *Empress Cars* case below, *R.* v. *Secretary of State for the Environment ex parte Standley* (1998) 10 JEL 93).

Reversal of the burden of proof is now also becoming more frequently included in conservation law. The international moratorium on whaling established under the 1946 International Convention on the Regulation of Whaling is, in effect, a precautionary measure which can only be overturned by the presentation of proof that harvesting of whale species will not be to the detriment of those species. In the USA applicants for permits to take marine mammals under the Marine Mammals Protection Act must show that the taking will not have adverse effects on the species (*Comm. for Human Legislation* v. *Richardson*, 540 F.2d 1141, 1145). Section 7 of the United States' Endangered Species Act requires environmental agencies to 'give the benefit of doubt to the species' in insuring that their actions are not likely to jeopardise the continued existence of any endangered or threatened species (Bodansky, 1994).

A weakness of the policy of reversal of burden of proof is that decision-makers, presented with evidence of safety, are faced with uncertainty concerning the reliability or comprehensiveness of such claims. Some suggest that this is because the complexities of environmental interactions are, by their very nature, not amenable to scientific understanding (Hunt, 1994). The decision-maker can never be entirely sure that the evidence presented is a guarantee of environmental safety. Furthermore, the manufacturer of a product or the proposer of some development may not have the resources to prove that some relatively safe course of action is in fact safe. Requiring proof that a course of action is 'safe' or presents no risk of environmental harm amounts to requiring proof of a negative which, philosophers and scientists agree, is difficult if not impossible to achieve (see Cross, 1996, p.853).

Cost-Effectiveness Application of the Best Available Techniques

It is sometimes suggested that the precautionary principle requires or can be given effect by application of the 'Best Available Techniques' (BAT) to which is often added, in order to achieve proportionality, 'Not Entailing Excessive Cost' (NEEC) giving us BATNEEC. This emphasis on clean technologies is considered to be a practical manifestation of the original *Vorsorge* principle (Boehmer-Christiansen, 1994). For instance the Commission of the 1974 Paris Convention for the Prevention of Marine Pollution from Land-based Sources adopted a resolution in 1989 stressing the importance of applying BAT as part of a precautionary approach (Freestone, 1991).

While clean technologies are likely to reduce pollution, and hence provide partial application of the principle, there is no guarantee that reliance on BAT alone will reduce pollution to any particular level which is compatible with the other elements of the principle such as respect for margins of ecological tolerance (Bodansky, 1991). Reliance on BAT-NEEC states nothing about whether action will be taken ahead of scientific certainty – the central element of the precautionary principle. There also remain considerable problems in definition elements such as 'best' and 'excessive cost'. In particular the problem of comparing the costs of taking precautions with the environmental benefits gained is complicated by the fact that costs are readily quantified whereas benefits are indeterminate and may not be possible to quantify in money terms at all. This relates to problems of risk which are discussed below.

Problems with the Precautionary Principle

Scientific Validity

Firstly, the requirement of taking action in advance of full scientific certainty is problematic. Taken literally nothing is scientifically certain so that the strong version of the precautionary principle is a recipe for paralysis. Moreover any precautions that we might take in conditions of uncertainty may have harmful side effects. Scientific method consists of theory *falsification* and not theory *validation*. Thus, although a scientific theory may be widely *accepted* by the scientific and/or wider community it can never be shown to be *true*. At any time empirical observation may render the theory invalid. An example of this 'paradigm shift' is Galileo's observation of the phases of Venus which, in 1610, refuted the previously dominant cosmology in which the earth was considered to be the stationary centre of the universe around which the sun and planets passed in circular orbits. As Talbot J. pointed out in *Jeffrey Nicholls* v. *Director National Parks and Wildlife Service Forestry Commission of New South Wales Minister for Planning* (Land and Environment Court of New South Wales [1994] NSWLR 13304) adopting the precautionary principle as a legal standard could have the potential to create interminable forensic argument. 'Taken literally in practice it might prove to be unworkable ... [because] scientific certainty is essentially impossible. It is only 500 years ago that most scientists were convinced the world was flat. The controversy in this matter further demonstrates that all is not yet settled.'

Risk

Secondly there is the problem of risk. As we have seen, because so-called 'scientific facts' can never be shown to be 'true' scientists prefer to deal with the '*risk*' of certain consequences of actions. Gradually the notion that environmental policy is about reducing environmental risks is becoming more pervasive in the legal context. For example, in the USA the role of the National Environmental Protection Agency is generally accepted to be the reduction of *risk* rather than actual environmental harm (Bodansky, 1994).

Risk assessment is, of course, beset by the very problems of scientific uncertainty that the precautionary principle is supposed to address. Often risks are unknowable (in such cases it is more appropriate to speak in terms of scientific *ignorance*: Faber *et al.*, 1992). For instance, one of the main risks that GMOs are considered to pose is that genes, designed to create pest or disease resistance in cultivated plants, will transfer to wild plants % creating 'super weeds' which disrupt natural ecosystems. This process could take several generations to occur – perhaps more than a hundred years. The very small number of releases that have thus far taken place provide no data set on which to judge the likelihood of future cross-over potential, hence no grounds for judging ecological tolerance. As Hill (1994, 179) observes:

'Since we have only a limited idea of the nature of the hazard, we can have no realistic knowledge of what the margins of tolerance might be. Some commentators have come forward with the notion of "genetic pollution", implying that any genes spread in the environment that would not have arrived there naturally should be considered undesirable. This implies a no "margin of tolerance" for GMOs and hence no releases under a precautionary approach.'

Risk is itself a complex concept incorporating at least three elements: *probability, magnitude* and *reliability*. 'Probability' refers to the chance of an outcome occurring. This could be the probability of occurrence of a one-off event (such as irreversible loss of the ozone layer) or multiple events (e.g. cancers caused by exposure to a given substance). For many events probability is simply not known. 'Magnitude' refers to the seriousness or irreversibility of the considered outcome. Some outcomes are bad but not too serious or irreversible (e.g. moderate pollution of a small pond); others are very serious and/or irreversible (e.g. loss of the ozone layer). 'Reliability' refers to the reliability of the assessments of probability and magnitude i.e. the *quality* of that data. This is sometimes referred to as our 'confidence' in the data. Some 'risks' are known with a very high degree of reliability (e.g. chance of throwing a six on a dice, risk of death through motor vehicle transportation). Other risk data are thought to be unreliable (e.g. assessments of safety of placing high-level nuclear waste in deep geological depositories).

Because errors can occur in assessment of any of these three elements, and because scientific evaluations are affected by political and ethical assumptions, it is unclear whether valid and reliable environmental risk assessments can be carried out (Shere, 1995). Scientific assessments of risk are sometimes shown, with the benefit of hindsight, to be unreliable. For instance, the maternity anti-sickness drug thalidomide was judged safe after being subjected to extensive testing, including animal experiments, before being issued. In the event it caused serious congenital abnormalities. Similarly, in the early post-war period CFCs were thought, with virtual certainty, to present no environmental problems due to their hyper-stable characteristics, the very characteristics which are now known to facilitate their role in causing ozone depletion.

Related to the practical objection that even paradigmatic scientific research does not and cannot require scientific certainty, is the challenge raised by those who object to basing actions on aversion to (uncertain) risks. Gray (1990) characterises this as rejecting scientific evidence, such as statistical predictions, in favour of 'mere suspicion of effects'. We might well ask 'why organise our lives around predictions unlikely to come true?' If mere uncertainty is in issue then one might just as easily side with Brunton (cited by Gullet, 1997, p. 56) who suggests adoption of, in effect, a 'reverse precautionary principle' i.e. that certain activities should not be prevented, since such activities might reap unknown *benefits*. Indeed, the history of science can be read, in part, as a chronology of accidental beneficial discoveries. Moreover, as we saw in Chapter 1, genuine public fear unsupported by scientific evidence might justify a decision.

There is considerable dispute concerning the degree and/or type of risk which should trigger the application of the precautionary principle. If the principle were to be applied to *all* risks then social administration would become extremely burdensome, possible grinding to a halt. Smith J. in *ex parte Duddridge* (above) was clearly perturbed by this implication when he observed that if the EC Treaty imposed a legally binding obligation on member states: 'That would entail the need to conduct cost-benefit analysis in respect of *every known risk to human health from the environment*. [Member States] would then be obliged to legislate in every case in which cost-benefit analysis showed that action would be reasonable' (emphasis added). The situation is possibly worse than Smith J.'s assessment since is no *logical* reason why the principle should be limited in its application even just to risks to 'human health'. The concept of risk depends upon our position on the anthropocentric/ecocentric spectrum.

Costs and Benefits

Even if it is accepted that a precautionary approach should be adopted this does not tell us what action should be taken. In *Greenpeace Australia* v. *Redbank Power Company* (1994, 86 LGERA 143) Greenpeace Australia appealed to the Land and Environment Court of New South Wales against consent for construction of a new power station. Greenpeace argued that emission of carbon dioxide would contribute to the greenhouse effect and that scientific uncertainty should not be used as a reason for ignoring the environmental impact of carbon dioxide emissions. Chief Judge Pearlman, who impliedly accepted that the precautionary principle was applicable to the case, said (at p. 154): 'The application of the precautionary principle [merely] dictates that a cautious approach should be adopted in evaluating the various relevant factors in determining whether or not to grant consent; *it does not require that the greenhouse issue should outweigh all other issues*' (emphasis added). Similarly, in *McIntyre* v. *Christchurch City Council* (1996, NZRMA 289) the Tribunal noted that the precautionary principle should be adopted at the stage of evaluating the various relevant factors in determining whether or not to grant a consent and that its influence on the evaluation and ultimate judgement is a matter of discretion – the weight to be given to the precautionary principle depending on the circumstances.

It may be desirable to restrict the application of the precautionary principle for political reasons. The UK government relies on cost-benefit analysis. The White Paper on environmental policy, 'This Common Inheritance', having stated that UK environmental policy is to be based on the notion of 'stewardship' (para. 1.14), states (emphasis added):

> 'Where there are *significant risks* of damage to the environment, the government will be prepared to take precautionary action to limit the use of dangerous materials or the spread of potentially dangerous pollutants, even where scientific knowledge is not conclusive, *if the balance of likely costs and benefits justifies it*. The precautionary principle applies particularly where there are good grounds for judging either that action taken promptly at comparatively low costs may avoid *more costly* damage later, or that *irreversible* effects may follow if action is delayed' (para 1.18).

Limiting the application of the precautionary principle to 'significant risks' of 'irreversible harm' or 'more costly damage' is, or course, in itself problematic since those concepts are beset by uncertainty. What is a 'significant' risk? 'Significant' is potentially a multiple referent with connotations in relation to all three elements of risk. In the context of *reliability* 'significant' may mean no more than 'established by studies carried out according to the normal canons of scientific method' (this is what scientists mean when they speak of 'statistically significant' results). In the context of *magnitude* it may carry a connotation of social or ecological importance. How are these to be judged? In the context of *probability* it refers to the likelihood of a given outcome. How large is this, something not entirely insignificant or something very substantial?

Even at this early stage in legal considerations of the precautionary principle disagreement and ambiguity seem to have arisen in relation to both the propriety and meaning of the 'significant risk' limitation. In *ex parte Duddridge* (above) the Secretary of State's decision not to regulate the emissions of radiation from the proposed electricity cables was based on his understanding that the proposed cables did not pose a 'significant risk' of causing cancers. The applicants objected that by effectively setting 'significant risk' as a threshold for action 'This Common Inheritance', and hence the Secretary of State, had misunderstood the precautionary principle. Smith J. rejected that argument on the basis that as there is no single authoritative definition of the principle, and as the UK government has adopted the principle voluntarily rather than by legal obligation, it is free to set the threshold for regulatory action at whatever level it thinks fit.

Similar uncertainties exist in relation to the other limiting criteria: 'irreversible effects' and references to cost. Are 'irreversible effects' to be understood as meaning those effects which literally, at any price, over all time scales, and by all human ingenuity, are irreversible or only those effects which are practicably, and within normal time/cost parameters irreversible? When are effects 'more costly' to endure than to prevent?

Which costs are to be included in such a calculus? This question raises once again the problem of incommensurable values and in particular the validity of methodologies which attempt to measure environmental costs – how, for instance, does one value the loss of a local population of deer, the loss of a rare species or loss of some aesthetic quality of a landscape? As we have seen economists try to circumvent this difficulty by use of 'contingent value methodologies' (CVM): techniques which encourage people to attach 'surrogate' monetary values to environmental entities (Pearce, 1990, pp. 141–58) thus locking into an anthropocentric mode. Although CVM is central to environmental economics many commentators believe that the process of 'economising' the environment is invalid as a means of determining its value (Sagoff, 1988).

Deference to cost-benefit analysis, which in turn is based on utilitarian philosophy, is difficult to square with the assertion in 'This Common Inheritance' that UK environmental policy is grounded on *stewardship* – a notion which implies a deontological ethical approach. Indeed, taken in an intergenerational context, utility maximisation approaches to environmental protection tend to endorse policies which are non-precautionary in approach (Howarth, 1995). Moreover DoE policy guidance stresses the subjective nature of risk assessment, treating the precautionary principle not as a reason for curbing development but as an insurance premium to allow development to take place (see DoE, 1995).

The Polluter Pays Principle

Simply put, the polluter pays principle (PPP) asserts that the costs associated with pollution should be borne by the person or entity that causes these costs. The principle has two distinct rationales one based on economic theory, the other based on notions of justice.

The Economic Interpretation of the PPP

The dominant interpretation of the PPP is that it is an economic principle based on utilitarianism, which aims to create a uniform and fair world trading system (Birnie and Boyle, 1992, p. 109). Early formulations of the principle considered that these ends could be attained by fixing the polluter with (merely) the costs of pollution prevention and control measures:

The principle to be used for allocating costs of pollution prevention and control measures to encourage rational use of scarce environmental resources and to avoid distortions in international trade is the so-called polluter pays principle. This principle means that the polluter should bear the expenses of carrying out the above mentioned measures decided by public authorities to ensure that the environment is in an acceptable state. In other words, the cost of these measures should be reflected in the cost of goods and services which cause pollution and/or consumption. Such measures should not be accompanied by subsidies that would create distortions in international trade and investment.

Whether the assumption of control costs could avoid such distortions is unclear. It is obvious that control costs vary from state to state according to the environmental standards adopted in each state: full economic equity would also require uniformity of environmental standards.

Later economic interpretations of the principle call for the polluter to be fixed not only with the costs of preventative or control measures but also the costs of pollution damage. Fixing the polluter with these additional costs can be justified by linking the PPP to a broader economic theory of environmental protection in which the internalisation of costs is viewed as a technique for maximisation of social welfare. Economists assume that the ideal level of pollution is not zero, but a level at which social benefits are maximised: too low a level of pollution will result in net social disbenefit because the welfare foregone by refraining from economic activity will greatly exceed the small costs of environmental damage; too high a level of pollution and the costs of environmental damage will significantly exceed the welfare obtained from such high levels of economic activity; only a medium amount of pollution can maximise welfare. In the absence of any liability or cost allocation regime, economic activity will not rest at this point but rise until there is no further private gain to be obtained for the individual polluter. At this level of pollution societal welfare will be significantly sub-optimal. If, on the other hand, individuals are made to bear the costs of pollution damage then welfare will be maximised because the rational polluter will pollute to a level at which the (marginal) profit obtained just equals the (marginal) costs of environmental damage (Pearce and Turner, 1990).

The Justice Interpretation of the PPP

The economic interpretation of the PPP is premised on welfare maximisation which, in turn, is underpinned by the philosophy of utilitarianism (pleasure maximisation). Utilitarianism, as was noted in Chapter 2, is not only contested as a basis for human ethics but also precluded from providing the conceptual foundation of wider biocentric and all ecocentric ethics.

An alternative justification for requiring individuals to pay for pollution damage or control is that such payment satisfies some notion of 'environmental justice'. The concept of justice has received a very significant amount of scholarly attention but can very roughly be considered as the idea that *individuals or entities are to be given their deserts*. This involves treating equal cases equally. Quite what any individual or entities' deserts are is, of course, a highly contentious matter, as is the question of judging who is the equal of whom. Perhaps a more helpful move is to consider justice as comprising *retributive* justice, *distributive* justice and *corrective* justice.

Retributive justice concerns the imposition of a proper punishment on one who has committed a wrong in order to exact some measure of societal retribution. Quite why society is justified in doing this is much debated. Retributive justice is sometimes thought of as unethical or uncivilised and closely linked to revenge; but many judges and legislatures hold this to be a valid objective of, at least, criminal law (e.g. *Pierson* v. *Secretary of State for the Home Department* [1997] 3 All ER 577). It is possible that the PPP, through the visible imposition of liability for pollution damage measures, exacts a measure of retributive justice. If this is so, then as suggested by the *Cambridge Water* case, fault is an important factor. Retributive justice may therefore clash with economic welfare.

Distributive justice concerns the correct distribution of social goods (or bads). It is more directly connected to the problem of social inequity than the imposition of blame or punishment: 'An obligation in distributive justice is placed on those administering the common stock of goods, the common resource and the wealth held in common which has been raised by taxation, to distribute them and the common wealth fairly and to determine what is due to each individual' (*John O'Reilly and Others* v. *Limerick Corporation and Others* [1989] ILRM 181). Distributive justice concerns the pre-existing state of affairs and not the obligation to compensate or remedy any harm done as such (these are matters of corrective justice). It is likely that, when viewed from a biocentric or ecocentric perspective, distributive justice does not yet exist between humankind and nature – indeed the situation is steadily worsening. However, the PPP contains elements of distributive justice because it asserts that, between humans, the resources used to compensate for environmental damage must be the polluter's own and not taken from some common stock or other person.

Corrective justice (sometimes known as 'restorative justice' or 'commutative justice') requires one who causes harm to make amends by 'correcting' or 'equalising' the harm caused. Assuming that some degree of distributive justice exists between humans and between humans and nature then corrective justice requires that the polluter shall pay for the maintenance of that balance. Whether corrective justice will actually prevail depends, to an extent on the degree of freedom that exists to expend payments made. In the case of preventative measures the payment is necessarily used for the benefit of the environment and, as such, 'correction' is automatically achieved. On the other hand, in cases concerning payment for actual pollution damage it can be argued that corrective justice is only obtained when the payments made by a polluter are actually employed to remedy the environmental damage caused. The general rule in English law is that the recipient of damages in tort or contract is free to use them as he chooses: consequently there is no certainty that, in the event of the polluter being made to pay, corrective justice will be done between humankind and nature. This problem is avoided by environmental statutes which empower authorities to carry out corrective work and charge the polluter for the costs of such work (e.g. Water Resources Act 1991, section 161) or to direct the polluter to carry out remedial work at his own expense (e.g. Environment Act 1995, section 57).

Legal Examples of the PPP

The PPP has gradually become more influential in the law governing the relations between states. A generally accepted principle of customary international law is that a state is liable if it fails to prevent its territory being used in such a way as to prevent unreasonable transboundary damage. The origins of this principle are usually traced to the *Trail Smelter* arbitration (33 *AJIL* (1939), 182 and 35 *AJIL* (1941) 684) and the *Corfu Channel* ICJ Rep (1949) 1 case. The *Trail Smelter* case concerned emissions from a smelter in Canada, emissions that were causing crop and property damage in the USA. The arbitral tribunal required Canada to take steps to abate pollution to avoid any future damage and to pay compensation for damage caused. Although the principle is accepted as a binding legal principle of customary law it suffers from ambiguity and uncertainty as to precisely how far states must go in preventing transboundary damage. As such it is usually interpreted as a duty of 'due diligence' rather than one of strict liability.

The 1972 Stockholm Declaration exhorted states to

'co-operate to develop further the international law regarding liability and compensation for the victims of pollution' (principle 22)

The 1992 Rio Declaration is expressed in clearer terms:

> 'States shall develop national law regarding liability and compensation
> for the victims of pollution and other environmental damage; they shall
> also co-operate in an expeditious and more determined manner to
> develop further international law regarding liability and compensation
> for adverse effects of environmental damage caused by activities within
> their jurisdiction or control to areas beyond their jurisdiction' (principle
> 13)

> 'States should endeavour to promote the internalisation of environ-
> mental costs and the use of economic instruments, taking into account
> the approach that the polluter should, in principle, bear the costs of
> pollution, with due regard to the public interest and without unduly
> distorting international trade and investment' (principle 16)

In international law there are a number of treaties that impose strict
liability for pollution damage:

— The International Convention on Civil Liability for Oil Pollution
  Damage, adopted under the auspices of the IMO in 1969, imposes
  strict liability on the owners of ships carrying persistent oil in bulk
  as cargo for damage caused by spillage of such oil.
— The 1971 Convention on the Establishment of an International
  Fund for the Compensation of Oil Pollution Damage provides
  additional compensation for oil pollution from a fund created and
  maintained by levies on oil importers.
— The 1960 Paris Convention on Third Party Liability in the Field of
  Nuclear Energy channels strict (but limited) liability for damage to
  persons or property onto the operators of nuclear installations.
— The Brussels Supplementary Convention of 1963 provides additional compensation for damage caused by nuclear installations
  payable out of the public funds of the contracting state in which the
  liable operator is situated, and further additional funds made available by all the contracting states according to a prescribed formula.

Many other international conventions refer to or endorse the PPP. For
example:

— Article 2.5 of the UN ECE Convention on the protection and use
  of transfrontier rivers and lakes states that

  > 'The Parties shall be guided by the following principles . . (b) the
  > polluter pays principle, by virtue of which the costs of pollution

prevention, control and reduction measures are to be borne by the polluter'

— Article 2.2b of the 1992 Convention for the Protection of the Marine Environment of the North-East Atlantic, provides that

'The Contracting Party shall *apply* . . (b) the polluter pays principle, by virtue of which the costs of pollution prevention, control and reduction measures are to be borne by the polluter'

The PPP has become a central feature of European environmental law and policy. In 1973 the PPP was incorporated into the first EEC action programme on the environment, article 5 of which asserted that 'the cost of preventing and eliminating nuisances must in principle be borne by the polluter'. In 1986 the Single European Act amended the Treaty of Rome to include Article 130R such that 'Community policy on the environment . . shall be based on the principles that ... environmental damage should as a priority be rectified at source and that the polluter shall pay'.

Some community environmental legislation refers to the PPP as a requirement and a justification for action. For example, EC Council Recommendation of 3 March 1975 regarding cost allocation and action by public authorities on environmental matters (OJ L 194,1 25 July 1975, p.1), states that indemnities given for the collection and/or disposal of waste oil must be in accordance with the PPP. The framework directive on waste, 75/442/EEC, requires that the cost of disposing of waste must be borne by the holder or producer of waste 'in accordance with the polluter pays principle'. The PPP is also the driving force behind the proposal for a Directive on Civil Liability for Damage Caused by Waste (Com(91)219 Final) and the Council of Europe Convention on Civil Liability for Damage Resulting from Activities Dangerous to the Environment.

There are many provisions of UK national law which provide for the costs of pollution prevention and control to be borne by the polluter. Most of the principal environmental legislation enables schemes of charges to be instituted for those engaging in polluting activities. Additionally some UK law creates liability for pollution damage. Some environmental statutes impose liability for pollution damage regardless of whether the person who caused the pollution was legally authorised to do so (e.g. section 161 Water Resources Act 1991 and section 57 Environment Act 1995). Other Acts either only expressly provide for civil liability in cases of illegal pollution (e.g. section 73 of the Environmental Protection Act 1990) or merely provide that authorisations issued under such legislation do not constitute a bar to civil liability (e.g. section 100 Water Resources Act 1991).

Problems with the PPP

Identifying the Polluter

The shibboleth that the 'polluter must pay' leaves unanswered the question of whom is to be regarded as the polluter. In cases of intentional pollution the polluter is clearly the person who causes or permits the pollution. However, in other cases, identification of the polluter or polluters may be less straightforward.

Many people and corporations may have some role to play in the production and consumption cycle that leads to some form of pollution. In a free market economy products and services are provided through the collaboration of many actors, driven by consumer demand or producer manipulation. Are the real polluters, in cases of atmospheric pollution caused by vehicle emissions the vehicle manufacturers, the petrol suppliers or distillers, or the vehicle drivers? In the economic interpretation of the PPP clear identification of a single polluter is not necessary since economic theory predicts that manufacturers will pass on any internalised costs of pollution to the consumer. However, a justice interpretation of the PPP may find such cost shifting less easy to countenance, especially if the consumer has little or no real choice over the consumption of a particular product or service.

Cost shifting may be exacerbated by the existence of insurance schemes whereby potential polluters agree to share out the cost of liability for pollution damage between contributing parties. Such cost sharing may be consistent with notions of distributive justice (since all share the risk) but may be difficult to square with notions of corrective justice (since the actual polluter bears no more of the costs than any other party). Ironically, corrective justice may, pragmatically, be better served by mandatory insurance as otherwise there is a serious risk of impecunious polluters failing to have sufficient resources to make good the damage that their pollution causes. Many pollution regimes now require operators to take steps to ensure their long-term financial credibility. Section 74 of the Environmental Protection Act 1990 takes a similar approach in excluding from the class of 'fit and proper person' who may hold a waste management licence any person who 'has not made and either has no intention of making or is in no position to make financial provision adequate to discharge the obligations arising from the licence.'

Where several actors all bear a measure of responsibility for pollution damage there is a danger that any civil action to recover compensation will become unwieldy or intractable. Consequently environmental liability regimes usually 'channel' liability exclusively onto one or more clearly identifiable parties. Sometimes liability is shared among such parties according to rough notions of equity. For instance, under the 1969 International Convention on Civil Liability for Oil Pollution Damage a set amount of liability for oil pollution damage is channelled onto the owner of the ship: above and beyond this compensation is available from a fund established by oil importers under the 1971 Fund Convention.

In cases where pollution damage may be caused by a material which is handled by many actors it may be necessary to define 'polluter' so as to include persons other than the originator of that material. Thus the proposed EC Directive on civil liability for damage caused by waste places liability onto the producer of the waste, and 'producer' is defined to include the importer of the waste and the person who had actual control of the waste when the incident occurred.

In cases where pollution damage is caused by a process run by several operators sequentially over a period of time it is theoretically possible to identify all of these as polluters or to channel liability onto one of these, e.g. the last operator. The Council of Europe Convention on Civil Liability for Damage Resulting from Activities Dangerous to the Environment uses the 'last operator' rule for closed waste sites and ceased dangerous operations but, where an incident consists of a 'continuous occurrence', fixes 'all operators successively exercising ... control' with liability.

Sometimes so many polluters will be identifiable that obtaining compensation through a civil action is likely to be difficult (e.g. vehicle drivers identified as polluters in relation to respiratory ailments caused by air pollution). In such cases liability regimes often ease the plaintiff's burden by allowing for joint and several liability, i.e. a rule whereby each party who has contributed to the pollution damage is held liable for the entire amount but (usually) may proceed against other liable parties for a contribution to damages awarded.

Sometimes it may not be possible to determine which of a number of parties connected to a material, process or site is responsible, to any extent, for the pollution damage. In such cases legal rules can adopt a liability rule which effectively imposes liability onto the party who is most able to bear it – a 'deep pockets' approach. This is most clearly exemplified by the United States' Comprehensive Environmental Response and Liability Act (CERCLA) which allows the costs of remedying pollution damage to be imposed on banks and other lenders who have invested in the polluted land, but who are morally blameless (*United States* v. *Fleet Factors* 901 F 2d 1550, 11th Cir. 1990). The imposition of remedial costs on the owner for the time being of contaminated land under s.57

Environment Act 1995 evinces a similar approach. Deep pocket liability rules have little basis in corrective justice but may be able to draw justification from distributive justice: pollution costs essentially falling on those who are most able to pay.

There are also cultural factors. For example there is evidence of an expectation among farmers that they should be paid *not* to pollute and indeed farmers do receive payments for voluntarily joining nitrate sensitive areas (S.I.1990 no1013, S.I. 1994 no 1729) although there are reserve powers of compulsion (WRA 1991, s.94(4)(d)).

There are several other circumstances which may make direct polluter liability difficult to operate: unbounded or latent damage; cumulative acts or incidents; unidentifiable liable parties; no basis for liability; no proof of causation; no interested party with legal interest to bring an action (Commission of the European Communities, 1993). In these cases the most common proposed solution is to require the establishment of a joint compensation fund, financed by all those who in some sense stand in the shoes of 'polluter'. This is achieved in the USA by the creation of a 'Post-closure Liability Trust Fund' under CERCLA, s.232 and a 'Hazardous Substance Superfund' under the Superfund Amendments and Reauthorization Act of 1986. The former was, originally, funded by a mix of US Treasury funds; a 0.79 cent per barrel tax on imported crude oil and petroleum products, a tax on the sale of forty dangerous compounds and clean-up costs recovered under CERCLA. The latter is financed by a broad-based corporation tax. The European Community has proposed that some form of joint compensation fund be created to deal with situations where pollution liability is not practicable.

Defining Pollution

What should a 'polluter' be made to pay for under the PPP? All human activities involve emissions or waste of some kind but many authorities consider that not all emissions or waste are to be counted as pollution (Commission of the European Communities, 1993). Contamination as such is not pollution. In part this is said to be because the environment has a natural assimilative capacity to degrade and render harmless certain levels of pollution. Furthermore, some economists (e.g. Pearce and Turner, 1990) consider that environmental degradation does not constitute pollution until it has some adverse effect on human welfare. If human health or happiness are not affected then 'pollution' does not occur. This anthropocentric approach could take into account indirect effects on other life forms insofar as they are valued by humans.

In nuisance actions there has been a reluctance to characterise low levels of contamination as actionable damage – although, of course, this is not quite the same thing as saying that low level contamination is not *pollution*. In *Salvin* v. *North Brancepeth Coal Co* [1874] 9 Ch App 705 James L.J. stated that, in order to succeed in nuisance, the plaintiff must show substantial, or, visible damage. Apparently damage is not 'visible', in this context, merely by virtue of the fact that it is ascertainable by some respectable scientific test or that it can be viewed through a microscope: it must, according to James L.J., be 'such as can be shown by a plain witness to a common juryman'. Furthermore, not only must such damage also be substantial (i.e. it must be actual not contingent, prospective, or remote) but, according to James L.J., 'damage' does not include gradual and imperceptible operations such as the accumulation of particles or dust (until visible damage effects occur).

Brancepeth Coal was cited with approval by the trial judge, Kennedy J., in *Cambridge Water Company* v. *Eastern Counties Leather* (unreported 23 Oct 1991) in which he stated that the spillage of chemicals which had subsequently leached into groundwater at very low concentrations would not have constituted an actionable nuisance were it not for the introduction, by the EC, of regulations declaring groundwater containing such chemicals to be unfit for human consumption. (The logic of such an argument is difficult to follow since the only actual damage consequent upon the introduction of such regulations was a form of economic loss which, in other areas of tort, is generally considered to be inactionable excepting special circumstances.) The effect of this approach, combined with the notorious difficulty of proof in pollution cases, is to substantially weaken the effectiveness of the PPP.

Whether one endorses an anthropocentric or an ecocentric approach to defining pollution there are serious questions to be answered about the meaning of this key term. Is pollution any different from 'contamination'? Is pollution just the introduction of some substance or energy into the environment which society disapproves of? If we take a typical case of serious pollution, say the extreme chronic contamination of a river, then the usual result is that aesthetically pleasing aerobic life forms are replaced by smelly unpleasant anaerobic bacteria. But, from a strictly ecocentric perspective, do these life forms have any less ethic status or right than their larger more common predecessors? The earth's atmosphere was originally oxygen deficient and, as a consequence, anaerobic life forms have a longer ancestral lineage than aerobic life forms. Indeed, originally oxygen itself was a 'pollutant' (Lovelock, 1986).

Legal attempts to define pollution often make reference to the effects that emissions have on other life forms or the risk that they pose to human health. For example, Article 1(4) of the United Nations Convention on the Law of the Sea defines pollution of the marine environment as 'the introduction by man, directly or indirectly of substances or energy into the marine environment, including estuaries, which results or is likely to result in such deleterious effects as harm to the living resources and marine life, hazards to human health, hindrance to marine activities, including fishing and other legitimate uses of the ocean, impairment of the quality of the use of sea water and reduction of amenities'.

To some extent such definitional approaches simply push the question back to one of agreeing the meaning of adjectives such as 'deleterious' and 'legitimate' or concepts such as 'harm' or 'environment'.

Assuming that agreement can be reached on the definitional question of 'pollution' there is the question of limitation: should a polluter pay for all of the costs associated with her pollution, even if these considerably exceed the benefit to the polluter of the operation in question? From an economic perspective the main argument against fixing a polluter with the full costs of pollution damage is that this may cause polluters to go out of business, thus reducing overall economic and social welfare. Some liability regimes have a financial limit (e.g. the 1969 International Convention on Civil Liability for Oil Pollution Damage); most have a temporal limit (e.g. the Limitation Act 1980). Corporate actors possess additional general limitation through the legal personality of the limited liability company. Ship owners have similar general liability restrictions.

Often liability regimes limit liability by exclusion of liability for what is generally termed 'historic pollution damage' i.e. damage caused by activities, carried out in the past, which were either authorised or assumed to be safe at the relevant time but which have subsequently turned out to be environmentally harmful. The common law deals with this problem by excluding liability for pollution damage which, at some relevant time, was not foreseeable by some relevant person.

The question of foreseeability is itself problematic: differing tests have been applied in different areas of law at different times. Although sometimes seen as equitable and just, limitation of liability by reference to the criterion of foreseeability provides a disincentive for research and inquiry into the effects of polluting activities, encouraging polluters to turn away from investigations which could lead to indications of the possible harmfulness of the activity in question.

Difficulties also arise with the notions of 'relevant time' and 'relevant person'. In *Cambridge Water Company* v. *Eastern Counties Leather plc* [1994] 2 AC 264 the House of Lords were presented with a claim for continuing nuisance due to contamination which leaked or escaped many years previously into soil or underground strata but which is currently dispersing further into water underlying the plaintiff's property. The House of Lords held that foreseeability, in such a case, is to be determined by reference to the time of the original escape and not the time of the ongoing dispersal. This has the effect of removing liability in many cases of historic pollution which amounts to an ongoing or continuing nuisance. The relevant person may not be the 'polluter'. In *Cambridge Water*, for example, the defendant – who we assume to be the polluter – was a corporate entity: the test of 'relevant person', by contrast, was 'the reasonable supervisor overseeing the operation of the plant'. There is a danger that the resources and cumulative intelligence attributable to a corporation may be significantly greater than those of an individual such as a reasonable supervisor.

The earliest and best-known legislative regimes for pollution liability – the US 'Superfund' legislation adopts a strict retrospective approach. However, presumably due to the perceived injustice of this situation, European regimes – the Council of Europe Convention and the EC draft waste directive – rule out retrospective liability. The EC Green Paper on remedying environmental damage (Commission of the European Communities) suggests that in cases of authorised activities it is reasonable that the authoriser (public authority) should pay for historic pollution damage. This, in effect, returns to the problem of the definition of 'polluter'. Where environmental or other agencies license polluting activities, and are or should reasonable be aware of the consequences, it would seem to be keeping with justice interpretations of the PPP to characterise such authorisers as polluters (see, for a common law example, *Scott-Whitehead* v. *National Coal Board and Southern Water Authority* 53 P–CR 263).

Damage

Next arises the issue of which *type* of pollution costs the polluter should pay for. This relates to the question of what is environmental harm. As pointed out above a significant problem in relation to environmental damage caused by pollution is that many aspects of the environment are unowned and/or not subject to transferability in the free market. As such they have no easily determinable economic value. One solution to this is to employ contingent valuation techniques to fix surrogate prices. However, as we have seen, these are subject to methodological and principled objections. Another is to adopt some form of arbitrary formula, which values pollution at a fixed rate per cubic metre of affected water.

A better way to avoid the cost problem may be to require the polluter to pay not for the value of the pollution damage caused, but for actual re-instatement of the environment. This is the case for example under the 1992 Convention on Civil Liability for Oil Pollution Damage. According to Article 1 'compensation for impairment of the environment other than loss of profit... shall be limited to costs of reasonable measures of reinstatement actually undertaken or to be taken.'

Even then difficulties arise. Should the polluter pay for a full restoration or just a partial restoration? It can be argued that cleaning pollution up to 'polished earth standards' is wasteful and inefficient and also involves the ethical problem of 'faking nature'. Consequently the approach to contaminated land in UK law and policy has been 'use-led' with the standard of decontamination being matched to the prospective use of the site. Because nature has a regenerative capacity, especially over long time periods, it may be argued that it is better to let nature take its course and undo pollution damage in a safe and natural way. Instructive in this respect is the *Zoe Colocotroni* case (*Commonwealth of Puerto Rico et al.* v. *The SS Zoe Colocotroni et al.*, 628 F. 2d 652.) This litigation arose from the grounding of the tanker *S.S. Zoe Colocotroni* off the coast of Puerto Rico on 18 March 1973. In order to refloat the ship the captain intentionally discharged 1.5 million gallons of crude oil which caused serious contamination of thick mangrove swamps that lined the adjoining shore. An estimated 92 million small marine animals (e.g. reptiles, snails, shrimps, worms, etc.), mostly resident in the mangrove swamp, were killed. The District Court awarded the plaintiffs damages of over $14 million for the costs of clean-up, restocking animals and mangrove trees, and scientific monitoring based on the actual average market cost of replacement organisms required to make the plaintiff's environment whole. The Court of Appeals, however, vacated the $14 million award on the ground that

> 'the primary standard for determining damages in a case such as this is the cost *reasonably* to be incurred by the sovereign or its designated agency to restore or rehabilitate the environment in the affected area to its pre-existing condition, or as close thereto as is feasible without grossly disproportionate expenditures' (emphasis added).

The Court of Appeals noted that determination of whether costs of reinstatement were 'reasonable' would depend on factors such as:

1. technical feasibility;
2. harmful side effects;
3. compatibility with or duplication of such regeneration as could be naturally be expected; and
4. the extent to which efforts beyond a certain point would become either redundant or disproportionately expensive.

Whilst the plaintiff's plan to purchase marine organisms from marine laboratories was technically feasible they had not undertaken to actually use the damages awarded to carry out the scheme. Furthermore the plaintiff's plan was *unreasonable* since not only would many of the organisms die if re-introduced into the contaminated mangrove swamps and sands, but also most of the creatures would in any case be replenished by nature's own regenerative capacity. There is also the problem of English law's relatively narrow approach to damages in tort. This will be discussed in the next chapter.

An environmental justice interpretation of the PPP may have some difficulty in dealing adequately with cases of irreversible environmental harm (e.g. permanent loss of some habitat or species). In such cases corrective justice, in particular, is difficult to achieve because the actual damage cannot be corrected or equalised. It may be that, in such cases, justice may still be done by endowment of a benefit on an entity similar to the entity harmed, or reversing a similar pre-existing harm e.g. paying for protective measures for another species or restoration of some other habitat. This is similar to the *Cy-Pres* doctrine in the law of trusts. Distributive and retributive justice can still, to an extent, be achieved because even if the particular harm cannot be undone society may still re-adjust the balance between the polluter and the environment as a whole (Wilkinson, 1993).

Subsidies

Because the PPP requires the polluter to pay for the costs of preventing or ameliorating pollution damage it seems, intuitively, that subsidies (i.e. state payments) must be inconsistent with that principle. Subsidies and other payments to those who exploit property rights to the detriment of the environment play a substantial part in UK environmental law. However, *in the short term*, the economic end of the PPP – maximisation of social welfare – is served just as well by the payment of subsidies as by the imposition of liability. Recall that, according to economic theory, the ideal level of pollution is not zero but rather the level at which social welfare is maximised. Consider a person who receives a subsidy for refraining from some part of her economic activity: an amount equivalent to the level of environmental damage *avoided*. Such a person should, in theory, restrict her level of economic activity to the level which maximises social welfare. This should occur because she will prefer to refrain from all units of economic activity for which the subsidy (hence the damage) is greater than the profit otherwise to be made from that unit. However, she will not reduce economic activity beyond the 'social optimum' because she will not refrain from any unit of activity for which the profit exceeds the subsidy. Subsidies will be discussed in Chapter 7.

Summary

1.   The precautionary principle broadly requires us to take action to protect the environment even in the absence of scientific proof. It has strong and

weak versions. The strong version would prevent us from damaging the environment unless we were sure it is. However strictly speaking we can never be sure of this. The weak version requires us to weigh the costs and benefits of our actions making allowances for uncertainty. The weak version has been adopted in the UK.

2. The precautionary principle has been said to include the following ideas: preventative anticipation, safeguarding ecological space, a weighting for uncertainty, duty of care on those who advocate change, promoting the cause of intrinsic natural rights and paying for ecological debt.

3. The precautionary principle has been recognised at international levels where it might have acquired the status of customary law. However, there are fundamental uncertainties as to the requirements of the precautionary principle which militate against this. The precautionary principle does not have the status of law in the UK.

4. The precautionary principle has many uncertainties. These revolve around the notion of risk and the difficulty of weighing costs and benefits. Environmental costs and benefits may be unquantifiable and are difficult to compare with direct human costs and benefits. The scientific uncertainty that attracts the precautionary principle also makes it difficult to evaluate risks. Political and moral assumptions must therefore enter into the risk assessment process. The precautionary principle might therefore act as a way of evaluating scientific judgements and as a brake upon human-centred economic cost-benefit analysis. It might therefore be a device for restricting the power of professional expertise in favour of participatory values.

5. The polluter pays principle (PPP) can be justified on the economic ground of advancing general welfare by allocating social costs to those who produce them and also on grounds of corrective and distributive justice. However, there are problems in identifying who is the polluter, in deciding what counts as pollution and in devising payment particularly in relation to environmental harm that has no direct economic value or in relation to irreversible damage.

6. PPP is implemented in a weak sense in the law of tort and to some extent through market mechanisms. In as much as tort liability is based on fault it raises conflicts between corrective justice and economic efficiency.

7. Subsidies fulfil similar economic purposes to those of the polluter pays principle but raise conflicts between questions of welfare and those of justice. Subsidies are discussed in Chapter 7.

Further Reading

Cameron, J. and Aboucher, J. (1991) The Precautionary Principle: a Fundamental Principle of Law and Policy. *Boston College International and Comparative Law Review*, **xiv**(1), 1–27.

Cross, F.B. (1996) Paradoxical Perils of the Precautionary Principle. *Washington and Lee Law Review*, **53**(3), 851–925.

Elworthy, S. and Holder J. (1997) *Environmental Protection, Text and Materials* (London: Butterworths), pp. 154–64.

Faber, M., Manstetten, R. and Proops, J.L.R. (1992) Humankind and the Environment: An Anatomy of Surprise and Ignorance. *Environmental Values*, **1**, 217–42.

Freestone, D. (1991) The Precautionary Principle. In R.R. Churchill and D. Freestone (eds) *International Law and Global Climate Change*.

Freestone, D. and Hey, E. (eds) (1996) *The Precautionary Principle and International Law: The Challenge of Implementation* (The Hague: Kluer).

Fullem, G.D. (1995) The Precautionary Principle: Environmental Protection in the Face of Scientific Uncertainty. *Willamette Law Review*, **31**(2), 495.

Gullet, W. (1997) Environmental Protection and the Precautionary Principal: A Response to Scientific Uncertainty in Environmental Management. *Environmental and Planning Law Journal*, **14**(1), 52–69.

Gundling, L. (1990) The Status in International Law of the Principle of Precautionary Action. *International Journal of Estuarine and Coastal Law*, **5**, 23–30.

Hey, E. (1992) The Precautionary Concept in Environmental Law and Policy: Institutionalizing Caution. *The Georgetown International Environmental Law Review*, **4**, 303–18.

Kuhlman, W. (1997) Can the Precautionary Principle Protect Us from Imperial Ecology? *Wild Earth*, **7**(3), 67.

McIntyre, O. and Mosedale, T. (1997) The Precautionary Principle as a Norm of Customary International Law. *Journal of Environmental Law*, **9**(2), 221–41.

O'Riordan, T. and Cameron, J. (1994) *Interpreting the Precautionary Principle* (London: Earthscan).

O'Riordan, T. and Jordan, A. (1995) The Precautionary Principle in Contemporary Environmental Politics. *Environmental Values*, **4**, 191–212.

Shere, M.E. (1995) The Myth of Meaningful Environmental Risk Assessment. *Harvard Environmental Law Review*, **19**(2), 409–92.

Tromans, S. (1995) High Talk and Low Cunning: Putting Environmental Principles into Legal Practice. *Journal of Planning and Environment Law*, September, 779–96.

Walton, W., Ross-Robertson, A. and Rowan-Robinson, J. (1995), The Precautionary Principle and the UK Planning System. *Environmental Law and Management*, February, 35–40.

Workshop

1.   Explain the difference between the strong and weak versions of the precautionary principle. To what extent has English law adopted the precautionary principle?

2. To what extent does environmental impact assessment embody the precautionary principle?

3. How can we assess risk in terms of costs and benefits in the face of scientific uncertainty?

4. To what extent can the precautionary principle be reconciled with traditional ideas of criminal and civil justice?

5. 'The difficulty facing the adherents of precaution is that is that there is no agreement over how serious the predicament is. At the root of this dilemma lie contrasting positions on the robustness of natural systems to withstand shock, the seemingly bountiful adaptiveness of human societies to cope with change of whatever kind, and the apparently inherent unwillingness to attach much importance to whatever may or may not happen beyond one's lifetime.' O'Riorden and Jordan. Discuss.

6. Discuss the case of *Envirocor* v. *Secretary of State* (1996) 8 JEL 355 in the light of the precautionary principle.

7. 'The polluter pays principle is fatally flawed since we do not know who is the polluter nor what it means to pay.' Discuss.

8. How can a polluter pay for destroying a rare species?

9. 'The polluter pays principle serves conflicting purposes and is therefore unhelpful as a guide to action.' Discuss.

7 The Range of Legal Techniques

Environmental issues straddle many areas of law. In this section we shall outline the various legal techniques that have been applied to environmental problems. In later chapters we shall discuss particular aspects of the main regimes. The details of the main regimes are covered in the standard texts.

A broad distinction can be made between pollution law and nature conservation law. Pollution clearly causes harm from an anthropocentric standpoint whereas the ethical basis of conservation law is less clear. It is not obvious that humans benefit from biodiversity even in the broad enlightened anthropocentric sense. Nor is there any agreed scientific model of what nature should be like, for example whether the notion of ecological balance is helpful or whether we should take positive steps to conserve ecosystems or respect the integrity of nature by leaving nature to look after itself. In the common law, pollution is regarded as 'wrong' whereas the exploitation of nature is regarded as an incident of private property. Nature conservation law relies, to a greater extent, upon voluntary mechanisms than is the case with pollution law and the powers of enforcement are less draconian. For example while there are stop and search powers in nature conservation law, there are only limited powers of entry to private land. More draconian powers apply in the case of pollution law and town and country planning law. We shall discuss conservation in more detail in a later chapter. In this chapter we shall outline the main environmental regimes and discuss some general questions of legal remedy.

Broadly speaking pollution law is interventionist. Conservation law is voluntarist but both are underpinned by the idea of balancing on the one hand environmental concerns and on the other hand the interests of private property. However, the distinction between voluntary mechanisms and compulsion is blurred in that, even where there are powers of compulsion, there is a strong tradition in English culture in favour of using techniques of negotiation and consent with compulsion as a last resort (see Hughes, 1996 p. 584; Lowe, 1997).

The pollution control procedures embody considerable official discretion and so encourages negotiation between regulator and polluter with the risk that working understandings form between polluters and regulators and the wider public are excluded from the process. In ethical terms this could be regarded as on the one hand endorsing the participatory, sustainable development ethos and on the other as giving weight to utilitarian concerns that are likely to favour the bargaining power (and the capacity to be responsible citizens) of the larger polluters (see Mehta, 1998). Indeed the Environment Act 1995 has facilitated the self-monitoring of pollution by the bodies that are subject to regulation. Section 111 of the Act relaxes what were previously strict evidentiary requirements relating to the taking of samples by the enforcer. However, this generates other ethical problems centring upon the protection which the law gives against self-incrimination (see Howarth, 1997).

Public Law Permissions

The most widely used public law instrument, sometimes called 'command and control' is the permission coupled with conditions and enforced ultimately through the criminal law. Permissions (variously called authorisations, consents, licences, etc.) form the centrepiece of the main pollution regimes. These are:

1. Integrated Pollution Control under the Environmental Protection Act 1990 Part I which applies to discharges into any environmental medium caused by processes and substances prescribed in regulations by the Secretary of State;
2. discharges into 'controlled waters' of trade or sewage effluent under the Water Resources Act 1991;
3. waste management regulation under the Environmental Protection Act 1990 Part II. This will be discussed in a later chapter.

Permissions also feature in nature conservation and animal welfare law (e.g. Animals (Scientific Procedures) Act, 1986) and are integral to general land use controls under the Town and County Planning Act 1990. There are also registration requirements, for example in connection with waste management or transport businesses. Registration operates as a general form of permission which is less restrictive than an individualised licence but which is intended to filter out undesirables.

The law targets different aspects of the process in particular contexts. There is usually a blanket prohibition upon the carrying out of defined acts, with the right to do so returned in the form of an individualised permit subject to conditions which can be further controlled by powers of revocation or overriding emergency prohibitions. In the case of integrated pollution control the permit system relates to prescribed processes. In the case of water pollution permits are required for discharges into controlled waters. In the case of waste disposal a permit is required for the disposal, keeping or treatment of controlled waste on land or by means of a mobile plant, thus targeting the chain of waste management operations. In the case of animal welfare legislation there are blanket prohibitions but subject to wide general exceptions with individualised licences applying in certain cases.

Enforcement is usually discretionary involving the initial service of an enforcement notice requiring the offending action to be stopped followed by criminal penalties. There may also be 'prohibition notices' which give overriding powers to close down an activity usually in an emergency, e.g. EPA 1990 s.14(1), integrated pollution control, EPA 1990 s.110, genetic engineering. There are also veto mechanisms which allow pollution unless specifically prohibited thus enabling control over activities that are not necessarily harmful (e.g. Water Resources Act 1991 s.86 – discharges on to land or self-contained pools).

Conditions attached to permissions are an important mechanism for implementing quality standards such as those prescribed by European Community law relating to water pollution. The precautionary principle is an important influence in this context. In accordance with the precautionary principle standards can be set according to perceptions of risk weighted to take account of scientific uncertainty (see Ball and Bell, 1997, pp. 439–47). Moreover standards and limits can reflect non-anthropocentric concerns by being set higher than is required for human needs.

Quality standards take many forms. Some are legally binding, others merely guidance to be taken into account when exercising discretion. they fall into four main groups. Firstly there are quality 'objectives' imposed upon the receiving medium, for example requirements as to acceptable levels of substances in a river or requirements as to the impact on fish or swimmers. Objectives sometimes take the form of 'limits' to what can be permitted by other standards. These have advantages of flexibility and are especially suitable for pollution from diffuse sources such as from farmland. They are, however, vulnerable to our limited scientific knowledge of cause and effect and the interaction between different substances. Secondly there are 'end of pipe' emission standards suitable for 'point source' pollution emanating from a building. These are usually relatively easy to monitor. Thirdly there are 'process standards' which regulate the operations of the polluting enterprise. The tall smokestacks of Victorian factories were an early example. Process standards are flexible in that they allow for choice between different environmental media. They are, however, intrusive in civil liberties terms and require wide monitoring powers. Fourthly there are product standards. These are appropriate to consumer goods, for example the requirement that vehicles have catalytic converters. These techniques depend to a large extent upon technical and administrative factors but also raise ethical considerations relating for example to the kind of interests that they protect, accountability and civil liberty.

Structuring Discretionary Power

Traditionally English law has relied heavily on broad discretionary powers to grant or refuse permission or to attach conditions. Subject to important qualifications where detailed European rules must be applied, this remains the case under modern legislation. In the case of town and country planning, for example, any matter relating to the development or use of land is a relevant consideration (*Stringer* v. *Minister of Housing* [1970] 1 WLR 1281). There is nothing in the Act which expressly excludes a non-anthropocentric ethic. However, according to the *Fewings* case (see p. 12) it is arguable that positive statutory authority would be required to justify an authority embarking on a moral crusade that is not reflected in established community values. On the other hand the law is entitled to reflect changing community values (see *Roberts* v. *Hopwood* [1925] AC 578, *Pickwell* v. *Camden B.C.* [1983] 1 All ER 602).

The main pollution regimes define pollution so as to include harm to non-human species although the discretionary nature of the power means that enforcement can in practice be geared to human concerns as is apparently the case with the contaminated land regime (below) and in connection with nitrate vulnerable zones (see Elworthy, 1998, p. 108). The only way to challenge a restricted policy would be to argue that a non-anthropocentric approach is either contrary to the purpose of the legislation or is irrational. EU legislation has not committed itself to non-anthropocentric ethics and public opinion is unlikely to support an irrationality argument.

The exercise of discretionary power is sometimes structured by a duty to carry out an environmental impact assessment. This applies to certain planning and other decisions where projects require the approval of a public body. The concept of BPEO (best practicable environmental option) involves a kind of environmental assessment. BPEO applies to integrated pollution control where a process involves discharge into more than one medium. It involves comparing the costs and benefits of alternative ways of dealing with the pollution thus embodying the notion of sustainable development (below). The law relating to genetically modified organisms also requires a risk assessment (EPA 1990 Part VI). This is an application of the precautionary principle since we have little scientific knowledge as to the likely long-term effects of tampering with genetic structures. Of course, humans have been involved in genetic manipulation for centuries but until scientists discovered how to isolate genes this could be achieved only by the slow and relatively limited technique of selective breeding. It is questionable whether apart from the risks involved there is any moral difference between the two activities.

The exercise of discretionary power is usually structured by policy guidance from the central government. Unless statute says otherwise (e.g. EA 1995 s.57 – contaminated land regime), such guidance must be taken into account but is not strictly binding (*Tesco Stores Ltd.* v. *Secretary of State* [1995] 2 All ER 134). Thus the decision-making process may be open ended in terms of ethical influences (see DoE, 1995). However, the Environment Agency is required to take an instrumental approach which balances costs against environmental objectives (see EA 1995 s.39). The Agency is also required to aim at achieving sustainable development but only to the extent required by the government. Nevertheless this is a vehicle for introducing an element of social justice into the exercise of discretionary powers, for example by taking into account the impact of polluting activity upon vulnerable people.

Integrated Pollution Control

Integrated pollution control (IPC) under Part 1 of the EPA 1990 embodies the general international and European policy in favour of a co-ordinated approach to environmental problems (EC treaty Article 3c). The traditional approach of English law to environmental issues had been to treat the environmental media of air, water and land as separate. They are, of course, interrelated firstly because a given discharge may affect more than one medium, for example a discharge into the air may find its way into the water table, and secondly because a restriction on a discharge into one medium creates pressure to discharge into another. IPC seeks a holistic solution that concentrates on the process in relation to all three media. Integrated pollution control is also influenced by sustainable development aims in that its environmental objectives are balanced against considerations of cost-effectiveness. These concerns are implemented mainly through the methods of BATNEEC and BPEO which we shall discuss below. We shall first sketch the regulatory system as a whole.

As in the case of other regimes the scope and intensity of control depends on executive discretion. IPC applies only to processes and substances prescribed in regulations made by the Secretary of State who can also prescribe quality objectives and emission standards (EPA 1990 ss.2.3). A distinction is made between matters prescribed for central control and those prescribed for local control (s.2(4)). The Environment Agency regulates central control matters that concern discharge affecting more than one medium. Local control matters are regulated by local authorities and concern only emissions into the atmosphere (Environmental Protection (Prescribed Processes and Substances) Regulations 1991 (S.I. 1991 no. 472 as amended)).

Control is based upon a power to grant authorisations for processes, to which conditions can be attached. A complex of processes within the same category under the regulations and carried out by the same operator on the same site requires a single authorisation. Applications for authorisations and for substantial variations to existing authorisations must be publicly advertised and representations considered (see Environmental Protection (Applications, Appeals and Registers) Regulations 1991, S.I. 1991 no. 507). The regulator's discretion to grant an authorisation is circumscribed by several factors, notably the need to apply BATNEEC and BPEO (below). In particular an authorisation must be refused if the authority considers that the applicant would be unable to comply with any condition which would be included in the authorisation (EPA 1990 s.6(4)).

Remedies include criminal offences relating to operating without or in breach of a permit, and failing to comply with a notice (s.23). There is also a duty to serve an enforcement notice requiring the operator to remedy a breach including one that in the authority's opinion is 'likely' to take place (s.13), and powers to revoke an authorisation where the authority has reason to believe that the process has not been carried on for at least twelve months (s.12). Where the authority believes that there is an imminent risk of serious pollution it must serve a prohibition notice even where there is no breach of an authorisation (s.14). The effect of this is to suspend the authorisation.

BATNEEC

The concept of BATNEEC (best available technique not entailing excessive cost) is at the heart of the integrated pollution control system. BATNEEC provides a method for balancing environmental goals against economic efficiency. BATNEEC is rooted in the utilitarian ethic and embodies the policy of sustainable development in that it is intended to balance the competing goals of environmental protection and economic welfare. BATNEEC also embodies a weak version of the precautionary principle. Like sustainable development BATNEEC faces both ways. BAT requires a high level of environmental protection albeit watered down by the notion of 'available'. NEEC puts a brake on environmental fervour by reminding us that the environment may not be worth paying for. The concept in itself provides no guidance as to how the balance should be struck and raises the familiar problem of how we measure environmental benefits in money terms. Moreover BATNEEC does not tell us who should bear the cost. In general BATNEEC is more comfortable with anthropocentric than with non-anthropocentric perspectives being compatible with the extreme technocratic attitude that we should not impose costs on business solely for environmental reasons. BATNEEC can justify a low level of environmental protection more easily than a high one.

BATNEEC developed out of the long-established UK concept of 'best practicable means' (BPM) and is now a widely accepted international standard. BATNEEC's main area of operation is in the law of integrated pollution control as a required condition of an authorisation. Specific conditions must be imposed in the cause of BATNEEC (EPA 1990 s.7(1)(2)) and a general BATNEEC requirement is implied (EPA 1990 s.7(4)(a)(b)). An authorisation must be refused if the authority considers that BATNEEC cannot be complied with (EPA 1990 s. 6(4)). BATNEEC also applies to genetically modified organisms under Part VI of the EPA 1990 (s.109(3), s.112(4)(c), (5)(c) and, in its older incarnation of BPM, as a defence in some cases of statutory nuisance, s.79(9), s.80(8)).

The purposes of integrated pollution control and therefore of BATNEEC are (a) to prevent the release of substances prescribed for any environmental medium into that medium (subject to BPEO (below)), or, where that is not practicable, to reduce the release of such substances to a minimum and to render harmless any such substance that are released; and (b) to render harmless any other substances that might cause harm if released into any environmental medium (EPA 1990 s.7(4)). We saw in Chapter 1 that the concept of harm is not limited to harm to human beings (EPA 1990 s.1(4)). Integrated pollution control gives the regulator considerable discretion so that the BAT part of BATNEEC could be used to pursue a non-anthropocentric agenda.

The use of the term 'practicable' in this context is difficult since it overlaps with BATNEEC itself. In other contexts 'practicable' has been held to include an element of cost-effectiveness (see *Edwards* v. *National Coal Board* [1949] 1 K.B.704) but in this context the element of cost will have been dealt with as part of the BATNEEC test. It could be that the personal financial burden to the polluter could be taken into account in deciding whether it is practicable to prevent the release. As we shall see the financial circumstances of the particular firm are not regarded by the government as relevant to BATNEEC. Another meaning of practicable might, however, be 'possible'.

The Act does not define the ingredients of BATNEEC except to specify that 'technique' relates to the controlled process and includes technical means and technology, the number, qualifications, training and supervision of staff and the design construction, layout and maintenance of the buildings in which the process is carried out (EPA 1990 s.7(10)).

The regulator therefore has considerable discretion to tilt BATNEEC in favour of political or ethical goals. In connection with the regulator's discretion the Act provides for a substantial political input. The Agency must take into account 'guidance' from the Secretary of State in relation to the meaning and application of BATNEEC (EPA 1990 s. 7(11)) and generally in relation to its functions (EPA 1990 s.4(2)). The Secretary of State also has power to give directions to the Agency in respect of international and European obligations, the imposition of quality standards imposed under other legislation, and in connection with the establishment of national or local emission limits or quotas (EPA 1990 s.7(2). Except in relation to these matters the Secretary of State has no power to override the general BATNEEC requirement (s.7(3)). The Environment Agency is not therefore independent of the central government and is far from being the kind of representative of nature's interests proposed by Christopher Stone (see Chapter 12).

In addition to the costs element built into BATNEEC itself, the Agency is required in exercising any of its powers to take into account the costs and benefits of its actions unless it would be unreasonable in the particular circumstances (EA 1995 s.39). This may entitle the Agency to weigh wider social and economic factors against the concerns of the environment in addition to the costs on the industry built into BATNEEC.

Non-statutory guidance issued by the DoE (1993) gives some indication of the government's ethical stance. This appears to be utilitarian but with emphasis on a precautionary approach. It is emphasised that the costs to the environment as a whole should be taken into account and that some risks of irreversible damage may be so serious that they cannot be permitted irrespective of economic concerns. It is not clear how far policy extends beyond traditional anthropocentric concerns although in the light of the government's contaminated land policy (below) it appears that human interests are the exclusive concern except where specific legal obligations are concerned.

'Available' does not mean in general use but rather general accessibility supported by business confidence. This again indicates a utilitarian balancing rather than a striving for a high level of protection. Similarly the notion of excessive cost is an attempt at identifying a general welfare. The financial circumstance of the particular firm is not as such relevant and the notion of excessive costs relates to the industrial sector as a whole although not apparently to social costs generally. However, if serious harm would result, a permit should be refused even if BATNEEC is satisfied.

In the case of new processes BATNEEC is to be applied in full but in the case of existing processes there is an element of distributive justice in that progress can be staged for up to four years taking into account general environmental conditions, the life of the plant and the economic conditions of the industry in question.

BPEO

BPEO (best practicable environmental option) is essentially procedural. It applies to integrated pollution control when a process is designated for central control by the Environment Agency and is likely to involve the release of substances into more than one medium (EPA 1990 s.7(1)). The Royal Commission on Environmental Pollution 11th Report (cm 310) described BPEO as 'the outcome of a systematic consultative and decision-making procedure which emphasises the protection and con-servation of the environment across land air and water. The BPEO procedure establishes for a given set of objectives, the option that provides the most benefit or least damage to the environment as a whole at acceptable cost, in the long term as well as in the short term.' Thus BPEO reflects the goal of sustainable development and the precaution-ary principle. However in the EPA 1990, BPEO is linked to BATNEEC so that its purpose is currently more limited than the Royal Commission suggested. BATNEEC requires an assessment as to the least harmful form of release but does not apparently include wider environmental concerns such as the consumption of energy or natural resources. In other words the negative question of harm is addressed but not the positive question of benefit. On the other hand BPEO invites an ecocen-tric approach. Harm includes harm to any living organism so that BPEO might for example require people to put up with a measure of air pollution in order to save a rare water species. However, unlike BAT-NEEC, BPEO is not a goal of the legislation but merely a factor to be taken into account in pursuing the aim of BATNEEC so that cost can legitimately prevail. In relation to the cost-benefit balance BPEO over-laps with BATNEEC in that costs must be considered as part of both. In particular it is it not clear how far the term 'practicable' allows personal financial circumstances to be taken into account (see above).

The EC Directive on Integrated Pollution Prevention and Control (96/61) which for new processes must be implemented by 14 October 1999 and for existing processes by 1 October 2007 broadens the scope of integrated pollution control in general and BATNEEC and BPEO in particular. Under the Directive BATNEEC is to include decommission-ing processes and to address itself to energy conservation and to the restoration of the site after the activity ceases in addition to the existing concern with preventing releases or harm (Article 3). However, the Directive is anthropocentric in tone. Its definition of pollution is signifi-cantly narrower than the usual approach of English law. Article 2 defines pollution in terms of harm 'to human health or the quality of the environment.... damage to material property.... impair or interfere with amenities or other legitimate uses of the environment.' On the other hand the Directive includes noise, and vibrations among polluting events.

Waste Management

In as much as pollution is usually generated by waste, all the pollution regimes and also the general law of town and country planning are concerned with waste. However, the concerns of waste management are not limited to pollution but involve broader questions of sustainability including in particular resource conservation through recycling waste and using waste as a source of energy.

A specific waste management regime is contained in Part II of the EPA 1990. This adopts a 'cradle to grave' approach to waste management that reflects the preventative principle (see Royal Commission on Environmental Pollution 11th Report, 1985 (cmnd 9675)). The waste regime implements the EC Framework Directive on Waste 75/442 amended by Directive 91/136 and imposes a licensing system on the waste management process and both civil and criminal liability upon persons who are involved in the waste disposal chain. Waste management is discussed in Chapter 10.

Water Pollution

Water pollution regulation falls within the integrated pollution control regime and is also governed by the Water Resources Act 1991. Water pollution regulation in English law dates from the mid-nineteenth century (Salmon Fisheries Act 1861) and is also a long-standing concern of EC regulation. The law is therefore relatively well developed and has reflected changing approaches to environmental regulation.

The water pollution regime is distinctive in that it creates a wide criminal offence of polluting 'controlled waters' (which comprise almost all inland and coastal natural waterways, lakes and groundwaters (WRA 1991 s.104) as well as more specialised offences (WRA 1991 s.85). Compliance with permission granted specifically under this regime or under other regimes such as integrated pollution control is a defence (WRA 1991 s.86). Criminal liability is discussed below. There is also a range of enforcement mechanisms including enforcement notices (which can be served in advance of a violation) requiring remedial work (WRA 1991 s.90B), power to recover clean-up costs (WRA 1991 s.161), and power to make regulations requiring precautionary measures (WRA 1991 s.92).

As in the case of the other regimes, the Environment Agency has a wide discretion in relation to the granting of permits and the imposition of conditions and there is provision for public advertisement of applications and for consultation (see WRA 1991 sched. 10, Control of Pollution (Applications, Appeals and Registers) Regulations 1996 (S.I. 1996 no. 2971)). The Secretary of State has power to set quality objectives and by means of regulations classifying waters by reference to their uses or substances in them or other specific characteristics (WRA 1991 s.82) and to impose by notice particular quality objectives in relation to each classification (s.83). The Agency has a duty to achieve these quality standards as far as 'practicable' thus allowing cost to be taken into account (s.84). The Secretary of State also has general power in s.40 of the Environment Act 1995 to give directions to the Agency relating to international and EC obligations. The content of water pollution conditions is therefore likely to be dominated by standards which derive from the large body of EC water pollution directives, these usually being implemented by regulations made under the European Communities Act 1972.

A discussion of specific water quality standards and objectives is outside the scope of this book but these powers seem to be wide enough to be used for non-anthropocentric ecological purposes (although where IPC overlaps with the water regime an IPC permit provides a defence (EPA 1990 s.28, WRA 1989 s.88(1)(b)). It seems that the concerns of water law have expanded from a focus upon the use of water by humans, with incidental benefit to other species towards concern for supporting life without direct human benefit (see e.g. Surface Waters (Fish Life) (Classification) Regulations 1997, S.I. 1997 no.331, Surface Waters (River Ecosystems) (Classification) Regulations 1994, S.I. 1994 No. 1057).

Clean-up Powers

There are free-standing clean-up provisions that impose liability to abate a nuisance or to remove pollution upon a designated person, again backed by criminal penalties. There are also powers that allow the court to order offenders to pay clean-up costs or the authority to carry out clean-up operations and to recover its costs from the polluter. The latter may be of limited effect because of the risk of not being able to recover the money. Examples of limited clean up powers in English law include planning (Town and Country Planning Act 1990 s.178, statutory nuisance (EPA 1990 s.80), integrated pollution control (EPA 1990 s.26, s.27), waste management (EPA 1990 s.38(9)), water pollution (Water Resources Act 1991 s.161)). Public law clean-up provisions avoid the difficulties of causation and damage that face the law of civil liability and also reflect the public interest in the environment by avoiding the need for an individual to bring an action. Consistently with the protection that the common law gives to property rights the courts have been concerned to ensure that the costs claimed are actually attributable to the pollution (see *Bruton and National Rivers Authority* v. *Clarke*, 1993 unreported, discussed by Hughes, 1996, p. 583).

The contaminated land provisions of the Environment Act 1995 s.57 (inserting new provisions into EPA 1990) provide a more far-reaching example of clean-up provisions. Local authorities are required to inspect their areas for contaminated sites, defined as sites where by reason of substances in, on, or under the land significant harm is being caused or where there is a significant possibility of significant harm or where pollution of controlled waters is being or is likely to be caused. All inland freshwater, groundwater and estuarine waters are controlled water.

The local authority or in more serious cases ('special sites'), the Environment Agency, then has a duty to require the 'appropriate person' to clean up the site at its own expense. Local authorities are responsible for requiring persons who caused or permitted contamination or, if they cannot be traced, the current owner or occupier to clean up contaminated land. However, contaminated land is defined by reference to the concept of 'significant harm' (EPA 1990 s.78A(2)), which by virtue of ministerial guidance (EPA 1990 s.78A(5)) relates to the proposed use of the land. Similarly the standard of clean up relates to the uses of the land; the overall aim being not to restore the environment in an absolute sense but to create a market in contaminated land. Remediation requirements must be 'reasonable' in the context of a cost- benefit assessment (EPA 1995 s.78E(4)).

The government's policies for contaminated land are implemented in the form of 'guidance' at present only in draft form some of which the Act makes binding including the crucial issues of whether land is contaminated (EPA 1995 s.78A(2)(8)) and the distribution of liability between two or more 'appropriate persons' (EPA 1990 s.78F(7)). The government requires remedial action only where there are 'unacceptable actual or potential risks to health or the environment and there are 'appropriate and cost-effective' means of remedy 'taking into account the actual or intended use of the site'. The government's objectives include the improvement of sites for development, encouraging an efficient market in contaminated land and encouraging the development of contaminated land. The government also stresses that the wealth-creating sectors of the economy cannot afford to deal with all contaminated land at once (see DoE, 1995, p. 22).

The appropriate person is the person who 'caused or knowingly permitted the contamination'. However, much contaminated land in the UK was contaminated many years ago and the polluter may be untraceable. In this case the appropriate person is the present owner or occupier of the land. However, officials who control the land in cases of insolvency (receivers, etc.) can be personally liable only in respect of their own, unreasonable, actions (EPA 1990 s.78X(3)).

There is provision for a breathing space of three months to enable the appropriate person and the authority to agree upon voluntary clean-up arrangements. The authority has the usual back-up powers of criminal sanctions and entry onto the land to do the work itself, recovering its costs as a debt secured against the landowner's property (s.78N). In principle a person who caused or knowingly permits a substance to enter land is responsible for the consequences even where the harm is the result of the combination of his substance with other substances put there by someone else. There might therefore be more than one liable person. In this case the Secretary of State can lay down guidance as to which of them should not be regarded as an appropriate person or as to the apportionment of responsibility (s.78F(6)). There is an exemption from liability in cases where the authority is entitled to do the work at its own expense. This includes, in particular cases, hardship but only while the hardship lasts. Guidance from the Secretary of State must be taken into account but is not binding (s.78H(5)(d), s.78N(3)(e), s.78P(2)).

Where a substance escapes from X's land onto other land owned by Y, X is responsible for the whole of the consequences while Y is responsible only for the state of his own land (s.78K). Unlike the case with civil liability forseeability is not relevant so that there is no state of the art or BATNEEC defence. However, the authority cannot serve a remediation notice if it is satisfied, in the light of guidance from the Secretary of State that the cost of the measures would outweigh the seriousness of the harm (s.78E(4)).

A significant feature of the contaminated land legislation is the wide discretion given to the Secretary of State to control the clean-up strategy. He can issue 'guidance' in relation to the key features of the regime, which in some cases is binding; at the time of writing formal guidance had not been published. Draft guidance suggests that the government is adopting a traditional anthropocentric stance based upon sustainable development. In particular the concept of contaminated land itself, which can be defined in guidance is made relative to the use of the land. This creates a market in contaminated sites since the chosen use determines the permitted level of contamination. This links the contaminated land regime closely with the local authority's planning powers. Ecological interests are apparently to be taken into account only to the extent required by other laws. The guidance is likely to use concepts of cost-effectiveness and risk assessment based on pollution pathways from source to receptors. (see Wolf, 1997, p.348 *et seq.*). Responsibility focuses on those with interests in the capital value of the land but with protection given to lenders again emphasising the economic thrust of this regime.

Overlapping Powers

Parliament has traditionally allocated the power to grant permits to many different public bodies. The Environment Act 1995 created the Environment Agency which is now responsible for many of the main pollution control regimes. However, the environmental jurisdiction of the Agency is not comprehensive. Nature conservation powers are vested in the Nature Conservancy Council (English Nature); some pollution powers including contaminated land, statutory nuisance and localised atmospheric pollution belong to local authorities. Town and country planning powers include both pollution control and nature conservation in as much as both these matters relate to the use of land. For example, a local planning authority might grant permission for a new factory subject to conditions relating to emission levels. Operational changes in relation to existing factories will not usually require planning permission and so will fall exclusively within the remit of the Environment Agency.

Where there are overlapping powers there is a risk of conflicts arising out of different political priorities and ethical perspectives. Section 28 of the EPA 1990 deals specifically with conflicts between integrated pollution control and other pollution regimes. However, little provision is made for broader conflicts between the pollution and waste regimes and the general planning regime which deals with all development of land without being limited to any particular purposes. There are overlaps with both in respect of new building, engineering or mining operations, including many waste deposits, or changes of use (see Town and Country Planning Act 1990 s.55(1)(3)(b)). An application for a waste management licence must be refused if there is no planning permission thus giving priority to the local planning authority (EPA 1990 s.36(2)).

It is through planning and its link with nature conservation that clashes between different ethics are particularly likely to arise. The Environment Agency is a national unelected body whereas town and country planning is primarily a response to local concerns albeit with substantial if unsystematic central input. For example a local planning authority may wish to favour local environmental interests over economic and social justice and impose higher standards upon a new factory than the Environment Agency would require. A local planning authority is an elected body and public and political perceptions of risk may be different from the scientific evaluations of the Environmental Agency. Ethical perspectives are likely to be influenced by the regulatory culture and the professional backgrounds of the decision-maker, and the range of interests to which the decision-making procedures are exposed. In recent years the Environment Agency and its predecessor the National Rivers Authority have encouraged the participation of a wide range of interests including environmental interest groups and the public. However, formal rights of participation are sometimes confined to public bodies although in the case of town and country planning and integrated pollution control there are public rights to make representations.

In *Gateshead MBC* v. *Secretary of State* [1994] 1 PLR 85, the Court of Appeal held that overlaps between planning and pollution control powers were matters of discretion. The law would interfere only to the extent that it would ensure that planning authorities consider whether the specific pollution control powers would be adequate to achieve their purposes and should use their broader planning powers only where this was not so. This approach is directed at efficiency concerns but does not address the problem of conflicting ethical priorities (see also PPG 23).

Agreements

Public law has also adopted private law techniques in the form of agreements or covenants between public bodies and polluters or developers. These are to be found mainly in connection with nature conservation and are also important in the case of planning obligations (Town and Country Planning Act 1990 s.106). Provisions for negotiation and agreement in relation to clean-up work are also built into the contaminated land regime of the Environment Act 1995 and the Water Resources Act 1991 s.95. Conservation is discussed in Chapter 9.

Agreements can provide detailed environmental management regimes fine-tuned to particular local circumstances, and have a strong moral basis in consent. Agreements with environmental interest groups could be a way of representing non-anthropocentric interests in the law. An agreement with a public authority might also be a vehicle for compensating individuals who are required to make sacrifices for the good of the environment. Command and control regulatory mechanisms cater for the general welfare in a utilitarian sense but are not designed to serve the interests of individualised justice. Civil liability can protect individual rights but is limited by a narrow approach to the question of what kind of damage can be compensated and does not in any case apply to injuries suffered as the inevitable result of lawful government measures. People who suffer as a result of environmental protection measures include people forced to live in 'brownfield' sites because of policies in favour of protecting the countryside and people living near pollution 'hot-spots'.

Planning obligations under s.106 of the Town and Country Planning Act 1990 are sometimes used to provide community benefits in return for planning permission. These can be environmental (e.g. *R* v. *Plymouth City Council* [1993] JEL 1099) or economic such as low-cost housing. Thus planning agreements can be used as a tool of sustainable development with a view to compensating for environmental damage and achieving social justice by providing benefits for people whose interests are damaged by pollution.

The benefits sought under a planning obligation must have a rational relationship to the subject matter of the application and unless the benefit is intended to overcome an objection to the application, the local planning authority cannot insist that a benefit be provided. It must, however, take into account any offers to provide benefits when considering the planning application (*Tesco Stores* v. *Secretary of State* [1995] 2 All ER 636). Planning obligations or planning conditions could also be used to authorise and fund the monitoring of the environmental effects of a project.

On the other hand planning and other environmental agreements have serious disadvantages. Even though the public authority party to an agreement represents broad community interests which could include those of future generations, the process of negotiation may lack mechanisms for objective fact finding that feature in formal regulatory processes. Third party interests may be excluded and public confidence may be weakened due to commercial secrecy and the risk of bias. It is not clear how far public law principles of fairness and rational justice apply to negotiated decision making.

Special Zones

Regulatory powers are sometimes supported by powers to designate special geographical zones within which there can be more stringent controls or where special agreements can be made or subsidies paid or where special weight must be given to ecological factors in the ordinary decision-making processes (e.g. Sites of Special Scientific Interest under the Wildlife and Countryside Act 1981, Environmentally Sensitive Areas under the Agriculture Act 1986, Water Protection Zones and Nitrate Sensitive and Nitrate Vulnerable Areas under the Water Resources Act 1991 ss.93, 94 and EC Directive 91/676). The creation of special zones with its rough justice facilitates a precautionary approach. Zone designation is a suitable vehicle for the ecocentric environmental ethic according to which value lies not in the individual but in collective entities such as habitats and ecosystems.

Information

Access to information is an important aspect of sustainable development and relates also to the precautionary principle. Particular examples of procedural devices designed to ensure that information is available to the public about environmental matters are discussed in context mainly in Chapter 12. They include public registers relating to planning and to the main pollution control regimes, requirements for environmental impact assessment in relation to planning, integrated pollution control, and genetic engineering, advertisement and consultation requirements, and public rights of access to environmental information held by public bodies. These provisions support public involvement in several ways including agreements, consultation, initiating legal proceedings, making complaints to public bodies and making market choices.

Civil Liability

The main civil law devices that we will meet in this book are property rights over environmental entities such as wild animals and water, the law of nuisance, restrictive covenants protecting amenities and charitable trusts for nature conservation. In this section we shall discuss the main liability issues with some examples. In the next chapter we shall examine property rights and liability in more depth.

Civil techniques are double edged in that they can be used both to advance and hinder environmental interests. Property law rights can promote environmental concerns because they provide incentives to conserve resources and confer power to protect the environment, for example by suing neighbours in respect of pollution. Environmental activists sometimes purchase land in order to protect it and the National Trust's property rights have been augmented by statute for this purpose (see National Trust Act 1937). Charitable trusts use property devices for public purposes, which to a limited extent can include environmental protection. The Lands Tribunal can discharge or modify restrictive covenants on public interest grounds taking into account environmental concerns (LPA 1925 s.85). Property holding no longer carries parliamentary voting rights but may still influence company policies. For example environmental activists – or 'shareholders from hell' (see Tromans, 1997) – might acquire shares in companies so as to vote at company meetings or even become directors.

On the other hand property owners have the incentive to maximise the productive use of their land at the expense of their neighbours or of nature. Property rights are also a barrier against the state's attempt to regulate the environment in as much as there is a moral claim to compensation in respect of the appropriation of private property for public purposes particularly in the case of agricultural land where traditional values do not regard pollution or killing wildlife as harmful. Much therefore depends upon the extent to which pollution or damage to nature is regarded as outside the scope of property rights and therefore the extent to which property rights can be restricted without compensation.

On the whole the English law of civil liability does not easily accommodate environmental principles such as precaution and polluter pays. Civil liability raises problems in connection with the precautionary principle in that the precautionary principle may require a lower standard of evidence than that which can be accommodated within traditional notions of justice. English law leans heavily on ideas of fault or foreseeability and is reluctant to adopt such precautionary ideas as reversing or lowering the burden of proof or presumptions in favour of liability. The common law of nuisance addresses itself to protecting private rights and preserving the *status quo* rather than to environmental precautions. Civil liability also leans against retrospective liability for historic pollution. This runs counter to the aspiration of the precautionary principle concerned with paying the debts of the past.

English law relies on notions of fault and strict views of causation. It is also influenced by the 'floodgates' policy of discouraging large numbers of claims which take a utilitarian view at the expense of individual justice (see *Merlin* v. *British Nuclear Fuels* [1990] 3 All ER 711 at 722). Civil liability is short term and individualistic in outlook focusing upon disputes about individual rights usually expressed in economic terms whereas environmental concerns emphasise long-term public and perhaps non-human interests which cannot always be evaluated in economic terms. Private law remedies concentrate on compensation in the form of damages intended to restore the winning party as far as possible to the position he was in before the injury. This raises problems in relation to clean-up costs and to environmental damage not directly relating to individual human loss such as loss of a species.

Liability is usually limited to foreseeable financial loss or compensation for human suffering. Clean-up costs may be recoverable only up to the market value of the land minus its value in its polluted state. For example under the Merchant Shipping Act 1995 the strict liability of a ship owner is limited to liability for contamination and reasonable clean-up costs and 'impairment of the environment' is limited to loss of profits and reasonable reinstatement measures (s.156(3)). This reflects an economic judgement that a 'polished earth' approach might not be cost-effective (International Convention on Civil Liability for Oil Pollution Damage (Cm 2657) 1992 Protocol; Council of Europe Convention on Civil Liability for Damages Resulting from Activities Dangerous to the Environment 1993

(Lugano Convention). There is probably no liability in English law in respect of loss of wild animals which are the subject of property rights other than those including, for example fishing rights. There could be liability for loss of plant life that is regarded as part of the land and therefore property but the measure of damages would reflect the market value of the plant and probably not its replacement costs.

In *Merlin* v. *British Nuclear Fuels* [1990] 3 All ER 711 Gatehouse J. took a narrow approach to the meaning of property damage for the purposes of liability under s.12 of the Nuclear Installations Act 1965. This Act implemented the Vienna Convention on Civil Liability for Nuclear Damage (cmd. 2333). The convention referred to 'property damage' but without defining it. The plaintiff claimed that his Lake District cottage had become unsaleable due to contamination of the air inside it by ionised radiation emanating from the nearby nuclear installation at Sellafield. According to the plaintiff there was a health risk from exposure to the levels of radiation that were detected in the house.

The Vienna Convention Art VIII left the question of compensation to the domestic law. Gatehouse J. held that the notion of damage was confined to proved mental or physical injury or physical damage to property. He applied common law concepts. In the common law damage has a strongly anthropocentric meaning of physical change that makes the article less useful or less valuable (see *Hunter* v. *Canary Wharf* [1996] 2 WLR 348, *Blue Circle Industries plc* v. *MoD* [1997] Env LR 347). According to Gatehouse J. damage does not include increased risk or pure economic loss of a kind not recoverable at common law. His Lordship recognised that there can be property rights in relation to airspace but thought that the idea of airspace as property in itself was far fetched (at p. 720). He also took a narrow view of what is meant by cause holding that the presence of contamination in the house does not itself cause damage (at p. 722). Injury is caused only where the particles are ingested so that liability arises only at that point. The decision in *Merlin* provides an example of the strict application of traditional concepts without taking account of either the precautionary principle or the polluter pays principle.

In *Marquis of Granby* v. *Bakewell* UDC (1923) LXXXVII JP 105 damages were recovered for the loss of wild fish on the basis that fishermen placed a higher value on catching these than on farmed fish. The value of damaged habitat was also recoverable but only as a resource for fishing purposes.

The remedy of injunction is sometimes available to prevent future environmental damage (e.g. *Pride of Derby Angling Association* v. *British Celanese Ltd* [1953] 1 Ch 149). The courts are reluctant to issue injunctions where damages would adequately compensate the parties.

Civil liability serves the objective of the polluter pays principle as a search for an individual upon whom to pin responsibility. However, pollution does not necessarily fit into this simple pattern. Pollution may have complex causes in the combination of many different substances put into the environment by different actors that react with each other in unexpected ways over long periods of time. As Teubner points out (1994, p. 22) 'small scale technological effects gradually accumulate and lead to sudden catastrophic changes. Several technologies may have unanticipated effects in their combination with each other.... situations of highly improbable co-incidence arise when two or more causal chains intersect in a non-foreseeable way.' Moreover pollution may affect many people but each individual only to a small extent. in all these cases the transaction costs of leaving the remedy to individual civil action is very high.

Pollution is often the result of a collective process for which it might be unfair to blame any one individual. Firms are usually liable only vicariously as employers. One approach is to relate liability to a 'risk pool' of the enterprise that creates the pollution risk, for example, the farming community. This would encourage members of the enterprise to regulate themselves (see Teubner, 1994). Another approach is Stone's proposal (see Chapter 12) of a right 'isolated' in nature enforced by an official human trustee.

The contaminated land scheme in section 57 of the Environment Act 1995 gestures towards enterprise liability in that it focuses upon the land itself, making its owner or occupier liable. The landowner or occupier's has secondary liability when the person who caused or permitted the contamination cannot be found. The authority has a wide discretion to specify cases where there shall be joint liability thus balancing the enterprise approach with consideration of fairness to individuals. The concerns of economic efficiency are also taken into account. For example, according to the Secretary of State's draft guidance, liability will not normally be imposed upon lenders, insolvency practitioners and other providers of financial services.

The draft guidance sets out the general principles that liability belongs to those who have an interest in the capital value of the land and that effect should be given to agreements between two or more parties in a liability group. Moreover, liability is related to 'significant pollution linkages' in the sense of a source and pathway relating to the use of the land rather than to a duty to clean up the environment as such.

The US 'Superfund' scheme relating to civil liability for waste is also to some extent based upon risk pooling. The federal government is responsible for cleaning up polluted sites recovering its costs from a 'superfund' made up from taxes imposed on relevant industries and compensation paid by polluters (see Comprehensive Environmental Response, Compensation and Liability Act 1980 (CERCLA), Superfund Amendments and Reauthorisation Act 1996, (SARA)). 'Covered persons' on whom liability is imposed include owners and operators of a site, both current and at the time of the disposal, generators of the waste who arrange for its disposal or treatment and transporters of the waste. Strict civil law principles of causation and fault do not apply and liability is joint and several when harm caused by different agents is indivisible (see *US* v. *Monsanto* 858 F. 2d 160). The scheme has proved expensive to administer and raises insurance problems (see Muller, 1998, p. 144).

The possession of a permit from a public body that authorises an activity such as pollution is not in itself a defence to a civil law action in private law. Unless the governing statute expressly creates such a defence, the polluter must show that it would be impossible to implement the purpose of the statute without overriding private rights or that in some other way the intervention of the statute has necessarily changed the conditions of liability. For example in *Gillingham Borough Council* v. *Medway (Chatham) Dock Co Ltd* [1993] QB 343 the *implementation* of a planning permission was held to change the character of the land against which a nuisance fell to be measured but the permission in itself provided no defence. (See also *Wheeler* v. *J.J. Saunders Ltd* [1996] Ch 19, *Hammersmith Railway Co* v. *Brand* (1869) LR 4. HL 171, *Allen* v. *Gulf Oil Refining Ltd* [1981] AC 1001.)

Criminal Liability

The pollution regimes create a range of criminal offences. These most commonly centre upon polluting without a permit or violating the terms of a permit (e.g. EPA 1990 s.23, integrated pollution control, s.33, waste management). The Water Resources Act 1991 s.85(1)(a) creates a general offence of causing or knowingly permitting any poisonous, noxious or polluting matter or any solid waste to enter controlled waters to which compliance with a permit is a defence. This also applies to the contaminated land regime (EPA 1990 s.78(K)). Sometimes statute places a duty on those involved with high-risk activities to take reasonable care as a vehicle for imposing socially determined standards, such as the precautionary or preventative principles. For example, anyone in the waste disposal chain under ss 33(7) and 34 of the EPA 1990. It includes a duty to prevent others contravening statutory waste management requirements, to ensure that waste is passed on only to a properly authorised person and to provide an adequate written description of the waste to anyone to whom it is transferred (see also Environmental Protection (Duty of Care) Regulations 1991 S.I. 1991 no. 2839). Similarly in the case of genetic engineering, those who import, acquire, keep, release or market genetically modified organisms have a duty to identify risks and prevent damage to the environment (EPA 1990 s.109).

To some extent criminal liability with its focus on the general public interest and its concern to deter rather than compensate meets the requirements of the precautionary principle. Most criminal offences are created by Parliament. Armed with this democratic mandate the courts seem to have been more willing to pursue environmental goals than has been the case in the common law settings that still dominate civil liability. Criminal law also has the advantage that, unless the governing legislation provides otherwise, any member of the public can bring a prosecution. The majority of pollution and wildlife conservation offences can be prosecuted by the public. Breach of planning control can be prosecuted only by the local planning authority after serving an enforcement notice.

The criminal law is less than precautionary in the sense that liability bites only after the damage has been done. It is possible to seek an injunction from the court in advance but only where there is strong evidence that that the ordinary criminal penalties would not be effective and that 'the defendant's unlawful operations will continue unless and until effectively restrained by the law and that nothing short of an injunction will be effective to restrain them' (*per* Bingham L.J. in *City of London Corporation* v. *Bovis Construction Ltd* (1988) 86 LGR 660 at 682). Similarly under s.24 of the EPA 1990 the Environment Agency can apply to the High Court for an injunction where there has been a failure to comply with an enforcement notice or a prohibition notice. According to *Tameside M.B.C.* v. *Smith Bros (Hyde) Ltd* [1996] Env LR 312 it must first exhaust other remedies. There is, however, a wider power under town and country planning legislation to obtain an injunction without first exercising other powers (Town and Country Planning Act 1990 s.187B).

Criminal liability can be imposed directly upon companies and, as is usually the case with pollution offences, upon individual managers and directors who consented or connived or were negligent (e.g. EPA 1990 s.157, waste management; integrated pollution control). Traditionally a company can be criminally liable only where the governing legislation or the definition of the offence necessarily creates vicarious liability or alternatively where the offending act is committed by someone who has sufficient responsibility within the company to be regarded as part of the company's 'controlling mind' (see *Tesco Supermarkets* v. *Natrass* [1972] AC 153).

However, in *National Rivers Authority* v. *Alfred McAlpines Homes East* [1994] 4 All ER 286 the Court of Appeal held a company liable for the acts of low-level employees who had allowed cement to be washed into a river. Moreland L.J. in particular relied on the purpose of the legislation, which was 'the keeping of streams free from pollution for the benefit of mankind generally and the world's flora and fauna', a rare example of a specifically non- anthropocentric dictum. It was concluded that parliament must have intended a company to be liable for the actions of its employees at all levels. His Lordship went on to say (at p. 300) 'I see no reason why Parliament as a matter of policy should not have placed on principals, whether companies or others, the responsibility of environmental protection. They are best placed to ensure that streams are not polluted during their activities by their servants or agents. They can do this by training, supervision and the highest standards of maintenance of plant.'

The courts have also taken a broad approach in relation to other aspects of the water pollution offences. For example in *R.* v. *Dovermoss Ltd* [1995] Env LR 258 the Court of Appeal took a broad precautionary approach to the meaning of polluting that included substances capable of causing harm to living things irrespective of whether actual harm was involved.

The House of Lords has also confirmed a broad precautionary approach to the question of what is meant by 'causing' pollution to enter controlled waters under s.85(1) of the Water Resources Act 1990. It had been established by *Alphacell* v. *Woodward* [1972] 2 All ER 475 that causing in this context did not require fault and that this was justifiable on environmental grounds (see Lord Salmon at p. 491). However, there was doubt as to the position where the pollution is the result of an unforeseeable outside agency such as the act of a trespasser who damages storage equipment. The *Alphacell* line of reasoning is that liability should fall on the person who controls the operations that create the risk thus furthering precautionary and preventative goals and preferring utilitarian to deontological ethics. (The polluter pays principle does not help in this context since the very question at issue is who is the polluter.)

In *Empress Car Co (Abertillery)* v. *National Rivers Authority* [1998] 1 All ER 481 the House of Lords held that a person 'causes' pollutant to enter controlled waters if he does a positive act which produces a situation where the polluting matter can escape even though other factors outside his control are also involved and even if his actions are not the immediate cause of the pollution. In this case the firm had maintained a diesel oil tank on their land which they had connected with an unlocked tap to a smaller tank which stood outside a bund designed to contain spillage from the larger tank. An unknown person had turned on the tap with the result that the whole contents of the tank ended up in the river. It was held that the firm was rightly convicted because it had actively set up the operation that created the risk and that it was irrelevant whether or not the particular chain of events was foreseeable.

According to Lord Hoffman (at p. 486) with whom three of the others agreed, the requirement of a positive act derives from the structure of s.85(1) and not from any moral distinction between positive and negative causes. The first limb of s.85(1) requires a positive act because the second limb which refers to *knowingly* permitting deals with omissions. Lord Clyde, however, warned against reliance on terms such as 'active' or 'positive' which are not in the Act itself. While agreeing that complete passivity does not constitute a cause his Lordship thought that actions such as abandoning a mine or failing to take precautions could be regarded as causing pollution (at p. 494).

Their lordships emphasised that 'causing' must be given a common-sense meaning related to the particular purpose of the legislation. In this case the legislation was designed to prevent the pollution of controlled waters and to encourage a precautionary approach. There can therefore be liability even in relation to unforseeable events such as an act of a third party or acts of natural forces such as the clogging up of a pump by leaves that happened in the *Alphacell* case. However, their Lordships qualified this by distinguishing between acts which 'although not necessarily foreseeable in the particular case, are in the generality a normal and familiar fact of life and acts or events which are abnormal or extraordinary such as a terrorist attack or a freak storm' (at p. 491). There would be no liability if the pollution was the result of such abnormal or extraordinary events.

Economic/Market Mechanisms

The use of economic mechanisms is currently favoured as a tool of environmental protection albeit in conjunction with traditional command and control methods. All regulation affects the market but market mechanisms are intended to provide voluntary incentives to encourage levels of environmental behaviour that maximise overall welfare thus helping to create the optimum balance between environmental protection and economic welfare contemplated by sustainable development. Market mechanisms deploy financial incentives, such as pollution charges, taxes, and subsidies. They also include the creation of property rights to pollute or to use scarce resources with a view to creating a market in environmental goods. They try to insure that the costs of pollution are made explicit and are borne by the polluter or its customers thus reflecting the polluter pays principle and promoting a rational market choice as to whether it is worth while degrading the environment (see Pearce *et al.*, 1989, chapter 7).

Market mechanisms cannot operate without the backing of state regulation since the state must ultimately decide what level of environmental protection is appropriate. The market mechanisms must be created and backed up by administrative and enforcement machinery just as is the case with traditional regulation. In particular the state must represent the interests of non-participants in the market such as future generations and non-humans. Moreover, although market behaviour is said to be better informed than the state could be, the market reacts to short-term concerns. State arrangements such as environmental impact assessment are therefore required in the interests of prevention and precaution. On the other hand the market is likely to be good at developing technology, so that market incentives may effectively re-enforce BATNEEC.

Market mechanisms rely on conventional economic assumptions notably that of rational self-interest. They are the product of the free market ideology which was dominant during the 1980s. They do not attempt to address problems of social justice or, of course, do they embrace non-anthropocentric concerns. Market mechanisms are a facet both of the idea of sustainable development and that of polluter pays. It is not clear whether the overall cost of the market approach is greater or less than that of other techniques. Nevertheless economic mechanisms provide another weapon in the armoury. They are generally regarded as complementing rather than replacing traditional legal techniques and presuppose an ethical climate that favours private transactions.

In accordance with the Rio Declaration Principle 16 and the Fifth Action Plan of the European Union (COM (92) 23 final, OJ 1993 C138/5, ch 7.4.) the UK government has adopted market mechanisms as a tool of environmental policy albeit in conjunction with other methods. In 1992 the government favoured a presumption in favour of market mechanisms, (See 'This Common Inheritance', Second Year Report, 1992 Cm. 2086) but this has since been diluted in favour of a pragmatic mix of techniques (see DoE, 1993, 1997).

Following the OECD, five main kinds of market instrument have been identified (see White Paper, 'This Common Inheritance', 1990, Cm. 1200, Annex A). These are charges, subsidies, deposit/refund schemes, market creation, for example transferable pollution permits, and enforcement incentives (such as paying informers).

A broad distinction can be made between mechanisms such as charges, subsidies and taxes which work within the context of existing market transactions by providing incentives, and mechanisms such as tradable pollution permits which create new markets by creating new kinds of property right. Charges and taxes do not necessarily reduce pollution but create an optimal level of pollution beyond which it becomes more expensive for a firm to clean up than to pay the charge and carry on polluting. They therefore aim to achieve the maximum welfare but this does not necessarily benefit the environment. Pollution costs bear more heavily on some firms than others and the consumer's willingness to pay also varies. Tradable permits by contrast involve a market in pollution created by the state which fixes overall variable thresholds below which permits can be traded. Holders of permits therefore have an incentive to drive down pollution levels as much as possible.

The discretionary nature of the regulatory system could also be sensitive to individual or local cost-benefit factors However, traditional economic analysis would claim that the participants in the market have better information than government officials and can produce a more efficient solution. A pollution charge should ideally cover all external costs imposed on the community by the pollution in question including the cost to society and future generations of a given level of pollution. In practice this is very difficult if not impossible to calculate and the charge may relate only to the perceived costs of administering the system and clean-up costs (see DoE, 'Economic Instruments for Water Pollution', consultation paper, 1997).

Taxes create special difficulties because of the conflict between the desire to raise revenue and the use of a tax to discourage anti-social behaviour. Tax revenues are traditionally put into the general government coffers and cannot be earmarked for particular purposes such as cleaning up the environment. Thus a tax may be less efficient than a charge. Moreover attempts to avoid taxes may distort environmental policy by transferring a problem elsewhere or create unintended side effects. For example the introduction of the Landfill Tax in 1996 may lead to waste being disposed of in other undesirable ways such as muckspreading and fly-tipping or to a shortage of materials for landscaping or infilling work because of fear of the tax. Socially desirable activities such as landscaping or recycling might be encouraged by means of detailed exemptions and reliefs but this entails a large administrative burden.

English law has not made systematic provision for market mechanisms but there are some examples (compare the 'pioneering' Resource Management Act 1991 (NZ); Richardson, 1998). The UK has introduced several examples of taxes and charges. The Landfill Tax created by the Finance Act 1996 is an attempt to combine taxation and charging concepts. Traditionally taxes in the UK have not been earmarked (hypothecated) for particular purposes. However, in the case of the Landfill Tax, the revenue is used to off-set employers' national insurance contributions and credits are available, although not to the full amount of tax payable, where the taxpayer makes a donation to a body concerned with the protection of the environment registered with ENTRUST a private body set up for the purpose (Finance Act 1996 s.53). There are several exemptions designed to encourage environmentally friendly ways of waste disposal or to favour other desirable activities. They include temporary storage pending re-use, mine and quarry waste, the reclamation of contaminated land (see ss.43, 43A, 43B, 44, 45, Landfill Tax Regulations 1996 S.I. 1996 no. 1527).

Charges to cover the cost of regulation feature in the town and country planning legislation and in the main pollution regimes (see e.g. Environment Act 1995 ss.41, 42). However, although sections 41 and 42 do not limit the purpose for which charges can be made current policy is to limit charges to administrative costs. These cannot therefore be regarded as market mechanisms in the present context.

Subsidies involve a transfer of capital from society to those involved in environmental harm. This capital can be used to invest in abatement and other 'clean' technology so that, in the future, environmental harm is lessened. EU law dealing with subsidies adopts this approach. Generally subsidies are prohibited by Article 92 of the EC Treaty. The Commission, which has the power to approve state subsidies in certain cases (Article 93), has as a matter of policy restricted payments to installation of anti-pollution technology for existing businesses.

Examples of subsidies can be found in a range of incentives to farmers and foresters mainly under EC legislation designed to encourage environmentally friendly practices (see e.g. EC Regulation 2078/92; Habitat (Former Set-Aside Land) Regulations 1994 S.I, 1996, no. 1242; Forestry Act 1979 s.1; Agriculture Act 1986, s.18; Rodgers, 1992). Under the Environment Act 1995 s.98, the government can pay grants to anyone for the anthropocentric purposes of conserving or enhancing the natural beauty and amenity of the countryside or promoting public enjoyment of the countryside.

In the short term the economic end of the maximisation of social welfare is served just as well by the payment of subsidies as by the imposition of liability. Recall that, according to economic theory, the ideal level of pollution is not zero but rather the level at which social welfare is maximised. Consider a person who receives a subsidy for refraining from some part of her economic activity: an amount equivalent to the level of environmental damage avoided. Such a person should, in theory, restrict her level of economic activity to the level that maximises social welfare. This should occur because she will prefer to refrain from all units of economic activity for which the subsidy (hence the damage) is greater than the profit otherwise to be made from that unit. However, she will not reduce economic activity beyond the 'social optimum' because she will not refrain from any unit of activity for which the profit exceeds the subsidy.

Subsidies have a number of disadvantages, both in terms of the goals of the polluter pays principle and wider social and environmental goals. One major drawback is that, by definition, subsidies involve wealth transfer to the recipients, which, if not channelled into pollution abatement, can be used to offset product costs. Consequently subsidy recipients are able to offer goods at a lower price than non-recipients. Subsidies tend, therefore, to be inconsistent with the demands of an economic 'level playing field' in relation to freedom of trade. Subsidies also have the undesirable long-term effect of attracting new entrants into the economic activity (or preventing the natural decline of numbers engaged in that activity) which it is sought to reduce (Pearce and Turner, 1990, pp. 107–09).

In order to avoid these undesirable consequences OECD policy suggests that subsidies should be limited to measures which do not significantly distort international trade and investment and which are not limited only to the abatement of existing pollution. Similarly Principle 16 of the Rio Declaration requires that 'the polluter should, in principle, bear the cost of pollution ...without distorting international trade and investment.' EU law dealing with subsidies mirrors this approach. Generally subsidies are prohibited by Article 92 of the EC Treaty. The Commission, which has the power to approve state subsidies in certain cases (Article 93), has as a matter of policy restricted payments to installation of anti-pollution technology for existing businesses.

Corrective justice would generally rule out the payment of subsidies, because these would reward rather than punish a polluter. Situations may arise, however, where the elements of corrective and distributive justice pull in the opposite direction. Consider, for example, payments made to developing countries under the Fund established by the Montreal Protocol to the Vienna Convention on Protection of the Ozone layer. In the main the ozone-depleting substances (ODS) that are currently causing ozone destruction are a product of developed states. Furthermore, developed states have received the vast proportion of the *benefits* from ODS technologies. They also, in general terms, possess the bulk of global financial and technological assets. It may, therefore, be thought as making a proper *distribution* of world goods for subsidies to be paid by developed states to enable developing states to avoid causing further unnecessary ozone damage.

Market creation involves turning pollution, energy consumption or development rights into property rights which can be traded between polluting firms. Pollution permits could also be bought up by environmental interests so as to reduce the available pollution capacity. The government can intervene by ratcheting down permissible overall pollution levels or buying up permits. A similar permit system could apply to energy use or to non-market environmental goods such as rare species. Under schemes adopted in the USA the state fixes an overall quota in relation to a given kind of pollution and allocates permits to individuals authorising pollution up to prescribed limits. The permits are transferable to other persons in other locations thus giving a polluter an incentive to pollute below the limit. Pollution permits therefore seem to address the need to drive down pollution more effectively than do charges, etc. but presuppose the existence of a market. The uncertainties inherent in the concept may make such a market difficult to establish.

On the other hand firms have an incentive to pollute where it is cheapest to do so thus creating pollution hot spots where permits are concentrated which may bear heavily on already disadvantaged communities.

Tradable pollution permits have not been introduced into English law. The Environmental Protection Act 1990 s.3 empowers the Secretary of State to fix overall quotas in relation to integrated pollution control but permits can be transferred only between persons and not between sites. The contaminated land scheme introduced by section 57 of the Environment Act 1995 involves relating the level of clean up required to the proposed use of the land. This creates the basis for a market in contaminated land rather than encouraging the clean up the environment.

Trade in environmental goods is sometimes forbidden. For example, the Wildlife and Countryside Act 1981 forbids the sale of specimens of most bird species and the CITES Conservation 1972 requires participating states to prohibit almost all imports of endangered species (Endangered Species (Import and Export) Act 1976).

Market mechanisms also include a range of devices for giving information to consumers and other stakeholders about the environmental practices of an enterprise. As well as furthering market goals, this provides an accountability mechanism although as with other market devices, broader public interests are not catered for. Examples are company reporting and audit, environmental resolutions at company meetings, eco-labelling and published standards against performance targets (Taubner, 1994; Elworthy, 1996, pp. 324–46; Hughes, 1996, pp. 30–4).

The EC Regulation on Eco-Management and Audit (Reg (EEC) No 1836/93, OJL 168, 10.7.93) introduces a voluntary scheme for industrial companies. Registration for the scheme commits the company to complying fully with all regulatory requirements, adopting and implementing a written environmental policy in relation to its site based broadly on the idea of BATNEEC, to monitoring its performance, to subjecting itself to an independent external audit, to seeking continuous improvement, and to preparing an environmental statement in non-technical language for each site. The environmental statement must be published 'as appropriate' and the site registered with the commission. The company must also disclose environmental information to anyone who asks for it. The Regulation includes the notion of sustainability but does not impose any specific ethical perspective.

Advantages and Disadvantages of Market Mechanisms

To summarise, market mechanisms are said to have six main advantages. Firstly, voluntary behaviour is preferable to legal compulsion. Secondly market mechanisms allow direct public participation in the form of consumer choice. Thirdly they may be cheaper for private firms than compliance with direct regulatory requirements. Fourthly they expose the environmental costs and benefits of transactions. Fifthly decisions taken by firms in the marketplace may be better informed than decisions taken by public officials. Sixthly they can raise revenue that can be used to clean up the environment.

Objections to market mechanisms include the following. They are not particularly democratic in that access to the market depends on income levels and therefore broad rights of participation on public interest grounds or by those who bear the brunt of pollution are excluded. Market mechanisms might also be seen as morally offensive in that they reinforce a belief that degrading the environment is not wrong but is simply a transaction with a price (see Rose, 1985). Could it seriously be suggested for example that there should be a market in rape? Market mechanisms are entirely anthropocentric. Market mechanisms might also lead to social injustice in that richer firms could afford to buy the right to despoil the environment putting poorer firms at a competitive disadvantage and perhaps creating 'pollution hot spots' concentrated in areas of low land value near low income housing.

The disadvantages of market mechanisms also include problems of the distortion of international trade by subsidies. On the other hand direct regulation such as a ban on the import of waste can also be a distortion of trade (see Basel Convention on the Transboundary Movement of Hazardous Waste 1989 29 I.L.M. 649; *Wallonian Waste* case, *Commission* v. *Belgium*, Case C-2/90, [1993] 1 C.M.LR. 365). Market mechanisms also raise the problem of imcomensurability between environmental goods and tradable goods which were discussed in Chapter 1.

Summary

1. We outlined the range of legal devices available to tackle environmental problems distinguishing broadly between pollution control devices and conservation devices. The latter tend to emphasise voluntary mechanisms such as agreements rather than state force. In practice both involve discretionary powers and even in relation to pollution there is a tradition of negotiation in preference to legal enforcement.

2.   Public law devices most commonly depend on grants of permission subject to conditions imposing quality standards. These standards range from the discretionary BATNEEC to precise requirements for the composition of water and include target standards, end of pipe standards, process standards and product standards.

3.   The main pollution regimes vary in their purposes and ethical and policy bases. Integrated pollution control reflects a utilitarian and precautionary approach. Waste management embodies a preventative and polluter pays approach and is also influenced by ideas of sustainable development. It therefore leans in favour of anthropocentric values. The water pollution regime has the greatest scope for an ecocentric approach since it does not specifically require cost balancing (but note EPA 1995 s. 39).

4.   Other public law devices include clean-up requirements illustrated by the contaminated land regime which reflects the polluter pays principle and the sustainable development policy. Here the leaning in favour of anthropocentrism arises out of the way in which the government exercises its wide powers to apply the Act rather than from the Act itself.

5.   Public law devices are backed by powers to designate special areas and powers relating to information. These are discussed in later chapters.

6.   Private law devices include liability in tort, the law of restrictive covenants and trusts. They are dominated by the concept of property rights. These are discussed more fully in the next chapter.

7.   Criminal penalties in relation to statutory offences reveal the courts taking a more positively pro-environmental stance than they are prepared to do in relation to common law civil liability.

8.   We drew attention to the main market mechanisms: taxes, charges, subsidies, and tradable permits. Taxes, charges and subsidies seek to balance the costs of pollution against those of environmental protection. Tradable permits seek to enlist the profit motive to drive down pollution levels or to enable a given pollution level to be attained at low cost. Market mechanisms raise problems of moral accountability, environmental valuation and social justice. They are not free standing but operate in conjunction with direct state regulation.

Further Reading

Ackerman, B.A and Stewart, R.B. (1983) Reforming Environmental Law, The Democratic Case for Market Incentives. *Columbia Journal of Environmental Law*, **13**, 171.

Ball, S. and Bell, S. (1997) *Environmental Law: the Law and Policy Relating to the Protection of the Environment*, 4th edn, chapters 5 and 6 (London: Blackstone Press).

Elworthy, S. and Holder, J. (1997) *Environmental Protection, Text and Materials*, chapters 6, 7 and 8 (London: Butterworths).

Leeson, J.D. (1995) *Environmental Law*, chapters 1 and 2 (London: Pitman).

Pearce, D., Markandya, A., Barbier, E.B. (1989) *Blueprint for a Green Economy* (London: Earthscan).

Purdue, M. (1991) Integrated Pollution Control in the Environmental Protection Act 1990: A Coming of Age of Environmental Law. *Modern Law Review*, **51**, 534.

Sunkin, M., Ong, D. and Wight, R. (1998) *Sourcebook on Environmental Law* (London: Cavendish), pp. 239–87.

Wolf, S. and White, A. (1997) Environmental Law, 2nd edn, chapter 1 (London: Cavendish).

Workshop

1. Compare the advantages and disadvantages of ambient standards, end of pipe standards process standards and product standards from the point of view of the main ethical perspectives and in relation to civil liberty.
2. What are the ethical bases of BATNEEC and BPEO?
3. To what extent is the UK waste management regime influenced by the precautionary or preventative principles?
4. For many years water had seeped into a disused mine on land acquired by Quickbuck plc. Quickbuck had not previously been responsible for the mine but on acquiring the land it installed a pump to keep the water level in the mine under control. One night an unknown person entered the land and tipped poisonous chemical waste into the mineshaft. That same night the pump failed due to an unforeseeable power cut. Contaminated water from the mine overflowed and entered a nearby river killing numerous fish. Advise Quickbuck as to any possible criminal liability.
5. Consider the benefits and disadvantages of using voluntary agreements to achieve reductions in pollution and nature conservation objectives.
6. Compare the criminal law with the law of civil liability for damages as means of furthering the polluter pays principle and the precautionary principle.
7. What role does agency discretion play in (a) setting standards and (b) enforcement? Is a conciliatory or a tough stance more likely to achieve compliance with standards? What are the major drawbacks of traditional 'command-and-control' regulation?
8. What are the ethical advantages and disadvantages of
    (a) environmental taxes;
    (b) marketable permits;
    (c) subsidies;
    (d) charges
    as methods of environmental regulation? To what extent do these devices feature in English law?

8 Property Law and the Environment

The Attitude of the Common Law

In this chapter we shall try to bring out the ethical standpoint of the common law and the possibilities of using ethical arguments within the common law framework. In measuring the common law against general principles such as 'sustainable development' or 'polluter pays' it would be wrong to take a simplistic approach that assumes a model of consistent and mechanical compliance with these principles and 'rates' the law against the model. Firstly the meaning of the principles is fluid and uncertain so that we are trying to hit a moving target. Secondly there is no particular reason why the common law should comply with environmental principles except to the extent that they are embodied in customary international law or in the ethical values of the community from which the common law derives its authority. By contrast relevant statute law can be legitimately measured against such environmental principles as are contained in treaties since there is a duty upon government to comply with international obligations.

Environmental law operates within the context of the common law of property both as a direct source of law and as the background to legislative intervention. On the whole it has been reluctant to adopt environmental principles. We have already seen an example of this in *R. v. Secretary of State ex parte Duddridge* (p. 153) where the court treated the precautionary principle as a matter for the exercise of discretion by the Secretary of State. More generally in *Cambridge Water Co Ltd v. Eastern Counties Leather plc* [1994] 1 All ER 53 at p. 76, Lord Goff thought that it was for Parliament rather than the common law to develop environmental principles. (This can be contrasted with the more activist standpoint that the courts have taken in criminal cases (p. 210).

'The protection and preservation of the environment is now perceived as being of crucial importance to the future of mankind; and public bodies both national and international are taking significant steps towards the establishment of legislation that will promote the protection of the environment. But it does not follow from these developments that a common law principle should be developed or rendered more strict.

On the contrary, given that so much well informed and well structured legislation is being put in place for the purpose, there is less need for the courts to develop a common law principle to achieve the same end and indeed it may well be undesirable that they should do so.'

In one sense Lord Goff is right. Parliament has created a large but by no means comprehensive body of environmental law and the European Union has imposed both detailed environmental standards and regulatory machinery. The court's job is to settle disputes not to regulate. Moreover the common law is orientated towards private rights whereas environmental concerns are often regarded as collective or public rights.

However, Lord Goff may be drawing too sharp a line in ruling out the common law. Firstly, the courts are necessarily involved in environmental disputes and cannot avoid laying down environmental principles. *Cambridge Water* is itself an example. The issue in the case was whether the water company could recover damages for pollution to a borehole caused by chemicals which over many years had been spilt from a company's leather factory onto the ground and seeped into the water table. The borehole had to be closed because the water quality broke European rules. The House of Lords held that the consequences of the pollution could not have been foreseen at the time of the spills so that the company was not liable. The court was in effect saying that in the absence of fault the cost of pollution should be borne by its victim or society at large. This may violate the 'polluter pays' principle but is still an environmental principle that might be defended.

Secondly, the common law and public law legislation are not hermetically sealed from each other. Legislation has to be applied and interpreted against a background of common law values attitudes and reasoning methods and the common law has to react to the impacts of legislation. There is a common law presumption that statutes should not be interpreted so as to impose burdens upon private property unless clear language is used. This could have repercussions in respect for example of clean up costs for pollution and where planning decisions impose costs on landowners.

In the context of planning decisions at any rate, the traditional common law attitude seems to be weakening. For example the courts have begun to accept the proposition that, in return for the right to exploit their land, property owners can reasonably be required to provide environmental compensation to the community in the form, for example, of contributions to local amenities (see *R.* v. *Plymouth City Council ex parte Co-operative Wholesale Society* (1993) 67 P and CR 78; *Tesco Stores* v. *Secretary of State* [1995] 2 All ER 636 particularly Lord Hoffman's speech).

A grant of planning permission under statutory powers is not in itself a defence to an action in nuisance at common law (see *Wheeler* v.

Saunders: [1995] 2 All ER 697). However, if it is acted upon, a planning permission might change the character of a locality so as to raise or lower the quality of the environment against which the reasonableness of the pollution must be judged. If the area is downgraded, as in *Gillingham Borough Council* v. *Medway (Chatham) Dock Co* [1992] 3 All ER 923, where a port expanded to the disturbance of local residents, the plaintiff may escape liability. If on the other hand a series of planning permissions upgrades a locality, for example by introducing executive housing into a run-down commercial area, existing businesses may find themselves vulnerable to a nuisance action (see *R.* v. *Exeter City Council ex parte Thomas* [1990] 1 All ER 413). In both cases the common law allows private rights to be extinguished without compensation.

Thirdly, it is arguable that the common law is especially well suited to dealing with environmental principles combining as it does general principle with pragmatism, and flexibility in the setting of a real dispute. Unlike statute law the common law is not tied to particular verbal formula but can express principles in many different ways. Environmental principles sometimes take the form of grandiose generalisations which cannot be directly applied such as 'sustainability'. The common law can take the core of good sense from a general principle and apply it case by case in an incremental way thus allowing the principle to be tested against reality and manipulated to meet new problems. Moreover the common law is an open system in the sense that it must give an answer to any problem, however novel. Through the medium of the action on the case any dispute can be raised in a common law court and the judge cannot refuse to adjudicate on the basis that there is no law. In other words he must give a positive reason in law or justice for denying a claimant a remedy. The common law must also respond to the changing social and political values of the community.

Furthermore the common law has both deontological and instrumental aspects. We suggested earlier in Chapter 2 that neither deontological nor instrumental approaches make sense on their own if only because the rigid application of either would produce outcomes that offend many people's intuitive sense of what is right. Both approaches play a part in addressing practical problems. The common law provides a technique for balancing incommensurable ethical approaches which is lacking in statute law which depends upon fixed forms of words.

The common law is often favoured by right-wing thinkers who advocate market solutions to environmental problems. Curiously, judicial intervention is not regarded by such advocates of the market as state intervention (see Simpson, 1995, chapter 7). By contrast deep ecologists would be ambivalent about the common law. On the one hand they might applaud its customary and community-based theory. On the other hand they call for a revolution in the way that we think of our relationship with nature whereas the common law is a conservative force that appeals to the established values and customs of the community. Moreover the formative influence of the common lawyers of the seventeenth-century Enlightenment, notably Sir Edward Coke and the polymath Francis Bacon, associate the common law with the same kind of rationality that conforms to the Christian tradition of man's domination of nature. The 'enlightened anthropocentric' approach advocated by Passmore (1980) who argues that environmental concerns can best be advanced by building upon established values and traditions also seems to endorse the common law view of the world.

The community basis of the common law has many ramifications one of which is that judges speak as individuals and not as the collective voice of an institutional court. For example dissenting judgements are taken for granted whereas in civil law countries public dissents are usually not allowed. Common law judgements can therefore stimulate new ideas or be platforms for later reforms of the law. There are many cases where yesterday's dissent became today's orthodoxy. The process by which the raw material of community values is translated into legal outcomes is complex and not fully understood. It is subject to the danger that the common law will reflect the vested interests of those who have access to the courts. Community values have to be filtered through the practices and attitudes of the legal profession from which the judges are recruited and through the short-term interests of their clients. These are overwhelmingly anthropocentric interests usually of a commercial nature. The question of ' environmental justice' – who has access to the court? – is therefore of crucial importance.

The common law could be a conduit for international principles although its track record has not so far been impressive. In practice the common law has sometimes been accused of insularity (Lucy, 1997) but in theory the common law can draw upon any material domestic or international as a persuasive authority. The common law is 'open law' in that it is open to any kind of argument. The main inputs of the common law are, of course, cases but the judges also take into account international agreements, foreign laws, ethics, economic theories, philosophy and even biblical sources, literature and poetry (see e.g. *Tesco Stores* v. *Secretary of State* (above per Lord Hoffman). The style of common law judgements is discursive and reasoned not prescriptive.

The common law is not tied to any particular attitude to the environment. However, its perspective has so far been anthropocentric treating nature as a resource for human exploitation and preferring economic values to those of amenity. For example in a case from the formative period of the common law of nuisance, *Salvin* v. *North Brancepeth Coal and Coke Co* (1873) 9 Ch. App 705 at 709–710, Sir W. James M. R. expressed hostility to the nature-loving romanticism of his time.

> 'If some picturesque haven opens its arms to invite the commerce of the world, it is not for this court to forbid the embrace, although the fruit of it should be the sights and smells and sounds of a common seaport and shipbuilding town, which would drive the Dryads and their masters from their ancient solitudes. If (the defendants) had been minded to erect smelting furnaces, forges and mills which would have utterly destroyed the beauty and amenity of the Plaintiff's ground, this court could not have interfered. A man to whom Providence has given an estate, under which there are veins of coal worth perhaps hundreds or thousands of pounds per acre must take the gift with the consequences and concomitants of the mineral wealth in which he is a participant.'

Similarly in *Hole* v. *Barlow* (1858) LJCP207, Sir John Byles said

> 'it is not everyone whose enjoyment of life and property is rendered uncomfortable by the carrying out of an offensive or noxious trade in the neighbourhood that can bring an action. If that was so... the neighbourhoods of Birmingham or Wolverhampton or of other great manufacturing towns of England would be full of persons bringing actions... to the great injury of the manufacturing and social interests of the community. I apprehend the law to be this that no action lies for the use, the *reasonable* use of a lawful trade in a convenient or proper place....'

These are typical expressions of the Christian anthropocentric tradition. Not only does economic development come before natural beauty but we have a moral obligation to exploit nature. (See also *Versailes Borough* v. *Mc Keesport Coal and Coke Co Ltd* 83 Pittsburg Legal Journal 379 (1935), 'the philosophy of the beautiful must give way to the realities of bread and butter existence' per Musmano J.)

The Role of Property Law

The concept of property is fundamental to environmental law. A property right entitles a person to control and transfer an asset and in its full sense is binding upon all. To an economist, property is a device for rationing consumption and directing it to its most efficient use thereby generating wealth. For example, according to Posner (1986, chapter 3), all resources should be owned by someone, except resources so plentiful that everybody can consume as much of them as he wants without reducing consumption by anyone else. Garrett Hardin (1968) argues that our environmental problems are caused by the 'tragedy of the commons' meaning that environmental resources cannot easily be reduced to private property so that there is no incentive to conserve them. Hardin regarded overpopulation as a primary cause of environmental disaster and, in the absence of the property incentive, suggests abandoning the ethical values of individual liberty and concern for the disadvantaged in favour of draconian state controls. Market devices such as transferable pollution permits can exploit the rationing function of property in the interests of pollution control.

To a lawyer, property is not necessarily limited by the economic perspective. The law does not regard property as a single 'thing' but as a bundle of rights in relation to a thing, the right to use it, the right to dispose of it, etc. The right to control an asset can be divided up by legal rules in many different ways, between different people for different purposes. The law can create property rights over any asset for any purpose including that of protecting the environment. Indeed transferable pollution permits have been pioneered in the USA making the right to pollute into a property right. English law has followed the economists' goals and concentrated upon commercial interests in particular the need for a property asset to be tradable. This privileges the interests of certainty and involves caution in restricting the landowner's ability to exploit the land. In *NPB* v. *Ainsworth* [1965] AC 1175 at 1247–8 Lord Wilberforce emphasised the qualities of clear definition, capacity for recognition and assumption by third parties, permanence and stability as necessary qualifications for a property right (see also *Victoria Park Racing and Recreation Ground* v. *Taylor* (1937) 58 CLR 479 – a spectacle cannot be owned because of the possible chilling effect upon development).

Property law points in two directions. On the one hand, according to the 'tragedy of the commons' thesis (an aspect of what economists call the prisoner's dilemma), property provides a rationing device and an incentive for conservation. In the absence of property or at least of local customary rules everyone would consume as much as possible because they could not stop others from doing the same thing. Traditionally English law has taken the view that environmental assets, in particular the air, were virtually unlimited and did not need the protection of property law. There can be use rights in relation to airspace but the airspace itself is apparently not property and its quality not protected in itself without proof of some further injury (see *Merlin* v. *British Nuclear Fuels* (above p. 206). By contrast water is in some circumstances capable of being property and its quality defended under the common law. The exploitation of other limited 'resources' such as game or fish has also been turned into property. Blackstone for example justified the common law principle that animals can be property by drawing on the belief that God gave man dominance over nature. Blackstone (quoted by Brooman, 1997, p. 51) also drew attention to the value of property as giving an incentive to conserve. There is no doubt that the desire to hand on assets to the next generation is a deep-rooted human instinct.

Pride of Derby Angling Association v. *British Celanese and Derby Corporation* [1952] Ch 149 provides an illustration of how exploitation rights can be used for environmental protection. A club with fishing rights in the River Derwent succeeded in nuisance against Derby Corporation whose sewage works were no longer able to cope with the city's increasing population so that effluent polluted the river. The Court of Appeal held that the club's proprietary right to fish entitled them to an injunction despite the health problems faced by the city. The effect of the injunction was to protect the fishes' habitat and the case is sometimes regarded as a triumph for the environment. However, its sole rationale appeared to be the existence of a private property right which in this case happened to be to catch fish. The interests of the fish were, of course, immaterial. Moreover the case involved a clash between different environmental interests, which was resolved by privileging private rights over public health interests.

Another example of the use of property in furtherance of environmental concerns comes from the USA during the *Lochner* era (after *Lochner* v. *New York* 198 US 45 (1905), when the thrust of constitutional law lay in subjecting governmental powers to external constraints based upon common law ideas such as property rights and freedom of contract. The federal courts managed to reconcile the protection of wildlife with the constitutional protection of free interstate trade by deeming wildlife to be the state's property which the state was therefore free to remove from commerce (see *Geer* v. *Connecticut* 161 US 519 (1896)). Modern constitutional law has turned this issue on its head by treating conservation interests as public concerns that can be weighed against property rights in deciding whether environmental restrictions constitute a 'taking' of property without compensation (see *Hughes* v. *Oklahoma* 441 US 322 (1979), *Spurhase* v. *Nebraska* 458 US 941 (1982), *Babbit* v. *Sweet Home Chapter of Communities for a Greater Oregon* (1996) 8 JEL 179).

It is sometimes said that property law acts as a neutral method of reconciling competing interests. For example, just as developers may exploit their land, pressure groups may use property power to advance an ethical agenda by acquiring land over which they can prohibit activities such as hunting. Similarly shares in companies can be acquired with a view to influencing company policy in favour of ethical investments or environmentally friendly practices by asking questions or proposing motions at company meetings or exercising voting power.

On the other hand property may be an obstacle to environmental protection. Neither the law nor the idea of property are neutral. The law fashions property rights to serve particular economic and political purposes. In English law this is arguably wealth maximisation. For example nuisance law is balanced in favour of the interests of development (below

p. 231) and property rights cannot exist in goods such as landscapes that are incapable of being traded. Trustees have a fiduciary duty to maximise financial returns within the constraints of prudence. It is not clear to what extent this can be overridden by ethical concerns in the absence of clear authority in the trust instrument. In *Harris* v. *Church Commissioners* [1993] 2 All ER 300, Sir Donald Nichols V. C. held that where property was held by trustees for the purpose of generating money to be used to further the work of the trust, the trustees must normally use ordinary investment criteria. While they are entitled to have an ethical policy they will only exceptionally be permitted to make a financial loss for ethical reasons. One such case would be where an investment conflicts with the aims of the trust, or where a particular investment might hamper the trust's work by destroying its credibility.

Thus property owners have an incentive to exploit their resources for short-term gain. It is in their interests to pass their costs onto the wider community by polluting or dumping waste, thereby creating what economists call 'externalities'. The law of nuisance, which depends upon the notion of a right to reasonable enjoyment of land, is one response to this but, as we shall see later, provides an imperfect solution. Also the claims of property owners to compensation may impede environmental measures taken in the public interest. In relation to this it could be argued that property is a gift of the state which the state can firstly restrict in line with the values of the community. On the other hand it is arguably unjust that the burden of environmental protection should fall on the property owner rather than on society at large.

A broad distinction might be drawn between the pollution and the nature conservation aspects of environmental law. Pollution regulation tends to be tougher than conservation regulation and to rely to a greater extent upon force exerted through the criminal law. There is no right to pollute unless it is granted as an easement by a neighbouring landowner who is therefore assigning his right to a clean environment. By contrast property owners can at common law freely exploit living things that happen to be on their land. Thus interfering with nature is not regarded as 'wrong'. For example under the Deer Act 1991 it is an offence to take, kill or injure deer without the consent of the owner of the land, the deer being valued, not for themselves but as part of the owner's assets. Attempts by the state to protect nature clash with property rights in a way that pollution control does not.

The Basis of Common Law Property Rights

The common law assumptions that underlie the law of property reinforce the law's narrow anthropocentric bias. The moral basis of English property law appears to lie in the belief that man is master of nature. We have already said that the common law does not recognise a right to environmental quality other than in respect of short-term damage caused by pollution. The common law also gives a landowner an automatic right to exploit all wild creatures that happen to enter his land. Houck (1995 at pp. 331–2) described this as a fiction writing that '(t)he idea that anyone through the payment of money and the completion of other rituals may dispose of the millions of living things that occupy his titled property, heedless of the role those things play in the life of everything around it is an anachronism supportable only in a world ignorant of its dependence on all life.'

The theoretical basis of title to land is the intention to control the land and to exclude others. The common law reflects the Hegelian notion that property is the expression of the human will to control and the need for self-expression, rather than the labour theory of John Locke, according to which by mixing his labour with a natural object a person extends his ownership of himself (which Locke takes for granted) to the object in question (see Waldron, 1988, pp. 350–65). A particular feature of Locke's moral underpinning of property is that the initial allocation of property presupposes that there is no scarcity in the sense that there is 'enough and as good' for everyone thus introducing the notion of sustainability.

For example, at common law title to property depends solely upon the claim to prior possession as evidenced by the systems of title documents, limitation periods and registration that have developed around the core concept. In the absence of a claim that is prior in time, a person acquires title by adverse possession, that is by controlling the land with a manifested intention to exclude the world at large. As Carol Rose (1985) puts it 'those who conquer resources are favoured over. Those who move lightly through [the land] living with the land and its creatures as members of the same family rather than as strangers who visited only to conquer the objects of value. The common law gives preference to those who convince the world that they have caught the fish and hold it first' (see e.g. *Buckinghamshire C. C.* v. *Moran* [1990] Ch 623). Apart from customary rights which exist in favour of local communities the common law has no concept of public property dedicated to the public interest (see *Mercer* v. *Denne* [1905] 2 Ch 538; *New Windsor Corporation* v. *Mellor* [1975] Ch 380; Rose, 1986, 1991).

According to the common law and also in equity, investing labour in land is neither sufficient nor necessary for the acquisition of title (see *Lloyds Bank* v. *Rossett* [1991] 1 AC 107) although in equity estoppel might come close to it. Use of the land as a resource is not in itself evidence of title and the courts are not concerned with questions of sustainability or efficiency. A landowner does not discontinue his possession merely by ceasing to make productive use of the land (*Leigh* v. *Jack* (1879) 5 Ex D 264 at 271) nor does productive use in itself constitute evidence of adverse possession. For example in *Powell* v. *McFarlane* ((1977) 38 PCR 452 at 476) the grazing of cattle was held insufficient to establish adverse possession. In the Australian case of *Milirrpum* v. *Nabalco City Council* (1971) 17 FLR 141, it was held that the common law had no room for the Australian aboriginal concept of customary access to land to meet grazing needs because aboriginal values did not include the essential element of an intention to exclude others from the land (see Gray, 1994, p. 182 *et seq.*). The ethics or economics of land use does not seem to be an important concern of the English law of adverse possession which is dominated by the interests of conveyancing certainty (see Dockray, 1985).

The ability to put resources to productive use occasionally influence property rights. For example, rights to use airspace exist only up to the limits of ordinary use (*Bernstein* v. *Skyviews* [1978] QB 479 at 488). Riparian rights in respect of the use of water flowing in a river or a stream are also limited. A landowner can sue his neighbour who deprives him of the use of the water. Except in the case of 'ordinary' use for the basic needs of life for which an unlimited quantity can be taken, a crude sustainability regime operates so that any water used, for example for industrial purposes, must be replaced in quantity and quality (*McCartney* v. *Londonderry and Lough Swilly Ry Co* [1904] AC 301.

On the other hand there is no right to the flow of water percolating through the ground so that a neighbouring landowner, however unreasonably, can take the entire resource running through or under his land (see *Bradford Corporation* v. *Pickles* [1895] AC 587).

The difference between percolating water and water in a defined channel seems to lie in the pragmatic problems of proof viewed from the perspective of a nineteenth-century court (see *Chasemore* v. *Richards* (1879) 7 HLC 349). Today, of course, the common law is overlaid by statutory licensing regimes governing abstraction and pollution. The pollution regime does not, however, affect common law liabilities.

A landowner does possess a right that any water, whether percolating or in a defined channel that actually enters his land be unpolluted (*Ballard* v. *Tomlinson* (1885) 29 Ch D 115; *Young* v. *Bankier Distilliery Co* [1893] AC 691). This is difficult to reconcile with the principle that there is no property right in percolating water. In *Cambridge Water Co* v. *Eastern Counties Leather plc* [1994] 1 All ER 53, which concerned historic groundwater pollution, Lord Goff said (at p. 68) that there is no natural right to percolating water except in as much as the landowner can abstract whatever water happens to enter his land. If this is so, then it is difficult to see why the owner has any rights in respect of the quality of percolating water. However, in *Cambridge Water* their lordships clearly accepted the proposition that if the pollution had been foreseeable the plaintiff would have been liable.

The common law relating to wild animals follows a similar pattern of control and exploitation. Wild fish, animals and birds cannot be owned while at large but are regarded as 'profits' of the land which can be reduced to ownership by being captured or killed. The owner of the land where the animals happen to be usually has the first claim to capture or kill them. This is apparently the basis of the widely held view that there is an ancient 'right' to hunt. And the cultural and economic importance of hunting to property owners is reflected in a large body of legislation buttressing common law rights (see Brooman and Legge, 1997, p. 289 *et seq.*). The law regards a profit to catch animals or fish as a distinct kind of property right which can freely be transferred separately from the land itself. The public has fishing rights in tidal waters but in other cases the landowner usually has the first claim to creatures captured on his land (see *Blades* v. *Higgs* (1865) 11 HL Case 621, *Attorney General for British Columbia* v. *Attorney General for Canada* [1914] AC 153). At common law game animals (deer, etc.) were in a special position in that by virtue of the royal prerogative the king had exclusive power over them as quasi-property which he could grant to others (see 2 Blackstone's Commentaries para 410).

Trees and other vegetation are regarded as part of the land and therefore under the absolute control of the landowner. Natural features such as trees are sometimes protected by the doctrine of waste which has elements of intergenerational equity. Under the doctrine of waste a limited owner such as a tenant or a holders of an interest under a trust cannot destroy the land to the prejudice of later owners. However, the doctrine concerns only items of economic value such as timber or trees planted for human enjoyment (see *Doherty* v. *Allman* (1878) 3 AC 709, *Re Harkers* WT [1938] Ch. 323). These features of the law clearly depend upon the overriding importance of resource exploitation (see *Dalton* v. *Angus* (1881) 6 AC 740 at 822, 824, 827).

It is not clear whether the common law recognises a right to pollute as a property right in the sense that it can be acquired by grant or prescription so as to run with the land. In principle a right to pollute could fall within the common law tests for an easement (see *Sturges* v. *Bridgman* (1879) 11 Ch D 852). Provided that the use is sufficiently definite it should not matter that it fluctuates in intensity from time to time (see e.g. *Waterfield* v. *Goodwin* (1957) 105 LJ 332, *Hulley* v. *Silversprings Bleaching Co* [1922] 2 Ch 268, 281). On the other hand the law is reluctant to recognise negative easements the content of which imposes restrictions on the landowner's ability to develop his land.

The common law does not recognise easements in relation to amenity values such as landscape. English law has usually resisted the creation of property rights of a kind that restrain building and development such as a right to protection from the weather or to a pleasant view or to a flow of air except through a clearly defined channel in a way analogous to an easement of light. The possibility of developing the law of easements in the direction of environmental values therefore seems remote. The underlying rationale of the law seems to be that of mediating between competing claims to exploit land and so to facilitate efficient development (see *Dalton* v. *Angus* (1881) 6 AC 740; *Hunter* v. *Canary Wharf*; *Bryant* v. *Lefever* (1879) 4 CPD 172; *Webb* v. *Bird* (1862) 13 CBNS 841; *Phipps* v. *Pears* [1965] 1 QB 76).

The common law cannot easily accommodate the moral perspective of those who claim the public should have the right of access to privately owned land (see *A.G.* v. *Antrobus* [1905] 2 Ch 188). The present government has promised to introduce such a right but as the law stands there are no public rights of access to private land other than linear rights of way. The notion of a 'right to roam' can be supported by enlightened anthropocentric arguments and ecocentric values which draw upon spiritual affinity with nature. There are dicta which could support a limited right to roam but these are inconclusive (see *R.* v. *Doncaster M.B.C. ex parte Brain* (1987) 57 P and CR 1; *Re Ellenborough Park* [1956] Ch 131).

The Law of Nuisance and Trespass

The law of nuisance combats the tendency of property owners to pass their costs on to others without their consent and could therefore serve the concerns of the polluter pays principle. However, English law has a more limited perspective. In the law of private nuisance any right to environmental quality is not a free-standing personal right but is an incident of a proprietary interest in the land. Only a person with a property interest in the land or at least a permanent occupier can sue in private nuisance and only in respect of interference with the use and enjoyment of property rights (see *Hunter* v. *Canary Wharf* [1997] 2 All ER 426). Non-property owners do, however, have limited rights to sue in public nuisance (below). The right to exploit land is also a proprietary right so that the law seeks an accommodation between the two concerns. This could be regarded as consistent with the ethos of sustainable development. However, as we shall see, the common law is not concerned with the social justice aspects of sustainable development. Moreover the law takes a restrictive view of what kind of environmental damage can be compensated.

Property law is typically concerned with disputes between competing private interests so that broader questions of public interest arise only indirectly. The law of nuisance is concerned with damage to property itself and with the comfort and convenience of the use of property but not with matters of amenity such as a beautiful landscape. Damages for nuisance are not general damages but relate to the value of the land affected so that it is not certain whether clean-up costs as such are recoverable. The value of plants destroyed by pollution is recoverable since plants are regarded as property which is part of the land. The economic value to the landowner of wild animals such as dead fish or game animals may also be recoverable but this is unlikely to include the existence value of rare species. A landowner has no property right in a wild animal until it is captured. If an animal is killed by pollution and its body lies on the plaintiff's land it becomes a chattel and becomes the plaintiff's property only once he forms the intention to control it (see *Parker* v. *British Airways Board* [1982] QB 1004; c.f. Theft Act 1968 s.4(4)).

Once more the problem arises of how we value things that cannot be replaced or sold on the market. On the one hand the courts sometimes take a narrow view of what counts as property damage. On the other hand the courts routinely award damages for pain and suffering and loss of reputation, qualities that are not always quantifiable in terms of financial loss. In the *Trail Smelter Arbitration* 33 AJIL (1939) 182, an international case which applied the law of the USA, it was held that wildlife and ecological concerns as such cannot be compensated as property interests. In *Commonwealth of Puerto Rico* v. *SS Zoe Colocotroni* 456 Fed Sup 1327 (1978) ecological concerns were recognised as compensatable in US law but only to the extent of requiring reasonable restoration costs to be paid (see also *Exxon Corp* v. *Hunt* 475 US 355 (1986)).

Nuisance law attempts to balance competing property rights rather than environmental concerns as such. It has created a number of control devices to limit liability. These have been applied pragmatically in different contexts and are broadly linked by the moral notion of fault in relation to commercial concerns. They include, 'reasonable' use of land, 'natural' use of land and foreseeability. In the absence of injury to health or physical damage to property, the question of what is a reasonable level of pollution varies according to the socio-economic character of the locality. The more degraded the area the higher is the acceptable pollution level (*St Helens Smelting Co Ltd* v. *Tipping* (1865) 11 HLC 642). The standard of comfort and convenience to be applied is that of the ordinary person who has no special sensitivities. These principles seem to run contrary to the social justice concerns of sustainable development and do not advance either the precautionary or polluter pays principle. Those who live in the vicinity of the pollution hot-spots favoured by the common law's zoning policy are likely to be low income people who are especially vulnerable to the impact of pollution on quality of life and health.

On the other hand nuisance law to some extent reflects the polluter pays principle in as much as, once it has been established that an activity is unreasonable in terms of its effect, the person whose activities directly cause a nuisance is strictly liable irrespective of fault or whether he has tried to take precautions. There is no 'state of the art' or 'best practicable means' defence (see *Cambridge Water Co* v. *Eastern Counties Leather* [1994] 1 All ER 53 at 70, *Graham and Graham* v. *Rechem International* [1995] 7 ELM 175).

However, the general no-fault approach was qualified in the *Cambridge Water* case where the House of Lords decided that there is liability in nuisance and under the rule in *Rylands* v. *Fletcher* (below) only for damage of a kind that a reasonable person in the defendant's position should have foreseen at the time of the escape. This introduces an element of state of the art defence but possibly only in relation to consequences not to the risk of escape itself. Moreover, where a danger is not caused by the activities of the landowner but is the result of a natural event or was caused by a predecessor, the court will take into account the owner's resources and knowledge (see *Leakey* v. *National Trust* [1980] 1 All ER 17). The same applies where a polluting substance remains in the defendant's land but cannot be recovered and later escapes causing damage (*Cambridge Water Co* v. *Eastern Counties Leather* [1994] 2 All ER 53 at 77). *Cambridge Water* does not therefore advance the polluter pays principle and is unhelpful to the notion of a duty to future generations.

Therefore, where pollution is historic or involves the interaction of different substances and pathways, difficult problems may arise. Property law with its individualistic bias is not well equipped to deal with them. In this connection it is worth noting that the public law regime for cleaning up contaminated land created by the Environment Act 1995 s.57 imposes a potential duty to clean up upon anyone who caused or knowingly permitted a substance to enter the land even if that person caused only a small part of the substance to be present or if the danger was created by the combination of his substance with others. The enforcing authority has power in the light of ministerial guidance to apportion liability between two or more polluters (EPA 1990 s.78F; see Lane, 1995, p. 146).

The rule in *Rylands* v. *Fletcher* (1868) LR 3 HL 330 which imposes strict liability for dangerous substances which escape from land is subject to similar property orientated values of the law of nuisance. In *Cambridge Water Co* v. *Eastern Counties Leather* [1994] 1 All ER 53 at 76 the House of Lords regarded *Rylands* liability as an extension of the law of nuisance to the particular problem of an isolated escape from land. Just as nuisance concerns the 'unreasonable' use of land, *Rylands* applies only to a 'non-natural use' of the land. This relates to risk. An activity might count as non-natural because it creates a serious risk as in the cases of the reservoir in *Rylands* v. *Fletcher* itself. However, the courts appear to balance this against a social value judgement as to the desirability of the use (*Rickards* v. *Lothian* [1913] AC 263 at 280). For example in *Read* v. *Lyons* (below) a war-time munitions factory was held to be a natural use of the land. However, in *Cambridge Water Co* v. *Eastern Counties Leather* [1994] 1 All ER 53 at 78 Lord Goff appeared to treat non-natural use as a general term which embraces the storage of dangerous substances such as chemicals and to treat natural uses as an exception perhaps embracing such activities as the provision of local services. This strengthens the common law as a means of environmental protection and reinforces the polluter pays principle.

According to the *Cambridge Water* case there is no liability for personal injuries in nuisance but the position under the related rule in *Rylands* v. *Fletcher* (above) remains unclear. We have seen that only a person with a property interest can sue in nuisance but this limitation may not apply under the rule in *Rylands* v. *Fletcher* (see *Read* v. *Lyons* [1947] AC 156).

There is criminal liability for public nuisance and in respect of a 'statutory nuisance' under the Environmental Protection Act 1990. Public nuisance allows a public remedy unrelated to property rights, the rationale being that it is sometimes unfair to expect individuals to have the responsibility for taking action in respect of ills that affect the whole community (see *A.G.* v. *PYA Quarries* [1957] 2 QB 169), but is confined to a nuisance in the common law sense. Statutory nuisance introduces public law controls in the form of liability to clean up enforced by the local authority. The authority has a duty both to inspect its area for statutory nuisances and to take action (EPA 1990 s.80(1); *R.* v. *Carrick D.C. ex parte Shelley*). If the authority does not act any individual can bring proceedings in a magistrate's court. Nuisance is defined in the same way as private nuisance so that environmental interests as such are not protected. Moreover in some cases there is a 'best practicable means' defence (EPA 1990 s.80(7), s.79(9)). This applies mainly to commercial activities.

Trespass to land can apply to pollution in the form for example of poisonous substances which contaminate goundwater. However, trespass is an ancient tort designed originally against direct physical invasions of property and is not sufficiently flexible as a modern environmental device. The invasion must be intentional or negligent and must be direct. The directness requirement limits liability to cases where the polluting substance inevitably enters the plaintiff's land. For example where fumes or oil pollution drift onto the plaintiff's land by virtue of the wind or the tide the fact that this might be foreseeable as a probability is not enough (see *Esso Petroleum* v. *Southport Corporation* [1956] AC 218; *Jones* v. *Llanwryst UDC* [1911] 1 Ch 393). On the other hand, in trespass unlike nuisance, there is no requirement of any specific injury. Any 'sensible alteration' in the land or in water quality is a trespass (see *Young* v. *Bankier Distilliary Co* [1893] AC 691). Trespass may therefore be a weapon in defence of ecocentric interests.

Property and Regulation

Property rights may inhibit the exercise of public law regulatory powers. The courts have in the past interpreted legislation with a presumption in favour of private property rights (e.g. *Hall* v. *Shoreham-by-Sea* UDC [1964] 1 All ER 1). This creates a difference between pollution law and nature conservation law. Destroying nature is not regarded as 'wrong' in the same way that pollution is so regarded. Public controls over pollution can be imposed without compensating the polluter because, in the absence of a grant or agreement there is no right to pollute the property of others. The polluter's behaviour is regarded as a violation of the rights of others, whereas conservation controls are typically regarded as imposing a burden upon an 'innocent' property owner for the public benefit. Thus pollution controls typically take the form of provisions under which a permit is required in order to discharge pollution the sanction being criminal penalties. In some cases notably under the Water Resources Act 1991 and the Contaminated Land Regime of the Environment Act 1995 cleaning up can be required without compensation. Abstraction of water is also regulated by a licensing system reflecting the limited nature of proprietary rights in water.

By contrast property law does not recognise interests in aesthetic amenities such as landscape or in wildlife which can therefore be interfered with by other property owners without legal redress. Some economists might support this by pointing out that the value of any right to a view would be far outweighed by the loss in the value of building rights on the large tracts of land that would be sterilised if the law did recognise environmental rights. Once again we are faced with the problem of how to place a value on interests that are inherently non-tradable. The practical result is that the law relies on voluntary arrangements as the main technique for conservation and compensation is often payable. However, Rowan-Robinson and Ross (1993) argue that in practice arrangements for compensation on environmental grounds are driven by short-term political expedience and are something of a lottery.

In some cases conservation duties are imposed on property owners without compensation albeit in a relatively weak form. The controls over development of the Town and Country Planning Act 1990 are an assertion of public interest values over property rights in that compensation is not normally payable in respect of restrictions upon new development unless an existing permission is revoked. However, there is nothing in the governing legislation to privilege environmental concerns. Decision-makers must certainly take environmental factors into account but are entitled to give them nil weight in relation to economic concerns (see *Tesco Stores* v. *Secretary of State* [1995] 2 All ER 636). Indeed the original purposes of planning control were as much economic as environmental, for example to locate development efficiently and to secure the food supply. On the other hand the important concept of the green belt was an early planning initiative and environmental interests such as the garden city movement and the Society for the Protection of Rural England were influential in the development of planning policy.

Moreover the planning legislation is biased towards private property interests. For example an applicant for planning permission can appeal to the Secretary of State against a refusal or a conditional grant of planning permission but no one can appeal against an unconditional grant of permission. Part 1 of the Wildlife and Countryside Act 1981 criminalises the killing of wild birds and of rare species of animals even by the landowner thus reflecting the principle that until they are captured or killed, they are not the subject of property rights. Even so there is a defence where the killing is the incidental result of a lawful operation and could not reasonably have been avoided (s.4(2)(c), s.10(3)(c))). Thus the ordinary activities of property owners (and road users) would seem to be protected. It is not clear what standard a court would apply to the question of whether a death could reasonably have been avoided.

US law has attempted to develop general principles as to when a restriction upon private property for environmental purposes can be justified in the public interest. This has been driven by constitutional protection against the 'taking' of property. The concept of taking has been extended to include some forms of regulation but the boundary between legitimate regulation and unlawful taking is controversial. One approach has been to attempt to decide whether interests such as nature conservation should be regarded as a public right or a public benefit. If conservation is a right, then a landowner whose activities restrict public regulation is causing harm analogous to a nuisance and should not therefore be compensated. If conservation is a benefit the state should pay the landowner for restrictions which it imposes (see *Lucas* v. *South Carolina Coastal Council*; Sax, 1993; Purdue, 1995; *Babbit* v. *Sweet Homes* (p. 226)).

A similar principle may underlie the practice of 'planning gain' according to which it is lawful for a developer to provide environmental or other public benefits in return for planning permission. In *Tesco Stores* v. *Secretary of State* [1995] 2 All ER 636 at 653, Lord Hoffman endorsed the policy that developers can offer environmental benefits as a means of compensating the community for the external costs imposed by their activities but did not go as far as to suggest that they can be required to provide benefits. The courts are not entitled to weigh the merits of the benefit offered. They do, however, prevent the unfettered sale of planning permissions by requiring that there be a rational link between the benefit offered and the development applied for.

Equitable Concepts

There are, however, three concepts generated by equity which could be used as the basis of environmental property rights. As the law stands at present these have been applied in an anthropocentric manner but they have the conceptual power to extend more broadly into nature. They are firstly the restrictive covenant, secondly the charitable trust and thirdly and most speculatively, more general notions of equitable moral duty deriving from the stewardship tradition.

Restrictive Covenants

Under the rule in *Tulk* v. *Moxhay* (1848) 2 Ph 774, equity has created a right to amenity in the form of a restrictive covenant. By entering into a restrictive covenant for the benefit of neighbouring land, a landowner can bind himself and his successors not to exploit his land. A restrictive covenant cannot impose a positive obligation to develop land and in this respect it is environmentally friendly. By means of a restrictive covenant a landowner can for example preserve a pleasant view even though as we have seen the common law does not recognise a right to a view.

The rule in *Tulk* v. *Moxhay* is sometimes regarded as an unprincipled confusion of property with personal contractual obligation. Its rationale is not primarily environmental but the protection of commercial property values. In particular the plaintiff must show, among other things, that he owns land in the area to which the covenant was originally attached and which at all times has benefited from the covenant. The development of the law of restrictive covenants has been dominated by the competing desire to give effect to the parties' intentions and the need for certainty in conveyancing particularly in relation to identifying the land to be protected by the covenant (see e.g. *Renals* v. *Cowlishaw* (1878) 9 ChD 125; *LCC* v. *Allen* [1914] 3 KB 642; *Federated Homes Ltd* v. *Mill Lodge Properties Ltd* [1980] 1 All ER 371; *Newton Abbot Co-op* v. *Williamson* [1952] 1 Ch 286). In W*rotham Park Estates Co Ltd* v. *Parkside Homes Ltd* [1974] 2 All ER 321, Brightman J. opened the way to environmental arguments by emphasising that the benefit to the land protected by a covenant did not have to be a financial benefit in terms of the market value of the land. The covenant in question entitled the landowner to approve layout plans for the development of open spaces in the neighbourhood. It was held that, even though the covenant did not affect the value of the land it remained enforceable provided that an estate owner might reasonably take the view that the covenant was of benefit to his estate (at 333). This makes it possible to argue that benefit includes a moral element that reflects the environmental values prevailing at the time it is sought to enforce the covenant.

There has been statutory intervention to enable the Lands Tribunal to discharge a restrictive covenant (LPA 1925 s.84). One of the grounds on which a covenant can be discharged is that of public interest. The Lands Tribunal has sometimes *upheld* a covenant on environmental grounds even when planning permission had been granted for development thus endorsing the environmental purposes of the restrictive covenant from a public perspective (see *Re Trollopes and Andrews Application* (1961) 14 P and CR 80; *Re St Albans Investments Ltds Application* (1958) 9 P and CR 536).

Restrictive covenants have sometimes been elevated by statute into environmental instruments. For example the National Trust can enter into covenants with landowners for the benefit of the Trust's concerns relating to amenity and natural beauty (National Trust Act 1937 s.8) which are enforceable 'as if the National Trust were interested in adjacent land'. The ambivalence of combining public and private law ideas in this respect was illustrated in *Gee* v. *National Trust* [1996] 1 WLR 170 where the Trust was held not to be able to enforce a covenant for the purposes of fund raising since this had no direct relationship to natural beauty. The Court of Appeal left it open whether the law had to treat the Trust as if it were a landowner of neighbouring land for this purpose so that the covenant would be enforceable only if it was capable of benefiting adjacent land hypothetically held by the Trust. If the Trust does have to be so treated then it would be unable to assert broad public environmental concerns and would be confined within a narrow anthropocentric perspective.

Under the Wildlife and Countryside Act 1981 s.39 a local planning authority can enter into a management agreement with a landowner for the purpose of enhancing the natural beauty and amenity of the land. The agreement is enforceable against successors in title but without reference to the notion of benefited land thus avoiding the pitfalls of private law. There are several other examples of statutory management agreements. The more recent legislation avoids the notion of benefited land and imposes liability directly upon successors. (Cf National Parks and Access to the Countryside Act 1947 s.16, Countryside Act 1968 s.15, Agriculture Act 1986 s.18, Town and Country Planning Act 1990 s.106, Forestry Act 1967 sched.16.) Management agreements are less common in relation to pollution (e.g. Water Resources Act 1991 s.95 (1)).

Charitable Trusts

A charitable trust is a vehicle for intergenerational equity. Property held under such a trust must be devoted to charitable purposes indefinitely and cannot be diverted to private gain. The rule against perpetuities which militates against future generations by preventing the tying up of property for more than about one generation does not apply to charitable trusts. Moreover charitable trusts are aimed at objects regarded as beneficial to the community rather than at persons thereby perhaps avoiding Parfitt's paradox (above p. 133). A charitable trust is essentially a fund that is permanently ring fenced by the law for certain purposes that are deemed to benefit the community. It does not therefore depend upon their being ascertainable human beneficiaries. To qualify as charitable a trust must be exclusively directed at an object within the 'spirit and intendment' of the categories set out in the Statute of Elizabeth of 1601 which itself is no longer in force but which the courts apply by analogy to new situations.

Charitable purposes set out in the statute include the relief of poverty, education, religion and other objects beneficial to the community. There is also an overall requirement of public benefit which is easier to satisfy in the case of the more specific objects but which is applied cautiously in the context of the fourth category of 'other' objects (see *Income Tax Special Purposes Commissioners* v. *Pemsel* [1891] AC 531).

Environmental trusts might fall within the specific object of education which includes research provided that there is some form of dissemination (*McGovern* v. *A.G.* [1982] Ch 321 at 352). However, the advancement of an environmental belief that involves changing the law, such as animal rights or 'deep' ecology might be regarded as a political object and therefore not charitable (see *National Anti-Vivisection Society* v. *IRC* [1948] AC 31). More generally environmental purposes seem to fall within the notion of other objects beneficial to the community. Recreation as such is not charitable but health can provide a charitable dimension.

The courts have adopted an anthropocentric perspective on the question of benefit. They have held that a charitable purpose must be of benefit to human beings so that benefit to animals or nature as such is not sufficient. There is, however, evidence of a gradually widening perspective. Earlier cases concentrated on animals that were of direct use to humans. However, in *Re Wedgwood* [1915] 1 Ch 113 at 112 a trust for humane animal slaughtering conditions was upheld on the 'enlightened anthropocentric' ground that brutality towards animals coarsens our natures and may spill over to our treatment of each other. In the *National Anti-Vivisection Society* case (above) the House of Lords held that the benefit to humans from carrying out animal experiments outweighed the harm to the animals experimented upon. The House of Lords was prepared to condemn cruelty to animals in the sense of hurting animals for enjoyment or causing unnecessary suffering but took the view that the value of a human always outweighed that of an animal.

In *Re Grove-Grady* [1929] 1 Ch 557 the court was reluctant to extend environmental trusts and held that a trust for an animal sanctuary intended to protect nature against man could not be charitable because there was no direct human benefit. However, it could be argued that there is direct human benefit in the 'existence value' of natural objects in that by knowing that a species is flourishing we enrich our sensibilities. There is no problem in regarding the preservation of the built environment as charitable or as treating landscape preservation as charitable for reasons of cultural heritage (see *Re Verrall* (1916) 1 Ch 100; Charity Commissioners Annual Report 1968 paras 67–72, 1973 para 40, 1979 paras 61–65; Broome, 1997, p. 58).

The Australian case of *A.G. for New South Wales* v. *Sawtell* [1978] 2 NSWLR 200 is sometimes regarded as a breakthrough. There a trust for wildlife conservation was held to be charitable and the court emphasised that the boundaries of charity can shift with changing public opinion, pointing to the development in environmental thinking during the last fifty years. This opens up the debate. However, the court's reasoning remained firmly anthropocentric, emphasising the scientific, medical, amenity, cultural and other resource value of biological diversity. It was also thought relevant for patriotic reasons that native animals were involved.

Stewardship

The notion of stewardship, which imposes a duty to look after and perhaps to improve the environment, has a basis in Christian tradition.

Stewardship also falls within the core equitable idea of 'trust' meaning that equity imposes a moral obligation on the legal owner to use the property in the interests of someone else which, in the case of a charitable trust need not be an identifiable person (see Gray, 1994; Lucy, 1996). According to the stewardship doctrine equity would impose a duty on a landowner not to damage the environment. The duty would be enforceable by a person affected by it or possibly by a public official on behalf of future generations. The concept of stewardship is closely related to that of sustainable development. Both require concern for future generations and both require that a landowner choose the most environmentally friendly way of achieving development. The White Paper 'This Common Inheritance', 1990 Cm 1200, para 1. 14, endorses the concept of stewardship as government policy. Stewardship restrictions can be placed upon property owners by means of planning controls, for example the green-belt policies that require developers to show that there is no feasible alternative to using the green belt (See PPG2; Millichap, 1993).

Except in the case of charitable trusts which are enforced by the state, trusteeship duties in English law arise out of voluntary assumptions of obligation and are owed to particular human beneficiaries who, if they are adult with full legal capacity are entitled to bring the trust to an end and transfer ownership to themselves even against the wishes of the founder of the trust (*Saunders* v. *Vautier* (1881) 4 Beav 115). However, a charitable trust is permanent, so that provided that the purpose is capable of being fulfilled, the trust cannot normally be broken.

There is an analogy between the concept of stewardship and the 'public trust' doctrine which has emerged in the USA and which claims a common law pedigree. Under the public trust doctrine, land that is owned by the state is impressed with the obligation to use the land for the benefit of the public even after the land is transferred to private hands. Public purposes can include environmental goals (see Sax, 1970; *Geer* v. *Connecticut* 161 US 519, 522–523 (1896); *Locate* v. *Dept of Conservation* 263 US 545, 549 (1924)). The public trust doctrine is said to derive from the old common law rule that the Crown owns the bed of tidal waters subject to a public right of navigation and fishing, a right which survives any transfer of the land by the Crown (see *Gann* v. *Whitstable Free Fishers* (1865) 11 HLCas 192; *Duke of Devonshire* v. *Patterson* (1887) 20 QB 263). The argument is that the public right of navigation is an example of more general public rights against the Crown. Unfortunately this involves a conceptual shift since the mediaeval Crown was not identified with the state, still less with the people and held land as a private person and certainly not as trustee for the people. Indeed a private landowner holds his land in a relationship of tenure with the

Crown under which the landowner theoretically owes duties to the Crown in its role as chief landowner and not as representing the people.

The public right of navigation was *sui generis* and there is a large jump from the limited notion of navigational rights to a broad concept of trusteeship. It is unlikely that an English court unprompted by Parliament would be willing to make such a jump. Even in the USA where judicial lawmaking is more widely accepted, the public trust doctrine has in many states been incorporated into legislation. On the other hand there is conceptual space for the public trust in as much as the Crown owns all land in England and Wales. Other persons have only an estate in the land, an estate being a bundle of rights and responsibilities defined by time. It does not matter in this context that the largest available estate, the legal fee simple absolute in possession, is indefinite in length. A legal fee simple can be made defeasable by attaching to it a right of entry exercisable in any circumstances other than those contrary to public policy.

Market Devices and Property Law

As we saw in Chapter 6, environmental policy makes use of economic instruments which provide incentives towards environmentally friendly behaviour. These include the creation of property rights, for example tradable pollution permits or tradable energy consumption permits, which can be sold in accordance with the polluter pays principle. The well-established notion of the *'profit a prendre'* which is a transferable right to natural produce provides a conceptual model for this. Easements to pollute are also well established but, unlike profits, can be transferred only with the land to which they were initially attached thus providing a method of quality control in the form of the notion of benefit to the dominant land. Tradable pollution permits are like profits in that they can be transferred between units of land provided that the quota is not exceeded.

Tradable pollution permits have been pioneered in the USA. They are said to have the ethical advantages of promoting equality and democratic values (see Ackerman, 1983). However, pollution control is more costly for some firms than others and the cost of buying a permit is in relative terms less for the rich than for the poor. Thus tradable permits can be regarded as allowing the rich to buy a right to pollute and raise problems of social justice especially where economic forces concentrate permits in 'pollution hot spots' which are likely to be in areas of low land values where low income people are forced to live. US law has also endorsed 'transferable development rights' which entitle a property owner who is refused planning permission on environmental grounds to build to an equivalent value elsewhere or sell the entitlement (see e.g. *Fred R French Investing Co inc* v. *City of New York* 350 N. E. 2d 381 (1976); *Penn Central Transportation Co* v. *City of New York* 366 N. E. 2d 1271).

A right to interfere with rare species or landscapes could possibly be turned into property. For example the 'elephant' as an abstract idea could be assigned to multiple private ownership as a form of intellectual property. Owners, not of the elephant itself, but of its elephantine qualities would be able to exploit the asset by means of film, tourism, etc. The owner of a permit or of a share in the conservation value of the elephant has an incentive to protect his investment because he can sell the remaining credit.

There are obvious cost and enforcement difficulties in putting natural resources such as water, air and species into private ownership and also in imposing equitable duties upon property owners in the way we discussed in the previous section. Also, as we saw earlier (p. 217), questions of social justice arise if we believe that environmental rights are marketable. We are moreover signalling that pollution is not wrong in itself. No one would presumably suggest that there should be a market in rape. There is also a danger of monopolistic control over pollution and energy as poorer people, faced with a choice between freezing or starving are forced to sell their credits.

On the other hand using the language of property raises the political stakes and underlines the importance of the environment as a human asset. McPherson (quoted by Gray, 1994, p. 210) states that 'we have made property so central to our society that anything and any rights that are not property are very apt to take second place'. Gray adds 'when you pollute our air or our rivers or exclude us unreasonably from wild and open spaces we can mobilise the enormous symbolic and emotional impact of the property attribution by asserting that you are taking away some of our property'.

Summary

1. The common law's attitude to nature is founded upon the Christian tradition of man's domination and upon enlightenment values of reason. However the common law is flexible and open to changes in societal values and cannot be ruled out as a vehicle for environmental legal principles.

2. Property law is ambivalent. On the one hand property rights can be used to encourage conservation, for example by creating rights over environmental assets or encouraging ethical investments. On the other hand the exploitative power of property encourages domination of nature and sets up claims to compensation in respect of state interference with

private rights. English property law places a higher value upon economic concerns than upon environmental concerns.

3. Property law to some extent regards pollution as wrong but, in relation to nuisance law takes a prodevelopment stance in relation to environmental standards and to some extent in relation to fault. This is consistent with the ethic of sustainable development. Property law concerns itself only with assets of economic value and is concerned to encourage trade. Notions of fault and foreseeability are regarded as important and applied with the effect of privileging commercial interests over the polluter pays principle.

4. It is difficult to apply traditional notions of compensation to environmental goods.

5. A limited sustainability principle applies to water rights in relation to water flowing in defined channels. In the case of percolating water a landowner has a common law right to abstract and is also protected against pollution but there is no right to a flow of percolating water.

6. Property law does not protect wildlife or amenity values such as landscapes except to the limited extent made possible by the law of restrictive covenants. Plants and animals can be the objects of property rights. Trusts for wildlife conservation must directly benefit human beings and trusts against cruelty to animals are evaluated according to human interests. Conservation measures therefore infringe property rights and are difficult to implement.

7. The analogy of the public trust in the USA together with the general theory of equity could support the development of a stewardship doctrine. However, the English law of charitable trusts is strongly anthropocentric.

8. Environmental assets can be made into property rights in accordance with the emphasis on economic instruments in environmental policy. This creates problems of social justice and weakens ecocentric positions but has the advantage of giving incentives towards environmentally friendly behaviour, and helping to bring environmental costs into the open.

Further Reading

Ball, S. and Bell, S. (1997) *Environmental Law: the Law and Policy Relating to the Protection of the Environment*, 4th edn (London: Blackstone Press), pp. 167–92.

Coquillette, D. (1979) Mosses From and Old Manse: Another Look at Some Historic Cases About the Environment. *Cornell Law Review*, **64**, 761.

Elworthy, S. and Holder, J. (1997) *Environmental Protection, Text and Materials* (London: Butterworths), pp. 47–60, 65–7.

Gray, K. (1994) Equitable Property. *Current Legal Problems*, **47**(2), 157–214.

Miller, C. (1998) *Environmental Rights, Critical Perspectives*, chapter 7 (London: Routledge).

Rodgers, C. (ed.) (1996) *Nature Conservation and Countryside Law*, chapter 1 (Cardiff: University of Wales Press).

Steele, J. (1995) Private Law and the Environment: Nuisance in Context. *Legal Studies*, **15**, 236.

Workshop

1. Do you agree with Lord Goff in the *Cambridge Water* case that the common law should not develop environmental principles? Why do the courts in criminal cases appear to be more sympathetic to environmental concerns? See also Chapter 7.
2. Your client intends to apply for planning permission to build a housing development in the countryside. In return for planning permission he offers to enter into an agreement with the local planning authority under which he will set aside a plot of land on trust for ever as a nature reserve in which rare species will be protected against human interference. Advise him whether this objective is lawful and how it might be secured.
3. To what extent does the law of nuisance serve to protect the environment?
4. Water rights embody the values of sustainable development. Do you agree?
5. To what extent does English property law reflect the view that man is entitled to exploit nature? Could existing property law concepts be used to advance the values of stewardship?
6. To what extent does the English law of civil liability embody the polluter pays principle?
7. Explain the advantages and disadvantages of tradable pollution permits. See also Chapter 7.
8. Jack owns a nature reserve on a patch of wasteland within an industrial estate. Jill who owns a neighbouring site is building an extension to her print works. This requires the groundwater under her land to be pumped away. Unknown to Jill the groundwater has for many years been contaminated by chemicals leaking from her printing machinery. Jill's pumping operations cause groundwater to seep onto Jack's nature reserve causing the loss of several rare species of plant and animal life.
   Advise Jack as to any legal remedies available to him. What further information about the circumstances would you require?

9 Wildlife and Nature Conservation

Introduction – The Purposes of Nature Conservation – Conflicting Values and Uncertainty

In this chapter we shall first look at some general ethical problems which underlie conservation law. These are the question of its purposes and of how far we are entitled to manipulate nature. We shall then discuss the attitude of the law to these matters in connection with the topics of animal welfare and nature conservation.

There is considerable agreement that nature conservation is a desirable policy objective but less agreement as to why this should be. Conservation raises the entire range of environmental perspectives. Conservation has clear anthropocentric advantages which were set out in the preamble to the Biodiversity Convention 1992. These include ecological, genetic and economic resources, educational, cultural, recreational and aesthetic value. A technocentrist utilitarian might favour preserving genetic material rather than keeping members of a species alive. More obscurely the Biodiversity Convention also referred to the intrinsic value of biological diversity irrespective of human interests. A 'Gaian' might claim that this is human arrogance and that we should concentrate on our own problems leaving nature to look after itself. Does nature have intrinsic value irrespective of human concerns? Do we value individual animals according to their similarity or attractiveness to humans? Is our purpose to protect nature against human intervention or to interfere with nature for the good of its health?

Conservation problems are made even more complex because fundamental assumptions about the scientific base are controversial and are therefore not strong enough to serve as a basis for consistent ethical guidance. We have seen that scientific statements about what the world is like cannot in themselves tell us what it ought to be like. For example diversity in itself is neither good nor bad even if Aquinas did argue that a universe containing angels plus other things is better than one containing angels alone (Passmore, 1981, p. 119). The importance of science in this context is to help us to apply our moral principles by predicting the consequence of our actions. Moreover although no scientific fact can dictate a moral value, the image we create of physical events is likely to influence our moral thinking. For example is an ecosystem like a community or more like a single organism?

In the case of conservation we are therefore doubly perplexed. It is not surprising that the anthropocentric approach seems to be the dominant approach even by those who claim otherwise. The absence of a coherent ethical basis may be one reason why conservation law is weak compared for example with pollution law which to a large extent has a conventional ethical base in human interests.

Basic Scientific Concepts

The most fundamental scientific concepts are probably species and ecosystem. The notion of habitat is also important but in a secondary sense as a support system for a species. There is nothing in the real world directly corresponding to a species or an ecosystem. Both are abstract ways of describing features which individual plants or animals have in common. We select these according to human purposes. As humans we are imprisoned by the mechanisms of our senses and by nature of our thought processes both of which are outside our control. It is impossible to think outside them so that we cannot know what the world is actually like. We depict nature in human terms dividing it into made-up categories such as species and ecosystem and labelling its characters as 'populations', 'native', 'alien', 'colony', all of which are terms borrowed from human societies. We also imagine nature as having organisation and purposes just as we have.

The most widely used definition of a species is 'a population whose members are able to interbreed freely under natural conditions' (Wilson, 1992) thus providing a genetic lifeline. While this usually works for animals it is less reliable for plants. Nor does it make sense from a time perspective between creatures such as humans and their remote ape ancestors who could never have met. Another approach is based on similarities of physical features but this is arbitrary except in relation to a given human purpose since every individual is unique. Indeed the variations between individuals which determine whether they are to be considered as separate species may be questions of degree which shade into each other. This is the case for example with the herring gull and the lesser black-backed gull which exist in a ring around the world. At one point on the ring the species are physically similar and can interbreed. They gradually differ as they move along the ring until in the UK they are different species according to both approaches (Dawkins, 1993).

An ecosystem is a collection of living things and non-living natural features which appear to be interdependent and to some extent self-regulating. Again this is a question of degree and involves the drawing of lines for our own purposes as when for example we try to define the boundaries of a Site of Special Scientific Interest (below p. 267). Since every component of the universe is possibly interdependent the line drawing may be arbitrary.

It is not known whether there is any validity in the notion of ecological balance which forms the mainstay of the land ethic (Clements, 1995). Does nature depend on systems in which the individual components support each other and maintain the system as a whole, as for example seems to be the case with the food chain or the cycle of the seasons? If we make sacrifices for future generations are we not merely temporarily staving off an inevitable collapse in which case why do we bother to make sacrifices? Until Darwin established evolutionary theory there was a belief in 'the great chain of being' in which life was organised in a hierarchy in which each species from bacteria up to man and beyond had its place. Darwinian evolutionary theory points both ways. Natural selection on the one hand harmonises species with their environment while on the other hand regards evolution as generated by random genetic changes. Some modern ecological perspectives using the insights of chaos theory and quantum physics emphasise the random aspects of nature and try to blur the distinction between individuals and larger units and sometimes between individuals and smaller units such as genes.

Our common-sense perceptions tell us that nature appears at least sometimes to be in a state of balance. Our dominant traditions from the Stoics of Ancient Greece through Christianity to the Enlightenment have depicted the universe as rational and balanced although there has always been an undercurrent which emphasises the capricious aspects of nature. Enlightened anthropocentrism assumes that nature should be respected because it is in human interests to do so and thus provides a relatively focused approach to conservation issues.

The precautionary principle is sometimes used to support conservation reminding us that our knowledge of ecological matters is limited and that consequences of our actions may be irreversible and damaging. Thus 'Extinction shuts doors and deprives us forever of the option to find value in that which we previously found valueless' (Kunich, 1994, p. 527). However, this cuts both ways. In the absence of scientific knowledge the preservation of any given species is equally capable of causing benefit or harm (Francis, 1996; Sober, 1995).

Given these uncertainties it is tempting to say that biodiversity or species conservation make sense only from an anthropocentric point of view which, of course, includes the enlightened anthropocentric perspective. If we think that nature is random then our conservation policy can legitimately be anthropocentric making sense of nature as a storehouse, a life-support system and a source of information and entertainment and taking a precautionary approach in the interests of future generations.

On the other hand if we believe that nature has an inherent order then, although as beneficiaries of nature we may still take an anthropocentric stance, the non-anthropocentric ethics are also opened up. On the face of it the ecocentric approach is an attractive way to support conservation objectives focusing as it does on collective entities such as ecosystems. However, as we saw in Chapter 2, ecocentric approaches are controversial breaking down as they may into human-centred arguments, mystical assertions, or disguised individualism.

Alternative Goals for Nature Conservation – Health or Integrity?

These considerations lead to two broad ethical alternatives underpinning wildlife policies. One concentrates on species and ecosystems taking the view that our job is to maintain the health and diversity of nature. This justifies for example the culling of elephants to reflect our ideas of the proper balance of nature and is easily explained from an anthropocentric perspective. Within this perspective, ethical differences may still lead to policy conflicts. In particular there may be a conflict between the idea of protecting an ecosystem as such and protecting a species. It may not matter which particular species form part of the ecosystem provided that the health of the system as a whole is maintained. Thus, the popular pre-occupation with rare species has no clear qualification. As we have seen the land ethic values a species only if it contibutes to the overall viability of the community. The main qualification for biodiversity seems to be human needs.

This perspective allows us positively to improve nature, for example by introducing foreign species which we think might support an ecosystem and exterminating harmful species for the greater good. Related to this is the 'plastic trees' problem, that is whether we are entitled to fake nature and whether an imitation of nature is as good as the real thing (Tribe, 1974). Is it not an abuse of nature's autonomy to presume to improve on nature? For example planning permissions sometimes include requirements to transpose features such as meadows to another site. Section 61(1) of the Environment Act 1995 provides that the purposes of designation as a national park include 'conserving and enhancing the natural beauty, wildlife and cultural heritage' of the area thus legitimating artificial 'improvements' upon nature. Similarly s.98 empowers the Secretary of State to make grants to persons for the 'conservation or enhancement of the natural beauty or amenity of the environment' or 'the promotion or enjoyment of the countryside by the public'. A grant would presumably not be available for the conservation of a rare but ugly species. Enhancing biodiversity is also recommended in government guidance to the Environment Agency (see DoE, 1995a.b).

The second ethical alternative concentrates on respecting the integrity of nature by leaving it alone even if the result would be damaging or species destroyed. From a human point of view this approach concentrates on the spiritual and aesthetic aspects of nature and so is less at home with economic cost-benefit analysis than the other approach. It would also worry less about individual creatures or species or even particular ecosystems but would concentrate on minimising human influences. The World Wildlife Fund has recently changed its name to the World Wide Fund for Nature possibly reflecting an ethical shift. Faking nature might be resisted even from an anthropocentric perspective by appealing to the aesthetic value of nature undisturbed by man along the lines of a work of art (Elliot, 1995). However, this seems to be a subjective preference not shared by everyone and it is not obvious that other human interests such as enjoying a theme park in which it is possible to observe a lion attacking its prey should give way to the interests of purists.

These different approaches may create policy dilemmas in the case of natural disasters such as fires or floods. Are these events part of nature's balancing mechanism or part of a random chaos? How should conservationists react to the aftermath of a forest fire? Should they replant the forest or leave nature to get on with it? This is a case where there might be confusion between ethical and scientific differences. Even those who favour health over integrity might believe that the best way to restore nature's balance would be to leave the forest alone.

Faking nature also raises problems where a trade-off is proposed between, for example, the destruction of a habitat and the provision of a new habitat for different creatures somewhere else. This might be possible by way of a planning undertaking (below). No version of human ethics other than the strictest utilitarian would endorse the killing of a human community with analogous 'compensation'.

In this context the terms 'conservation' and 'preservation' carry different moral messages. Preservation implies leaving nature as it is except possibly for the purpose of remedying damage. Conservation is human centred and implies saving nature as a resource and also includes the positive goal of maximising nature's advantages or enhancing nature. The Huxley Report (1947), which laid the foundations for the present law, regarded nature conservation as analogous to farming (p. 11) and thought that the scientific and the aesthetic perspectives were not in conflict.

Conflicts Between Ethical Perspectives – Interest Balancing

The narrow anthropocentric perspective, the enlightened anthropocentric perspective, the individualistic biocentric perspective and the ecocentric perspective are incommensurable but not always uncombinable. They sometimes support the same outcome which is capable of buttressing policy. For example a concern for animal rights supports a policy of preserving habitats and ecosystems as life support for individuals and for valuing species instrumentally as mechanisms for sustaining individuals. Enlightened anthropocentrism would do the same in the interests of prudence, admiration, or scientific interest so that even if, as is sometimes suggested, biotechnology were able to produce and store all possible types of gene so as to manufacture any natural resource, we would still value natural objects since admiration for nature may be intrinsic to our human natures. Conversely concern for rare species would justify provisions ensuring that individual specimens are properly cared for when being transported, etc. by humans (see CITES (1973) Arts III 2(c), 4(b), IV 2(c), 5(b),6(b), V 2(b), VIII 3).

The ethics conflict where the interests of species diverge from those of individuals. From the animal rights perspective it is wrong to harm individual creatures for the purpose of preserving a species. A case in point is that of the indigenous red squirrel which is threatened with extermination because the proliferating grey squirrel, an immigrant from America that many people find unattractive, is seizing its food supplies. The animal rights perspective would leave both species alone. The ecocentric perspective, 'health' version, would cull the grey squirrels while the 'integrity' version would probably agree with the animal rights version and leave nature alone. The anthropocentric perspective is likely to cull the grey squirrel on the basis that grey squirrels are unattractive. The tuna–dolphin dispute in the USA (see Chapter 11) involved clashes between animal rights perspectives, ecocentric perspectives and anthropocentric perspectives. One issue was whether it is better to avoid stress to dolphins even at the expense of killing other sea creatures such as turtles; the problem being that the techniques used for tuna fishing were likely to cause harm to one or other species. The interests of the tuna do not seem to have been weighed in the balance. The tuna–dolphin dispute suggests that where ethical arguments conflict human-centred utilitarianism is used to produce a solution.

Within the anthropocentric perspective, conservation raises questions of social justice particularly on an international level. Even if conservation is a general public good it has to be paid for in terms of loss of other opportunities. On the whole the wealthy gain most and lose least from conservation. For example the 'Debt for Nature' exchange schemes promoted by the World Wide Fund for Nature and the US government allows the multinational bodies to interfere with the lives of indigenous communities who do not necessarily benefit from the paying off of their country's foreign debt. The poorer nations provide most of the world's genetic resources which the richer nations are able to exploit and thus convert into value. Both groups can justly claim to be rewarded for their input. Transfer of knowledge and technology between richer and poorer nations is therefore a feature of the Biodiversity Convention because this helps to lessen inequality of bargaining power.

On a domestic level the sacrifices to be made by the wealthy are proportionately less than those of the poor. For example, unlike pollution control, wildlife conservation is not perceived as a good by everyone. Should poor urban communities subsidise public services for rich people who happen to live in remote areas which are protected against development. Are local communities entitled to the fruits of resources that happen to lie in their area? Unlike for example the case of oil or minerals, bioprospecting of plants for use in medicine does not generate significant local employment. Is it right that the cost of nature conservation should be borne by low-income people denied access to affordable housing or jobs in the countryside? The cost-benefit methods required of the Environment Agency do not address problems of social justice.

Perhaps the most important function of public law in relation to conservation decisions is to ensure that all relevant ethical perspectives can be put forward with a view to establishing areas of practical agreement. In public law the courts attempt to ensure that decision-makers take into account all relevant factors but the courts do not weigh the competing factors (see *Tesco Stores* v. *Secretary of State* [1995] 2 All ER 636). In private law by contrast the courts are required to do the balancing exercise for themselves. We have seen that they are prepared to do this by relating the standard of reasonableness in nuisance cases to the existing character of the neighbourhood but where damage to a property right is concerned they are not prepared to weigh competing social and moral factors nor give effect to the public interest against an established property right (see *Pride of Derby Angling Co* v. *Derby Corporation* [1953] Ch 149; *Elliot* v. *Islington BC* [1991] EGLR 167).

In private law and in the case of the charitable trust, as we have seen, the English courts have effectively ruled out non-anthropocentric approaches. In public law they have equivocated. It is not clear whether a government decision-maker can take into account non-anthropocentric considerations. As the law stands it seems that there must be a positive indication in the governing legislation in favour of non-anthropocentric concerns (see *R.* v. *Somerset County Council ex parte Fewings* [1995] 3 All

ER 20). It also seems that the courts do not take a deontological approach but apply instrumental reasoning.

The experience of the Endangered Species Act 1973 of the USA (16 USC 1531–1543) illustrates the problem of balancing competing interests. The Act is explicit in its human-centred approach declaring that 'various species of fish, wildlife and plants have been so depleted in numbers that they are in danger or threatened with extinction. These species are of esthetic, ecological, educational, historical, recreational and scientific value to the Nation and its people.' Nevertheless the Supreme Court has interpreted the Act to give strong protection to nature conservation over other human interests. The Act prohibited the 'taking' of any of the species listed in the Act and requires public authorities to ensure that 'actions authorized, funded or carried out by them do not jeopardize the continued existence of such endangered species'. The Act makes one exception that of 'the Class Insecta' determined by the Secretary to constitute a pest whose protection would present an overwhelming and overriding risk to man (16 USC 1531). This seems to be a self-defence exception and the interest balancing approaches recommended for example by Taylor are conspicuously absent.

In *T. V. A.* v. *Hill* 437 US 153 (1978) the Supreme Court ruled that the ban on interfering with endangered species was absolute so that a scheme to build the Tellico Dam which would economically regenerate a large community but at the expense of the snail darter, a rare and obscure species, could not go ahead. It is important to note that the reasoning in *Hill* was not deontological. The Supreme Court did not consider that the snail darter had rights. The matter was treated as an instrumental one which depended on the intention of the legislator. This made the interpretation of the statute crucial. The court held that the intention of the legislature was to give almost absolute protection to the endangered species although it was not clear why. One danger with this absolutist approach is that the interests of nature can be used as a cover for human concerns such as NIMBYism. After the *Hill* case the Act was amended firstly to allow protection to be overridden by a special committee albeit no criteria were set out for this and secondly to require an economic assessment before designating certain critical habitats. The Supreme Court did its own balancing act in *Babbit* v. *Sweet Homes Chapter of Communities for a Greater Oregon* (1996) 8 JEL 158 where it held that the Act's concept of 'harm' protected endangered species against any modification of their habitat not only against direct injury and that this overrode private property rights.

English conservation law relies on executive discretion and is therefore a forum for canvassing of different ethics. We have already drawn attention to the approach of the Environment Act 1995 to the functions of the Environment Agency. Town and country planning law is more open ended in that it requires the interests of sites designated for conservation purposes (below) to be taken into account by decision-makers as 'material considerations' but does not specify the weight to be attached to conservation concerns (see Town and Country Planning Act 1990 s.70(2), PPGN 2 (Green Belts), PPGN 7 (Countryside), PPGN 9 (Nature Conservation)). The Countryside Act 1968 s.11 in anthropocentric spirit requires public authorities in exercising any of their functions to 'take into account' the natural beauty and amenity of the countryside. This might conflict with the desire to preserve the habitat of a rare but unpleasant species.

There have been attempts to inject a statutory weighting element. The most important concerns the Habitats Directive 1992 (below). Another example is the Environment Act 1995 s.61, which amends the law relating to national parks. The concept of a national park was introduced into English law by the National Parks and Access to the Countryside Act 1949 as part of the post-war package of planning reforms. The policy emphasis was upon human amenity and tourism balanced against the economic interests of those who live and work in the parks (see Hobhouse, 1947). The 1995 Act has amended s.5 of the National Parks and Access to the Countryside Act 1949 to embrace the following objectives (a) conserving and enhancing the natural beauty, wildlife and cultural heritage of the areas [designated as national parks] (b) promoting opportunities for the quiet enjoyment and understanding of the special qualities of those areas by the public. Where there is a conflict between these objectives (a) must be given greater weight (s.11A(2)). The Act therefore tips the balance in favour of environmental and arguably even ecocentric concerns (Edwards, 1991). However, economic and social factors must also be taken into account (s.11A(1)). By contrast in the USA and many other countries national parks are regarded as wilderness areas to which people have access under controlled conditions.

The Attitude of the Law

We saw in Chapter 7 that English property law does not regard it as wrong to exploit nature and indeed often regards the exploitation of nature as an incident of property rights. Conservation law is therefore less prescriptive than pollution law and seems to have an anthropocentric bias. Conservation law relies heavily upon voluntary mechanisms, it pays landowners compensation, and it confers discretionary powers rather than duties upon decision-makers, for example to designate protected areas and the weight to be given to conservation values.

English public law in so far as it announces its purposes at all is utilitarian and places emphasis upon the recreational and aesthetic approaches in the form of human interest in 'natural beauty and amenity and access to the countryside' (see Environment Act 1995 s.7; Countryside Act 1968 s.11; Agriculture Act 1986 s.17; Town and Country Planning Act 1990 ss.12(3A), 31(3)). The emphasis of the Environment Act 1995 upon sustainable development and cost-benefit principles also gives an anthropocentric bias since costs and benefits are difficult to assess except from an anthropocentric perspective (see s.4, s.5(3)b, s.39). Where ministers or the Agency formulate or consider 'proposals' relating to pollution control they need only 'take into account' the aims of conservation thus entitling them to impose lower standards (EPA 1990 s.7(1)(b)). We have also seen that when exercising powers, as opposed to specific duties, the Agency must be guided by cost-benefit analysis. The Agency's pollution control powers include ecological concerns and there is a general requirement to consider the environment as a whole taking into account any likely costs of protective measures (EA 1995 s.4). The Agency's non-pollution control powers mainly concern water management (s.6). Here conservation is given greater weight in that the Agency must exercise these powers with the objective of furthering conservation goals (s.7(1)(a)).

The law does not give significant ethical guidance over and above its anthropocentric bias but leaves this kind of choice to the discretion of decision-makers. For example the government's 'Guidance to the Environment Agency' (DoE, 1995(a),(b)) goes no further than to stress the need to balance relevant factors including costs and benefits and the 'requirements' of human beings, enterprises, natural habitats and fisheries. The ethical cultures both within and between the different regulatory agencies are therefore crucial.

As regards regulatory culture we have seen that environmental regulation is the responsibility of many different agencies each of which may approach its work from a different ethical perspective. In England for example, local planning authorities, the Nature Conservancy Council, the Countryside Commission and the Environment Agency have overlapping responsibilities. The departments of the environment and agriculture are both directly concerned with conservation issues. Indeed the sustainable development principle means that any government agency might also be concerned with conservation. One of the law's most important functions is to reconcile different perspectives and at least to ensure that different points of view get a hearing.

Under s.40 of the EPA 1995 the Secretary of State can give directions to the Environment Agency for the purpose of implementing international and European obligations. International instruments and in particular European law have hesitantly begun to adopt a more prescriptive and less anthropocentric approach which runs counter to the English tradition. However, this tendency should not be overstated. It is evidenced mainly by grand declarations at the policy formation stage or in preambles or instruments that are not legally binding.

International conservation instruments stretch back at least to the Convention for the Uniform Regulation of Fishing in the Rhine of 1875 although as with the earlier English gaming laws the concern was to protect human resources (see Birnie and Boyle, 1992, p. 421; Thompson, 1990). The modern instruments introduce in a not entirely consistent way the concerns of human amenity and of biodiversity as an end in itself (see Biodiversity Convention 1992; Ramsar Convention on Wetlands 1971; Bonn Convention on Migratory Species 1979; The Convention on Trade in Endangered Species 1973; The Berne Convention on European Wildlife and Natural Habitats1979; The Wild Birds Directive1979; The Habitats Directive 1992).

The Biodiversity Convention provides an example of inconsistency. Its preamble treats nature as a resource for life support, raw materials, medicine, entertainment, research and education and also as having value in itself irrespective of its value to humans. The Convention then concentrates on the resource perspective. Nations are invited to exploit their resources (Article 3) and conservation obligations are to be carried out only 'as far as possible and appropriate' (Articles 8–14). The Convention gets down to business in dealing with the transfer of genetic resources, money and technology to developing countries (Articles 15–21) and makes it clear that in the case of developing countries economic and social development is the top priority (preamble). The Convention endorses genetic modification concentrating on safety and the use of profits.

Animal Welfare

We feel a moral obligation to animals but may not know why. Nozick (1947, p. 37) compares a man who swings a baseball bat and does not bother to move when a cow stands in the way, thus smashing the cow's head, with people eating meat for pleasure. The former but not the latter would be widely regarded as wrong. Wherein lies the difference? Christian ethics can be read as regarding duties to animals as incidental to duties to humans. St Paul for example explains the Old Testament prohibition against working oxen on the Sabbath in terms of human welfare and the tale of the Gadarine swine suggests that we can ill-treat animals for our own ends. Mediaeval theologians and philosophers believed that animals were essentially instruments of human purposes and this was reinforced by enlightenment rationalist philosophers.

Animal welfare law in Britain developed from the early nineteenth century originally in the context of captive, useful or attractive animals culminating in the Protection of Animals Act 1911 which, as amended, is still in force but does not apply to animals in the wild. During the twentieth century conservationist concerns became prominent influenced by preferences in favour of attractive species. Birds for example enjoy long-standing support from the RSPB and have wide protection. The Wildlife and Countryside Act 1981 protects all wild birds other than game and pest species, with an enhanced level of protection for endangered species scheduled in the Act. The Badgers Act 1973 now consolidated in the Badgers (Protection) Act 1992 was a curious House of Lords bill based ostensibly on the interests of conservation and opposition to particularly horrific forms of ill-treatment but seemingly informed by anthropomorphic sentiment associated with the persona of 'Mr Brock' (see H. L. Deb. vol. 857 col. 1692 (1973); H. L. Deb. vol. 864 col. 22 (1973); H. L. Deb. vol. 867 col. 43 (1973)).

The Scott-Henderson Report on Cruelty to Wild Animals 1951 (Cmnd 8266) took a decidedly anthropocentric approach tinged by virtue ethics when it said 'we think that there should not be an undue restriction on anyone's right to kill wild animals: but that it is not asking too much that any person exercising this right should do so with due regard to the dictates of humanity, viz. to kill without causing unnecessary suffering.' In other words killing animals is morally neutral. It was not until the Wild Mammals Protection Act 1996 that there was general, albeit limited, protection for mammals. The Act became law only after extensive compromises with the hunting lobby including the removal of the words 'torture and mistreat'.

Statutes protecting animals against cruelty provide good illustrations of attempts at balancing competing interests with a strong human bias and of the use of ethical arguments to mask selfish agendas. Sometimes criminal offences are created and the balancing takes the form of general exceptions or defences. Typically these statutes cater for human-centred values and vested interests. Overrides vary from statute to statute in accordance with the rarity, utility and attractiveness to humans of the species in question. They usually include public health, the defence of property, medical, scientific and agricultural purposes, education and game sports. Captive or pet animals enjoy wider protection than wild animals under the Protection of Animals Act 1911. It is debatable whether this should be interpreted as an anthropocentric bias towards creatures with which we are familiar or a virtue ethics response to mitigate the fact that we have enslaved them.

It seems reasonably safe to suggest that the strict animal rights perspective is not reflected in the law. We saw in Chapter 8 that animals can be owned and that only human interests can benefit from the law of charities. The RSPCA and other voluntary bodies whose functions include the prosecution of offenders have charitable status but this requires them to act only in the interests of the human community.

In introducing the Wild Mammals Protection Bill in the Commons, Michael Fabricant M.P. took an animal rights stance.

'One of the most elegant pieces of English law based on the Judaeo-Christian ethic is the duty of care. We owe a duty of care to each other and this place has a duty of care to its citizens. In that context we cannot rule out the duty of care that we as mammals ourselves owe to other mammals.'

However, the resulting Act is heavily compromised. It applies only to specified acts of cruelty (mutilating, kicking, beating, nailing or impaling, stabbing, burning, stoning, crushing, drowning, dragging or asphyxiating) and then only to the intentional causing of 'unnecessary' suffering (s.1). Moreover there are exceptions for mercy killing, hunting and sporting and poisoning even it seems where the suffering is unnecessary. One sponsor of the Bill expressed his objectivity by revealing that he was a fisherman (see H. C. Deb. vol. 270 no. 37, 26 June 1996).

It may be possible to analyse animal welfare law in utilitarian terms but there is no serious attempt at interest balancing. There are invariably overrides for human interests and these seem to include most socially acceptable activities. For example harm to animals is often justifiable as an 'incidental' result of a lawful operation which could not reasonably have been avoided (e.g. Wildlife and Countryside Act 1981 s.4(2)c; Badgers (Protection) Act 1992 s.8(2)). This suggests a form of utilitarianism incorporating an element of proportionality that privileges any human activity, however trivial, that is not positively forbidden by law. The Animals (Scientific Procedures) Act 1986 regulates scientific experimentation using live animals and is explicit in its utilitarian ethos. Section 5(3) lists various purposes for which the Home Secretary can grant licences. These are mainly human purposes such as medicine research and education but also include the protection of the natural environment in the interests of the health and welfare of humans and animals. Section 5(4) requires the Secretary of State to weigh the likely adverse effects on the animals concerned against the benefits of the programme to be specified in the licence. This seems to suggest that the *total* suffering to the animals can be aggregated against human goals in an instrumental way. A deontological element is, however, introduced by the Act's requirements that the experiment must be essential and there must be no non-animal alternatives. Similarly the Badgers (Protection) Act 1992 contains overrides in favour of the protection of property and, subject to licensing requirements, for scientific, educational and conservation purposes, for the purposes of zoo-keeping, tagging, marking or ringing or preventing the spread of disease.

The successful opposition to the Wild Mammals (Hunting with Dogs) Bill 1997 mobilised around utilitarian concerns evoking the supposed social and economic benefits of fox hunting as well as the part hunting is said to play in conservation. It was suggested that foxes experience less pain by being hunted than would be the case if they were culled by other means. The instrumental role attributed to animals is revealed by the argument that hunting-dogs would be killed if there were no longer a job for them. The pro-hunting lobby also raised deontological concerns in favour of property rights in the face of evidence that a large majority of the population favoured a ban on hunting (see *The Guardian*, 16 December 1997).

The virtue ethics approach may provide an appropriate analysis of animal welfare law. This is illustrated by requirements in legislation including the Wildlife and Countryside Act 1981 and the Wild Mammals (Protection) Act 1996 that there must be an intention to cause suffering. As we have seen the 1996 Act focuses on particular acts of cruelty rather than harm to animals as such. According to the virtue ethics approach we can use animals as instruments of our own well being provided that we do not inflict 'unnecessary' suffering judged against our own concerns. The concept of 'unnecessary' suffering is a common device in animal welfare legislation. For example the Protection of Animals Act 1911 s.1 states that 'if any person (a) shall by unreasonably doing or omitting to do any act, or causing or procuring the commission or omission of any act, cause any unnecessary suffering, or, being the owner, permit any unnecessary suffering to be so caused to any animal, such person shall be guilty of an offence of cruelty within the meaning of this Act'. The concept of necessity is question begging, giving us no clue as to what interests the necessity should be measured against. Is it for example necessary for a fox to suffer in order for people to enjoy the hunt to the full?

In *Roberts* v. *Ruggiero* (unreported 3 April 1985, QBD) the Divisional Court held that whether keeping veal calves in crates amounted to unnecessary suffering depended on the context of the particular enterprise. Unless the suffering was deliberately inflicted and went beyond what was a normal consequence of the system of farming in question the justices were entitled to acquit. On the other hand in *Hall and Anor* v. *RSPCA* (unreported 1993), Holland L.J. took the view that a farmer who allowed pigs to live with arthritic joints until they reached optimal weight for the market was causing unnecessary suffering because he had the option of slaughtering them earlier. According to this view suffering is necessary where it is needed to serve the human purpose despite proper husbandry. *Ford* v. *Wiley* (1889) 23 QBD 203 concerned the dishorning of cattle. The defence had succeeded before the magistrates in establishing that dishorning, despite causing pain and suffering was reasonably necessary in order to rear the cattle to their full potential. The Divisional Court in a judgement given by the Lord Chief Justice, Lord Coleridge, held that there were alternative methods of preventing the mischief at which dishorning was aimed and in the course of his judgement he posed the case of a farmer who cut the hooves of his cattle to stop them straying and said that in such a case the justices would surely have been able to consider the alternatives of fencing or penning, tethering, store yards, etc. These cases suggest that the courts are aware of the moral concern with letting an animal flourish in accordance with its own nature but only up to the point of collision with a human interest.

Miscellaneous provisions responding to specific problems could be analysed in virtue ethics terms. These single out particular forms of cruelty, for example the Protection against Cruel Tethering Act 1988, the Abandonment of Animals Act 1960, the Animals (Cruel Poisons) Act 1962, and the Protection of Animals (Anaesthetics) Acts 1954 and 1964. They also regulate particular activities. Examples include the Animal Boarding Establishment Act 1963, the Riding Establishment Act 1964, the Pet Animals Act 1951 (Pet Shops), the Agriculture (Miscellaneous Provisions) Act 1968, the Animal Health Act 1981 (Transport), the Welfare of Animals (Transport) Order 1997 SI no 1480, the Slaughterhouses Act 1974, the Slaughter of Poultry Acts 1967–1971), the Cinematograph Films (Animals) Act 1937, the Performing Animals (Regulations and Rules) Act 1975.

International law is mainly concerned with conservation and the treatment of animals used for economic or domestic purposes (e.g. European Convention for the Protection of Animals Kept for Farming Purposes (1976), European Convention on the Protection of Animals Used for Slaughter (1979), Convention for the Protection of Vertebrate Animals Used for Experimental and Other Scientific Purposes (1986)). These outlaw particular forms of cruel treatment but on the whole strike only against suffering that is not necessary for human purposes. They have not all been incorporated directly into the law but can be used as aids to interpretation.

The European Convention for the Protection of Animals During International Transport (1968) serves as an example. This applies to five categories of animal namely:

1. domestic animals of soliped, bovine, ovine, caprine and porcine species;
2. domestic birds and domestic rabbits;
3. domestic dogs and domestic cats;
4. other mammals and birds;
5. cold-blooded animals.

Animals in class 1 are covered by detailed provisions regarding fitness to travel, the separation of hostile species, construction and marking of containers, means of attachment of animals, feeding, rest and watering in transit, need for attendant and veterinary attention (Articles 3–37). Animals of class 2 covered by most of those provisions (Articles 38 and 39), as are animals of class 3 except when accompanied by the owner or his representative (Articles 40 and 41). Animals of class 4 are similarly covered, with special provisions for wild animals (Articles 42–45). Animals of class 5 are covered briefly (Article 46).

There are also many European instruments regulating the treatment of animals for particular purposes notably in connection with agriculture (e.g. Community Directive on the Transport of Animals Between and Within Member States 91/628 EEC 11.13.1991, amended by Directive 95/29 EEC; see Broome, 1997, p. 189 *et seq.*). Article 36 of the treaty allows national governments to restrict the free movement of goods on grounds which include 'the protection of health and life of humans, animals or plants'. It is not clear how far this includes moral concerns. At the time of writing an action is proceeding in the European Court concerning the question whether the government can restrict the export of calves for the purpose of rearing them in veal crates (see also *Minister of Agriculture ex parte Roberts* [1991] 1 CMLR 555, *R* v. *Minister of Agriculture ex parte Hedley Lomas (Ireland) Ltd* [1996] 3 WLR 787, *Ken Lane Transport* v. *North Yorkshire County Council* [1995] 1 WLR 1416).

On the whole then animal welfare law seems to comprise an eclectic use of ethical principles which allows us to be kind to animals without sacrificing human interests approved by the community or negotiated in the particular case (see Harrop, 1997). Animal welfare law may be regarded as an application primarily of 'virtue ethics' supplemented by a loose utilitarianism weighed in favour of ourselves. The identification of human interests that override animal interests is not entirely a rational process but depends on the state of public opinion, economic and social class factors or the influence of vested interests. For example, cruelty to animals for entertainment is generally regarded as abhorrent yet, although some sports such as cock fighting and badger baiting are universally condemned, hunting is controversial and angling is widely accepted.

Endangered Species

The Endangered Species Act 1992 in the USA bites only at the point where a species is under serious threat so that legal powers are a last resort means of saving it. An endangered species is defined by the Act (16 USC 1532(6)) as a species in danger of extinction throughout all or a significant portion of its range. This approach is often called deathbed conservation. It has been described as akin to a deathbed repentance in that we find ourselves respecting nature only when we have no opportunity to sin again (Kunich, 1994). A lesser degree of protection is given to 'threatened species' defined as 'a species likely to become an endangered species within the foreseeable future' (16 USC 1532(20)).

Kunich (1994) argues that intervention at the stage when a species has been reduced to the verge of extinction by years of neglect and exploitation has a high probability of failure. The strict controls which the Act imposes once a species has reached crisis point may also give landowners an incentive for 'pre-emptive slaughter' by using up habitats such as forests in order to avoid designation.

The flexible approach of English law may help to avoid these problems. English law seems to be more broadly ecocentric in that it includes ecosystems and habitats without exclusive concentration on species. For example the Wildlife and Countryside Act 1981 Part 2 is concerned with the protection of Sites of Special Scientific Interest. Designation is based on the 'special interest of the site by reason of any of its flora, fauna or geological or physiographical features' (s.28(1); see also s.29). Intervention would therefore be possible at an earlier stage and on broader scientific grounds. However, certain powers are limited to deathbed cases.

English law protects particular rare species by the device of scheduling a list which can be altered by the Secretary of State. Earlier legislation singled out particular species according to criteria of usefulness or attractiveness to humans (see Protection of Birds Acts 1925, 1933, 1954, 1967; Protection of Lapwings Act 1928; the Quail Protection Act 1937). The Wildlife and Countryside Act 1981 introduced more general protection for rare species but falls far short of protecting wildlife generally. All wild birds enjoy protection against being killed, injured or having their eggs taken or destroyed by humans (s.1) with special penalties in respect of rare birds listed in schedule 1. However, certain birds associated with sporting can be killed outside their close season (schedule 2, part 1). Other kinds of animal listed in schedule 5 are also protected. This includes all native reptiles and amphibians. Other animals have no protection except under s.11 which applies to all wild animals and prohibits certain cruel methods of trapping and killing. However, the Wild Mammals (Protection) Act 1995 gives more general protection.

The main overrides for rare species under the 1981 Act are:

1. ministerial orders under agricultural legislation;
2. where the creature is disabled in order to tend it or to kill it if the accused shows that it has no reasonable chance of recovery;
3. the incidental and unavoidable results of lawful activities;
4. if necessary in the interests of health and safety or preventing serious damage to agricultural resources. (see Wildlife and Countryside Act 1981 ss.4,10).

Wild plants are protected under the Wildlife and Countryside Act 1981 s.13. However, unlike animals, except in the case of certain rare species, plants can freely be destroyed by the landowner or on his behalf (Wildlife and Countryside Act 1981 s.13(1), s.27(1)). This is because plants are capable of being private property and are therefore owned by the landowner.

Town and Country Planning Controls

Conservation law exists within the framework of town and country planning law governed by the Town and Country Planning Act 1990. This relies upon the discretionary powers of local authorities to prohibit development of land by refusing planning permission. The detailed machinery of the Act is outside the scope of this book which will concentrate upon the ethical values embedded in the legislation.

The Town and Country Planning Act 1990 does not set out any particular objectives but can undoubtedly be used to advance environmental goals. On the other hand the Act need not favour the environment. The Act confers political discretion which can be used for any purpose relating to the use of land (see *Stringer* v. *Minister of Housing* [1970] 1 WLR 1281). Policy goals can be set by the central government exercising its power to call in development plans and decisions for approval and through appeals against the refusal or conditional grant of planning permission. Sustainable development policies are currently incorporated both in development plans and in Planning Policy Guidance Notes (e.g. PPGN1 (General Strategy), PPGN2 (Green Belts), PPGN3 (Housing), PPGN7 (Countryside)). Environmental concerns are embedded in the Act itself to the extent that development plans must contain policies in respect of the conservation of the natural beauty and amenity of the land and the improvement of the physical environment (s.12(3A), s.31(1)). The development plan must be followed in deciding individual planning applications 'unless material considerations indicate otherwise' an obscure provision which at best seems to raise a weak presumption in favour of the plan (see 5.54A, PPGN 1 para 27, *Loup* v. *Secretary of State* [1996] JPL 22).

On the other hand there are features in the Act that militate against environmental values. Firstly agricultural and forestry uses of land are not development within the meaning of the Act and are therefore outside control (s.55(2)(e)). When the original planning legislation was drafted after the Second World War the importance of the domestic food supply was a primary concern and it was widely believed that farming was compatible with rural conservation. Modern high energy and industrialised agricultural techniques have invalidated both beliefs.

The Town and Country Planning Act 1990 also favours property interests in that there is a right of appeal to the Secretary of State against a refusal or a conditional grant of planning permission (s.78), but there is no right of appeal to anyone against an unconditional grant of planning permission. Thus environmental interests can challenge decisions only by judicial review: a forum where the merits of the issues cannot be canvassed. There are, however, provisions for public consultation as part of the planning application process (s.65, General Development Procedure Order Article 8). In some cases an environmental impact assessment is required (s.71A).

Town and country planning controls include provision for developers to enter into agreements or unilateral obligations with planning authorities (s.106). These can be used to provide environmental benefits such as landscaping or diverting a watercourse. It is not clear how far non-anthropocentric benefits can be secured by this means or by a condition attached to a planning permission under s.70 of the Act. A s.106 obligation must concern the physical use of the land or take the form of a payment of money. A condition is not so restricted but both obligations and conditions must serve planning purposes, have a logical relationship with the development and not be unreasonable (see Purdue, 1992).

In the case of obligations the relevance requirement has been broadly interpreted to include the provision of environmental amenities including ornithological facilities as part of a supermarket development (*R.* v. *Plymouth City Council* [1993] JPL 1099) and the House of Lords has been sympathetic to the general principle that developers should compensate for their environmental damage (see *Tesco Stores* v. *Secretary of State*). This could be regarded as endorsing the 'weak sustainability' version of intergenerational equity. The courts are in effect saying that environmental damage can be traded off against benefits of a different kind leaving it to the executive to deal with the problem of valuation.

Trees and Hedgerows

The only specific nature protection provisions in the Town and Country Planning Act 1990 relate to trees. Section 197 imposes a general duty on planning authorities to ensure that planning permissions include 'where appropriate' conditions for the preservation or planting of trees. Section 198 makes provision for Tree Preservation Orders with similar controls extended to any tree in a conservation area (s.211). It is a strict liability offence for anyone to destroy or damage a tree protected by a Tree Preservation Order without the consent of the local planning authority except to prevent a nuisance or where the land is under the control of the Forestry Commission. There are requirements to plant replacements (s.206). However Tree Preservation Orders are concerned solely with the amenity value of trees and must make provision for compensation in respect of loss or damage caused by a refusal of consent or a conditional consent (s.203).

Tree Preservation Orders control overlaps with the powers of the Forestry Commission to regulate the felling of trees under the Forestry Act 1967. It is an offence to fell a protected tree without a licence from the Forestry Commission. The main purpose of the Forestry Act is to protect commercial interests in forestry. Section 1(3A) requires the Forestry Commission to balance the interests of forestry against the enhancement of natural beauty and the conservation of flora and fauna and geological or physiographical features of special interest, but according to s.10 a condition can be attached to a felling licence only in the interests of good forestry or agriculture or the amenities of the district. Forestry Commission control does not apply to fruit trees or to trees in orchards, gardens or public open spaces or in certain other cases. It makes use of property law incentives by making arrangements for landowners to enter into 'forestry dedication covenants' binding on successors in title. These give the landowner various privileges in return for co-operating with a Forestry Commission management scheme.

Compensation is payable for refusal of consent under both the forestry and the Tree Preservation Order regimes. However, in the case of Tree Preservation Orders, the level of compensation reflects the loss of the value of the land while, in the case of forestry, compensation is limited to the value of the timber (see *Bell* v. *Canterbury City Council* [1989] JEL 90). Where there is an overlap between the two regimes the Forestry Commission can either decide the matter itself and pay compensation at the lower rate or refer the matter to the local planning authority to decide according to the Tree Preservation Order regime. A grant of a licence by the Forestry Commission counts as Tree Preservation Order consent. However, the local planning authority must be consulted and if it objects to the grant the matter is referred to the Secretary of State. The land must be re-stocked unless the Commission waives the requirement.

The legislation does not provide comprehensive protection in that there is no requirement to maintain protected trees. Moreover the emphasis is on trees conceived as individual objects or groups of trees or woodlands rather than as habitats or ecosystems.

The Environment Act 1995 s.97 introduces a certain ecocentric element by empowering the Secretary of State to make regulations protecting hedgerows. The Act confers wide powers to introduce any provisions comparable to those contained in the planning Acts. This could include criminal penalties and perhaps powers of entry and power to require restoration (see Hedgerows Regulations 1997, SI, no. 1160). Under these regulations the consent of the local planning authority within 28 days is required for the removal of a hedgerow. Consent can be refused only on the ground that the hedgerow is 'important'. A hedgerow counts as important if it is at least 30 years old and is the habitat of defined numbers and types of species. This legislation, although embodying the values of sustainability, is likely to be expensive and may be impracticable to operate.

Sites of Special Scientific Interest

The main conservation method is the designation of special sites. In most cases designation imposes few legal obligations on the landowner. The purposes of designation are to raise public awareness and to link in with the various regulatory systems – planning, pollution control, contaminated land – so that the special features of the designated area are taken into account. Designation also may trigger a power for the landowner to enter into management agreements with a public authority which are capable of binding future owners and occupiers of the land thus becoming property obligations. There are also various agricultural grant and management agreement schemes some of which are general and others applicable to designated environmentally sensitive areas (see Agriculture Act 1986 s.18; Commission Regulation (EC) 762/94). The dice are loaded in favour of anthropocentric concerns in that the Countryside Act 1968 s.37 imposes a specific duty on public authorities to 'have due regard to the needs of agriculture and forestry and to the economic and social interests of rural areas.'

The most important designation is that of Sites of Special Scientific Interest under the Wildlife and Countryside Act 1981. Under section 28(1) 'Where the Nature Conservancy Council are of the opinion that any area of land (including land covered by water) is of special interest by reason of any of its flora, fauna, or geographical or physiographical features, it shall be the duty of the council to notify that fact' to the local planning authority, every owner and occupier of the land and the Secretary of State. The power to designate is therefore open-ended and, unlike the US Endangered Species Act is not tied to deathbed conservation. The concept of 'special interest' allows the decision-maker to take both anthropocentric and ecocentric perspectives. The SSS1 designation is used both for domestic purposes and to comply with international obligations. In particular SSSIs include 'Ramsar' sites designated under the 1971 Convention for the Protection of Wetlands and sites designated under the EEC Wild Birds Directive (1979) and Habitats Directive (1992).

In *Sweet* v. *Secretary of State* (1989) JPL 927, Scheimann J. took an ecocentric approach to designation of an SSSI. He emphasised that the proper approach to identifying the size of the area that could be designated lay in the notion of a 'single environment' which could include an area of land which did not actually contain the rare species that was to be protected but which was ecologically interdependent. The court will not, of course, make this ecological judgement for itself but will ensure that the decision-maker has a rational basis for its decision. The concept of a single environment is of course open-ended in that every piece of land is ecologically related to every other particularly from the Gaian perspective. The focus in this kind of case would be on the support mechanisms needed for the species in question but even this might involve large or separate areas of land.

There are no public consultation provisions before a site is notified. Nor is there a right of appeal although a period of at least three months is available after notification during which representations or objections can be made (s.28(2)). Within nine months the Nature Conservancy Council (NCC) may withdraw or confirm the notification with or without modifications. Otherwise the notification lapses at the end of nine months (s.28 (4A)). In Scotland there is a right to make representations to an independent advisory committee although its recommendations are limited to the scientific basis of the notification and are not binding (Natural Heritage (Scotland) Act 1991 s.12).

The consequences of designation as an SSS1 are limited. There is no requirement to maintain the site. The Act merely prohibits the landowner or occupier but not third parties (see *Southern Water Authority* v. *NCC* [1992] 3 All ER 481), without the consent of the NCC from carrying out or causing or permitting to be carried out any operation of a kind specified in the notification which appears to the Council to be *likely* to damage the special features of the site, for a period of four months. During this period the NCC can negotiate a management agreement with the landowner (s.28(5)). After the expiry of four months the landowner is free to carry out the operation. (Note that the word 'likely' may contradict the precautionary principle.)

Management agreements can be made under s.16 of the National Parks and Access to the Countryside Act 1949 for the establishment of a nature reserve or under s.15 of the Countryside Act 1968 relating to areas of special scientific interest. The purpose of a nature reserve can be exclusively the human purpose of study and research but can also be that of conservation as such.

Management agreements can be made to bind successors in title. However, some of the relevant provisions are obscure where they use the private law mechanism for enforcing restrictive covenants by making the contract enforceable against successors in title as if the authority owned land benefited by the agreement (see National Trust Act 1937 s.8, National Parks and Access to the Countryside Act 1949 s.16(4), Countryside Act 1968 s.15(4), Conservation (Natural Habitats etc) Regs 1994, SI 1994 no. 2716 reg. 16 (4)). This perhaps illustrates the anthropocentric assumptions implicit in environmental law. It is surely inappropriate to regard restrictions imposed to protect the environment as conceptually grounded in the notion of the benefit to be gained by the 'reasonable landowner' (see *Wrotham Park Estates* v. *Parkside Homes* [1974] 1 WLR 798).

The use of restrictive covenant law means that only negative obligations can run and that the obligation must be of a kind that is capable of benefiting a neighbouring landowner rather than benefiting the environment as such. If this is correct then management agreements cannot be used to pursue non-anthropocentric goals. *Gee* v. *National Trust* [1966] 1 WLR 170 concerned a covenant made with the National Trust to erect only certain farm buildings on land. The Court of Appeal held that the covenant had to be of a kind which benefited neighbouring land so that the Trust could not oppose an application to modify it to allow the construction of a dwelling on the ground that the modification might hamper the Trust's fund-raising activities. Their lordships left it open whether the Trust had to be treated as if it owned specific land in the neighbourhood.

A local planning authority can enter into a management agreement with any person with an interest in the land but only for the human purposes of 'conserving or enhancing natural beauty and amenity' or promoting public enjoyment (Wildlife and Countryside Act 1981 s.39). Management agreements can also be made under s.18 of the Agriculture Act 1986 relating to 'environmentally sensitive areas' designated by the Minister of Agriculture and under s.94 of the Water Resources Act 1991 in relation to Nitrate Sensitive Areas designated by the Secretary of State and the Minister of Agriculture jointly. Section 18 protection goes beyond nature conservation and includes the human interests of natural beauty and the built environment. These provisions do not refer to the restrictive covenant mechanism and are capable of binding successors in title without drawing upon restrictive covenant law (s.39(3)).

Management agreements are also vulnerable to the argument that, because they are in form private transactions, they are not exposed to public scrutiny. Indeed for the purposes of disclosure of environmental information (Chapter 12) they could be protected by commercial confidentiality.

The Act's financial arrangements illustrate the traditional attitude that ecological damage is not a wrong. Management agreements require payment to the landowner the amount of which, is fixed by the offeror taking into account ministerial guidance (s.50). Agreements are negotiated individually whereas in other case such as agreements with farmers in Environmentally Sensitive Areas (below) there are fixed rates. The financial arrangements have been criticised on the grounds of inefficiency in as much as they involve individual negotiations. They are generous to landowners including as they do payment for loss of future profits (see Wildlife and Countryside Act 1981 s.50). However, the government is considering limiting payments to cases where the landowner takes positive environmental measures (DETR, 1998). This may be unfortunate in that payments based on natural loss (akin to damages in contract) provide an incentive to maximise environmental protection.

There is also power under section 98 of the Environment Act 1995 to make grants to persons who do or who undertake to do anything that in the opinion of the minister is conducive to the 'conservation or enhancement of the natural beauty or amenity of the countryside (including its flora and fauna and geological and physiographical features)'. This appears to be limited to anthropocentric concerns. Section 98 is not limited to special zones. The power is exercisable through regulations and grants can be made conditional with power to modify any conditions and to claim back a grant where the recipient defaults.

Planning permission overrides SSSI protection thus privileging development over conservation. The local planning authority need not in law give any weight to SSSI status or any other designated status provided that they do not ignore the matter. Where, as is usually the case, an SSSI is identified in the development plan the plan must be followed unless there is a specific planning reason not to do so thus creating a weak presumption in favour of the SSSI. It is hardly surprising that in the *Southern Water* case (above at 484), Lord Mustill described the SSSI regime as 'toothless' requiring no more from the owner or occupier than a little patience and depending only on moral pressure. Moreover non-occupiers such as water authorities can perform what Lord Mustill (at 485) described as ecological vandalism since they fall outside the criminal offence.

There are slightly more stringent powers in s.29 of the Wildlife and Countryside Act 1981. The Secretary of State can make a 'Nature Conservation Order' for the purposes of securing the survival in Great Britain of any kind of animal or plant, or for complying with an international obligation or where the Secretary of State considers the site to be of national importance. compensation is payable. No person may carry out a forbidden operation and the court may require a convicted person to restore the land. The waiting period is three months but is extended to twelve months where the NCC offers to acquire the land or to enter into a management agreement. Again planning permission is a defence to prosecution. The NCC can also acquire the land compulsorily.

European Sites

Under the Habitats Directive 1992 (92/43 EEC), which builds on the Berne Convention (1979), the European Commission draws up a list of 'Sites of Community Importance' from proposals submitted by member states. The criteria for designation relate to conservation and biodiversity. Conservation status is widely defined in Article 1 of the Habitats Directive as 'the sum of the influences acting on the habitat or species that may affect its long-term distribution, structure or function or abundance of its population'. The Habitats Directive is aimed at ensuring the stability of the population of a species, its variety and its long-term survival as a viable component of its habitat. Human concerns are matters to be taken account of but not objects in their own right albeit the Directive places itself within the context of sustainable development. Member states are required to designate sites that contain the habitats and species listed in the Directive (see Article 4). The Secretary of State is then under a duty to designate each European Site as a 'Special Area of Conservation' (SAC) as soon as possible and in any event within six years.

The Habitats Directive 1992, and its predecessor the Wild Birds Directive 1979, could be regarded to some extent as ecocentric. The Directives have been implemented in English law by being grafted on to the SSSI regime and town and country planning law (see Conservation (Natural Habitats) Regulations 1994, S. I. 1994 no 2716). The Wild Birds Directive conferred protection which could be overridden on the grounds of 'a general interest superior to the general interest represented by the ecological objectives of the Directive'. This formula could allow any interest to override an ecological concern. However, in *Commission* v. *Germany* [1991] ECR 1 883 (*Leybucht Dykes* case) it was held that the protection of people against flooding was sufficient but the economic interests of the local fishing community were not. Partly as a result of pressure from the UK government, the Habitats Directive Article 6(4) makes it clear that the superior interest can include social and economic factors.

Under the English regulations sites protected under the directive are called 'European Sites' (regs. 10, 11). Special Protection Areas (SPAs) designated under the Wild Birds Directive also fall within the regulations. All European Sites must be registered by the Secretary of State and designated as SSSIs. There is a four-month freeze on potentially damaging operations notified to the owner or occupier. If the NCC considers that there is a risk that an operation may be carried out without consent it must notify the Secretary of State who can then make a Special Nature Conservation Order under reg. 22 and 23. This makes the freeze permanent on any operation specified in the Order subject to a similar consent provision as above but with provision for referring the matter to the Secretary of State (reg. 24).

The Habitat Directive Article 2 imposes general obligations in relation to all threatened species but this can be balanced against economic, social and cultural requirements. Stricter obligations apply to European sites. These sites must be designated and, at designation stage, there is no right to balance economic, social and cultural factors against ecological factors. In *R.* v. *Secretary of State for the Environment ex parte RSPB* [1995] JEL 267, House of Lords [1997] QB 206, [1997] JEL 168 ECJ, the question was whether in deciding to designate Lappel Bank, an important bird habitat, the Secretary of State could take into account human economic and social factors or whether he was limited to biological considerations. A majority of the House of Lords initially held that social and economic factors were relevant. Therefore, the Secretary of State could take into account the desirability of creating jobs by expanding a nearby port. The ECJ held that at *the designation stage* economic and social factors were not relevant and the decision should focus on biological factors alone (see also *Commission* v. *Spain* [1993] ECR 1, *Santona Marshes* case). Whether this is an indication of a developing non-anthropocentric jurisprudence or merely a way of structuring a many layered decision-making process remains to be seen. In any event the Directive seems to override s.37 of the Countryside Act 1968 (above p. 266).

In accordance with the requirements of Article 6(4) of the Habitats Directive, the Secretary of State can direct the NCC to give consent only on certain grounds (reg. 24). These grounds are:

1. there must be no alternative solution; and
2. there must be imperative reasons of overriding public interest. These can be social or economic reasons.

3.   compensatory measures must be provided of which the Commission must be notified.

Within the general designation there are special categories of 'priority habitats' and 'priority species' chosen by the Commission which qualify for protection even before the site is designated as an SAC. Where there is disagreement between the Commission and the member state in relation to a priority species or a priority habitat Article 5 of the Directive provides for consultation. Meanwhile the site falls within the protective regime and the NCC can give consent to an operation only in special circumstances. These are as follows (regs 19, 20):

1.   the operation is directly connected with or necessary to the management of the site; or
2.   the operation is unlikely to have a significant effect on the site; or
3.   having carried out an environmental impact assessment, the NCC takes the view that the plan or project will not adversely affect the integrity of the site.

After designation, in the case of priority habitats or priority species, the only considerations that can outweigh the designation are considerations relating to human health, public safety, and beneficial consequences of primary importance for the environment or other imperative reasons of overriding public interest permitted by the Commission. In two recent opinions concerning a motorway project in Germany that formed part of the important trans-European transport network and which invaded several important habitats, the European Commission took the view that it is for the national government to assess whether the social or economic goals of the project are sufficiently important to count as imperative reasons of overriding public interest (see Nollkaemper, 1997). However, it is not clear whether, having decided that there are imperative reasons, a balance then has to be struck between these and the conservation interests or whether a finding of imperative reasons is in itself sufficient to justify consent. In the motorway cases the Commission took a strict approach to the question whether there was an alternative solution thus enabling it to police the process of environmental impact assessment.

As regards compensation it seems that under the Habitats Directive an environmental loss can be traded for an environmental gain elsewhere. In *Commission v. Germany* (above) for example the European Court held that it was lawful to build a new canal to a port for flood protection and recreational purposes even though this destroyed an important bird habitat. Completion of the project would produce compensation in the form of new wetland areas and the closing of some existing navigational channels. This reflects the notion of sustainable development and takes a broad ecocentric and utilitarian standpoint. Such an approach is difficult to justify from an individualistic respect for life perspective.

As in the case of the ordinary SSSI regime an operation can be carried out in an emergency or under a planning permission and the NCC can enter into management agreements. However, in the case of a European Site the planning process requires an environmental impact assessment and planning permission must be refused unless the integrity of the site is not affected subject to similar provisions relating to the overriding public interest as outlined above.

Finally the NCC has compulsory purchase powers. These can be used if the NCC cannot enter into a management agreement on terms which appear to be reasonable or if a management agreement is broken and not remedied within a reasonable time where the breach prevents or impairs the satisfactory management of the site (reg. 32). It is, however, questionable whether delegated legislation such as this is capable of creating powers of compulsory acquisition without clear authority in the parent Act.

Other Special Sites

Areas important for landscape or conservation reasons can be designated under miscellaneous legislation. These designations do not usually entail restrictions on the rights of landowners. They must be taken into account by decision-makers in relation to planning and pollution control decisions. They sometimes attract grants, there is sometimes power to enter into management agreements and in some cases there is a power to make bylaws regulating access. The main designations are as follows.

1. *Environmentally sensitive areas* (Agriculture Act 1986 s.18). These can be designated by the Minister of Agriculture for a mixture of human-centred and ecocentric reasons including the familiar 'conservation and enhancement of natural beauty', the conservation of flora or fauna or geographical or physiographical features and also the protection of the built heritage. The Act requires these factors to be balanced against agricultural stability and efficiency, social and economic interests and public enjoyment of the countryside (s.17). The protection given to ecocentric concerns is therefore significantly weaker than in the case of SSSIs. The Act's main instrument is a management agreement made with persons with an interest in agricultural land under which they adopt environmentally friendly practices in return for payments. Public access to the land might also be required (s.18(4)). There are also grants relating to sustainable

agricultural practices and 'set aside' land (EC Agri- Environment Regulation 2078/92/).

2. ***National parks*** (National Parks and Access to the Countryside Act 1949 Part II). We have already seen that national parks' designation is intended to be primarily anthropocentric and to balance the aim of preserving natural beauty, itself an anthropocentric idea, with the interests of tourism and with the economic and social interest of those living or working in the park. National parks are not therefore wilderness areas. There are special planning authorities for national parks, some modifications to development permitted under the General Development Order, and special financial provisions. Under s.42 of the Wildlife and Countryside Act 1981 the Secretary of State can designate areas of moor and heathland which can be protected against agricultural or forestry use for up to twelve months.

3. ***Areas of outstanding natural beauty*** (National Parks and Access to the Countryside Act 1949 s.87). These differ from national parks in that no special finance is available, tourism is not one of the statutory objects and there are no special authorities.

4. ***National nature reserves*** (National Parks and Access to the Countryside Act 1949 s.15). These are concerned with study and research or conservation or both. Management agreements and compulsory purchase powers are involved.

Summary

1. The common law does not provide for nature conservation and does not regard exploiting nature as wrong. Hence conservation legislation tends to be weak and dependent upon voluntary mechanisms.

2. The ethical basis for nature conservation is obscure and the different ethical perspectives of anthropocentrism, individual biocentrism and ecocentrism sometimes conflict. We do not know what is a 'right' state for nature to be since we cannot reason from 'is' to 'ought' and have no objective measure other than our own interests of what nature is meant to be like.

3. The scientific basis of conservation policy is also uncertain. It is not clear what a species is or whether nature is in a state of balance.

4. International instruments vacillate between anthropocentric and non-anthropocentric concerns. Animal rights perspectives conflict with environmental concerns. It is not clear how we balance human interests against those of nature given that we are natural predators and that we cannot know what nature's interests are.

5. It is not clear whether our responsibility is towards the well being of natural systems or towards their integrity. If we respect nature are we entitled to improve it?

6. English legislation does not embody an animal rights concept but comprises a pragmatic mixture of largely human-centred ethical values best explained on a 'virtue ethics' basis.

7. English law prefers to leave the task of interest balancing to administrative discretion. However, European law is beginning to establish priorities which may point in an ecocentric direction. A broad ranking order is emerging of public health and related matters (self-defence?), conservation concerns, and ordinary social and economic concerns.

8. Protection given to species and their habitats is limited and relies upon treating conservation concerns as material factors in planning decisions supported by agreements and payments to landowners. It is not clear how far current environmental agreements escape the restrictions of property law.

Further Reading

Broonman, S. and Legge, D. (1997) *Animal Law: Text, Cases and Materials*, chapters 1, 2, 8 and 9 (London: Cavendish).

Clark, S.R.L. (1979) The Rights of Wild Things. *Inquiry*, **22**, 171–87.

Des Jardins, J.R. (1997) *Environmental Ethics: An Introduction to Environmental Philosophy*, 2nd edn, chapters 5, 6, 8 and 9 (Belmont, CA: Wadsworth).

Elliot, R. (ed.) (1995) *Environmental Ethics*, chapters II, III, XI, XII and XIII (Oxford: Oxford University Press).

Elworthy, S. and Holder, J. (1997) *Environmental Protection, Text and Materials*, chapter 11 (London: Butterworths).

Garner, R. (1994) Wildlife Conservation and the Moral Status of Animals. *Environmental Politics*, **3**, 114–29.

Hargrove, E.C. (1987) Foundation of Wildlife Protection Attitudes. *Inquiry*, **30**, 3.

Harte (1997) Nature Conservation: The Rule of Law in European Community Environmental Protection. *Journal of Environmental Law*, 168.

Norton, B.G. (1987) *Why Preserve Natural Variety?* (Princeton: Princeton University Press).

Passmore, J. (1980) *Man's Responsibility for Nature: Ecological Problems and Western Tradition*, 2nd edn, chapters 4 and 5 (London: Duckworth).

Rodgers, C. (ed.) (1996) *Nature Conservation and Countryside Law* (Cardiff: University of Wales Press).

Warren, L. (1991) Conservation, a Secondary Environmental Consideration. *Journal of Law and Society*, **18**, 64.

Workshop

1. 'English conservation law is based largely on the voluntary approach'. Is this correct? Why should this be and do you think this is an effective and ethically valid approach?

2. A fire has destroyed a large tract of forest which was host to many species, some of them rare. You are the local authority considering an application for planning permission to use the site as a 'nature theme park' to be filled with plastic trees, artificial vegetation, and imported animals 'of attractive and friendly disposition'. The developers propose to promote the site for holidays for the urban poor. They are also prepared to provide the local community with a nature reserve in another part of the county to be set aside for the scientific study of ecosystems. However, two local environmental pressure groups, Boffins for Bio-Diversity and Nerds for Nature have alternative proposals. Boffins want to encourage the forest to regenerate by introducing new species. Nerds want the site to be left exactly as it is so as to let nature take its course. Your Chief Planning Officer, A. N. All, is very keen on cost-benefit analysis. What legal and ethical factors would inform your decision and how would you decide?

3. To what extent is there a conflict between animal rights and conservationist approaches to environmental ethics?

4. To what extent has section 37 of the Countryside Act 1968 (p. 266) been affected by European law?

5. What legal devices are available (a) to a private landowner; and (b) to a local planning authority dealing with an application for planning permission for commercial development, to ensure that land be set aside for nature conservation purposes?

6. The Secretary of State proposes to give grants under section 98 of the Environment Act 1995 to landowners who are prepared to provide habitats for a rare species of toad. The species in question is noisy and smelly and is in the habit of wandering along roads at night. Joan, the secretary of the local traders association fears that the initiative will discourage visitors to the area which contains several hotels and tourist shops. She wishes to challenge the legality of the proposal but without appearing to be environmentally unethical. Advise her.

7. To what extent does the law relating to animal welfare adopt a coherent ethical perspective?

8. Examine the Wild Mammals (Protection) Act 1996 in the light of Regan and Singer's approaches to animal welfare.

10 Waste

Developed societies produce vast amounts of waste (around 390 kg per person per year in Europe) and the amount produced is rising steadily. Waste is a serious problem which law is justified in addressing.

In European law the main directive governing waste management is Council Directive 75/442/EEC on waste (1975 OJL 194, p. 39). This requires member states to establish a general system of authorisation and supervision of waste disposal operations (Article 5) and to draw up one or more waste management plans (Article 7). Installations or undertakings treating, storing or tipping waste on behalf of third parties must obtain a permit from the competent authority (Article 8). A lower, less onerous, system of regulation applies to undertakings transporting, collecting, storing, etc. their own waste; undertakings collecting or transporting waste on behalf of third parties; and in certain circumstances, undertakings which carry out waste recovery. For these activities the Directive does not require that a permit be obtained; it requires only that the undertaking be registered with and subject to periodic inspection by the competent authority designated by the member state (Articles 10–12).

In the UK, as we saw in Chapter 7, there is a dedicated waste management regime under Part II of the Environmental Protection Act 1990 (hereafter EPA) supplemented by the Waste Management Licensing Regulations 1994 (SI 1056 as amended, hereafter 'the 1994 Regulations') which imposes controls upon the keeping, treating or disposal of waste. Most of these controls apply only to 'controlled waste' which is defined by s.75(4) EPA to mean 'household waste, industrial waste and commercial waste or any such waste': terms which are themselves defined by ss.75(5)–(7). Waste from mines or quarries and waste from any premises used for agriculture are not controlled waste (s.75(7)(c)). An inclusive list of controlled wastes is provided by the Controlled Waste Regulations 1992 (SI 1992 no. 588, as amended). In order to qualify as controlled waste a substance or object must first be waste according to the s.75 definition and, additionally, fall within the categories of controlled waste listed in s.75 and the 1992 Regulations (*Thanet District Council* v. *Kent County Council* [1993] Env LR 391).

An important function of the EPA is to establish and define the responsibilities of the waste institutions. The Control of Pollution Act 1974 (hereafter 'COPA') established Waste Disposal Authorities

(WDAs) – local authorities, mainly county councils – but these had been criticised on the ground that they both operated and regulated waste disposal sites: thus having conflicting 'poacher' and 'gamekeeper' roles. This conflict of responsibilities was removed by s.30 EPA which established (mainly) county councils as both Waste Regulation Authorities (WRAs) and WDAs but, at the same time required them to keep their waste regulation and waste disposal functions separate (s.30(7) EPA). Section 32 EPA further assisted in the separation of functions by requiring WDAs to transfer their operational functions either to private companies or to 'arm's length' companies set up by local authorities themselves known as Local Authority Waste Disposal Companies (LAWDCs). Local authority WRA responsibilities were ultimately transferred to the Environment Agency by s.2(1)(b) Environment Act 1995 (hereafter 'EA'). Waste collection is carried out both by Waste Collection Authorities (WCAs) and by private waste collection companies. District councils are established as Waste Collection Authorities by s.30(3) EPA.

Private waste collectors require to be licensed as waste carriers under the Control of Pollution (Amendment) Act 1989 and the Controlled Waste (Registration of Carriers and Seizure of Vehicles) Regulations 1991.

Two examples illustrate the roles of these institutional actors. First, it is the duty of each WCA to arrange for the collection of household waste in its area (s.45(1) EPA), for which no charge shall be made (s.45(3)) and to deliver that waste for disposal to a place where the WDA for the area directs (S.48(1)). In order to satisfy this duty the WCA may require the householder to place the waste 'in receptacles of a kind and number specified' that it specifies (separate receptacles may be required for waste which is to be recycled (s.46)). Complimenting the WCAs' 'duty to collect' the waste the WDA is obliged to arrange for the disposal of controlled waste collected in its area by WCAs and to provide places where household waste may be taken for deposit by members of the public (s.51).

Industrial waste may be collected either by a private waste carrier, which must be registered under the 1989 Act and 1991 Regulations, or a WDC. Both will charge for this service: the former to make a profit, the latter because they are obliged to charge a reasonable amount for the collection of non-household waste (45(4) EPA). Either collector will typically take the waste to a disposal site run by a LAWDC or a private company – a provision that will form part of the WDA duty to arrange for the disposal of controlled waste in its area. In either case the waste disposal contractor incurs a tax under the Finance Act 1996 as supplemented by the Landfill Tax Regulations 1996 and the Landfill Tax

(Qualifying Substances) Order 1996. In the case of a private waste collector the costs of disposal including the cost of the tax will be met directly and usually passed onto the customer as an element of charges. In the case of the WCA the costs of disposal will be met by the WDA.

The main elements of the waste management regime are as follows. Section 33(1)(a) EPA creates an offence of depositing controlled waste (or knowingly causing or knowingly permitting the same) and s.33(1)(b) creates offences of treating, keeping or disposing of controlled waste (or knowingly causing or knowingly permitting the same) - in both cases except in accordance with a valid waste management licence. Section 33(1)(a) applies to any deposit whereas s.33(1)(b) applies only to the disposal and recovery operations in Annex I of Directive 75/442/EEC. Section 33(1)(c) creates a new offence of treating, keeping or disposing of controlled waste in a manner likely to cause pollution of the environment or harm to human health and this offence applies regardless of the existence of and compliance with a waste management licence. There is a (due diligence) defence (s.37(7)).

Section 36 imposes limitations on the grant of licences. A licence shall not be granted for use of land for which planning permission is required in the absence of such permission or an established use certificate. An licence application can be rejected if the WRA is not satisfied that the applicant is a 'fit and proper person' or that rejection is necessary in order to prevent pollution of the environment, harm to human health or serious detriment to the amenities of the locality. A person is not a 'fit and proper person' if she has been convicted of a relevant offence (i.e. a pollution offence), if the activities would not be in the hands of a technically competent person or if she 'has not made, has no intention of making or is in no position to make financial provision adequate to discharge the obligations arising from the licence' (s.74). Regulation 3 of the 1994 Regulations lists the relevant pollution offences. Regulation 4 includes (hence effectively defines) as technically competent a person who holds an appropriate certificate of technical competence issued by the Waste Industry Training and Advisory Board (WAMITAB) (see also the Waste Management Licensing (Amendment) Regulations 1997 SI 1997/2203).

Regulation 16 *excludes* completely from the licensing regime processes prescribed for IPC control under Pt.I EPA, waste incineration subject to local control, disposal of liquid waste subject to consents and the deposit of waste at sea under the Food and Environment Protection Act 1989. These exclusions apply regardless of whether they the processes involve categories of hazardous waste known as "special waste". They are all processes which are subject to other forms of legislative control. Regulation 17 *exempts* a large number of exemptions from the full application of the waste management licensing system. Regulation 17 exemptions differ from reg.16 exceptions in that the offence in s.33(1)(c) continues to apply and, generally, they do not extend to cases involving special waste. Several of the prescribed exemptions do not apply unless:

(a) the activity is carried on by the occupier or with the consent of the occupier of the land where the activity is carried; or
(b) the person carrying on the activity is entitled to do so on that land for some other reason which renders the consent of the occupier superfluous.

Exempt processes still need to be registered with the Environment Agency (reg.18).

A problem with the waste disposal regime previously obtained under COPA 74 was that waste disposal licences could be surrendered at any time, releasing the previous holder from all regulatory responsibilities. Section 39 EPA alters that by providing that a site licence may only be surrendered if the WRA accepts the surrender. WRAs are required, before accepting surrender, to carry out a survey to satisfy themselves that the condition of the land, as a result of waste treatment, etc. is not such as will cause pollution of the environment or harm to human health.

The requirement in Directive 75/442/EEC to produce one or more waste management plans was reflected in s.50 of EPA 1990. This required WRAs to produce plans for their area detailing the 'arrangements which are needed for the purpose of treating or disposing of controlled waste ... so as to prevent or minimise pollution of the environment or harm to human health'. Section 50 was repealed by the 1995 Act as from 1 April 1996, and the Secretary of State was given the responsibility to formulate (in consultation with the Environment Agency and other relevant bodies) a national waste strategy (1990 Act s.44A, inserted by EA s.92) although existing s.50 plans continue in force until a national strategy is formulated (EA, s.23, para.16(1)). So far only a draft national waste strategy has been produced: *Making Waste Work: a Strategy for Sustainable Waste Management in England and Wales* (Cm 3040).

Waste also falls within other pollution regimes in so far as polluting substances happen to comprise waste. As mentioned activities authorised under the appropriate other regimes are exempt from the waste-licensing regime under the 1994 Regulations. Waste also falls within town and country planning and nature conservation regimes in so far as activities involving waste constitute development or other controlled operations in relation to land. In particular the deposit of refuse or waste materials on land involves a material change in its use notwithstanding that the site is already used for that purpose if: (i) the superficial area of the deposit is extended; or (ii) the height of the deposit is extended and exceeds the level of the land adjoining the site (Town and Country Planning Act 1990 s.55(3)). Moreover under s.215 of the same Act a local planning authority can serve an 'amenity notice' upon an owner or occupier requiring the condition of the land to be remedied as it appears to them that the amenity of a part of their area or of an adjoining area is adversely affected by the condition of the land. Waste therefore straddles three major concerns of environmental law viz. the prevention of pollution, the protection of amenity, and sustainability; the latter raising the question of whether waste should be recycled or re-used. Waste also illustrates a holistic approach in that it is widely accepted that the entire process of waste management should be dealt with in a co-ordinated way. The concerns of waste management law appear to be largely anthropocentric although habitat preservation might be indirectly served by controls designed for the benefit of human amenity. On the other hand waste controls might be positively harmful to non-human entities by denying them the opportunity to feed on human leftovers.

The Problem of Waste

Waste is acknowledged to be an environmental problem worthy of legal regulation because it presents a risk of causing environmental harm. The *kind* of risk posed by waste is peculiar to that class of objects or substances: it a risk of harm due to the *likelihood of escape or abandonment*. The risk of escape or abandonment is much higher for things which are waste because these things are not valued by the persons who control them.

'Abandonment' is used here to mean a deliberate severing of the link between controller and object without any attempt to control the subsequent use of that object. To abandon an object is to discard it. Abandoning or discarding could include consigning an object to a chain of events which would lead to eventual landfill disposal, aquatic or gaseous emissions, incineration or recovery. Abandonment can also take less well-managed routes, especially direct abandonment – dumping or fly-tipping.

'Escape' implies negligent rather than deliberate behaviour. In the absence of ethical attitudes towards the environment, a person is likely to fail to take precautions to prevent the escape of any substance under his care which he does not perceive to be of value. A substance which is regarded as having positive value, on the other hand, is likely to be subject to protective action to preserve its 'attached' value.

'Environmental harm' has many contested meanings. One of the most commonly cited 'problems' of waste is that of aesthetic displeasure (i.e.

unsightly waste mounds, litter, objects carelessly deposited or blowing around, unpleasant smells) but it may be difficult to explain why, from a non-anthropocentric perspective, loss of human aesthetic quality should count as 'harm' at all. Waste can cause environmental harm through pollution (harmful interaction of contamination with living organisms) and by other mechanisms.

Different types of waste present differing magnitudes of pollution risks. Some substances are intrinsically likely to pollute if released into the environment (e.g. radioactive waste or toxic chemicals). Some substances pose only context-specific risks of pollution, e.g. milk is generally harmless but if spilt into a river presents a serious risk to aquatic life due to its tendency to rob the water of available oxygen. Some substances almost never pollute (e.g. water vapour).

Waste can cause both *direct* and *indirect* pollution. Direct pollution occurs when waste itself becomes a contaminant which inflicts environmental harm. Landfill, for example, creates a risk of direct environmental harm through the leaching of pesticides, organic compounds, cyanide and heavy metals into substrata. These contaminants can infiltrate and contaminate groundwater. Landfill sites also give off methane gas which has a powerful greenhouse effect and emits noxious odours. Incineration creates air pollution in the form of sulphur dioxide, nitrous oxides, organic compounds, dioxins and heavy metals. These may present public health risks and 'fall out' onto nearby land or water. Incineration produces its own forms of waste – toxic ash which ultimately has to be disposed of to landfill. Fly tipping of waste creates an obvious hazard for organisms coming into contact with the tipped substances.

Indirect pollution occurs when waste substances are not themselves the contaminant. It is taken for granted in capitalist economies that things that are abandoned as waste can and should be replaced. Accessing resources and the production of new substances or objects creates a risk of pollution: often in excess of the risk associated with re-use or the original object or regeneration of the original substance. Waste also causes indirect pollution through transportation to disposal or recovery sites.

Waste can cause harm by processes other than pollution. In the case of non-renewable resources, the very act of drawing on resources to replace waste items leads to the diminution of the resource stock which may be classed as 'harm' if viewed from the perspective of future generations. This is recognised by the preamble to Directive 75/442/EEC which notes that 'the recovery of waste and the use of recovered materials should be encouraged in order to conserve natural resources.'

Waste can also cause harm through loss of habitat, ecosystems or species due to the proliferation of waste sites.

Given that waste can cause environmental harm, does that mean that creating or disposing of waste is ethically unacceptable? The answer to this question will depend upon (a) the type of ethic that we adopt (b) the type of waste involved and (c) the context of disposal concerned. If, for example, we adopt a biocentric or ecocentric ethical approach then waste which affects humans may be of relatively little importance, except to the extent that it also affects these organisms. From an ecocentric perspective leachate from a waste disposal site which contaminates an aquifer, thereby rendering it unusable as a source of potable supply would be of relatively little concern.

If, on the other hand, we adopt an anthropocentric approach to waste then waste which affects only animals and plants will be of relatively little importance, except to the extent that harm to animals and plants indirectly impacts on humans. Enlightened anthropocentric positions would require careful waste management because waste tends to diminish and demean the environmental conditions for human kind. This kind of reasoning is quite non-specific about actual waste policies because a variety of different approaches might lead to the least diminution in human welfare/satisfaction.

Any anthropocentric ethic concerning waste will have to take into account the need for equity between various parties affected by the overall waste cycle. This can be problematic. Difficult question of equity can arise, for example, in the law and policy concerning the siting of waste disposal sites. Welfare can be maximised in many cases if waste disposal sites are constructed in relatively accessible places in the vicinity of, or near by, large urban areas. But the aesthetic dis-amenity which accompanies the waste disposal site will impact differentially: being very significant for neighbouring residents and insignificant for those living further away. The response to proposals for waste disposal sites is often Not In My Back Yard (NIMBY). RCEP (1985) commented:

'We see NIMBY as a potentially serious obstacle to sensible waste management. In some areas the level of public opposition is apparently so overwhelming that governments and regulatory authorities are tempted to take the easy way out...'

If equity in the matter of siting waste disposal sites is to be construed via utilitarian principles, then the wishes of a local minority cannot be presumed to outweigh the greater good of those living in a larger area. At present decisions about the acceptability of waste sites are taken by county councils as local planning authorities under the Town and Country Planning Act (TCPA) 1990. The TCPA 1990 requires planning authorities to draw up development plans: both county-wide 'structure plans' under ss.30–35C, 36–45 and local plans under ss.36–45 which implement the structure plan. Except in the case of national parks and other areas where waste is not a county matter, waste is not included in the local plan. However, a local planning authority must prepare a special waste plan and also include its waste policy in its minerals local plan (s.38). As the RCEP report implies, decisions reached by local planning authorities on waste treatment sites may not produce the most equitable or ethical result in overall terms. (The underlying problem is an old one of defining the relevant constituency in the application of the utilitarian calculus.)

If approached from the perspective of deontological anthropocentric ethics, it might be desirable that waste law should focus on a number of key 'waste duties' owed to other humans. Waste law does indeed contain a number of duties of this kind, most importantly the duty of care under Part II EPA. In their eleventh report (1985) the RCEP commented

> '...responsibility lies...in our judgement...with the individual or organisation who controls the wastes. The producer incurs a duty of care which is owed to society, and we would like to see this duty reflected in public attitudes and enshrined in legislation and codes of practice...we believe that the waste producer's or handler's legal obligations towards the environment need to be classified and strengthened, with particular reference to the requirement to satisfy himself, when passing on the waste to somebody else, that it will be correctly dealt with...'

These expressions of ethical obligation are given legal form through s.34 EPA which provides that:

> '...it shall be the duty of any person who imports, produces, carries, keeps, treats, or disposes of controlled waste or, as a broker, has control of such waste, to take all such measures applicable to him in that capacity as are reasonable in the circumstances-
>
> (a) to prevent any contravention by any other person of section 33 above;
> (b) to prevent the escape of the waste from his control or that of any other person; and
> (c) on the transfer of the waste, to secure-
>
> (i) that the transfer is only to an authorised person or to a person for authorised transport purposes; and
> (ii) that there is transferred such a written description of the waste as will enable other persons to avoid a contravention of [s.33] and to comply with the duty under this subsection as respects the escape of waste.'

The duty to prevent any other person committing a contravention of s.33 refers to the main criminal offences in relation to waste: depositing controlled waste, or knowingly causing or knowingly permitting the deposit of waste without a licence. The obligation to prevent the escape of waste is designed to deal with situations of carelessness which are probably more commonplace than outright abandonment. Because it applies not only to producers but also to importers, transporters and holders of waste, the s.34 duty is in some respects wider than the obligations recommended by RCEP. It is important to note that s.34 imposes only a criminal duty of care with no attached civil liability.

Another duty-based approach to waste is, if interpreted as based on corrective 'justice', the polluter pays principle. Under principles of corrective justice one who causes damage or injury has an obligation to correct that state of affairs by restitutional remedies. In relation to waste the polluter pays principle is applied through rules of civil liability. Several statutory schemes for liability in relation to waste have also been proposed or incepted. The proposal for a Directive on Civil Liability for Damage Caused by Waste (COM(91) 219 final) fixes the 'producer' of waste with strict civil liability for damage and impairment of the environment caused by that waste. The producer is, initially,

'any person who, in the course of a commercial or industrial activity, produces waste and/or anyone who carries out pre-processing, missing or other operations resulting in a change in the nature or composition of the waste'

However, the importer of the waste, the controller of the waste (if he cannot identify the importer) and the person responsible for a waste installation are all deemed to be the producer in place of the actual producer. The proposed Directive thus fixes a variety of persons with a duty to pay for environmental damage caused by waste. Whether all of these persons are conceptually the 'polluter' or ethically responsible for waste damage is another matter. Article 14 of the proposal for a Directive on the landfill of waste, COM(91) 102 final, envisages imposition of strict civil liability on the operator of a waste disposal site for impairment of the environment caused by landfilled waste.

Civil liability for waste may also arise under common law. For example in *Blackburn and Another* v. *ARC Limited (formerly Amey Roadstone Corporation Limited, t/a Greenways Landfill)* (Unreported QBD Decision, 27 November 1997, LEXIS transcript) the defendants, who were engaged in backfilling a quarry as a waste disposal site, incurred liability in nuisance even though the site had planning permission and the operation had statutory authorisation on the basis that the smells and litter created by their operation went beyond a 'reasonable user' of the land. In *Gertsen* v. *Municipality of Toronto* ([1973] 41 DLR (3d) 646) the defendants incurred liability under the so-called rule in *Rylands* v. *Fletcher* for personal injury caused to the plaintiff when methane gas from landfilled waste caused an explosion in the plaintiff's garage.

Under s.59 EPA a WRA or WCA can require an occupier to remove any waste deposited in contravention of s.33(1) EPA subject to a defence in s.59(3) of 'innocent occupier'. If a person served with a notice to remove waste does not do so, the waste authority may remove it and claim the expenses reasonably incurred from the occupier. Immediate action may be taken by the authority in cases where such waste poses an environmental threat and the costs recovered from anyone who deposited or knowingly caused or knowingly deposited the waste or, in limited cases, the occupier of the land. Section 73(6) EPA 90 further imposes strict civil liability for any damage caused by waste which is deposited so as to commit an offence under s.33(1) or s.63(2) EPA.

The Concept of Waste

In this section we explain what we consider waste to be and consider the usefulness of that concept as a basis for regulation. In essence, waste is

anything which lacks value for its holder

The concept of waste can be more precisely defined as:

any object or substance under the control of a person who perceives it as having zero or negative net value

'Substance' includes all types of matter (solids, liquids and gases). Energy is capable of constituting waste because it manifests problems similar to those presented by material waste.

Control over objects or substances is frequently (but not necessarily) provided through ownership. Substances cease to be property when abandoned and thus, for the time being at least, fall under no one's immediate control. But property and control are not co-extensive since one may control a substance which one does not own, and own a substance which one does not immediately control. For instance, in *Cheshire County Council* v. *Armstrong's Transport (Wigan) Ltd.* [1995] Env LR 62 a demolition contractor contracted to remove concrete from a site owned by a housing association, crush it and return it to the site for use as infill for the foundations of new flats. The demolition contractors passed the concrete to the respondents, who deposited it on another site which did not have the benefit of a waste disposal licence, in order to carry out the crushing. The respondents were charged with depositing waste on a site without a licence contrary to the Control of Pollution Act 1974. In holding that the concrete was not waste the Divisional Court relied on the fact that ownership of the concrete never left the housing association and/or the demolition contractors. Consequently, the respondents never regarded the concrete as waste to be disposed of. Furthermore, they could not have sold it or disposed of it in any way they chose and were under a contractual obligation to return it to the original site. In this case the controllers (the respondents) controlled material that they did not own and the owners (the housing association) owned material which they did not control, but at no time did the *controllers* regard the material as lacking value.

The only 'value' which should be of importance in determining whether a substance is waste is *perceived* value (i.e. value identified at a personal level) of the person in whose control it lies at a given time. A substance or object not perceived as valuable may be mistreated and thereby create a special risk of environmental harm. Only the controller's perceptions of value should be relevant in classification of objects as waste as the perceptions of any other person have no direct bearing on whether the substance or object is likely to be handled carelessly. In cases where waste is produced by one person but passed to another the attitude of the recipient not the donor should, conceptually, determine whether the substance remains categorised as waste. This is not, however, the approach taken in *Meston Technical Services Ltd* v. *Warwickshire County Council* [1995] Env LR 380. The appellants, who traded in liquid wastes for reprocessing and subsequent resale, had received some drums of liquid waste from companies which regarded them and their contents as waste and had deposited these in an area not covered by their waste licence. Faced with a charge of causing controlled waste to be deposited the appellants argued that the drums and the liquids contained in the drums were not waste since they, the appellants, regarded them as valuable. The Divisional Court rejected this view on the grounds that the status of the drums and liquids as waste was to be determined by focusing on the state of mind of the persons who consigned the liquid wastes and not the appellants.

Accidental escape does not, of itself, cause an object or substance to become waste since even after escape it may still be valued. If, however, a substance has accidentally escaped or been lost then it may thereafter be difficult to recover and, for that reason, become to be regarded as non-valuable. For that reason lost or escaped things typically fall within the conceptual definition of waste. In *Cambridge Water Company*, for example, the chemicals which polluted the groundwater were not, conceptually, waste at the time of their escape but probably became waste when their irrecoverability led to a perception of negative value.

Defining waste in terms of perceived value raises the epistemological problem of obtaining 'real' knowledge concerning the valuation of others. Perception of value (rather than value in any objective sense, should it exist) lies in the realm of personal attitude or beliefs. In the real world it is not possible to determine accurately the attitudes and beliefs of others; only to make informed judgements about such matters by reference to observable factors such as statements and behaviour. Although objective or market value is irrelevant to waste classification *except* where such value stimulates perceived value in the controller, market value nevertheless acts as an indicator of likely perceived value since, in the absence of an information deficit or high transaction costs, a rational person regards anything which has market value as valuable.

Certain types of substances are inherently more likely to lack perceived value. Byproducts and residues, for example, are often (although not exclusively) perceived as non-valuable because they have, in effect, arrived free of charge in the hands of the controller and because they take up valuable space or require effort to manage. Hazardous substances are also likely to be regarded as non-valuable since, having the capacity for causing harm, they require handling and storage with particular care the cost of which might outweigh the benefit.

Value is a multi-dimensional concept: a person may perceive a variety of elements of value and disvalue in an object. What is important for waste classification is the *net* perceived value of an object. Net value takes account of different *types* of value: *instrumental* value (direct usefulness to the controller), *economic* value (being exchangeable for a price paid by others and so of indirect use to the controller) and *intrinsic* value (value regardless of usefulness or potential for economic exchange). So, on the positive side, a person may see the overall positive value of an object as a composite of instrumental, economic and intrinsic value. Value is often associated with property – a person will tend to value anything which she owns and tend not to value things that are owned by others or which are unowned. This is the basis for the traditional 'tragedy of the commons' thesis.

Net value also takes into account any *disvalue* in a substance (e.g. costs of managing, storage, handling, etc.) The disvalue of an object to a person must include the costs of retention or protection measures which will be required to ensure that the substance is not lost or does not escape. If the perceived disvalue of retention measures outweigh the perceived value of the object or substance then it is likely that the controller will not take care to prevent its escape.

Singular objects, i.e. those which for practical purposes are indivisible (e.g. a chair) either have or do not have a perceived positive net value. Substances and composite objects, on the other hand, being divisible, always contain some fraction which has no perceived net value. Diamond cutters, for instance, regard some proportion of the dust created in the cutting process as essentially worthless, i.e. waste. Similarly, farmers regard some fraction of field soil as expendable, e.g. the soil blown away by the wind or removed attached to crops. All substances and composite objects, even those generally regarded as 'resources' or 'products', contain some proportion which has no net value and which thus presents some risk of careless handling, escape or abandonment and concomitant environmental harm. Consequently, it is artificial to attempt to divide the world neatly into waste and non-waste. The best method of dealing with this somewhat paradoxical situation is to regard objects or substances as non-waste unless they are *mainly* of net negative value. If a situation arises in which the non-valued fraction becomes clearly identifiable and/or separate from the rest then that fraction should be regarded as waste.

Two examples may make this clear. First, consider a pile of ash which, as a whole, is regarded by its controller as having positive net value. A proportion of the ash may be at risk of being blown away by the wind but, because the pile of ash as a whole is valued, it would be unwise to describe the ash pile as waste. Taken as a whole the ash is not at any greater risk of escape or abandonment than a 'resource' of similar physical characteristics with similar perceived value. While the proportion that may be blown away is indistinguishably mixed into the whole pile it should not be regarded as waste. It becomes waste, however, once it has been separated by the wind and dispersed into the environment because it ceases to be regarded as having value. Contrast this with a pile of old paper which is regarded as useless and, therefore, properly regarded as waste. If a use is found for a fraction of the pile (e.g. using some paper for lighting a fire) then that paper, once separated, is no longer properly regarded as waste but the pile of paper as a whole remains waste.

One of the most difficult issues surrounding the legal and conceptual definition of waste is determining whether a substance which has been collected for recycling or for direct re-use should, thereafter, be considered as waste. Conceptually, the answer depends upon whether, post-transfer, the substance or object is perceived as valuable by its new controller. Substances transferred for re-use or recovery are likely to be valued because, as Judge Chapman observed (*Long* v. *Brooke* ((1980) Crim LR 109), 'one man's waste may be another man's valuable material'. However, it is possible that even in the hands of a new controller some substances will be perceived as having negative net value. This may occur when, due to its hazardous nature, control measures required to reduce environmental risks to an acceptable level are costly, when the value of the substance is very low or negative to the new controller, or when the recycling or recovery undertaking has only accepted the substance by virtue of a legal obligation to do so. In such circumstances the substance should generally be regarded as waste although if the new controller is legally obliged, either by contract or statute, not to abandon the substance or to allow it to escape then different considerations may apply.

It is legitimate to enquire whether waste is particularly useful as a concept for framing regulatory laws. Environmental law's justification in imposing regulatory controls on waste is that, as we stated at the outset, waste poses a peculiar risk of escape or abandonment. But since waste, as we interpret it, includes anything which is not valued by its controller then it will inevitably include many things which, while they may escape, pose little or no risk of environmental harm. Waste presents a risk which is uniform in type variable in magnitude. Some objects are dangerous if they escape or are handled carelessly but others are benign. Waste is, therefore, as a concept, over-inclusive. Waste is also under-inclusive since many substances or objects which are not waste (because they are valued) nevertheless pose a serious risk of causing environmental harm. For instance, oil which escapes from a tanker onto the coastline is not waste at the time of its escape. Similarly, the PCE and PCT chemicals which escaped from the Eastern Counties Leather site by dripping onto the ground were not waste but a valuable resource. In other words not all dangerous substances are waste.

We suggest that a concept which may be more useful than that of waste is 'environmental hazard' (hazard meaning risk of harm). If laws regulating to use and fate of substances were grounded on environmental hazard then waste which poses no significant risk of environmental harm would not be over-regulated and non-waste substances which poses a significant risk of environmental harm would be subject to commensurately stringent regulation. The concept of environmental hazard also has the advantage of being context-specific so that substances or objects used in a particular way which reduces or increases risk can be subject to commensurately stringent regulation. Although the idea of environmental hazard may be preferable to the concept of waste as a basis for environmental law, nevertheless the concept of waste is pragmatically useful since objects which are waste are generally (although not always) environmentally hazardous.

The Legal Definition of Waste

International Definitions

International and European attempts to define waste have centred around the concept of disposal and the promulgation of lists.

The Basel Convention on the Control of Transboundary Movements of Hazardous Wastes and their Disposal defines wastes as

'substances or objects which are disposed of or are intended to be disposed of or are required to be disposed of by the provisions of national law.'

OECD Council Decision C(88) 90 Final of May 1988 defines wastes as:

'materials other than radioactive materials intended for disposal, for reasons specified in table 1.'

Table 1 of Decision C(88) 90 lists sixteen 'reasons why materials are intended for disposal'. These include 'off-specification products', 'products whose date for appropriate use has expired' and 'residues or industrial processes' and (reason 16)

'Any materials, substances or products *which the generator or exporter declares to be wastes* and which are not contained in the above categories.'

European Definitions

The original definition

In EC law waste was defined by Directive 75/442/EEC as

'Any substance or object which the holder disposes or is required to dispose of pursuant to the provisions of national law in force.'

'Disposal' was, in turn, defined in Article 1(b) in exceptionally broad terms as:

'– the collection, sorting, transport and treatment of waste as well as its storage and tipping above or under ground,
– the transformation operations necessary for its re-use, recovery or recycling.'

Several types of waste were expressly excluded from the Directive definition by Article 2(1)(b):

(a) gaseous effluents emitted into the atmosphere;
(b) where they are already covered by other legislation:

(i) radioactive waste;
(ii) waste resulting from prospecting, extraction, treatment and storage of mineral resources and the working of quarries;

(iii) animal carcasses and the following agricultural waste: faecal matter and other natural, non-dangerous substances used in farming;
(iv) waste waters, with the exception of waste in liquid form;
(v) decommissioned explosives.

The use of the phrase 'disposes of' rather than 'ceases to perceive as of value' surmounted, to an extent, the epistemological problem of perceived value since disposal is likely to be a good indicator of perceived non-value. However, the phrase also created problems.

First, by focusing on the act of disposal rather than the controller's perceptions the definition missed the central element in the concept of waste. This much is clear from the Opinion of Advocate General Jacobs in *Zanetti and Vessoso* (Joined Cases 206/88, 207/88 and 359/88, 1990 ECR 1-1461).

> 'Neither definition contains any suggestion that the intention of the holder is relevant. For them to do so would, in my view, be inconsistent with the purpose of the directives, for the question whether a substance or object poses a threat to human health or the environment is an objective, not a subjective, one.'

A.G. Jacobs' view is inconsistent with the conceptual definition of waste because it overlooks the question of value. Although the question of whether a substance which is waste poses a risk to the environment is pertinent to the need to regulate that substance, nevertheless the personal attitude of the holder of the object is (or should be) central to the logically prior question of whether that substance or object is waste at all.

Second, the definition failed to include most objects which the holder regards as waste but which have not actually been disposed of. Non-valued non-disposed objects should be regarded as waste because they create a risk of causing environmental damage through escape or abandonment.

Finally, the Directive definition left room for differing interpretations between member states. This was in part due to its circularity (waste defined in terms of disposal defined in terms of waste) and, in part, due to the lack of precision concerning the elements of the various disposal operations.

The amended definition

Directive 91/156/EEC comprehensively revised Directive 75/442/EEC including a new Article 1 definition of waste:

> '"waste" shall mean any substance or object in the categories set out in Annex I which the holder discards or intends or is required to discard.'

'The Commission, acting in accordance with the procedure laid down in Article 18, will draw up, not later than 1 April 1993, a list of wastes belonging to the categories listed in Annex I. This list will be periodically reviewed and, if necessary, revised by the same procedure.'

According to the preamble to 91/156/EEC the purpose of that redefinition was to achieve a 'common terminology and a definition of waste'. The provision of a common terminology of waste is seen as important for the proper operation of the internal market in waste (Commission, 1997, p. 4). It is doubtful, however, whether this has been more than partly achieved.

A major problem with the amended definition of waste is that it does not explain the meaning of the central term 'discard'. Directive 91/156 has not, therefore, resolved the potential for differing interpretations of waste between EC member states. Indeed, the Commission has noted the existence of,

' ... major terminological disparity among the Member States. With regard to the classifications of waste, these vary considerably from one Member State to another, both in classification and in content' (Commission, 1997, p. 4).

The use of the word discard may even have created an additional new uncertainty viz. the difference, if any, between the concepts of 'dispose' and 'discard'. Cheyne and Purdue (1995) have suggested that 'discard' may encompass a narrower range of actions than 'dispose'; discarding may be limited to the 'getting rid of' unwanted objects, whereas disposal may also include the transferral of wanted objects and on the face of it seems to have nothing to do with waste as such. The French language version of the Directive is, however, identical in both original and amended form (the verb used in both is 'de se defaire') which may suggest that no major change of meaning was intended by the amending legislation. The best view seems be that in the Directive 'discard', hence waste, is to be interpreted by reference to the earlier concepts of disposal and recovery. It is for this reason that the amending Directive 91/156 contains a new Annex II comprising lists of disposal and recovery operations (Annex IIA and IIB, respectively).

According to A.G. Jacobs in his Opinion for *Tombesi* (Case C-304/94) [1997] CMLR 673) the term 'discard', as employed in the definition of waste in Article 1(a), has a *special* meaning encompassing the disposal of waste and its consignment to a recovery operation. Unfortunately, this does not remove all ambiguity because of the element of circularity noted by A.G. Jacobs: whether there is 'recovery' depends on whether there is 'waste', which in turn depends on whether there is recovery'. It is also unclear whether 'discard' should include *any* disposal and recovery operation or only those listed in Annex II. Cheyne and Purdue (1995) point out that the list of disposal operations in Annex IIA are not the only ways in which substances or objects can be disposed of.

An intriguing element of the amended definition of waste is that in order to be waste a discarded object or substance must also be a member of one of the categories set out in Annex I. This requirement could have provided EC law with a useful mechanism for narrowing the range of materials which may qualify as waste. However, this opportunity was lost due to the wording of the categories. The list of sixteen categories given in Annex I repeat virtually verbatim the sixteen 'reasons why materials are intended for disposal' from OECD Decision C88(90) (above p. 291) but with one important alteration: category 16 is:

> 'Any materials, substances or products which are not contained in the above categories.'

Note the absence of the italicised words (above p. 291) from the OECD's 'list of reasons'. This omission has the unfortunate effect of making the categories inclusive of all material objects.

Theoretically lists can be used to authoritatively determine that certain substances or objects are or are not to be regarded as waste. This is not, however, the effect of the Article 1 requirement that the Commission draw up a list of wastes belonging to the categories specified in Annex I. The Commission has drawn up a list of wastes (Commission Decision 94/3/EC, OJ No L 5/15, 7.1.94) known as the 'European Waste Catalogue' (EWC), but the preamble to the EWC states that:

> 'inclusion of a material in the EWC does not mean that the material is a waste in all circumstances. The entry is only relevant when the definition of waste has [already] been satisfied.'

Thus the only value of the EWC seems to be provision of a form of uniform nomenclature and categorisation of wastes which, in turn, can provide transparency and assist in developing markets in waste. Markets in waste are desirable because they facilitate the re-use and recycling of waste. This limited goal can only be achieved if all member states adopt the EWC as the basis for the national categorisation of waste which, so far, is not the case (Commission, 1997, p.16).

As we have seen, conceptually, market value is irrelevant in determining whether a substance or object is waste. ECJ cases which have dealt with the relevance of market value confirm this view. In *Zanetti and Others* (Cases C-206/88 and 207/88 [1990] ECR I-1461), for instance, the defendants, who faced charges in an Italian criminal court of handling waste without a licence, argued that the substances concerned should not be considered as 'waste' because they were capable of economic reutilisation. The ECJ rejected this position on the ground that several articles of the EC Waste Framework Directive 75/442 are specifically designed to lead to the recycling, recovery or re-use of waste, and that consequently substances capable of economic reutilisation cannot be excluded from the concept of waste. In *Tombesi* the ECJ was asked, *inter alia*, whether the concept of waste, in EC law, includes substances which may be the subject of a legal transaction or which are quoted on public or private commercial lists. In reply the court observed that because Directive 75/442/EEC lays down a system of control for recycling and other treatment of waste it 'is intended to cover all objects and substances discarded by their owners, even if they have a commercial value and are collected on a commercial basis for recycling, reclamation or re-use'.

We have also seen that, from a conceptual perspective, objects consigned to recycling should not be perceived as waste if, as is usually the case, they are valued by their recyclers. Decisions of ECJ have not adopted this view. In *Tombesi* the court ruled that the fact that a substance is a residual material or a reusable residue cannot, *per se*, exclude it from the category of waste. This, the court reasoned, is because the system of control set up by Directive 75/442/EEC is intended to cover substances and objects subject to the recovery operations listed in Annex IIB of the Directive. Reusable residues and materials will often be subject to these operations and must, therefore, be eligible for classification as waste. This reasoning is sound but it indicates that Directive 75/442/EEC is not merely a 'waste' Directive but is also, in part, a 'dangerous substances' Directive. This would be acceptable if the Directive expressly sought to regulate environmentally hazardous substances (a concept suggested above) but since it ostensibly only purports to regulate 'waste' the reasoning creates confusion. The basic problem is that the Directive is incoherently structured: on the one hand it is worded so as to apply only to 'waste' – on the other hand it seeks to apply controls to substances subject to recovery operations regardless of the current status of those substances.

We also noted above that substances or objects which are directly re-used should not, conceptually, be regarded as waste since they will be valued by their new controllers. EC law in relation to directly re-used materials is somewhat different from that for recycling. As A.G. Jacobs pointed out in his *Tombesi* Opinion:

'It may ... be inferred from the term "recovery operation" itself and from the list in Annex IIB ... that what is entailed by "recovery" is a process by which goods are restored to their previous state or transformed into a useable state or by which certain usable components are extracted or produced. It follows that ... goods which are transferred to another person and put to continued use in their existing form are not "recovered" in the above sense. Thus a second-hand motor vehicle sold to another person for continued use as a motor vehicle does not constitute waste.'

It should be noted, however, that several kinds of direct re-use are included in Annex IIB: re-use of oil, use of waste as a fuel and re-use of any waste on land for agricultural improvement. Substances re-used in these ways would, by parity of reasoning with the court's treatment of recycling, constitute waste.

National Definitions

EC member states are required, as a matter of EC law, to give effect in national law to Directive 75/442/EEC as amended including the definition of waste. In this task they have the choice of either transposing the definition into equivalent national terms or by simply referring verbatim to the Directive definition. Transposition has the advantage of coherence with existing national law but is likely to lead to discrepancies between national definitions of waste:

— Italian law defines waste as 'any substance or object deriving from human activity or natural cycles which is abandoned or destined to be abandoned.'
— French law defines waste as 'any residue of a production, processing or use process, any substance, material product or, more generally, any property abandoned by its owner.'
— Luxembourg law defines waste as 'any substance or object which falls within the categories established by that law, and more generally, any property which the owner abandons or intends or is required to abandon.'

It is not self evident that these definitions are equivalent or exactly equivalent to the Directive definition. On the other hand the verbatim approach, which involves merely referring back to the Directive definition, does nothing to solve the problems of interpreting the meaning of the verb 'discard' and places the onus on national courts and national policy-makers to interpret that definition. The verbatim approach is followed by Danish and Irish legislation.

In the UK 'waste' was defined by s.30 of COPA 1974 to 'include' (so the definition was non-comprehensive):

(a) any substance which constitutes a scrap material or an effluent or other unwanted surplus substance arising from the application of any process; and

(b) any substance or article which requires to be disposed of as being broken, worn out, contaminated or otherwise spoiled.....

Section 30 added that

'for the purposes of this Part of this Act any thing which is discarded or otherwise dealt with as if it were waste shall be presumed to be waste unless the contrary is proved'.

The COPA definition was included in s.75 EPA 1990. It became clear, however, that these terms were not identical to the amended Directive definition and that a number of legislative amendments were required in order to rectify the disparity.

First, s.75(2) EPA was amended by both the Waste Management Licensing Regulations 1994 and the Environment Act 1995. The 1994 Regulations revolve around the term 'Directive Waste' which is defined by reg.1(3) in terms identical to those used in the Directive (above p. 292). Schedule 4, para.9 of the 1994 regulations provides that in Part II EPA any reference to waste shall include a reference to Directive Waste. Section 75(2) was further amended by the Environment Act 1995 (hereafter 'EA 95') sch.22, para.88, such that 'waste' is now, in Part II EPA:

'any substance of object in the categories set out in Schedule 2B to [the] Act which the holder discards or intends or is required to discard ...'

'Holder' and 'producer' are defined by s.75 in terms identical to those used in the Directive. Schedule 2B, inserted by s.95 EA 95, repeats verbatim the categories of waste listed in Annex I to the Directive (above p. 294). S.75(11) EPA, added by the sch.22 EA 95, expressly adds that the s.75(2) definition and Schedule 2B are to be construed as giving effect to the Directive definition of waste. It is likely, therefore, that future judicial interpretations of the term 'waste' will need to make reference to the Directive itself, and its stated objectives (especially Article 4 which requires States to:

'ensure that waste is recovered or disposed of without endangering human health and without using processes or methods which could harm the environment, and in particular:

– without risk to water, air, soil and plants and animals,
– without causing a nuisance through noise or odours,
– without adversely affecting the countryside or places of special interest.'

Second, the concept of 'controlled waste' which, as mentioned above, limits the application of most the provisions of Part II EPA, was redefined to bring it into line with the Directive definition. Regulation 24 of the 1994 Regulations amends the 1992 Controlled Waste Regulations so that for the purposes of Part II EPA waste which is not 'Directive waste' shall not be treated as household, industrial or commercial waste.

Guidance to the interpretation of the term 'Directive waste' is given by Annex 2 of Department of the Environment Circular 11/94. The key test according to Circular 11/94 is that waste comprises

> 'those substances or objects which fall out of the commercial cycle or out of the chain of utility'

This test is useful but, from a conceptual perspective, under-determinative since, as mentioned above in relation to economic value, the location of an object within the commercial cycle or chain of utility is only indicative of the controller's perceived value of that object. In *Tombesi* the European Commission argued that the content of 'waste' should not be determined according to a utility or commercial cycle test but rather on a case-by-case basis.

As mentioned, difficult issues arise in the categorisation of substances destined for recycling or direct re-use. In relation to direct re-use Circular 11/94 indicates that substances subjected to recovery processes should cease be regarded as waste once they can be re-used 'in the same way as raw materials of non-waste origin by a person *other than a specialised recovery establishment or undertaking*' (paragraph 2.47). This view does not fit the conceptual definition of waste because substances which are re-used as raw materials by specialised recovery establishments are quite likely to be perceived as valuable by those establishments. It is, however, in keeping with Directive 75/442/EEC which, as discussed above, applies controls to discarded substances subject to the specialised recovery operations listed in Annex IIB of the Directive regardless of whether they are currently valued.

Circular 11/94 attempts to deal with direct re-use by stating that a person *does not discard* a substance when he transfers it to another person knowing and intending that the person to whom he transfers it intends to use it (a) in the form in which it was transferred or (b) in the same way as any other raw material *without its being subjected to a specialised recovery process* (paragraph 2.35). Conceptually, this is incorrect since a person may discard an object (because she abandons it) even though she knows that it will be directly re-used. For instance, a person who throws a chair onto a skip abandons it even though she may know that another person will remove the chair for personal use. Objects which are directly re-used should cease to be regarded as waste not because they have not been discarded but because the person who now controls them them also values them. The view expressed in the circular is, however, consistent with A.G. Jacob's view in *Tombesi* that discard means, in the context of the waste Directive, disposing of or consigning an object to a recovery process.

A series of cases show that the approach of UK courts in the matter of direct re-use is to examine the relationship between the producer and the material, and not to focus on the recipient's valuation of that material. In *Long* v. *Brooke* [1980] Crim LR 109 the appellant, who was the occupier of a disused quarry, allowed a construction company to dispose of a large quantity of subsoil and clay into the quarry. When the material had been deposited the defendant spread it over the shale slopes of the quarry with a bulldozer to make ready for grassing over. He was convicted by magistrates of knowingly permitting the deposit of controlled waste under s.3 COPA. The Crown Court held, dismissing the appeal, that although one man's waste may be another man's valuable material, on its true construction the Act defines waste from the point of view only of the person discarding the material.

Long v. *Brooke* was approved and followed in *Kent County Council* v. *Queenborough Rolling Mill Co. Ltd.* ([1990] Crim LR 813). In this case a third party, who had been contracted to clear broken pottery from a site, offered and supplied that material to the respondents. The respondents arranged for the broken pottery to be set down on their site to stabilise that land which, being near a river, was liable to subsidence. The respondents were charged with depositing waste without a licence under the COPA 1974. The magistrates concluded that the usefulness of the material on the infill site precluded its classification as 'waste', and dismissed the charges accordingly. The Queen's Bench Division, however, held (i) that the material in question had been 'waste' for the purposes of the 1974 Act when it was removed from the original site, and (ii) that its character was not subsequently changed by its usefulness to the respondents for infill purposes.

In *Ashcroft* v. *Michael McErlain Ltd* (unreported, Lexis transcript, 30 January 1985) the defendant was charged with causing controlled waste (soil) to be deposited on land. The defendants had been contracted to take soil to a riding establishment and spread it over a paddock in order to raise the site in an effort to improve the drainage. The soil had been excavated from a field which was being levelled as part of a separate development scheme. The prosecution alleged that the soil was waste because it was 'an unwanted surplus arising from the application of a process' and because it was waste to the developer of the factory and the intended new road. Dismissing the prosecutor's appeal the Divisional Court stated that whether a material is waste is a question of fact – thus falling to be determined on a case-by-case basis – and that although soil was capable of being waste on the facts of the case it was excavated as part of the process of levelling the paddock and had not been discarded by its owners.

Long v. *Brook* and *Queenborough Rolling Mill* are undesirable judgements since in each case the material determined to be waste was valuable to the respondents who had control of it at the time its deposition. As such it would not have posed any greater risk of causing environmental damage than an equivalent primary resource. The focus on the regard or intention of the original producer is also difficult to reconcile with the approach of A.G. Jacobs and the ECJ which, as we have seen, is that it is not the intention of the holder of the material which determines whether a substance is waste, but rather whether that material has been subject to a disposal or recovery operation.

Principles of Waste Management

Whether they be grounded in anthropocentric or more progressive environmental ethics, waste law and policy have evolved around a number of central principles. These are collectively known as the 'waste management hierarchy'. In *A Community Strategy for Waste Management* (Communication from the Commission to the Council and the Parliament, SEC (89) 934 Final, 18 September 1989) the EC Commission gave the following order of priorities to be followed in relation to waste:

1. Prevention
2. Recycling and re-use
3. Optimisation and final disposal
4. Regulation of Transport
5. Remedial Action

This ordering has been re-adopted more recently in Council resolution of 7 May 1990 on waste policy (OJ No. C 122, 18/05/1990, p.2) which states that:

> 'the production of waste should, where possible, be prevented or reduced at source, particularly by the use of clean or low waste technologies and products; ... waste that cannot be recycled or reused has to be disposed of in the most environmentally safe manner; ... it is important for the Community as a whole to become self-sufficient in waste disposal and it is desirable for Member States individually to aim at such self-sufficiency'

The waste management hierarchy is, however, not set in stone. Whether the prevention of any particular waste is the environmental best option is contingent. Waste prevention often requires increased energy use and/or technological capital: both of which have their own environmental costs. Some waste is very difficult to prevent yet relatively harmless (e.g. water vapour). Whether waste should be prevented depends, in ethical terms, very much on the kind of harm that it is likely to increase the risk of causing. Likewise, whether re-use is a better environmental option than disposal, all things considered, is not an *a priori* certainty. For example, the process of producing the energy required to manufacture, deliver, collect, clean and redistribute glass bottles may cause more environmental harm than the disposal to landfill of light-weight cardboard drink cartons.

It is increasingly recognised that individual waste streams will have their own management priorities which depend upon the overall benefits and drawbacks of the different types of action. To this end the preamble to Council Directive 94/62/EC of 20 December 1994 on packaging and packaging waste – 'The Packaging Waste Directive') observes that 'life-cycle assessments should be completed as soon as possible to justify a clear hierarchy between reusable, recyclable and recoverable packaging'. Article 10 of the Directive requires the Commission to promote the preparation of European standards for criteria and methodologies for life-cycle analysis of packaging.

Prevention

According to the waste hierarchy prevention is the preferred option. This policy preference surfaces in Art. 130S of the EC Treaty (now Art. 174):

> 'Community policy on the environment shall aim at a high level of protection *[and] shall be based on the principles that preventative action should be taken*, that environmental damage should as a priority be rectified at source' (emphasis added).

Waste prevention is also a specific goal of the Fifth Community Action Programme on the environment, *Towards Sustainability*, which aims to stabilise EC waste production at the 1985 level by 2000. A few examples of law can be found which requires waste prevention but these are not common:

— Article 9 and Annex II of the Packaging Waste Directive require States to take steps to ensure that packaging is manufactured so that volume and weight are limited to the minimum adequate amount to maintain the necessary level of safety, hygiene and acceptance for the packed product and for the consumer is placed on the market. Article 4 of that Directive requires 'other preventive measures' to be taken which may consist of 'national programmes or similar

actions ... designed to collect and take advantage of the many initiatives taken within Member States as regards prevention'.
— The proposed Directive on the Landfill of Waste (OJ C 156 , 24/05/1997, p. 10) requires that the amount of biodegradable municipal waste going to landfills must – as far as possible – be reduced to 75 percent of the total amount (by weight) of biodegradable municipal waste produced in 1993 , by 2002, to 50 percent of that amount by 2005 and to 25 percent by 2010.

Generally member states are free to prevent waste by prohibiting products which they consider create unnecessary waste so long as such measures are compatible with Treaty provisions on free trade. In the *'Enichem Case'* (Case 380/87 [1989] E.C.R. 2491, [1991] CMLR 313) the ECJ held that nothing in Directive 75/442/EEC prohibited member states from imposing prohibitions on the sale or use of non-biodegradable products (in this case, plastic bags). In UK law there are, as yet, no specific obligations to prevent waste from arising. It is likely that waste minimisation will be a feature of the National Waste Strategy when it is produced under s.44A and Schedule 2A of the Environmental Protection Act 1990. In the meantime the draft National Waste Strategy sets some rather weak non-binding waste prevention targets:

— to stabilise the production of household waste at 1995 levels by 2000;
— in due course to identify waste reduction targets for particular waste streams or for particular industrial sectors.

Sections 39–70 and Schedule 5 of the Finance Act 1996 create a 'landfill tax' which exerts an indirect pressure on waste producers to reduce the amount of waste destined for landfill.

Most laws which deal with waste prevention are hortatory rather than mandatory . For example, Article 3 of Directive 91/156/EEC amending the Framework Directive on Waste merely requires member states to take 'appropriate measures' to 'encourage' the prevention or reduction of waste production and its harmfulness including 'the development of clean technologies more sparing in their use of natural resources'. The lack of mandatory waste prevention measures can, in part, be explained by an underlying adherence to an anthropocentric/technocentric worldview. In the anthropocentric/technocentric worldview human welfare is deemed to possess a higher status than nature protection, and human welfare, in turn, is posited to require a continuation of the existing high levels of economic-technological production. From the deep ecology perspective it is the unquestioned adherence to continuation of patterns of high consumption life (and inevitable waste) which is responsible for most of the world's environmental problems (Naess, 1989, p. 23). In a world founded on an assumption of the desirability of constant or increasing production it is unlikely that firm steps will be taken to prevent waste from arising. Indeed as the EC Council have observed (Council resolution of 7 May 1990 on waste policy, OJ No. C 122, 18 May 1990 p. 2), the amount of waste produced in the Community is steadily *increasing*.

The position of waste reduction at the top of the waste hierarchy is, in any event, probably unattainable since basic laws of physics dictate that production necessarily creates waste. In particular the second law of thermodynamics states that every system is inefficient i.e. from every process of production a penalty is exacted. The penalty, *entropy*, is an increase in the 'mix-up' of material and the amount of energy which is unavailable for useful work. All bounded systems, except systems in equilibrium, involve a unidirectional flow from a state of low entropy to state of high entropy (Georgescu-Roegen, 1971). Mixed-up materials or materials with little or no available energy are generally non-valued hence waste. (Consider the example of the burning of paper – the carbon is released and 'mixed-up' as smoke: the available energy is reduced since ash will not burn.)

Given the difficulties in achieving significant quantitative reductions in waste production a complimentary solution is for law to focus on reducing the harmfulness of the waste. For example, Article 3 of Directive 75/442/EEC requires member states to take appropriate measures to encourage prevention or reduction of, *inter alia*, the harmfulness of waste through 'the technical development and marketing of products designed so as to make no contribution or to make the smallest possible contribution, by the nature of their manufacture, use or final disposal, to increasing the ... harmfulness of waste and pollution hazards'. Article 4 requires member states to

'take the necessary measures to ensure that waste is recovered or disposed of without endangering human health and without using processes or methods which could harm the environment, and in particular:
– without risk to water, air, soil and plants and animals,
– without causing a nuisance through noise or odours,
– without adversely affecting the countryside or places of special interest.

This requirement is transposed into UK law by schedule 4 of the Waste Management Licensing Regulations 1994 which imposes a duty on 'competent authorities' to discharge their specified functions, insofar as they relate to the recovery or disposal of waste, with the 'relevant objectives' mirroring those specified in Article 4 of the Directive.

Article 4 does not, however, create a binding obligation to follow the waste hierarchy. In *Ministere Public* v. *Traen* (Joined Cases 372 to 374/85 1987 ECR 2141) the ECJ held that, so long as member states have due regard to the objectives mentioned in Article 4 of Directive 75/442/EEC, they have freedom to organise the supervision of the waste disposal and recovery as they wish. In *Comilato di Coordinamento per la Difesadella Cava* v. *Regione Lombardia* (Case C-236/92 [1994] ECR-I 483) the ECJ held that Article 4 does not give individuals subjective rights which national courts may be required to protect which would enable them to object to national waste policies which are biased towards disposal rather than re-use or recycling.

There are other, more specific, elements of EC law which aim to reduce the hazardousness of waste or of waste treatment. Council Directive 75/439/EEC on the Disposal of Waste Oils requires waste oil to be collected and disposed of so as to cause no avoidable damage to man and the environment. Council Directive 91/157/EEC on batteries and accumulators containing certain dangerous substances requires member states to take appropriate measures to prohibit the sale of batteries with high lead and cadmium content. The Packaging Waste Directive 94/62/EC contains several measures aimed at reducing the hazardousness of packaging waste. The Preamble states that 'the presence of noxious metals and other substances in packaging should be limited in view of their environmental impact (in particular in the light of their likely presence in emissions or ash when packaging is incinerated, or in leachate when packaging is landfilled)'. Article 10 of that Directive requires the EC Commission to promote the preparation of European standards for methods for measuring and verifying the presence of heavy metals and other dangerous substances in packaging and their release into the environment from packaging waste. Article 11 requires heavy metals in packaging to be kept within certain specified limits and Annex II requires packaging to be designed so as to minimise its impact on the environment when disposed of.

Re-use

Second in the waste management hierarchy is re-use. Clearly re-use is an efficient method of dealing with waste since there is very little secondary environmental harm associated with the option. Objects may need to be collected and redistributed and, in certain cases, cleaned or lightly refurbished. As with prevention there are relatively few laws which positively require the re-use of materials or objects:

—

The Waste directive as amended by Article 3 of Directive 91/156 requires member states to take 'appropriate measures' to 'encourage', *inter alia*, the recovery of waste by means including re-use.

— Article 5 of the Packaging Waste Directive permits (but does not require) member states to encourage re-use systems of packaging 'which can be re-used in an environmentally sound manner, in conformity with the Treaty'. Annex II of that Directive specifies that packaging which is designed for re-use must be designed, produced and commercialised in such a way as to permit its re-use (or recovery, including recycling) including physical properties which 'enable a number of trips or rotations in normally predictable conditions of use'. The Directive does not, however, require packaging to be designed for re-use.

One problem with mandatory re-use systems is that they are generally uneconomic without prior standardisation around a small number of product types and specifications (witness the milk bottle). When a member state requires such steps to be taken competitors, especially importers, may be effectively 'locked out' of the market. This problem arose in the 1980s when Denmark introduced a compulsory deposit and return system for drink containers. The Danish system required the use of certain 'approved containers' apart from a very limited exception for imported drinks. Importers of drinks complained that because of the extra costs to them of changing to the approved type containers the system effectively discriminated against imports. Denmark was brought before the ECJ on the grounds that requiring drink containers to be of a certain type (in order to facilitate collection and re-use) created, effectively, a barrier to trade in conflict with Article 30 of the EC Treaty which states that:

> 'Quantitative restrictions on imports and all measures having equivalent effect shall, without prejudice to the following provisions, be prohibited between Member States.'

The ECJ ruled that protection of the environment through the imposition of a re-use scheme was an allowable exception to Article 30, as an extension of the 'mandatory requirement' exceptions established in the case *Cassis de Dijon* (case 120/78 [1979] ECR 649), but that such exceptions had to be non-discriminatory and proportionate. On the facts the ECJ indicated that some aspects of the Danish re-use scheme were not proportionate.

The Danish bottles legislation prompted the Drinks Containers Directive 85/339/EEC which required member states to draw up programmes for reducing the weight and/or volume of drink containers in waste disposal. These measures included:

— developing consumer education;
— facilitating refilling and recycling of containers;
— promoting selective collection of non-refillable containers and re-covery of materials used;
— encouraging technical development and marketing of new containers and maintaining and, if possible, increasing the proportion of re-filled and recycled containers.

The Directive suffered from weakly worded provisions which effectively allowed member states to rely on industry-led initiatives alone and was repealed by Article 23 of the Packaging Waste Directive.

Re-use of materials is a key feature of the Proposed Car Dismantling Directive. This aims to make the dismantling of vehicles more environment friendly and to increase the quantities of materials recycled. Discarded vehicles currently result in 8–9 million tonnes of waste each year in the EU, and the Directive aims to reach a level where 95 percent of vehicles' weight should be re-used and/or recovered by 2015. It applies the principle of producer responsibility by enabling the final owner of an end-of-life vehicle that cannot be recycled to reclaim the costs of transferring it to an authorised dismantling and treatment facility from the manufacturer. This is seen as a means of encouraging manufacturers to produce new vehicles that are easier to dismantle and reuse. The Commission also intends to propose changes to vehicle type-approval Directives with this aim.

We have seen above that according to A.G. Jacobs in *Tombesi* 'goods which are transferred to another person and put to continued use in their existing form are not "recovered" in the [Directive] sense' and thus do not constitute waste. A small number of forms of re-use are, however, listed in Annex IIB and, consequently, subject to the requirement of general rules, registration and supervision. These include the use of wastes obtained from most of the recycling operations listed in the Annex and the re-use of waste oil.

We have also seen that according to Circular 11/94 objects consigned to direct re-use are not 'discarded' and so not waste for that reason. Material which *has* been discarded, and which is therefore waste, but which is subject to 'beneficial use' is exempt from the waste management licensing regime if

(a) it is put to that use without further treatment; and
(b) that use of waste does not involve its disposal (sch.3, para.15 to the 1994 Regulations).

Certain waste materials are commonly re-used by being spread on agricultural land to improve soil or crops. Waste spread on land resulting in benefit to agriculture or ecological improvement is listed in Annex IIB of Directive 75/442/EEC and so is exempt from the need for a permit. In the UK sch.3, para.7 to the 1994 Regulations exempts from the waste management licensing regime the spreading on land which is used for agriculture of waste food, drink, blood and guts from abattoirs, waste lime, lime sludge from cement manufacturing, waste gypsum, waste paper or pulp, dredging of inland waters, textile waste, sludge from biological treatment plants, and waste hair and tannery effluent sludge.

Faecal matter is especially suitable for re-use on land. To encourage this 'faecal matter and other natural, non-dangerous substances used in farming' are excluded entirely from the ambit of 75/442/EEC (Article 2(1)(b)(iii)). The Urban Waste Water Treatment Directive requires sewage sludge (the semi-solid end product of filtration and other processes carried on in sewage treatment plants) to be reused 'whenever possible'. However, a problem with re-using sewage sludge is that in most European countries household faecal material is transported in the same sewers and treated in the same plants as industrial waste; consequently the resulting sludge tends to contain toxic substances, especially heavy metals. If sewage sludge is applied in large quantities to farmland this can result in a build-up of heavy metals in crops which enter the human food chain. The EC has addressed this problem through Directive 86/278/EEC on the protection of the environment, and in particular of the soil, when sewage sludge is used in agriculture. This is transposed into UK law by the Sludge (Use in Agriculture) Regulations 1989 (SI 1989/1263 as amended). The Directive and the Regulations set maximum concentrations for heavy metals and other elements in soil subject to sewage sludge spreading. To encourage sewage sludge re-use on *non*-agricultural land sch.3, para.8 to the 1994 regulations exempts this activity from the need for licensing if the concentrations of substances set out in the 1989 regulations are not exceeded and if the use results in ecological improvement.

Soil, rock and crushed building material can often be directly re-used. Waste resulting from prospecting, extraction, treatment and storage of mineral resources and the working of quarries are exempt from the application of Directive 75/442/EEC (Article 2). Schedule 3, para.9 to the 1994 Regulations exempts from the waste licensing regime the spreading of waste consisting of soil, rock, ash or sludge, dredgings from inland waters, or waste arising from construction or demolition work in certain circumstances. The exemption applies only where the land is incapable of beneficial use without such treatment and where it will result in agricultural or ecological improvement.

Recycling

As with prevention and re-use, despite the apparently fixed position of recycling in the waste management hierarchy, the environmental preferability of recycling varies according to the facts of each waste stream. The case of newspaper recycling provides a well-known example. EC Council recommendation 81/972/EEC of 3 December 1981 Concerning the Re-use of Waste Paper and the Use of Recycled Paper observes that

'the Community's present deficit of raw materials for paper and board manufacture has to be made up by imports from third countries, both of pulp as well as paper and paper based products, the latter being principally manufactured from virgin fibre.'

and that

'the use of waste paper instead of cellulose or wood pulp in manufacturing paper and board products enables substantial savings of energy and fresh water to be made, produces fewer effluents and less atmospheric pollution and contributes towards easier waste disposal.'

But some waste policy analysts maintain that the energy costs of collection plus the chemical burden of regenerative treatment outweigh the benefits of reduced disposal and reduced reliance on virgin fibre. Use of virgin fibre is not necessarily an environmental 'bad' since forests maintained as a 'crops' for paper production provide sinks for carbon dioxide thus contributing to the fight against global warming. Monoculture pine forests are admittedly low in biodiversity but may be preferable, even in ecological terms, to alternative land uses.

Any policy determination of the desirability or otherwise of recycling should also take into account intergenerational equity. In relation to intergenerational equity the considerations which arise in the case of waste which uses up non-renewable resource such as oil may be different from those which arise in the case of renewable resources such as trees.

The Waste Directive (as amended by Directive 91/156) requires member states to take 'appropriate measures' to encourage the recovery of waste 'by means of recycling ... or reclamation or any other process with a view to extracting secondary raw materials' (Article 3). In order to encourage recycling member states may allow establishments that carry out waste recovery to be exempt from the requirement for a specific permit so long as the state's competent authority has adopted general rules for each type of activity and the types or quantities of waste and methods of disposal or recovery are such that the conditions imposed in Article 4 are complied with (Article 11).

The Packaging Waste Directive furthers recycling by setting concrete recovery and recycling targets. Specifically, by June 2001, 50–65 percent of packaging waste must be recovered, and 25–45 percent of packaging waste must be recycled with a minimum recycling rate for each material of 15 percent. Under that Directive member states must also ensure that systems are set up to provide for:

> '(a) the return and/or collection of used packaging and/or packaging waste from the consumer, other final user, or from the waste stream in order to channel it to the most appropriate waste management alternatives;
> (b) the re-use or recovery including recycling of the packaging and/or packaging waste collected, in order to meet the objectives laid down in [the] Directive.'

In the UK the obligations of the Packaging Waste Directive are transposed by the Producer Responsibility Obligations (Waste Packaging) Regulations (SI 1997 No.648) made under ss. 93–95 EPA. These apply to businesses which, broadly speaking, are concerned with manufacturing raw packaging material, which produce, handle or supply more than 50 tonnes of packaging per year and which have a turnover of more than £5 million (from 2000 the regulations will apply to businesses with turnover of only £1 million). Affected businesses must either register individually or join a 'compliance scheme' which assumes legal responsibility for meeting recovery targets. Evidence of compliance is in the form of 'packaging recovery notes' issued by reprocessors of packaging waste. In 1998 and 1999 affected businesses must recover 38 percent of packaging and recycle 7 percent of each material. In the year 2000 these targets rise to 43 percent recovery and 11 percent recycling for individual materials. It is likely that the provisions under s.93 EA 1995 (which empowers the Secretary of state to make regulations concerning producer responsibility) will be used to encourage recycling and recovery of other products and substances (Ball and Bell, 1997, p. 370).

One of the key problems with legislating for recycling is that, in the absence of market forces, recycling can create a glut of low-value or unwanted materials. A partial solution to this problem is to intervene at the consumer end of the market by requiring or encouraging the use of recycled waste materials. To this end Council recommendation 81/972/EEC on waste paper recommends that member states and Community institutions:

> 'define and implement policies to promote the use of recycled paper and board and in particular to:
> (i) encourage the use of recycled and recyclable paper and board, especially in Community institutions and national administrations, public bodies and those national official services which can set an example;

(ii) encourage, where feasible, the use of recycled paper and board containing a high percentage of mixed waste paper;

(iii) re-examine in the light of recent technological advances the existing specifications for paper products which restrict, for reasons other than adequacy of a product for its purpose, the re-use of waste paper and the use of recycled paper and board;

(iv) implement programmes of consumer and manufacturer education to promote paper and board products made from recycled paper and board;

(v) develop and promote uses for waste paper other than as a raw material for the manufacture of paper and board.'

Similarly, the Packaging Waste Directive, exhorts member states, 'where appropriate' to 'encourage the use of materials obtained from recycled packaging waste for the manufacturing of packaging and other products' (Article 6(2)) and requires the Commission to promote the production of European Standards for criteria for a minimum content of recycled material in packaging (Article 10).

Barriers to recycling can also arise from the nature of the waste itself. Sometimes the constituents of waste reduces its compatibility with recycling technologies. Thus Council recommendation 81/972/EEC on waste paper recommends the adoption of policies to 'encourage the use of products (inks, glues, etc.) which do not preclude the subsequent recycling of paper and board'.

In other cases barriers to recycling arise due to the non-distinguishability of waste materials. Plastics in particular suffer from very low recycling rates because different plastic polymers cannot be processed together and the polymer composition is not normally marked on plastic products – thus preventing separation at source. Environmental law can alleviate this difficulty by requiring clear marking of materials or substances which may become waste. For instance the Batteries Directive requires member states to ensure, *inter alia*, that batteries are marked to indicate their suitability for recycling and their heavy metal content. Article 10 of the Packaging Waste Directive requires the Commission to promote the production of European Standards in criteria for the marking of packaging.

In the UK recycling is carried out by the waste institutions, by industry and on a voluntary basis by individuals. As we have seen the three principal institutions for waste management created by the EPA 1990 were the Waste Regulation Authority (WRA), the Waste Disposal Authority (WDA) and the Waste Collection Authority (WCA), although the EA has now taken over the WRAs' responsibilities. The WRAs, in drawing up their waste disposal plans under the now repealed s.50 EPA, were obligated to consider what arrangements can reasonably be made for recycling waste. WDA contracts for disposal of waste should have regard to including terms to maximise the recycling of waste (Schedule 2, para.19 and s.50(7) EPA 1990). WCAs have to draw up Waste Recycling Plans for their area (s.49). Local authorities can borrow extra funds to pay for capital investment in new recycling infrastructure through the Supplementary Credit Approvals scheme. As recycling can often be best achieved if waste is separated at source it is significant that, under the terms of the EPA 1990, WCAs may require separate receptacles to be used for different types of waste (s.46(1) and (2)). Recycling is an activity that carries efficiency of scale and WCAs are empowered to buy or acquire waste with a view to recycling it (s.55).

An unfortunate disincentive to recycling is effected by s.45(3) EPA 1990 which prohibits WCAs from imposing any charge for the collection of household waste. (Household waste collection costs are factored into local taxation.) Furthermore, not only are current 'wheely-bins' larger than pre-exising 'dust bins' but most WCAs allow households to request additional containers if payment is made. The government is considering changing this aspect of the legislation to provide for household waste to be charged according to weight or volume produced. By contrast WCAs have a duty, under s.45(4) EPA, to levy a 'reasonable charge' for the collection of non-household waste.

The most important initiative for recycling by the waste institutions is the 'Recycling Credits Scheme'. Section 52 EPA requires WDAs to pay a sum, fixed initially by the Environmental Protection (Waste Recycling Payments) Regulations 1992 and increased by the Waste Management (Miscellaneous Provisions) Regulations 1997, to WCAs in respect of waste that they have collected and recycled. The theory is that this reduces the amount of waste that WDAs have to arrange to dispose of resulting in a cost saving which can be passed on to the WCAs. WCAs thus have an economic incentive where recycling costs are less than the amounts received under the Regulations. In practice most local authorities provide facilities for collection and recycling of used paper, glass bottles and aluminium cans under the Recycling Credits Scheme.

As far as voluntary recycling is concerned recycling facilities can, and often are, situated at the civic amenity sites provided by local authorities, originally under the Refuse Disposal (Amenity) Act 1978 and latterly under s.51 EPA. These often provide for the recycling of larger or more hazardous items such as refrigerators, cookers and used engine oil. Voluntary organisations who collect waste for recycling can receive payments under the Recycling Credits Scheme representing savings both in WCA collection costs and WDA disposal costs. Unfortunately, unlike the situation between WDAs and WCAs, payment to voluntary organisations is not mandatory and some local authorities do not utilise the option.

One way to encourage recycling is to subject it to a less stringent and burdensome administrative regime. To this end Directive 75/442/EEC Article 11 permits member states to exempt undertakings that carry out waste recovery from the requirement to obtain a permit so long as

(i)   the member states have adopted general rules for each type of activity laying down the types and quantities of waste and the conditions under which the activity in question may be exempted from the permit requirements; and

(ii) the types or quantities of waste and methods of disposal or recovery are such that the conditions imposed in Article 4 are complied with.

Exempt undertakings must also be registered with and subject to appropriate periodic inspections by the competent authorities. This relaxation is reflected in some of the exemptions from the UK waste management licensing regime (1994 Regulations, para.17 and sch.3): for example, dismantling motor vehicles and scrap metal recycling activities (para.45)

Efforts to promote recycling have not yet been very successful. Currently around 85 percent of controlled waste in the UK goes to landfill (see DoE, *Sustainable Development: The UK Strategy Cm 2426, p150*). The draft national waste strategy, *Making Waste Work*, contains some non-legally binding recycling targets:

—   to recycle 25 percent of household waste by the year 2000;
—   to increase the use of recycled wastes as aggregates in England from 30 mt p.a. to 55 mt p.a. by 2006;
—   provision of close-to-home recycling facilities for 8 out of every 10 households by 2000.

It is likely that future legislation will promote recycling more vigorously.

Energy Recovery

The term 'recovery', in the context of waste, is understood to mean both material recycling and energy recovery. Energy can be recovered during, for example, the process of incineration. Waste can be burnt and, if incinerator technology allows, the resultant heat used to provide direct heating to nearby buildings or to create electricity. This, in turn, reduces the environmental costs associated with 'normal' energy production technologies. Article 3 of Directive 75/442/EEC requires member states to take appropriate measures to encourage, *inter alia*, the use of waste as a source of energy. The use of waste 'principally as a fuel or other means to generate energy' is included in the list of waste recovery processes in Annex IIB to that Directive. As such it benefits from exemption from the requirement for a permit (Article 11). This is reflected in regulation 17 of and sch.3 to the Waste Management Regulations 1994 which exempt from the licensing regime when burnt as fuel:

— straw, poultry litter, wood, waste oil or solid fuel formed from waste (para.3(a));
— tyres (para. 3(d));
— waste burnt in small incinerators (para.5(1));
— waste oil as a fuel in the engine of an aircraft, ship or vehicle (para.6(1)).

Under Annex II of the Packaging Waste Directive packaging waste which is processed for the purpose of energy recovery shall have a minimum inferior calorific value to allow optimisation of energy recovery. In UK law the Objectives for the purpose of the National Waste Strategy include use of waste as a source of energy. Similarly, the 'relevant objectives' to which local authorities are directed in exercising their plan-making functions under the Town and Country Planning Acts include encouraging 'the use of waste as a source of energy' (schedule 4 of the 1994 Waste Management Regulations).

Composting

Organic wastes can be dealt with either at source or at a central composting unit. The composting process produces useful soil enrichment product and avoids the use of landfill or incineration. Currently there are no EC requirements to compost waste. However, composting and other biological transformation processes are listed as Annex IIB recovery operations in Directive 75/442/EEC and, as a consequence, may be exempt from the requirement for a permit. This is reflected in sch.3, para.12 to the 1994 Regulations which exempts composting of biodegradable waste from the UK waste management licensing regime.

Annex II of the Packaging Waste Directive specifies that packaging waste processed for the purpose of composting 'shall be of such a biodegradable nature that it should not hinder the separate collection and the composting process or activity into which it is introduced' and, further, that biodegradable packaging must be 'capable of undergoing physical, chemical, thermal or biological decomposition such that most of the finished compost ultimately decomposes into carbon dioxide, biomass and water'.

In *Making Waste Work* the government adopts a target of recycling or composting 25 percent of household wastes by the year 2000. Some

WCAs have introduced household composting initiatives as part of their waste recycling plans under s.49 EPA and as part of the recycling credits scheme.

Disposal

Waste disposal is generally considered to be bottom in the list of waste management priorities. Yet, at the moment around 80 percent of waste in the UK is subject to disposal through landfill or through incineration.

It is important to be clear that disposal is not destruction. It is impossible to destroy waste. The *first law of thermodynamics* states that energy and matter cannot be destroyed or created – although each can be transformed into different forms or, occasionally into one another. The difference between matter and energy is, in any event, blurred by quantum physics that asserts that the two are, in essence, the same. The immediate consequence of the first law of thermodynamics for the concept of waste is that all talk of 'destroying' or 'eliminating' waste is mistaken.

Disposal, then, is understood to mean relatively long-term and fairly irreversible deposition or transformation through incineration. Whether this is, in fact, more harmful for the environment than prevention, re-use or recycling is contingent on the details of individual waste streams. For example, in relation to radioactive waste, long-term underground disposal may or may not be environmentally dangerous than attempts to recycle or treat.

The overall desirability of disposal depends, in significant measure, on whether the practice is carried out in an environmentally sound manner. Significantly, as we have seen, Article 4 of Directive 75/442/EEC requires member states to 'take the necessary measures to ensure that waste is recovered or disposed of without endangering human health and without using processes or methods which could harm the environment...' Member states must prohibit the abandonment, dumping or uncontrolled disposal of waste. Article 5 requires member states to establish 'an integrated and adequate network of disposal installations, taking account of the best available technology not involving excessive costs' (BATNEEC) which will 'enable the Community as a whole to become self- sufficient in waste disposal and the Member States to move towards that aim individually, taking into account geographical circumstances or the need for specialised installations for certain types of waste.'

The 'proximity principle', as it is usually described, is upheld by the additional requirement that 'the network must also enable waste to be disposed of in one of the nearest appropriate installations, by means of the most appropriate methods and technologies in order to ensure a high level of protection for the environment and public health.'

We have already seen that in the UK waste disposal without a licence is a criminal offence contrary to s.33 EPA 1990, and that there are stringent conditions imposed on the operators of waste disposal sites including the requirement that the holder of the licence be a 'fit and proper person' and have sufficient financial resources to carry out their obligations in relation to the disposal operation.

Hazardous Waste

Waste regimes often apply additional or alternative regulations to a sub-set of waste classified as 'hazardous waste'. As we indicated above waste is only subject to legal control because, in some cases, it presents an environmental hazard so in a sense any attempt to classify waste into two simple groups – hazardous and non-hazardous – is futile and misleading: waste varies in hazardousness along a continuum from benign to extremely hazardous. RCEP (1985) comment that:

> '"hazardous waste" as a term on its own has little meaning since hazard is related to the situation and circumstances rather than just to the properties of the materials ... Most materials have the potential to be hazardous if incorrectly handled.'

It is also the case that much environmental hazard is presented by substances or objects which are not waste: the criteria used for determining the hazardousness of waste in the EC hazardous waste Directive(Directive 91/689/EEC, as amended by 94/31/EC) are the same as those used in EC legislation concerning hazardous chemicals. However, some wastes are clearly more hazardous than others and this fact justifies more stringent regulation.

In international law hazardous waste is now subject to strict transportation restrictions. In the 1970s and early 1980s large quantities of hazardous waste were shipped to developing countries which accepted them for disposal or storage in return for badly needed foreign currency earnings. Waste was less expensive to dispose of in developing countries because of the lower environmental standards obtaining in such countries. A series of highly publicised incidents involving rejected waste shipments, most notably the *Karin B*, and very dangerous disposals, led to calls for new controls on international movement of hazardous waste. The principal results were:

— The 1986 Basel Convention on the Control of Transboundary Movements of Hazardous Wastes and Their Disposal.

— The 1989 Lome Convention (29 ILM 809).
— The 1991 Bakamo Convention on the Ban of the Import into Africa and the Control of Transboundary Movment of Hazardous Wastes Within Africa (30 ILM 775).

The Basle Convention provides a system of 'prior informed consent' whereby the shipper of waste has to inform and obtain the consent of the authorities in the importing state prior to shipment. If it transpires that the recipient of the waste cannot handle the waste in an environmentally sound manner then the exporter is obliged to re-import the waste. Originally the Basel Convention allowed for hazardous waste to be exported from OECD to non-OECD countries for recycling, but this 'recycling loophole' has now been closed.

The 1989 Lome Convention, which is one of a series of conventions negotiated between the EC and African, Caribbean and Pacific Countries states, bans the movement of hazardous wastes from the EC to those states. The Bakamo Convention bans imports of waste into African states but permits movements of waste between African states subject to certain restrictions.

The EC Directive 84/631/EEC, as amended by Council Directive 86/279/EEC, established a system of supervision and control of the transfrontier shipment of hazardous waste. On 30 March 1992 the OECD Council issued a Decision dealing with the transfrontier movements of wastes for recovery. This creates three lists of waste: the green, amber and red lists. The controls over movement of waste required by the OECD decision vary according to the status of the waste concerned within the three lists. Waste not on one of the three lists, and which is not considered hazardous by any concerned country, is uncontrolled by the OECD system. The EC adopted the OECD Decision and replaced Directive 84/631 with Regulation 259/93 on the Supervision and Control of Shipments of Waste within, into and out of the European Community. Regulation 259/93 substantially reflects the regime created by the 1992 OECD Decision although differing in some elements. Important differences include the definition of waste, treatment of unassigned wastes and differentiation according to the type of state. The definition of waste applied by Regulation 259/93 is that provided by Directive 75/442/EEC which, as we have seen, is phrased in terms of 'discard' rather than 'dispose'. In Regulation 259/93 wastes not assigned to one of the three lists are treated as if they were red list wastes thus adopting, in effect, the precautionary principle in relation to the classification of waste.

The rules and procedures for the shipment of waste set out by Regulation 259/93 vary according to three factors:

(i)   whether the waste is shipment involves another EC state or a non-EC state;

(ii) whether the waste is being moved for disposal or for the purposes of recovery; and

(iii) the type of waste being moved.

Waste which is moved for recovery is divided into three categories (Annexes II, III and IV) reflecting the OECD's green, amber and red lists. The link between the EC Regulation and the OECD Decision is further strengthened by the provision (Article 42 (3)) that the lists contained in the Annexes to 259/93 can only be amended to reflect changes already agreed by the OECD's review mechanism of the OECD.

Since green list waste is waste which should 'not normally present a risk to the environment if properly recovered in the country of destination ....' (preamble) the Regulation requires merely that it be accompanied by certain basic information (Article 11.1: the name and address of the holder; the usual commercial description of the waste; the quantity of the waste; the name and address of the consignee; the operations involving recovery as listed in Annex II.B to Directive 75/442/EEC; and the anticipated date of shipment).

Amber list wastes are subject to more elaborate controls: the exporting state competent authority must give prior notification along with detailed information including the source, composition and quantity of the waste (Article 6.5). The importing state competent authority must acknowledge the notification within three working days. The importing state competent authority has 30 days to make a reasoned objection to the planned shipment, in the absence of which the shipment 'tacit consent' which is valid for one year (Article 8).

Waste on the red list and wastes not yet assigned to one of the three lists are subject to the procedures for amber list waste but, additionally, require the consent in writing of the competent authorities concerned prior to the commencement of shipment.

Exceptionally member states may treat green list wastes as amber or red list wastes if they exhibit any of the hazardous characteristics listed in Annex III to the Directive on Hazardous Waste. Decisions to treat green list wastes as amber or red list wastes must be determined in accordance with Article 18 of the 1975 Waste Directive (Art 1.3 (c) and (d)): the Commission must be notified immediately, other member states must be notified as appropriate, and reasons must be given. The Commission may confirm such decisions.

Shipments of waste effected in contravention of the Regulation are deemed to be 'illegal traffic' which member states are required to take appropriate legal action to prohibit and punish. In the UK Article 12 of the Trans-frontier Shipment of Waste Regulations 1994 creates offences reflecting contraventions of the provisions of the Shipments Regulation.

One problem with the OECD decision and the EC Regulation is that neither deals expressly with mixtures of wastes of different types but which are all from one of the three lists (mixtures between lists are regulated). In *R* v. *Environment Agency, Ex parte Dockgrange Limited and Another* (Queens Bench Division, *The Times* 21 June 1997) the applicant sought judicial review of a decision of the Environment Agency requiring it to treat mixed green list wastes, which it imported, as red list waste. The court held that this was an inappropriate interpretation of the Regulation.

The EC has promulgated more general legislation for the control of hazardous waste. Control was originally provided by Directive 78/319 /EEC on toxic and dangerous waste (1978, OJ L 84, p. 43) but this was replaced by Directive 91/689/EEC on hazardous waste. Article 1(3) of Directive 91/689/EEC defines 'waste' in terms of the definition in Directive 75/442/EEC and 'hazardous waste' as waste which either is included in a list of hazardous wastes (Council Decision 94/404/EEC) or waste which displays certain properties which makes it hazardous (explosive, oxidising, highly flammable) listed in Annex III to the Directive. Although most of the fourteen properties listed in Annex III concern the effects of waste on humans it is notable that category H14 prescribes, as hazardous, waste which is 'Ecotoxic', i.e. 'substances and preparations which present or may present immediate or delayed risks for one or more sectors of the environment'. The regulations are not, therefore, entirely anthropocentric.

More specific EC controls include Council Directive 76/403/EEC on the disposal of polychlorinated biphenyls and polychlorinated terphenyls; Directive 75/439/EEC on the disposal of waste oils and Directive 86/278/EEC on the protection of the environment, and in particular of the soil, when sewage sludge is used in agriculture (see above).

In the UK controls over hazardous wastes began with the Deposit of Poisonous Waste Act 1972. This created an offence of depositing on land poisonous, noxious or polluting waste in circumstances in which it could give rise to an environmental hazard. The Act required notification to the WDA prior to movement or disposal of such waste. The 1972 Act was repealed and replaced by COPA 1974 but the prior notification requirement was carried through into the Control of Pollution (Special Waste) Regulations 1980 made under s.17 COPA. These took the approach that special waste is waste that has:

(i) the ability to be likely to cause death or serious damage to tissue if a single dose of not more than 5 cm^3 were to be ingested by a person of 20kg bodyweight

(ii) the ability to be likely to cause serious damage to human tissue by inhalation, skin contact or eye contact on exposure to the substance for 15 minutes or less, or

(iii) a flash point of 21 degrees centigrade or less.

It is notable that these characteristics related to human health effects rather than the effects on wildlife, species or ecosystems. Ethically this was dubious since, from a biocentric or ecocentric perspective, the effects of waste on natural entities or systems should be at least as important as the effects on humankind. The anthropocentric bias of the Special Waste Regulations 1980 has now been rectified since the Special Waste Regulations 1996 (SI 1996/972 as amended), which replace them, now define special waste to include hazardous waste as defined by Directive 91/689/EEC which, as we have seen, includes (category H14) waste with ecotoxic properties.

A particular form of hazardous waste which raises very challenging ethical issues is radioactive waste. Radioactive waste is, in the main, derived from the use of radioactive material in civil nuclear reactors for the production of electricity. The principal environmental benefit of nuclear energy is the production of electricity without the use of fossil fuels. Nuclear energy could contribute significantly to a reduction in global warming. Global warming is likely to have not only human impacts (e.g. crop failures, flooding and desertification) but also impacts on nature – loss of species and ecosystems as the world climates shift. Critics of nuclear waste production point out, however, that these benefits can be replicated by so-called 'soft technologies' (e.g. solar or wind power) without any of the concomitant risks.

The drawbacks of nuclear energy are several – increased amounts of bomb grade nuclear material, potential for nuclear accidents such as Chernobyl, increased death through cancers caused by radioactive emissions, etc. – but these principally affect human populations. Due to the long half-lives of many radioactive isotopes, the environmental risks of radioactive waste extend over a considerable period of time and hence number of generations. This sets up a complex ethical framework. The tensions in radioactive waste management extend along three principal axes:

(a) equity between humans and non-human nature;
(b) equity between human populations of this generation;
(c) equity between human generations.

Problems of equity between humans and non-human nature may arise because activities which result in radioactive waste may be of net benefit to the non-human aspects of the environment but relatively disadvantageous to humankind. If so, should environmental interests be allowed to outweigh those of human populations? Deep environmentalists may even welcome the risk of human mortality associated with radioactive waste since any lowering of the human population may be seen as ethically advantageous.

Problems of equity within the existing generation of humans arise in at least two ways. First, the concentration of radioactive materials at a number of plants for use or treatment increases the risk to surrounding populations from certain types of cancer while the benefits of such activities accrue to the population fairly evenly. Is it ethically acceptable to subject local populations to disproportionate risks for the benefit of the wider population? This raises, in an acute form, the problems of NIMBYism discussed above in relation to waste sites generally. Shrader-Frechette (1994, p. 133) argues that this imbalance of risks which occurs when radioactive waste is stored or treated in a small number of locations 'fails to take account of persons' rights to equal consideration of their interests, to due process, and to free informed consent'. Secondly, and conversely, the global population is subject to risks of nuclear accident and risks associated with nuclear proliferation resulting from energy programmes which immediately benefit only a few countries. Is it ethically acceptable to subject global populations to disproportionate risks for the benefit of local populations? Perhaps it is since Rawls, for one, maintains that material inequities are to be tolerated if they make even the worst-off groups better off.

Policy on the distribution of risks within existing populations in the UK was set out in the 1984 'Green Book', *Disposal Facilities on Land for Low and Intermediate-Level Radioactive Wastes: Principles for the Protection of the Human Environment* and is restated in the 1995 Department of the Environment publication, *Review of Radioactive Waste Management Policy*. The 1995 review states that

> 'The guiding principle in authorising discharges from a particular site is the need to restrict the radiation doses that may be received by the most exposed members of the public, or "critical group", since adequate protection of this group will ensure that others are also protected' (DoE, 1995, para.37)

Beyond that general rule the review sets out three specific Radiological Protection Principles: *justification*, *optimisation*, and *individual dose and risk limits*.

The principle of justification, as mentioned in the review, means that 'no practice involving exposures to radiation should be adopted unless it produces sufficient benefit to the exposed individuals or to society to offset the radiation detriment it causes' (DoE, 1995c). In *R* v. *Secretary of State for the Environment ex parte Greenpeace and Lancashire County Council* (the 'THORP case') ([1994] 4 All ER 352) Potts J. ruled that

Articles 6A and 13 of the Euratom Safety Standards Directive requires justification to be considered in granting authorisation of a nuclear waste treatment plant. In general terms it is unclear that nuclear energy, hence nuclear waste, is indeed justified on a test of excess of benefits over detriments (Schrader-Frechette, 1984). Some opponents of nuclear energy argue that the alleged justification for nuclear fission are based on unfounded assumptions that radioactive waste can be practically and cost-effectively disposed of or treated: assumptions which they claim are at best uncertain and at worst untrue. Justification involves weighing up and balancing risks and benefits but opponents claim that these risks either cannot be properly measured and/or that low risks of high magnitude catastrophes are routinely ignored in such calculations (Schrader-Frechette, 1994). Other commentators point out that justification is essentially utilitarian but that any attempt to apply a utilitarian test to the creation and management of radioactive waste is bound to fail since there is 'no practical guide as to how to determine when it is that the advantages outweigh the disadvantages sufficiently to ensure a result which would be considered by most people as an overall gain' (Strohl, 1990).

Optimisation, as used in the review, means that the magnitude of the dose received or likely to be received from any particular *source* within a practice should be kept As Low As Reasonably Achievable (ALARA). Government policy on optimisation is that the dose to members of the public from a *single new source* should not exceed 0.3 mSv/y (millisieverts per year). The review also endorses the introduction of a threshold for risk from radioactive identical to that accepted in relation to nuclear power plants: namely, 1 death per million people per year (broadly the same as the risk of death by accidental electrocution in the home and far lower than the risk of motor accident death). Determination of whether a given risk is ethically acceptable is, of course, more complex than simply comparing risk statistics (Schrader-Frechette, 1984): many very risky activities are considered ethically justifiable (e.g. car driving) but generally higher risks are tolerated and seen as ethically acceptable when they are voluntarily assumed. The risks associated with radioactive waste are not usually voluntarily accepted.

This second principle is qualified by a third: that 'the exposure of individuals resulting from the combination of *all the relevant practices* should be subject to dose limits, or to some control or risk in the cases of potential exposures'. The review accepts the NRPB recommended dose limit of 1 mSv/y from all man-made sources other than medical exposure (this compares with an average radiation dose of 2.2 mSv/y from natural background radiation and an average of 0.3 mSv/y from medical exposure).

As between generations the major problem for nuclear waste is that while most of the benefits of nuclear fuels (probably) accrue to the present generations the risks attached to the resultant wastes extend over many thousands of years. Is it ethically acceptable to subject future generations to environmental and health risks in return for present benefits? One of the problems associated with making an ethical determination of this question is that the risks to future generations are not well understood. In particular the resilience of containment systems for nuclear waste over periods of hundreds or thousands of years is not reliably known. Routley and Routley (1978) have argued that creating long-life nuclear wastes is akin to placing a package containing a highly explosive and toxic gas on board a crowded long-distance train in circumstances where the sender knows that the package may well leak before the train arrives in its destination, i.e. ethically outrageous.

The ethics of radioactive waste may depend upon the chosen disposal option. Deposit in deep geological vaults may protect members of the present generations but critics of deep geological disposal of radioactive waste maintain that leakage from these vaults is likely within a relatively short period of time (only several hundred years) creating permanent health and safety risks for future generations (Shrader-Frechette, 1994). An alternative solution, which is endorsed by the 1995 review, may be long-term above-ground storage. Above-ground storage creates a greater risk to members of present generation (e.g. from emissions or sabotage) but provides future generations with the greatest range of options. Not cutting off any major disposal option may be the fairest solution for future people.

Government policy in the matter of intergenerational equity, as contained in the Green Book, was that present and future generations should be afforded equivalent environmental protection. The Green Book did not, however, specify the period of time or number of future generations over which this parity should extend. The 1995 review states that radioactive waste management should be based on the same basic principles as those which apply more generally to environmental policy, and in particular on the principle of sustainable development, which it defines in Brundtland terms. The review specifically mentions that the UK interpretation of sustainable development (*Sustainable Development – the UK Strategy* (Cm 2426)) endorses a number of subsidiary principles:

— decisions should be based on the *best possible scientific information* and analysis of risks;
— where there is uncertainty and potentially serious risks exist *precautionary* action may be necessary;
— ecological impacts must be considered, particularly where resources are *non-renewable* or effects may be *irreversible*;

— *cost implications* should be brought home directly to the people responsible – the *polluter pays principle*.

In addition to the above, the review endorses a 'not worse off' principle of intergenerational equity:

'radioactive waste should be managed in such a way that predicted impacts on the health of future generations will not be greater than relevant levels if impact that are acceptable today'

The 1995 review gives no indication of the limit, if any, to the number of generations over which the parity principle should applied: we should bear in mind that nuclear waste can have harmful effects for a million years or 30,000 generations. It does, however, observe limitations in scientific method that would enable predictions of effects over long time periods. More particularly it notes that site-specific calculations relating to the biosphere and human behaviour should not extend beyond 10,000 years into the future and that beyond a few million years, at the most, risk assessments should concentrate on qualitative issues.

Summary

1. Waste is a term with contested conceptual and legal meanings. Conceptual interpretations focus on the notion of value whereas legal interpretations tend to be fashioned to fit the range of activities which legislation has been designed to cover. This raises questions about the desirability of basing environmental regimes around the concept of waste.
2. Waste policy is ostensibly based on a hierarchy of waste management options: prevention; re-use; recovery and finally disposal. Existing law, however, tends to be built up pragmatically from the other end of this list so that the most complete legal structures are those which regulate disposal and the least complete are those which deal with prevention of waste.
3. The desirability of each of the options is contingent upon the facts obtained for given waste streams.
4. Ethical issues arise in relation to waste in a number of areas. In particular ethical debate focuses around the siting of waste facilities, the impact of waste on human versus non-human life, and the ethics of radioactive waste. The long-lasting risks that accompany radioactive waste raise serious questions of intergenerational equity.

Further Reading

Ball, S. and Bell, S. (1997) *Environmental Law: the Law and Policy Relating to the Protection of the Environment*, 4th edn, chapter 13 (London: Blackstone Press).

Bontoux, L. and Leone, F. (1997) *The Legal Definition of Waste and its Impact on Waste Management in Europe* (Institute for Prospective Technological Studies: Sevilla)

Cheyne, I. and Purdue, M. (1995) Fitting Definition to Purpose: the Search for a Satisfactory Definition of Waste. *Journal of Environmental Law*, **7**(2), 149–67.

Routley, R. and Routley, V. (1978) Nuclear Energy and Obligations to the Future. *Inquiry*, **21**, 133–79.

Shrader-Frechette, K.S. (1984) Ethics and Energy. In T. Regan (ed.) *Earthbound: Introductory Essays in Environmental Ethics* (Waveland Press: Illinois).

Shrader-Frechette, K.S. (1994) Equity and Nuclear Waste Disposal. *Journal of Agricultural Ethics*, **7**(2), 133–56.

Strohl, P. (1990) Radioactive Waste Management: Ethics, Law and Policy. *Nuclear Law Bulletin*, December, part 46, 10–24.

Tromans, S. (1991) The Difficulties of Enforcing Waste Management Licencing Conditions. *Journal of Environmental Law*, **3**, 281.

Workshop

1. Devise and then justify a legal definition of waste which does not over-regulate benign substances or substances consigned for re-use or recycling.
2. Do you consider that it is necessary to base environmental laws around the concept of waste?
3. Compare the legal provision for recycling and re-use with that which exists to govern disposal?
4. What if any barriers exist to increasing legislative controls to prevent wastes from arising?
5. Consider and critically discuss (a) the Opinion of A.G. Jacobs in *Tombesi* and (b) the judgement in *Queenborough Rolling Mill.*
6. Justify or criticise the production of radioactive waste in terms of intragenerational and intergenerational equity.
7. To what extent does waste law have an anthropocentric bias?

---

11 International Trade and the Environment: Ethical Issues

The purpose of this chapter is to examine the interplay of law and ethics in the context of the international law of trade and its relationship with domestic environmental laws. It will primarily focus on a case study, namely a dispute over attempts by the USA to protect dolphins from certain tuna fishing practices by using import bans and restricting the right to use eco-labelling.

Background: The Basis of the International Trade Regime

The modern international trade regime rests upon liberal economic theory. This holds that economic competition is desirable because it allows states to specialise in those productive activities that they can perform with the greatest efficiency margin over other states. Thus, if State A can manufacture 100 widgets for the cost of £10, whereas State B needs to spend £20 in order to manufacture the same number of widgets, it is more efficient for State B simply to buy widgets from State A and put the money it saves to other uses. This is the concept of absolute advantage. The theory of comparative advantage takes this idea further by suggesting that a state that is more efficient than another in producing more than one type of good should specialise in the product in which it has the greatest advantage. By doing so, it maximises the efficiency of its resource allocation. To liberal economists, therefore, competition and ensuing specialisation permit the most efficient use possible of scarce resources. In addition, since all states have different resources and factors of production, e.g. skilled labour, fertile soil or sunny climate, all states can find their niche and exploit what they do best.

Thus, to liberal economists, free trade and competition constitute an essentially harmonious and mutually beneficial system that benefits both individual members and the community as a whole (Gilpin, 1987, p. 30). However, the general welfare benefits are aggregate in nature. In other words, although the community is expected to be more prosperous overall, some individuals or groups of individuals may find themselves worse off. For example, if consumers buy products that are made more cheaply abroad, domestic producers of the same products may lose their jobs. In ethical terms, therefore, it is an essentially utilitarian belief system because it favours whatever benefits the majority.

In order for this liberal trade regime to work, however, there must be as few restrictions on trade as possible, and it is this aspect of trade rules that creates an inherent tension between free trade policies and environmental protection regulation. Liberal economists view environmental 'damage' as a case of market failure, in other words, that environmental goods have not been appropriately valued and paid for. Provided that the costs of using or damaging environmental goods are internalised, i.e. that they are met by producers and reflected in the price of the products derived from them rather than being inflicted on society at large, for example in the form of pollution, the market itself will determine how much damage it is prepared to accept. If consumers assign a high value to the environment, it is argued that they will be prepared to pay higher prices for a product that tries to avoid environmental damage. If, on the other hand, consumers are prepared to pay a higher price for a product which costs more because its manufacture *causes* environmental damage, it is apparent that they have made a choice which puts other priorities above that of preserving the environment (Helm and Pearce, 1991, pp. 6–10). This is the same rationale that underlies the market mechanisms discussed in Chapter 7.

There are some obvious criticisms of this approach, for example that it is not always possible to calculate an appropriate value for environmental goods, particularly for those with aesthetic or existence value, that the theory is based on the premise of a perfect market which does not exist in practice, and that the contemporary market may choose not to value goods that might be highly valued by future generations. Despite the considerable work that has been done to develop this theory, therefore, it remains controversial (Bowers, 1995, p. 36). It is also entirely anthropocentric, regarding non-human components of nature as instruments of human desires (see above Chapter 1).

Another major concern is the large gap between the economic prosperity of developed and developing countries. Besides the moral issues raised by the existence of poverty in proximity to wealth, this gap has significant implications for environmental protection because of the acknowledged link between poverty and environmental degradation, for example soil erosion caused by tree felling for fuel (Beckerman, 1993, pp. 18–19). Economic development is usually seen by liberal economists as the key to strong and long-lasting environmental protection. In this school of thought, poverty itself is perceived to be the problem and the key to achieving environmental protection is the creation of prosperity through international trade, assisted by other elements such as aid through governments and international organisations, and foreign investment by private companies. However, this broadly market-based approach to development and environmental protection has been criticised on the grounds that it ignores the political, social and cultural elements of individual states that may create obstacles to free markets and yet be defensible on other value or belief systems. In addition, it does not necessarily accommodate concerns that increased trade and modification of traditional agricultural and manufacturing practices might themselves lead to environmental degradation (OECD, 1994).

Besides liberal economic theory, there is another important belief system called economic nationalism which holds that the overriding needs of a state are security and power in the international system and that economic policies are a means of achieving these goals. Typically, this approach takes the form of protectionist policies that protect domestic industries from foreign competition and deny other countries access to the national market. Indeed, in its most aggressive form, economic nationalists actually intend to harm competing states by using economic (and political) power against them. The desire to protect domestic industries is likely to be very strong when there is internal political lobbying by specific industrial sectors that feel threatened by foreign producers, labour groups concerned about unemployment, and others who fear, or may genuinely suffer from, change caused by the need to adapt to trade competition. Economic nationalism is therefore an inevitable temptation even among those states that overtly promote the liberal economic model of free trade (Gilpin, 1987, p. 34).

In order to counteract the temptation for governments to intervene in trade in order to protect their own producers, a charter of principles known as the General Agreement on Tariffs and Trade was adopted in 1947 (GATT 1947). GATT 1947 was intended to promote free trade and reduce or eliminate trade barriers such as tariffs, quantitative restrictions, subsidies and discriminatory practices that are intended to benefit domestic goods over imported goods, or one country's imports over those of another. Although GATT 1947 was remarkably successful in promoting international trade, continuing pressures towards protectionism led to new arrangements for the strengthening and enforcement of GATT disciplines being agreed in recent negotiations, known as the Uruguay Round. The 1994 World Trade Agreement sets up a permanent institution, the World Trade Organisation (WTO), reaffirms the principles of the GATT in a new version (GATT 1994), and consolidates and extends specialised agreements. More importantly, perhaps, it also establishes an effective and speedy dispute settlement procedure. Under GATT 1947, disputes were settled largely by negotiation and, although a formal procedure of setting up dispute panels had been developed, their recommendations could only be adopted by unanimity with the result that the 'losing' party could block any panel report it found unacceptable. Under the new arrangements in the WTO Agreement, panel recommendations can only be *rejected* by unanimity, effectively making them compulsory. As we have seen, international law has no dispute resolution machinery specifically for environmental matters.

Environmental groups lobbied hard for the inclusion of environmental protection to be integrated into the GATT regime during the Uruguay Round negotiations. The results were disappointing, amounting to a few concessions in areas such as standards and subsidies, and the resurrection of a committee on trade and environment which had originally been set up under GATT 1947 but rarely used. One of the reasons for this comparative failure was that many environmentalists had only just become aware of the potential threat of the international trade rules to modern-day environmental policies. Their concern was largely sparked off in 1991 by a dispute dealt with under the auspices of the old GATT dispute settlement procedure, concerning US restrictions on tuna imports aimed at protecting dolphins from unsafe fishing practices. This dispute encapsulates many of the issues of contention between the trade and environment lobbies and an examination of the way in which they were dealt with, both within the GATT system itself and in public discussion, provides some insight into the relationship between law and ethics.

Case Study: The Tuna–Dolphin Dispute

Factual Background

The activity at the heart of the *Tuna–Dolphin* dispute was the use of purse seine nets in fishing for yellowfin tuna in the Eastern Tropical Pacific Ocean (ETP). In this area, yellowfin tuna are often found swimming beneath schools of dolphins and fishers use this fact to locate the tuna. When a school of dolphin is spotted, it is chased with motorboats, sometimes with helicopters and explosives to herd the school together, until the dolphins are too exhausted to try to escape. The chase may last anything up to an hour. The purse seine net is placed around the dolphins and tuna, and the cable at the bottom of the net is then pulled together in order to form a 'purse' which captures the tuna fish and everything around them. The method was developed by US tuna fishing boats in the 1950s and by the early 1970s they were estimated to be causing the deaths of more than 300,000 dolphins a year (Buck, 1997).

As a result of increasing concern and revulsion in the USA at the level and cruelty of these dolphin deaths, the US government passed the Marine Mammal Protection Act of 1972 (MMPA) with the intention of reducing as much as possible the incidental killing or injuring of marine mammals, including dolphins, in the course of commercial fishing. US fishermen were required to observe limits on the number of incidental killings of dolphins. The Act also required a ban on the importation of fish or fish products caught with commercial fishing technology resulting in incidental killing or injuring of marine mammals that exceeded US standards.

Under the MMPA regime, estimated dolphin mortality caused by US tuna fishers dropped dramatically from 368,600 in 1972 to 5,083 in 1990. This was due in part to improved techniques for avoiding entanglement and for releasing dolphins from the net, but it also appears to have been a result of commercial pressure. In 1990, after graphic publicity was given to the killing and injuring of dolphins in the course of purse seine fishing, US tuna canning companies representing approximately 80 per cent of the US market announced that they would no longer be buying and selling tuna unless it was 'dolphin-safe'. In the same year, the Dolphin Protection Consumer Information Act was passed in order to set standards for the labelling of tuna as 'dolphin-safe'. The definition could only be applied to tuna that had not been caught by the method of encirclement, that is, by setting nets on dolphins. The International Dolphin Conservation Act of 1992 later prohibited the sale, purchase, transport or shipment in the USA of tuna that was not classified as 'dolphin-safe'. About this time, many US tuna seiners chose to move their activity elsewhere in the Pacific where tuna could be caught without such a high probability of dolphin involvement. By 1995 and 1996, US figures of dolphin mortality in the ETP had reached zero (Buck, 1997).

At the same time as US tuna fishing boats were reducing their number of dolphin kills, however, the entry of a growing number of foreign tuna seiners into the ETP area led to a renewed increase in the levels of dolphin mortality. The US Congress amended the MMPA twice in the 1980s in order to set standards for foreign tuna fishing boats wishing to export their catch to the USA, including a permitted level of dolphin kills calculated by reference to the US kill rate for any one year. However, as the US dolphin mortality levels dropped and US-registered boats left the fishery, it became increasingly difficult for foreign tuna fishers to meet the required comparability standards even though they successfully and steadily reduced their own figures.

In 1990, Mexico brought a complaint under GATT 1947 against an American ban on the imports of tuna caught by Mexican fishing boats. The dispute was considered by a GATT panel in *United States – Restrictions on Import of Tuna* Panel Report, GATT BISD 39S/155, 30 ILM 1594 (1991), ('*Tuna-Dolphin I*'). The panel report found that the USA was in violation of its obligations under the GATT. Although the report's adoption was blocked by the US government, the panel's findings caused outrage among environmentalists. One of their favourite insults was to call the GATT 'GATTzilla' and portray it as a ravening monster trampling the environment underfoot. Up to this point, environmentalists had largely ignored, or had been ignorant of, the possibility that the MMPA measures could be challenged under international law. There had been a widespread assumption among environmental NGOs and some policy-makers that the USA could use its considerable economic power to determine which environmental values were to be protected internationally. Now, however, they discovered that unilateral trade measures could not be used in order to combat environmental problems in the global commons, such as ozone layer depletion, or within the territory of other states, such as destruction of rainforests. The movement against the use of unilateral trade sanctions to attain environmental objectives was also underlined by the language of the 1992 Rio Declaration and Agenda 21 which assert the need for international consensus on environmental values, the need to avoid unilateral trade actions that operate outside the jurisdiction of a state, and the desirability of free and open trade in order to promote environmental protection in the long term.

To make matters worse for those environmentalists who thought that the USA should be able to set the international environmental agenda, the EEC (and other states) brought another action under the GATT in 1992. They complained about import bans being placed on their processed tuna because it came, or might have come, from fishing fleets that did not comply with the MMPA standards of dolphin safety. The second panel report (*United States – Restrictions on Imports of Tuna* Panel Report, 33 ILM 839 (1994) ('*Tuna Dolphin II*'), though indicating that the panel was aware of the hostile reaction occasioned by the first panel report, also found that the US measures were in violation of the GATT.

In the same year as the EEC complaint, the governments involved in tuna seining in the ETP negotiated the La Jolla Agreement which established the International Dolphin Conservation Program (IDCP), to be administered by the Inter-American Tropical Tuna Commission (IATTC). It set permitted levels of dolphin mortality which decreased each year, from 19,500 in 1993 to 5,000 in 1999, with the aim ultimately of achieving 'levels approaching zero'. Each individual seiner was also given a permitted limit, after which it was required to stop fishing. The La Jolla Agreement provided for observers on each boat and for a research and education programme to be established to develop fishing techniques that did not endanger dolphins.

There are, however, several criticisms that could be made of the Agreement. One is that it penalised the US fleet disproportionately because their limits were set very low and even careful seiners could find themselves no longer able to fish. In fact, the participation of US fishing vessels dropped dramatically during this period. At the same time, however, there was increasing concern that the majority of tuna fishers were now from foreign flag states, and that enforcement of the La Jolla restrictions was variable and generally weak. In addition, some were critical of the voluntary nature of the Agreement, and the fact that it permitted a level of dolphin mortality which was higher than it was in practice. For example, seiners were permitted by the Agreement to kill up to 19,500 dolphins in 1993, when the actual deaths that year were recorded as 3,601.

In 1995, a year after *Tuna Dolphin II*, five major environmental groups (including Greenpeace and the World Wildlife Fund) conducted negotiations with the Mexican government, leading to an agreement between the 12 major fishing countries in the ETP. This agreement, known as the Panama Declaration, was an attempt to consolidate the improvements gained under the La Jolla Agreement, and to encourage non-US fishers to stay within its scheme in the face of their increasing frustration with continued lack of access to the US tuna market despite their considerable success in lowering dolphin mortality. The parties to the Panama Declaration agreed to accept the IDCP under the La Jolla Agreement as a binding legal commitment, provided that two conditions were fulfilled. First, the USA would have to lift its import ban on tuna if it was caught in compliance with the IDCP (including its permitted mortality limits). Secondly, US legislation would have to be changed so that the meaning of 'dolphin-safe' labelling included tuna caught by dolphin setting, provided that no dolphins were observed being killed. Pressure was put on the USA to implement these legislative changes by the threat of various Latin American countries to pull out of the IDCP and the potential threat of a resulting increase in incidental dolphin deaths.

By 1995 onwards, therefore, there was considerable motivation for the USA to amend its legislation in order to acknowledge and reward the improvements in dolphin mortality that had been achieved by foreign tuna fishers. A number of bills were proposed in Congress that culminated in the passing of the International Dolphin Conservation Program Act of 1997 (Public Law 105-42). The debate leading up to the Act, both inside Congress and outside, revealed strong divisions of opinion. The Act represents a compromise that removes tuna import prohibitions against states who comply with the International Dolphin Conservation Program under the auspices of the IATTC. It also provides that the definition of 'dolphin-safe' will be altered in the future to include tuna caught by dolphin setting if observers certify that no dolphins were killed or seriously injured during their chase and encirclement, but only if a research study indicates that no long-term harm will be caused to dolphin populations by the dolphin-setting technique.

Legal issues before the GATT Panels in the Tuna–Dolphin dispute

The legal provisions that formed the basis of the complaints by Mexico and the EEC were Article XI and Article III of the GATT. Article XI prohibits the use of import restrictions and the US bans were therefore *prima facie* in violation of this provision. The application of Article III, however, was much more controversial. This article contains the so-called national treatment principle, which provides that importing countries will not discriminate in their treatment between domestic and imported 'like products'. There must be no protective effect or intention to provide protection for the domestic goods. The provision relates to a range of internal measures, such as any affecting the sale and distribution of goods, which would include the US conditions for the sale of tuna.

The key argument under Article III related to the meaning of 'like product' and it highlighted a fundamental disagreement between trade lawyers and environmentalists. The USA argued that all tuna caught in the ETP, including those caught by US tuna fishing boats, were subject to the same restrictions. The national treatment principle was therefore satisfied because there was no discrimination against tuna imported from other countries. However, both of the GATT panels found that Article III referred only to 'products as such', by which they meant that any discrimination between products had to be based purely on differences in their physical characteristics. Where products were closely similar or identical physically, they were by definition 'like products' and any discrimination between them on other grounds would automatically constitute a failure to afford national treatment to imports that were entitled to receive it. Thus, there was no scope for discriminating against products on the basis of their production or process method (PPM) and a method of fishing which was being targeted on environmental grounds could therefore not be tackled by trade restrictions under the GATT rules (GATT Panel Report 1991, paras. 5.10–5.11; GATT Panel Report 1994, para. 5.8).

The USA, having lost the argument on Articles XI and III, raised possible defences under Article XX. The two most relevant defences were paragraph (b), which provides that trade restrictions must be 'necessary to protect human, animal or plant life or health', and paragraph (g), which provides that they must be measures 'relating to the conservation of exhaustible natural resources if such measures are made effective in conjunction with restrictions on domestic production or consumption'. As defences, the burden of proof lay on the state relying upon them, and they had to be construed narrowly.

Although the jurisdictional reach of Article XX(b) and (g) is not conclusively decided by this wording, the panels took the view that neither paragraph permitted a state to take measures which were designed to protect the environment outside its own domestic interests. At most, states could enact and enforce measures within their jurisdiction, including their fishing fleets in the high seas. But they could not use trade measures which would only indirectly achieve their environmental objective by coercing other states to adopt a standard which was not mutually agreed (GATT Panel Report 1991, paras. 5.27–5.28; GATT Panel Report 1994, paras. 5.26–5.27). This interpretation, along with that of Article III, automatically excludes the consideration of a large number of ethical considerations by focusing on potential direct harm to the state or its immediate environment. It emphasises property rights in that it protects the right of other states to exploit shared resources in the quantity and manner that they choose. This is fundamentally an instrumental view of nature which assumes a basic right to exploit natural resources, although it also accommodates any desire on the part of states to exercise self-restraint in their own acts – a form of enlightened anthropocentrism or, perhaps, virtue ethics.

The Role of Ethical Values in the Conduct of the Tuna–Dolphin dispute

Even assuming that states are by their very nature capable of ethical behaviour, the discourse employed in their international legal relations is only occasionally located in ethical concepts. When ethical approaches are made explicit, they tend to occur during the negotiation of policy and principle, in the justification of state practice leading towards a finally binding legal obligation such as *lex ferenda* or 'soft law', or in explanatory clauses in treaty preambles. International environmental law depends heavily on the gradual development of shared values and objectives, and this is reflected in a significant reliance upon soft law and general principles. Where this process has largely already taken place, resulting in agreement on specialised and detailed rules, any ethical values that might have been considered in their development tend to be left unvoiced. In the case of international trade, the decision of what values to protect and what objectives to pursue has already largely been made. As one might expect, therefore, the discourse of the WTO/GATT system is primarily one of rights and duties without reference to ethical analysis.

The actors in the *Tuna–Dolphin* dispute ranged from concerned individuals (represented largely by NGOs) to government representatives (principally from the USA, Mexico and the EEC) to the quasi-judicial dispute panels. As issues were raised, discussed and interpreted, the explicitness of ethical values became progressively diluted as more formalistic legal arguments became increasingly dominant. It is to be expected, therefore, that the legal discourse of the GATT panels in the *Tuna–Dolphin* dispute did not, as a rule, incorporate ethical concepts. Indeed, both panels explicitly distanced themselves from any consideration of the appropriateness of the conservation policies in question. They consciously remained within the strict limits of formalistic reasoning, venturing outside the interpretation of plain words only to ensure that agreed rights and duties were observed.

In finding that the US trade restrictions could not be justified under the GATT, the panels explicitly followed a legalistic interpretation of the provisions based on techniques of *travaux preparatoires*, literalism, purpose and consequences. The nature of the forum itself necessarily dictated what issues the panel could consider and what rules it had to apply. The detailed reasoning of the panels is self-consciously legal in tone and content, and no indication of the ethical grounds for their findings is evident from the reports, other than their dedication to the aims and objectives of the GATT system of free trade. Thus, they denied the relevance of a different set of normative values for the settlement of this particular dispute, which they identified as being limited to the question of compliance with the GATT rules. Both panels acknowledged the right of the USA to determine and implement environmental policies and stated only that such implementation should be done with the agreement of the other parties to the GATT where their mutual rights and obligations were involved (GATT Panel Report 1991, paras. 6.1–6.2; GATT Panel Report 1994, para. 5.42). The ends, in other words, could freely be determined by individual states, whereas the means were limited by commitments previously made. As it turned out, however, the GATT could not allow the ends to justify the means if it involved breaching legally binding obligations.

Some ethical resonance can be found in the arguments of the individual parties to the dispute although, since they were designed and articulated to fit within the discourse of a trade law forum, what ethical references there are seem faint in comparison to the explicit ethical positions taken by the environmental groups who made their views known in the debate following the panel reports. From an ethical point of view, therefore, any attempt to analyse the formulation of the issues at stake and the applicable legal principles as presented by the panels and participating governments is an inherently speculative task. The most that can be attempted is to bring an ethical perspective to the conceptual framing of the arguments in advocacy and adjudication, their discoverable policy motives, and the subsequent actions of the parties.

Analysis of the *Tuna–Dolphin* dispute is complicated by the existence of two issues of debate. The first is the importance of conserving dolphins or protecting them from death or injury. This in itself is complicated by having both conservation and animal rights aspects. The second is the legality of using trade restrictions in order to achieve these aims. In the rhetoric of the NGOs, and to some extent in the defences raised by the USA, the two points are inextricably linked. In the panel report, however, they were deliberately separated and the first point excluded from consideration. This exclusion itself outraged many NGOs and other voices of public opinion, who felt that the ends were so important that they could be used to justify the means.

Participants in the debate outside the panel itself were able to look more closely at the issue of whether it was right to protect dolphins and, as a result, the ethical issues are more clearly laid out in their arguments. To find more explicit suggestions of what ethical issues might underpin the *Tuna–Dolphin* dispute, therefore, it is necessary to look at the arguments presented outside the panel's reasoning, namely the arguments of the parties and the public debate that took place in the wake of the panel reports, both inside and outside the US Congress.

The Arguments of the Parties

The role of ethical considerations in the conduct of argument was raised by the parties in two different ways. First, the USA made an attempt to introduce ethical issues by arguing that the existence and importance of environmental concerns reduced the appropriateness of applying trade rules and achieving a settlement within a trade dispute forum. However, the other parties and the panel itself rejected the US argument, which would have assigned greater priority to an urgent ethical issue than to the protection of free trade or compliance with previously agreed obligations. In any case, Mexico accused the USA of having imposed the tuna restrictions as a protectionist act. The implication was that any arguments based on ethical grounds were a disguise for other motives. Mexico claimed that American tuna fishers had substantially moved their operations from the ETP to other waters and, although this was denied by the USA, that the stiff restrictions under the MMPA had only been introduced after their move.

Secondly, the dispute arose because there was no common agreement about the ethical values to be protected or the means by which any protection was to be effected. One of the major questions of how to interpret Article XX was whether conservation or protective measures could be applied extrajurisdictionally. The USA argued that its measures were necessary in order to make the restrictions imposed on its own fleet effective. It did not say so explicitly, but it was clear that the USA was using its considerable economic strength as an effective weapon with which to coerce foreign fishing fleets to comply with US environmental requirements. The problem, therefore, was that the US measures were unilateral rather than based on a community standard. In support of its stance, the USA claimed that it had tried for over 20 years to reach multilateral agreement on purse seine fishing in the ETP without success. It implies therefore that coercive unilateral acts were acceptable in the light of failure to achieve a community standard. Against this view, the EEC argued that it was important to put a narrow interpretation on the word 'necessary' in Article XX(b) in order to avoid over-emphasis on national values. That is to say, it could not be left entirely or even largely up to individual states to determine what they thought was 'necessary', and the question should therefore be subject to review by the community as a whole (in this case, other GATT contracting parties).

The lack of commonly agreed standards was evident with regard to two issues: the extent to which dolphins should be protected and the ethical justification for killing dolphins as a result of fishing activity. With regard to the first, the parties took a firmly anthropocentric approach in their legal arguments. They all categorised the dolphins as a 'resource', although the USA went further than the other parties by describing them as 'a unique global commons resource' of common interest to all states. The categorisation of dolphins as a resource seems to imply that the major, or sole, value of the dolphins was their capacity for exploitation, but this may be qualified in two ways. First, the word 'resource' is derived from the wording of the defence under Article XX, which refers to the need to conserve 'exhaustible natural resources'. The use of the word might therefore be nothing more than an adoption of terminology appropriate to the forum. Secondly, the type of exploitation for which dolphins may be conserved could be their existence value to human beings. The anti-animal rights connotation of exploitation implied by the term 'resource' may therefore not apply in this context. Even given the most respectful interpretation of dolphins' rights, however, the classification as a resource rests upon an anthropocentric, instrumental view of dolphins.

Mexico challenged the claim that dolphins, which were acknowledged by all the parties not to be endangered, should be considered as 'exhaustible natural resources' for the purposes of Article XX(g). It argued that the phrase only referred to non-renewable sources; it could not encompass anything living because any species was liable to extinction in circumstances which were beyond the control of humanity. It did not make sense to say that states were able to take trade measures to achieve an end that was not, in essence, within their control. This can be seen as a consequentialist view under which protecting dolphins would not be ethically supported; this argument would not, however, invalidate a rights-based or virtue approach.

The USA did not accept this argument. It pointed out that dolphins would become extinct if a high rate of mortality continued. In any case, it argued, it would be absurd to suggest that a species must be in danger of extinction before it could be protected under Article XX(g). (This is the 'deathbed conservation' problem discussed in Chapter 9.) Otherwise, there would be no point in introducing conservation measures which, once they had successfully deflected the danger of extinction, would immediately expose the species to the danger from which it had just been saved. The USA was therefore asserting that dolphins had a right not to be killed or that they possessed a value to humans that made their deaths wrongful in itself.

From this it might be inferred that the USA placed value on each individual dolphin life, perhaps on the basis of animal rights. However, the MMPA restrictions were based on permitted levels of dolphin kills, amounting to a total of 20,500 at the time of the Mexican complaint with an ultimate goal of zero kills to be sought at some time in the future. This suggests an ecocentric ethic. Mexico pointed out that a country had two options. It could try to protect animals as an entire species, which would only make the US restrictions necessary if the species as a whole was in danger of extinction. This was not the case for the dolphins in the ETP as the US itself had acknowledged. Or it could try to protect individual members of a species, which meant that it should demand no deaths at all. Since the US legislation was based on keeping dolphin deaths to a permitted minimum, the US position was inherently illogical and could not be maintained on an ethical or any other basis. Mexico therefore argued that Article XX(b) only provided for the protection of humans, animals and plants as a population, not as separate individuals.

Whether it was accepted that dolphins should be protected as a species or as individuals, it was clear that there was a certain ranking implicit in the parties' recognition of values. Thus, for example, the US displayed certain preferences. It chose to protect the welfare of individual dolphins as being more important than the welfare of Mexican fishermen who would be required to get rid of their present fishing equipment, spend more money buying different equipment, and reduce their catches and their income by changing their fishing techniques. In addition, the US was only interested in the protection of the dolphins and expressed no concern for the tuna, thus revealing its anthropocentric stance given that dolphins are generally regarded as attractive to humans whereas tuna are not. In doing so, it was making judgments about the relative worth of dolphins and tuna, and the welfare of dolphins as opposed to the welfare of Mexican fishermen.

Another aspect of the argument over the right way to approach the question of purse seine fishing concerned the ethical justification for killing dolphins. Much of the US argument in support of the import bans was based on the virtue ethics idea of the 'needless' nature of the dolphin deaths. In other words, dolphins should not be killed simply as 'innocent bystanders' and, since there was technology available which could easily reduce dolphin mortality, many of the dolphin deaths which occurred at the hands of foreign fishers were avoidable and therefore wasteful. This in itself was seen by the US to be ethically wrong; it is worth pointing out in this context that many legal systems, including English law, do not prohibit the incidental killing of animals in the course of lawful human activity.

Indeed Mexico claimed that the killing of dolphins during purse seining was purely incidental and was therefore not wrongful. However, the US pointed out that killing of dolphins while tuna fishing was deliberate in that the dolphin were targeted and the nets were specifically set around them in order to catch the tuna below. In other words, it would be misleading to say that dolphin kills were simply incidental since they were inherent in the fishing method as practised by countries like Mexico.

The Congressional Debates

There was, unsurprisingly, an intense public debate after the panel reports had become public. One part of this debate was conducted in the US legislature over a series of bills proposed in order to accommodate the GATT rulings and to implement the La Jolla Agreement and Panama Declaration. Opposition to the bills outside and inside the US Congress was fierce, but matched by the determination of its proponents to see it made law.

In general, both sides appeared to have been genuinely committed to the goal of dolphin protection but were divided on the means to be employed to achieve this goal. The original question to be decided appeared to be a relatively simple one, namely how best to continue to fish for tuna while at the same time protect dolphins. However, it became very clear after the GATT panel reports that the issue could not be put so simply. The question of tuna fishing and its effects on other species of marine life as argued in these debates therefore demonstrates the extreme difficulties involved in protecting one species from killings during the exploitation of another resource of value to humans within a complex ecosphere.

Part of the concern behind the new legislative proposals was the likelihood that the US would ultimately be required to comply with the

GATT dispute settlement finding. Although both existing panel reports could be blocked by the USA, the new dispute settlement procedure would mean that a similar finding by a WTO panel would almost certainly become binding on the USA. In addition, there was concern that the progress already achieved through the voluntary La Jolla Agreement and the Panama Declaration would be lost if the USA proved inflexible in the face of demands to soften its legislative stance.

Besides these rather practical considerations, the law as it stood raised considerable ethical difficulties. Some of its consequences were both unintended and unpredicted. Restrictions on dolphin setting had apparently led to an increase in the use of two other means of catching tuna, namely log setting and school setting. Tuna like to swim under logs and other debris which float on the water and log setting involves encircling the floating material with the purse seine nets to catch the tuna swimming below. School setting is the encirclement of shoals of tuna that are found swimming freely in the sea. Unfortunately, both methods result in a high rate of bycatch, that is, the killing of other species such as sharks and seaturtles and the taking of immature tuna. Some of these species are endangered, and it is possible that catching immature tuna which have not yet reproduced will also eventually affect the viability of the tuna stocks themselves. In other words, attempts to protect dolphins were not just making life difficult for tuna fishers, but actually causing damage to other species.

At the same time, fishing techniques had been developed which successfully reduced the killing of dolphins, particularly the letting down of the back of the nets to allow dolphins to escape. Dolphin setting was therefore no longer as directly dangerous to dolphins as it had been earlier. By the time of the debate that followed the *Tuna–Dolphin* panel reports, therefore, the ethical issues had shifted to a significant degree and posed rather different policy questions.

In terms of the legislation, there were two issues to be addressed. One was the question of whether the ban on imported tuna could continue on the same basis, and the other was what method of fishing could be used for tuna sold as 'dolphin-safe'. The law at that time prohibited both the import of tuna caught as a result of dolphin sets and the labelling of such as 'dolphin-safe'. The proposed changes in the meaning of 'dolphin-safe' would allow dolphin setting, provided that it was certified that no dolphin deaths had occurred. Tuna fishing would be monitored through a system of observers, one of whom would be present on each fishing vessel. Any observed death of a dolphin during the process would exclude any catch taken on that trip from using the 'dolphin-safe' label. In other words, the existing legislation focused on the method of fishing by prohibiting the system of dolphin setting altogether, which might mean that dolphins were killed by other fishing techniques but that the resulting catch of tuna would still qualify for the 'dolphin-safe' label. The proposed legislation, on the other hand, was designed to target the actual killing of dolphins regardless of the method employed.

As suggested above, private and non-governmental groups and individuals were far more explicit in raising ethical issues in their arguments, both before and after the *Tuna–Dolphin* reports, since they were debating in the public sphere without the limitations of the more legalistic forum of the GATT and its dispute settlement panels. None the less, many of the ethical approaches adopted by such groups and individuals were assumed rather than defended by *a priori* argument. What follows, therefore, is an identification of the ethical views and assumptions that appeared to be at the root of most of the discussion.

The Role of Ethics in the Congressional Debates

It is not clear from the record how important the ethical arguments were to each Congressional speaker, or the extent to which they might have been used in order to persuade reluctant listeners, both in the Congress and outside. In other words, it was possible that ethical considerations were genuinely at the root of some of the speeches or that they were merely used to disguise or supplement viewpoints which were essentially economically or politically based. Even the environmental groups involved in the debate could not be assumed to be entirely concerned with environmental values, bearing in mind their need for financial support and their strategic choices about influencing policy decisions from within mainstream political institutions. At least two of them were explicitly accused of adopting their positions out of financial motivation, a charge which was made in return against one of the environmental groups opposing the bill (Cunningham, 1996, 1997; Marshall, 1997). Accusations were also made that the proposals for change were being made purely as a result of pressure from other countries – a political point, perhaps, but one that might be turned into a question of whether the legislature was in fact free to act ethically in its own right.

One of the most notable characteristics of the debates, therefore, was the inextricable link between the ethical and the political, with the result that the distinction between ethical positions and other policy considerations was significantly blurred. Some speakers simply used non-ethical arguments as a means to persuasion, leaving their main motivation ambiguous. Even those speakers who most strongly argued for a high level of protection of dolphins usually acknowledged what the effects would be in other policy spheres, such as the possible reaction of other countries or the likely effect on American jobs. Most speakers argued firmly for one view, with little ambivalence about the conflicting values and arguments that permeated the debate as a whole. However, some did make a plea for compromise and the achievement of practical results rather than being guided by extreme views (including, presumably, ethical views). One speaker suggested that the choice was between 'ideological purity and practical impact' and that, while it would feel good to vote for a measure which would prevent any dolphins becoming entangled in nets, other considerations such as non-co-operation by foreign fishers and loss of other species through bycatch had to be taken into account as a matter of practicality (Boehlert, 1996).

In other words, the ethical arguments employed in the Congressional debates were used for their rhetorical power, and some were very likely not the most important basis for the speaker's position. The motives which might have been behind some of the ethical rhetoric included the desire to protect or create jobs, and it is notable that the final Act was endorsed by major trade unions whose primary concerns may be assumed to have been their members' livelihood.

An example of how the proponent of dolphin protection used a number of different reasons combining ethics, politics, social policy and economics was given by Senator Boxer in her defence of the existing legislation and its definition of 'dolphin-safe'. She gave four justifications for the law as it stood:

— First, for the consumers, who were opposed to the encirclement of dolphins with purse seine nets and wanted guarantees that the tuna they consume did not result in harassment, capture and killing of dolphins;
— Second, for the US tuna companies, who wanted a uniform definition that would not undercut their voluntary efforts to remain dolphin safe;
— Third, for the dolphins, to avoid harassment, injury and deaths by encirclement; and
— Fourth, for truth in labelling (1996, 1997).

The first suggests that the original legislation was passed in order to implement the community's wishes based, presumably, on a common ethical choice. It would therefore rest on a utilitarian basis and, in turn, on the enlightened anthropocentrism or virtue ethics of consumers. The second is an economic issue which was concerned with making it easier for companies who had already made an ethical choice to continue their practices. It may be questioned, of course, whether their original change of policy was indeed truly ethical or merely a response to market forces, and whether the need to assist them in continuing their policy confirms this suspicion. Such a justification for an import ban therefore directly raised the question of whether the ban was primarily protectionist in nature. The third justification appears to recognise rights inherent in the dolphins themselves. In this case, the US Congress would have appointed itself their representative, although it might also mean that the legislature itself (representing the American community) had recognised and constituted a legally enforceable protective regime for anthropocentric purposes. The final justification may be seen as an ethical position going beyond the simple question of protecting dolphins, and can also be interpreted as a point of constitutional law, political desirability or an economic condition for a properly functioning free market.

The Ethical Issues in the Congressional Debates

The activity at the heart of the debate, namely tuna fishing, is a good example of a widely accepted right to exploit a resource. Running throughout the public discussion was a belief that tuna fishing was a legitimate form of exploitation. (This would not necessarily be true in some personal belief systems.) Tuna were therefore never considered as having a right to life or a right not to suffer in the process of being caught. The only concern expressed about the well-being of tuna was about the possibility of driving them to extinction as a result of catching immature tuna in log and school sets (e.g. Goss, 1996). In other words, the only problem with regard to tuna was the possible loss of viable stocks to exploit. The right to exploit tuna and the superiority of human interests was unquestioned, at least in so far as taking food was concerned (Gilchrest, 1997).

According to one speaker, the right to exploit meant that it was perfectly reasonable that people should not only want jobs exploiting tuna (and incidentally posing a threat to dolphins), but also to have a certain quality of life. Thus, he supported the proposed legislation on the grounds, *inter alia*, that it would 'protect the livelihood of individuals that fished throughout the Pacific Ocean, especially the eastern tropical Pacific Ocean, to pay their mortgages and raise their children and have a quality of life and standard of living that all of us would want to achieve' (Gilchrest, 1997). Since his view also incorporated the need to protect dolphins, he acknowledged that there was no absolute right on either side to exploit or be free from exploitation and so, as an ethical position, it might be identified as a form of enlightened anthropocentrism.

More controversial, of course, was the question of whether this right to exploit tuna could justify the incidental killing of dolphins. (The question of directly exploiting dolphins did not arise in the context of this particular debate.) The main questions were whether dolphins had an absolute right to be protected from death or injury, either as individuals or as a species, whether limits on dolphin kills should be derived from other principles such as proportionality, self-restraint and precautionary action, and whether dolphins should be given greater protection than other species.

No Congressional speaker argued against the protection of dolphins in these debates, and most speakers explicitly or implicitly favoured the goal of achieving zero mortality. Some made it clear that dolphin kills should be kept to the lowest possible level by criticising the Panama Declaration and the proposed legislation for permitting a threshold of 5,000 dolphin deaths a year although in practice dolphin deaths were already much lower than that figure. Some of these speakers, and others who supported the bill, were prepared to accept a permitted level of dolphin kills and a movement towards the goal of zero mortality over a period of time. On the other hand, there was also a strong strand of argument which entirely rejected the acceptability of any dolphin death occurring. Some of the lobbyists against the return of dolphin setting took this as their starting point. They wanted zero dolphin kills immediately, and were frustrated by the fact that the problem of continuing dolphin mortality now lay with foreign fishing boats beyond the reach of US jurisdiction. They would have to wait for US commercial pressure to have its effect, and did not want to make concessions until their desired goal had been completely achieved. In practical terms, therefore, they had to accept that it would take time to achieve zero mortality, but their ethical standpoint was that dolphin kills should stop immediately.

When looked at closely, however, the difference between those that accepted a level of kills while working towards zero mortality and those who wanted zero mortality immediately was not necessarily as great as first appeared. When the former group argued that dolphin setting with an observer system and a no-death requirement would be a more effective means of protecting dolphins, they were largely arguing about the most practical method of achieving zero dolphin mortality. The question of zero mortality and the need to protect the life of each individual dolphin was therefore a value shared by most of the protagonists, based on enlightened anthropocentrism or a narrow spectrum of animal rights.

Other participants in the debate, however, explicitly based their arguments on an acceptable level of dolphin kills calculated according to their impact on the future viability of dolphin populations. For example, a letter from a group of scientists presented to Congress stated that the permissible level of kills provided for under the Panama Declaration was low enough to allow dolphin populations to grow substantially. The limit of 5,000 kills a year would represent 0.1 per cent of the estimated population and, since the mortality rate had already fallen below that level, they considered it to be 'below levels of biological significance' (Bilbray, 1996). Another version of this idea was that the deaths of 'an extremely small number of dolphins' was acceptable if they made it possible to conserve tuna stocks, avoid needless bycatch of other species, and comply with international obligations (Kolbe, 1997). The approach of this group appeared to be an ecocentric one, that no irreversible harm should be done to dolphin populations but that individual dolphin kills were otherwise ethically acceptable. When it was convenient to reach a zero level of mortality, all other things being taken into account, this would be desirable but was not ethically imperative.

There was another view that accepted that killing was not an absolute wrong but, in accordance with the virtue ethics perspective, held that causing death or injury to dolphins should not be wasteful or needless. Thus, one speaker used the phrases, 'senselessly killed', 'senseless slaughter' and 'needless massacre' (Biden, 1997). The concepts of 'senseless' or 'needless' rely upon anthropocentric views of the rightness of acts, and acknowledge that any right to exploit is limited to methods which achieve the desired results with the fewest incidental consequences on other species. It suggests a belief that there is a duty not to waste resources and that human acts should be guided by principles of proportionality and self-restraint.

The question of what level of protection was owed to dolphins was not, of course, to be considered in isolation. Other species were involved because of the problem of bycatch, and this immediately gave rise to the problem of the comparative value of dolphins to species other than tuna. It might have been a relatively simple question had the choice been between the death of dolphins set against the death of other animals and fish. It was, however, made more complicated by the fact that some of the other species whose members were being killed in preference to dolphins were actually endangered, whereas the dolphins at issue were not. That fact alone would have significantly shifted the ethical problems involved. The final complication, however, was that these other species were not being threatened to avoid killing dolphins (accepting for the time being that dolphin deaths could be effectively prevented by the proposed scheme), but instead to prevent dolphins being subjected to the stress of the chase and encirclement by nets before being released.

One strong reaction to this choice was, of course, that capturing dolphins but letting them escape would be more desirable than the high rates of incidental killing of other species and the possible endangering of tuna stocks as a result of taking immature tuna. Limited harm to one species should not be allowed to trump irreversible harm to another (Gilchrest, 1997).

This view was not, however, universally held. Some maintained that dolphins should still be assigned a higher value than other species because they were not persuaded by the bycatch problem. In some cases, this was because they were not convinced that there was sufficient scientific evidence that it constituted a serious threat to those species (Boxer, 1996, 1997) or because they believed that it had been raised as an issue to serve a political purpose (Miller, 1997a). Others felt that a return to dolphin setting would inevitably result in dolphin deaths and injuries, and they were not convinced that the observer system would be able to record them or would result in effective enforcement action (Boxer, 1996, 1997; Biden, 1997). On balance, therefore, they were not persuaded that the bycatch problem was sufficient to warrant the risk to the dolphins. This view did not necessarily mean that they considered dolphins as a species to be superior to other species, but clearly gave higher value to individual dolphins than to the individuals of other species. In other words, they would prefer to see the death of turtles, sharks and other individual animals or fish rather than the death of a dolphin, at least until they could be convinced that those other species were genuinely endangered. They therefore favoured one species over another (speciesism) but could be swayed on an ecocentric basis.

Even some of those who did accept that there was a serious problem of bycatch still felt that there was an overriding need to protect the dolphins from the stress caused by the chase and encirclement by nets even if followed by release. They explicitly gave a higher value to protecting dolphins from stress than to the actual death of other species or the threat to tuna stocks by the catching of immature tuna. There were two principal reasons why it could be argued that dolphins should not be subject to stress by chase and encirclement. One was that the stress would lead to physical harm which might result in individual deaths and even threaten the ability of dolphins to survive as a species. The other was that it was cruelty to a species capable of suffering.

As mentioned earlier, the chase preceding the deployment of a net is carried out at high speed by helicopters and speedboats, sometimes using explosives, until the dolphins are too tired to continue swimming. It is probable that the same group of dolphins can be involved in this process several times in the same day. Mothers can become separated from their calves, while exhaustion and stress may cause injury, death or reduction of the ability to reproduce (Myrick, 1996). Whether this caused suffi-ciently dangerous levels of stress to justify the continued ban on dolphin setting proved surprisingly controversial. Two different scientific reports presented to Congressional committees came to opposite conclusions as to whether there was evidence of lasting damage caused by the stress of chase and encirclement. One speaker therefore argued that the alleged stress caused to dolphins by chasing and encirclement could not form the basis of policy decisions because of the lack of scientific knowledge (Gilchrest, 1997). Another speaker, a marine scientist, felt that the scientific evidence pointed towards clear physical changes caused by stress and, in any case, it should be assumed that dolphins were significantly affected by it until proved otherwise. However, he still felt the need to represent the question in human terms, on the assumption that such an exercise would allow us to 'know' what it was like for the dolphins on the basis of 'common sense'. Thus the audience was invited to imagine,

> '. . . a mixed group of unwilling people to run on foot, for half-an-hour, over an unavoidable course through scattered areas devoid of oxygen for short distances. The humans are driven by fear of injury or death to run ahead of armored vehicles. These tanks are moving at unrelenting speeds of 12 to 15 miles per hour, detonating small explosive charges near, and maneuvering close to would-be stragglers and escapees to keep the terrified and tiring herd together. The vehicles are studded with intimidating prods or projections and programmed to force the human herd into a confining structure, which itself is forebodingly cramped and unstable and subject to collapse at any moment' (Myrick, 1996).

When this process of chase and encirclement was put in the context of whether tuna caught using such methods should be labelled 'dolphin safe', several speakers argued that this would be extremely misleading for consumers. This point both contained and deflected the issue of cruelty. It was clear that many speakers who argued that consumers would be horrified to know that 'dolphin-safe' tuna had been caught by subjecting dolphins to a high-speed chase until they were exhausted did so because consumers, particularly children, would think it was cruel. However, this argument became much weaker in the face of the competing claims by other species threatened as bycatch and, in the legislation that was finally adopted, it was superseded by concern to avoid damage to dolphin populations as a whole.

The proponents of the new legislation acknowledged that money should be spent on research into the question of dolphin stress and, most importantly, that their proposals should be changed in order to safeguard dolphins from stress if evidence of its existence were to be found (Gilchrest, 1997). Even these speakers, therefore, assigned a very high value to the avoidance of stress to dolphins and were prepared to give a higher priority to that value than to the problem of bycatch of other species. Thus, there was ultimately a convergence between two apparently opposite positions, expressed strongly by those absolutely opposed to dolphin sets and weakly by those willing to be swayed in the light of future scientific evidence. This suggests an instrumentalist view of the issue – both sides wishing to act ethically, but in disagreement about the factual consequences of their policies.

This convergence of views is now contained in the new legislation which delays the introduction of permitted dolphin setting until scientific studies are conducted and there is no evidence of stress causing 'adverse significant effects on any depleted dolphin stock'. Interestingly, there- fore, the question of whether chase and encirclement is cruel (regardless of whether individual physical harm is caused) has now been dropped from the legislation. The only issue is whether it causes a significant number of deaths or failure to reproduce in a stock which is already depleted and may therefore become endangered. The neglect of the cruelty issue may be partly a result of an urgent need to find a political compromise, but may also reflect an ethical choice between saving dolphins from non-fatal suffering and saving other species from death or endangerment.

Another approach put forward to the bycatch problem was the view that the protection of a single species should not take precedence over environmental management of the whole ecosystem (Bilbray, 1996). One speaker put the debate into an international context, namely the efforts within the United Nations to protect the marine environment. 'Wasteful bycatch' represented 'a major threat to biodiversity' (McDer- mott, 1996). This holistic approach was, however, the exception rather than the rule in the public debate.

It is clear from the above discussion that dolphins were unanimously accorded a special status, reflected in the comparatively high level favoured by most Congressional speakers and other interested parties. This can be termed speciesism, but various ethical positions can be identified in the course of the public debate which might explain how this came about.

Dolphins appear to have been classified as resources, albeit in need of particular protection. The term resources does not, however, appear to have excluded a recognition of a wide range of values, including aesthetic and existence values, as justifying the protection of dolphins. Speakers that expressly considered the issue of whether they should be protected at all (as opposed to how much they should be protected) often did so by reference to the special nature of dolphins and their attractiveness to humans. These speakers took an enlightened anthropocentric view of dolphins, based on human values. Other speakers argued that they should be given less protection because of the effects of the dolphin-set- ting ban on other species as bycatch, and therefore took a directly instrumentalist approach on the basis of conflicting interests.

For the most part, the special status of dolphins was simply assumed by speakers, even by those who expressed the need to separate the emotional appeal of dolphins from the need to look at the whole ecosystem from a scientific point of view. Even those who claimed to take an ecocentric approach could acknowledge that dolphins were pretty, swam well and made the sea more attractive by their presence (Young, 1997). Others spoke of their feelings for dolphins, that they cherished, treasured or loved them (Goss, 1996; Gibbons, 1996). This is a common theme in individual views expressed on the Internet where dolphins are described, for example, as spiritual beings or as 'cute little dolphins' with personal names. Anthropomorphism of animals, with particular emphasis on 'cute' species and individual members given names and attention by the media, such as Keiko (the whale used in the film *Free Willy* for whom a successful campaign for release into the sea has been vigorously fought), has been fiercely criticised by one activist campaigner who argues that such campaigning draws attention and crucial resources away from the real problems of less charismatic species and anonymous mass killings (Watson, 1995). However, the anthropomorphic identification with species such as dolphins is a powerful force. It can be seen, for example, in the Flipper 'dolphin-safe' label introduced by an environmental organisation, Earthtrust, which pictures a friendly-looking dolphin with a smile on its face and a fin raised in greeting.

In Congress, this anthropomorphic identification with dolphins was very evident among some speakers. For example, the representative for American Samoa referred to them as 'one of the most beautiful mammals in the world', thus placing their appeal firmly in their satisfying of human aesthetic senses (Faleomavaega, 1996a). He had recently voyaged in a reconstruction of an ancient Polynesian canoe, using traditional navigational methods. In the context of going back to ancient, pre-industrial ways, he had discovered various aspects of dolphins that explained their special appeal to humans. He assigned to them a partnership role as he learned about 'the interaction among those who live in the sea and those who live on and above it'; they had a 'gentle, helpful nature' and were 'of tremendous psychological benefit'. Not only were they not threatening to humans, they had sometimes saved human lives. Humans had, for their part, betrayed dolphins by killing them and this had been made worse by the fact that they were not killed for food but merely because they swam with tuna (Faleomavaega, 1996b). It should be noted, however, that he did not go on to consider the teleological view of this relationship with tuna, i.e. that it might be their natural function to guide predators to tuna and to perish with them. It can also be pointed out that there is increasing evidence that dolphins do not necessarily have gentle natures and that they can sometimes be dangerous to humans. Neither are they necessarily as intelligent as some have suggested (Klinowska, 1994).

The same speaker gave added value to dolphins by reference to the sacred status of dolphins in Polynesian history which he suggested arose from the same knowledge of dolphins as modern humans are only now acquiring. What is more, ancient Polynesians would rather have died of starvation than kill a dolphin (Faleomavaega, 1996b). This cultural reference is of particular importance, since it reminds us that environmental and ethical values are essentially cultural constructs. It may therefore be instructive to mention here another cultural value that can be examined as a contrast. The Makah Nation, a tribe of indigenous people living in Washington State in the US, has recently sought the right to kill four grey whales a year in order to carry out religious and cultural practices. Canadian Inuits are planning to hunt bowhead whales as part of their ancient cultural tradition. These claims, made by those who are normally called in aid by environmental activists, have caused consternation in some quarters and challenged some assumptions long held by the environmental movement.

The representative from American Samoa also asserted the need (in line with Stone, see below Chapter 12) for dolphins to have a representative, a post that he and some others claimed to fulfil during the debates. He chose to give a message on their behalf which was a warning, vague in its import but specific in its menace, that failure to protect dolphins would lead to 'mankind' being 'held accountable for its actions'. (Faleomavaega, 1996b). It is interesting to speculate what other 'representatives' might decide were the thoughts and desires of dolphins, though a brief review of published opinions from different quarters suggests that they might like anything from larger swimming tanks to the ability to communicate spiritual guidance to devoted disciples.

Since protagonists offered justifications for their views ranging from enlightened anthropocentrism to extreme reverence, how could a solution to the practical problem of tuna fishing be reached? Ultimately, it was decided by reference to American consumers and their ethical preferences. Thus a utilitarian approach was decisive, assuming that it was genuinely known what the majority of consumers actually wanted. The reliance on consumers was almost always linked with the question of whether they were given sufficient knowledge to make a choice and the focus therefore turned to the question of truth in labelling. In ethical terms, of course, lack of accurate knowledge would, or could, have the effect of turning the intended ethical act of buying tuna which had been caught without any cruel or physically harmful effects on the dolphins into an act which actually promoted harm to dolphins. In other words, a consequentialist view would mean that the information implied in the label 'dolphin-safe' would be crucial to the ethical position taken by consumers.

Consumers were always referred to in the debates as a homogenous body, with no variation in ethical views or behaviour among its members even though it was extremely likely that some, perhaps many, consumers were not interested in, or might have been ignorant of, the issues surrounding the catching of tuna. They might have actively preferred to buy tuna if it was cheaper, which would probably be the case if no efforts were made to avoid injury to dolphins. They might simply have been misled about the issues.

Any doubts on this scare were trumped by references to the role played by American schoolchildren in the campaign to prevent dolphin setting. American schoolchildren, it was said, led the demand by American consumers for dolphins to be protected (Miller, 1997b). To change the meaning of the 'dolphin-safe' label would be a 'fraud perpetrated on America's kids!' (Stark, 1996). The implication here was that the ethical views and beliefs of children were more authoritative, more precious or more in need of satisfying than those of other actors, most especially foreign fishermen. The need not to mislead children, as well as other consumers, was a strong theme in the Congressional debate. This is largely an emotive argument, but it might be classified as an aspect of virtue ethics. It suggests that adult ethical actors should be led by the feelings of right and wrong of younger, less experienced members of community who might be more 'pure' in their motives. A cynic might suggest, of course, that the key role of children in the sale of tuna in the USA is that of consumer and that it was important not to alienate them from the idea of eating tuna altogether.

Even environmental groups, who might be expected to above political or commercial pressures, were ambivalent in their approach. The Panama Declaration had been negotiated by five major environmental organisations, but others ranged themselves against it and the proposed implementing legislation. The division between environmental groups broadly indicates the difficulty in determining a clear ethical approach to the complex problem presented by tuna fishing, assuming that the fishing activity itself and the need to use nets were accepted as legitimate. It neatly illustrates the problem of knowledge and of representation of non-human species. None of these groups knew precisely what any of the species involved actually wanted, but they were guided by their own views of how species should be ranked.

The reasons for favouring dolphins over other species clearly spring from a strong affinity with dolphins, most often seen in the assertion of dolphins' intelligence, gentleness, beauty, humour, altruism and their ability to communicate with other species, including humans. These characteristics have long been assumed by dolphin supporters, but are now being doubted by scientists. It remains to be seen whether a shift in conventional thinking about the nature and capacities of dolphins will be sufficient to change the strong anthropocentrism which has so far characterised the *Tuna–Dolphin* debate.

Summary

1. The regime of international trade is based on utilitarianism, and the triumph of the GATT rules over environmentalists' attempts to use trade restrictions to further their objectives is essentially a utilitarian result. However, this is partly because those rules are institutionalised by formal rules and procedures. The GATT panels were unable to extend their consideration to other preferences in so far as they existed outside the narrow confines of the legal dispute put before them. They therefore deliberately excluded any ethical considerations other than those implicit in the GATT rules and the purpose of the international trade regime.

2. Although ethical rhetoric was more evident in the public debate outside the GATT panel hearings and reports, distinctions between ethical and other policy views, and between ethical and factual arguments, became extremely blurred in the debate itself. Even arguments that appeared to be clearly ethical in nature could easily be suspected of disguising other policy motives. However, some clearly defined ethical issues can be identified.

3. All groups agreed that, where possible, dolphins should not be killed. Some went further and argued that no dolphin should be killed, thus assigning an absolute value to the individuals of the species. Other groups, who accepted that some kills were inevitable until techniques and procedures could be developed to eliminate them completely, still assigned value to individual dolphins by asserting their need for protection from needless death or injury, despite the absence of any threat of extinction to the dolphins as a species.

4. The principal division of opinion lay in whether the dolphins should be protected, not just from death and physical injury, but the stress resulting from the chase and encirclement. Protection of the dolphins from stress, however, would probably result in the incidental killing of other species, some of them endangered, because of increased log and school setting. Thus the value placed on dolphins by those arguing for the need to avoid harassment and stress would be higher, for example, than the value placed on sea turtles or sharks. The International Dolphin Conservation Program Act of 1997 accepts in principle that the chasing and encirclement of dolphins is preferable to threatening other species, but ultimately it still places a higher value on dolphins by making the change in the dolphin-safe label conditional on there being no significant adverse effects. However, since these effects have to be felt by dolphin popula-

tions as a whole, this is an ecocentric approach rather than one that values individual members of the species.

5.   The views identified above are anthropocentric and instrumental. There is little sign of a deontological approach. Those who argued for superior protection to be given to dolphins did so on the basis of a system of human values that could be characterised as speciesism. Others who considered that it was necessary to choose in favour of causing stress to dolphins rather than the death of other species took an enlightened anthropocentric approach by not ranking one species higher than another. Some of this group, however, might still have given dolphins a superior ranking but for the fact that the other species faced possible extinction. The need to avoid irreversible harm may trump other considerations. This is another product of anthropocentric values that relate to human wishes for certain species to continue to exist in our world and, possibly, extended to include the possible wishes of future generations. If, however, it is proved that the stress levels suffered by dolphins are sufficiently high for them to be threatened with endangerment themselves, the choice between the threatened species is, according to the new legislation, weighted again in favour of dolphins.

Further Reading

Esty, D.C. (1994) *Greening the GATT: Trade, Environment, and the Future* (Washington, D.C.: Institute for International Economics).

GATT Symposium on Trade, Environment and Sustainable Development, Geneva, 10–11 June 1994, *Trade and the Environment*, 28 July 1994.

High   North   Alliance,   Marine   Mammal   Management   Debate   at http://www.highnorth.no/

Kittichaisaree, K. (1993) Using Trade Sanctions and Subsidies to Achieve Environmental Objectives in the Pacific Rim. *Colorado Journal of Environmental Law and Policy*, **4**, 296.

Schoenbaum, T.J. (1992) Agora: Trade and Environment. *American Journal of International Law*, **86**, 700–27.

Schoenbaum, T.J. (1997) International Trade and Protection of the Environment: The Continuing Search for Reconciliation. *American Journal of International Law*, **91**, 268-308.

Weiss, E. (1992) Agora: Environment and Trade as Partners in Sustainable Development. *American Journal of International Law*, **86**, 728.

Workshop

1.   How can the international trade regime as established through the WTO be justified from an ethical point of view? What criticisms can be made against it in the context of environmental protection?

2. Was a GATT panel the appropriate forum in which to settle the *Tuna–Dolphin* dispute? What ethical arguments were excluded as a result?

3. The USA has also prohibited imports of shrimp unless they have been caught with fishing equipment and techniques that avoid killing sea turtles. In 1998, a WTO dispute panel found that this import ban was also in violation of the GATT. The panel's grounds included finding that measures could not be saved under Article XX if they 'undermine the WTO multilateral trading system'. The sea turtles are listed as endangered by the US Endangered Species Act and in CITES. To what extent can this dispute be distinguished from the *Tuna–Dolphin* dispute? Would any differences be crucial from an ethical perspective?

4. The EC has banned the import of furs of animals caught with leghold traps or other trapping methods that do not meet 'international humane trapping standards'. Both the USA and Canada had threatened to bring a complaint before a WTO panel and it was probable that any panel report would find against the EC for the same reasons given in the *Tuna–Dolphin* reports. The dispute has been resolved by an agreement on acceptable standards of trapping, including for example time limits. This has been heavily criticised by animal rights groups as a compromise that legitimates cruelty. Do you agree? To what extent can this dispute be distinguished from the *Tuna–Dolphin* dispute? Would any differences be crucial from an ethical perspective?

5. Many developing countries are openly suspicious of environmental policies being placed on them, either in common areas or in their own territories. This is partly because they believe that there are other more important values to be considered, including economic development, education, and a higher standard of living. What ethical choices are they making? To what extent are Western countries entitled to determine what environmental values should be protected?

354

12 Environmental Rights

The ethical and legal issues that we discussed in earlier chapters come together in the concept of environmental justice. The notion of justice has several meanings but centres upon giving to every person what is due to them. Justice is also associated with equality. In the present context we are concerned with corrective justice in the sense of ensuring that entities that have value have equal access to the legal system so that their claims can be weighed against those of others. We shall be particularly concerned with whether it makes sense to talk about environmental 'rights'. As we have seen, English public law relies heavily on discretion and is not at home with the idea of a 'right' at least in the sense of a fixed entitlement protected by rules. Private law relies on rights but these are intimately bound up with the idea of property.

Legal rights are not the same as moral rights. For our purposes we shall adopt Christopher Stone's definition of a legal right. According to Stone (1996, chapter 1), a legal right has four components:

1. that 'some public authoritative body is prepared to give some amount of review to actions that are inconsistent with that "right"';
2. that the thing that holds the right must 'be able to institute legal actions at its behest';
3. that in granting relief 'the court must take account of injury to it';
4. that 'the relief must run to the benefit of it'.

In this sense a legal right is a procedural notion concerning access to the courts. It does not necessarily mean a fixed entitlement that invariably overrides other concerns. In principle anything can have a legal right provided that there is a spokesperson for its interests. Indeed Stone famously argues that natural objects such as rivers or landscapes should have rights (below p. 369). Environmentalists often object to the use of the language of rights basing their objections on a mixture of ethical and practical grounds that we shall discuss in their context. Legal rights need not be the same as moral rights but the two can support and reinforce each other.

It is more difficult to decide what the basis of a moral right should be. Consequentialist ethics, such as utilitarianism deny the importance of rights as such. They argue that what matters is the sum total of happiness, preferences or welfare, valuing individuals not as ends in themselves but as vessels containing welfare. Utilitarianism is therefore not inconsistent with a holistic ecocentric ethic such as Aldo Leopold's land ethic. Utilitarianism is also used by Singer who focuses on the avoidance of suffering as the basis of an animal welfare ethic. Rights enthusiasts object to this approach for many reasons (see e. g. Regan, 1983, chapter 6), among which is the perception that utilitarianism might be able to justify actions which most people regard as abhorrent, for example performing scientific experiments on people without their consent.

A method used by Regan is that of 'reflective intuition'. This starts from widely shared moral beliefs subjecting them to tests of rationality, consistency and clarity in order to assess their validity. From this perspective for example many people accept Regan's argument that at least the higher animals have rights by analogy with the factors which persuade us that human beings have rights; what Regan calls the capacity for a 'welfare of their own'. It would therefore be 'speciesism', a notion inconsistent with the basic principles of equality and of respect for the individual to give ourselves rights while denying rights to animals. Human welfare is not, of course, the same as animal welfare and the content of the particular rights of different kinds of being need not be the same. Moreover, where rights conflict, some may be more important than others. In this way Regan and other supporters of environmental rights find ways of privileging human beings (see below).

Where you end up depends on where you started. Regan suggests autonomy as a starting point drawing upon established ideas of human rights. Taylor starts from the idea of respect for life and therefore extends moral concern to all living things – teleological subjects of a life – and has to call upon elaborate priority rules in order to produce a coherent scheme. Stone's approach which extends to non-living natural objects seems to be based upon a teleological notion of a proper state of being, supported by a pluralistic approach to moral theory (Stone, 1985).

A further complication is the distinction between positive rights and negative rights. A negative right is a right not to be interfered with, for example freedom of speech. A positive right is a right to a benefit, for example decent housing. Negative rights fall more clearly into the sphere of legal enforcement in that positive rights involve public spending which is not easily justiciable (see e. g. *R.* v. *Cambridge Health Authority ex parte B* [1995] 2 All ER 129). Environmental rights may be both positive and negative. Wenz (1988) suggests that the distinction between positive and negative rights is one way of marking the limits of our duty towards animals. According to the negative rights perspective, we must not harm animals but need not provide welfare services for them or protect them against each other. Principle 1 of the Stockholm Declaration 1972 is an example of a mixture of negative and positive rights. It refers to 'the fundamental Right to.... adequate conditions of life, in an environment of a quality that permits a life of dignity and well being....' (see also Ksentini Report, 1994, beloe p. 379). However, in the environmental context the distinction between positive and negative rights is blurred because we do not have a clear notion of what counts as damage, what interests are worthy of protection and what is the 'right' level of environmental quality. We cannot expect a completely pure environment.

Rights and Duties – Direct and Indirect Duties

Rights and duties are not necessarily two sides of the same coin. It is true that a right presupposes that someone has a duty to give effect to that right, but a duty can exist in isolation without anyone having a corresponding right. A duty might be enforceable by the state through the criminal law and, the notion of right is superfluous. The statutory duty of care owed by a holder of waste under s. 34 EPA to take reasonable measures to prevent waste escaping and to control others in the waste chain (below p. xxx) is a typical example of a duty without a corresponding right. It is enforced by criminal sanctions. By contrast, the deposit of waste without a licence gives rise to a right in the form of a civil action (EPA s.33, s.73(6)). Indeed there can be duties without there being any enforcement mechanism. For example the Resource Management Act 1991 (NZ) s. 17(1) states that 'everyone has a duty to avoid, remedy or mitigate any adverse effect on the environment arising from an activity carried out by or on behalf of that person'. For this reason even if we deny that nature can have rights we might owe duties in respect of nature without having to find a human right holder to fill the gap.

The duties approach is congenial to those environmentalists who regard the notion of rights as insufficiently holistic and excessively confrontational. In *R.* v. *Brown* [1993] 2 All ER 75 at 115, the sado-masochism case, Lord Mustill said that 'emphasis on human duties will often yield a more balanced and sharply focussed for protection for the individual than the contemporary preoccupation with human rights'. There is considerable interest in mediation as a method of resolving environmental conflicts which avoids the absolutism and aggression of the rights approach but which brings other problems. These include uncertainty, a lack of objectivity and perhaps privileging private over public interests (see Harrison, 1997).

Duties might be direct or indirect. The indirect duty argument claims that duties can be owed only to human beings. Therefore we owe duties to other people in respect of the environment but cannot owe duties to the environment itself. The enlightened anthropocentric perspective favours this approach. The most influential version of the indirect duty approach is that of Kant who argues that we should not be cruel to animals but only because being cruel to animals might encourage us to treat human beings cruelly. Only human beings can be valued as ends in themselves other beings are at best instruments of human purposes. Kant and other thinkers, notably Rawls, base their idea of justice upon the consent of autonomous and equal members of a rational community. According to this view, which is endorsed with hesitation by Passmore (1980, p. 115), it makes no sense to talk about rights or duties except between human beings.

According to Regan direct duties can be owed to non-humans who accordingly possess rights. However, only rational beings can possess duties. A moral duty cannot be owed by a being who does not know what a duty is. Thus even if chickens have rights, there is no duty on foxes or other animal predators to respect them. Even duties of strict liability such as those that arise under section 85 of the Water Resources Act 1991 embody a concept of conscious control (see above p. 210).

Regan challenges the indirect duty analysis as arbitrary. Indeed even Rawls regards it as wrong to harm animals but does not clearly indicate why this is the case (Regan, 1983, p. 163; see also Brooman, 1997, p. 99 *et seq.*). Finnis (1980, p. 194) is prepared to be openly speciesist by arguing that human beings are so different from other species as to make the idea of rights appropriate only to humans. However, Darwinian ideas of evolution mean that what counts as making us different may be a subjective matter.

'Difference' does not mean that animals cannot have rights at all. Difference could affect the content of rights in that rights are generated by particular desires or interests. For example animals cannot have political rights or rights based on promises such as contract. On the other hand an animal could have a right to life, freedom and security of habitat and perhaps rights based upon restitution and unjust enrichment. One of Taylor's governing principles, that of 'fidelity' requires that we should not deceive or betray wild animals. This can be compared with the legal concept of a fiduciary duty generated by an equitable right. In the case of domesticated or captive animals the reliance principle can generate rights. Moreover, unlike humans, animals cannot easily be taken to consent to an interference with their rights.

Deontological and Utilitarian Approaches to Rights

A utilitarian would regard the notion of a right as no more than a legal mechanism for the purpose of giving effect to an interest or a unit of welfare the overall aim being to produce the maximum aggregate happiness, welfare or interest satisfaction. From the utilitarian perspective individuals are valued only as units of well being of whatever kind. Bentham famously described the concept of a right other than one created by positive law as 'nonsense on stilts'. As we saw in Chapter 2 the strict deontological approach requires us to respect rights or fundamental interests as ends in themselves whatever the cost. In practice, however, deontological and utilitarian approaches run together. In human rights law, rights are rarely absolute. The law requires us to respect intrinsic rights until a threshold is reached at which the cost of doing so is disproportionate. At this point the right can be overridden by the public interest as expressed in such phrases as necessary in a 'democratic society' or 'compelling governmental interest'. It could be argued that this is utilitarianism in disguise since in order to decide when the threshold is reached we have to balance the right against other goals such as the public interest according to some common denominator such as general well being. We must therefore offer some utilitarian reason why it is desirable for a right to be respected at all. Conversely even where our starting point is utilitarian it is possible, as Mill did, to regard values such as individual equality, autonomy and property as having special weight.

Rights proponents such as Regan regard utilitarianism as defective because it does not necessarily protect animals or indeed any individual being. A utilitarian is dependent on a cost-benefit approach. A utilitarian might justify, say, factory farming on the ground that the overall welfare achieved by adding up the relatively trivial benefits to millions of humans in the shape of jobs and cheap food outweighs the suffering and death of the animals. According to Regan's rights analysis, factory farming and indeed meat eating are always wrong and in most cases animal experimentation is wrong in that a right is infringed with no countervailing right at stake. Weight of numbers is immaterial. What matters is the degree of harm to each individual taken separately.

However, in the famous example of a lifeboat containing four humans and a dog where one individual must be jettisoned, both persuasions would kill the dog. This is because there are two rights in competition. According to Regan a single human life has greater value than that of a dog because of its comparative richness of experience and this is true against one dog or a million. But this argument carries the implication that some human beings, the more intelligent or those with 'superior' capacities to experience life are of greater moral worth than those who are less favoured. The same is true with the Kantian argument that rationality carries a special entitlement to moral consideration. On this basis if the boat contains four poets and a mentally sub-normal person the latter would be tipped overboard. To return to the example of the dog, while it is true that, from a human point of view, the dog has less capacity to experience life, is not the dog equally entitled as any human to enjoy life to the maximum capacity open to it, such as it is?

Advantages of Rights

The rights approach gives particular interests the political and moral high ground and on a legal level confers standing before the courts. To call something a right underlies its importance both legally and politically. Lord Mustil's preference for duties (above, p. 356) seems to overlook the possibility that it might be easier to focus a duty where there is a corresponding right holder with a vested interest in enforcing it. The concept of a right is also a means of accountability since the environment gets an independent voice. A public duty imposed on officials is vulnerable to bias and inefficiency and reliance upon an administrative response to public opinion or pressure group activity may be unreliable. The notion of a right is also valuable in providing a framework for the development of changing values and attitudes.

Christopher Stone's suggestion that rights should be conferred upon natural objects is relevant here (Stone, 1972, 1985, 1996; below p. 369). His proposal includes a list of 'preferred objects' such as habitats subject to a strong presumption against interference. This can operate at the public law level by giving *locus standi* directly to environmental interests. Stone goes further and would also confer private law rights on natural objects. The mechanism for this would be a trust fund. A human being who violates the rights of nature would be required to pay compensation into the fund. Conversely the fund would have to compensate human beings in respect of damage which nature causes to humans. Traditional ideas of causation and responsibility would have to be modified but some existing notions, for example, that of restitution might be a fruitful basis for development.

Objections to Rights

Objections to the notion of environmental rights are of three kinds. First, there are those such as Frey (1983) who deny the validity of the concept of rights regarding a claim of right as a rhetorical cloak for personal preference. However, even if this is true of moral rights, the concept of a legal right as described by Stone (above) has a valid meaning.

Secondly, it has been said that only a human being can have 'rights' (see Passmore, 1980, p. 115 *et seq.* ; Huffmann, 1992; Elder, 1984; Redgwell in Boyle, 1996). According to this view a right is a claim or interest that gives the right holder moral, political or legal power against others which the right holder has a choice whether or not to assert. It is said therefore that a right only makes sense in the hands of an equal being that is knowingly participating in the moral system. The notion of rights, it is said makes little sense, where we, the so-called duty holders, say what those rights are and who should have them. From an enlightened anthropocentric perspective Passmore (1980, p. 116) says that '(t)he idea of "rights" is simply not applicable to what is non-human' although he adds that he is uneasy about the dogmatism of this.

Even if we accept that only human beings can have moral rights, we could argue that it still may be convenient as a technical device to confer legal rights upon animals, etc. even though we may regard this as a fiction. It is often argued, for example, that the device of a company is a convenient fiction that enables us to treat a large organisation as a person separate from its members. The argument that only humans can have rights seems to deny rights to some human beings including young children and the mentally impaired. As we have seen, this is often raised as an objection to anthropocentric arguments.

Thirdly it is said that the rights approach is legalistic, individualistic and self-centred and damages broader ecocentric concerns that stress balance, compromise and harmony between the components of the environment (Theron, 1996). In particular, sustainable development does not easily fit within a rights perspective and the animal rights argument does not place any special value on a species because it is rare.

However, Regan (1983, p. 361) suggests that there will often be no conflict. 'Were we to show proper respect for the rights of the individuals who make up the biotic community, would not the community be preserved?' (p. 363). On the other hand take the case of the red squirrel, the existence of which in the UK is threatened by the proliferation of grey squirrels, an import from the USA. The rights perspective values all right-holders equally and would not be prepared to cull the grey squirrel to save the rare species. Thus the rights approach might threaten the ecological balance by preventing us from destroying predators or from culling excessive populations.

Another objection to the rights approach is that it goes too far (see Wenz, 1988, p. 148). It is said, for example, that if animals had rights we would have to provide them with welfare resources such as housing and medical care and also protect weaker animals against predators. This would destroy the idea of environment as wilderness.

However, it does not follow from the fact that all entities have rights and that the content of each right is the same The rights of each entity depend on the needs of that entity such as they are. Regan (1983) suggests that the main interest of animals is to be left alone and the provision of services to animals would require unacceptable compulsion. Regan also argues that we have no duty to protect animals against predators because animals cannot have duties so that the wolf that attacks the lamb is not infringing the lamb's rights. However, we would certainly feel morally obliged to save a young child against the wolf and we do not know that an animal would prefer to be left alone. Wenz (1988) relies upon a distinction between positive and negative duties arguing that we have negative duties to everyone including animals, but owe the stronger positive duties to help others only to those close to us, in this case a sliding scale of human beings culminating in our families. This is a traditional distinction in human rights law but what is its ethical basis? The good Samaritan would presumably disagree with Wenz.

It has also been objected that the 'interests' of nature are utterly unknowable and that, by giving nature rights, we are merely superimposing our own interests upon natural objects. There is no reason for thinking that nature is good or bad except by reference to human interests (see Sagoff, 1974; Elder, 1984). According to this line of reasoning, enlightened anthropocentric ethics is as far as it is possible to go. Indeed Christopher Stone's main policy suggestions which are to give greater weight to environmental criteria and to extend environmental impact assessment does not require radical philosophical changes in our relationship with nature. We might argue that, as part of nature ourselves, we can make a reasonable attempt to guess what nature's interests are. Although we are prisoners of our human condition and can therefore never know the truth we are at least doing the best we can and being aware of our human biases can try to compensate for them.

Finally, it can be argued that the language of rights is self-defeating in many environmental contexts. Because of the complexity of environmental issues rights are rarely absolute and might be overridden so readily by economic or political concerns as to become discredited. Even Regan accepts that animal rights are weaker than human rights. No right is entirely absolute but it is characteristic of a right, that it should normally override the general welfare.

Weighing Environmental Rights

For the lawyer the most important aspect of environmental ethics is how it affects disputes between competing interests. As we saw in Chapter 1 environmental values are sometimes incommensurable and environmental goods uncombinable. Strictly speaking a right should be an absolute constraint upon the implementation of a social or economic policy but in practice rights usually give way to what the state regards as a good which in utilitarian terms outweighs the right in issue. In the environmental context this approach would load the dice in favour of human concerns because human beings can marshal more preferences than other creatures particularly as humans decide what counts as a preference. An ecocentric version of utilitarianism would seek the good of the ecosystem as a whole. This has unfortunate implications for human beings. It might for example require us to cull the human population. Moderate ecocentrists, however, recognise that, as in the case of a human community, group interests and individual interests have to be balanced and priorities established thus leaving the ecocentric goal merely as one among competing factors. At the anthropocentric extreme, we saw in Chapter 1 that economists claim to find a common denominator of value in human preferences expressed in money terms which can be evaluated using cost-benefit techniques.

Environmental ethics raises the problem of balancing competing interest in a complex form. There are several different kinds of balancing to perform. Stone (1997) calls these:

1. international equity meaning social justice between rich and poor nations;
2. intranational equity meaning social justice between different domestic human groups;
3. species equity meaning the task of balancing the interests of one *non-human* species against another or a species against an individual;
4. intergenerational equity; and
5. planetary equity.

Planetary equity concerns the balance between human interests and those of the rest of nature and is the most obvious setting for policy conflicts. As we have seen there is no common measure with which we can compare the value of a human activity, say cutting down a forest to provide houses, with the interests of the forest. Sometimes, of course, human interests can be combined with biological interests as in the case of a well-managed wildlife reserve. Indeed this is one of the driving forces of sustainable development. In other cases human interests must be sacrificed in order to preserve a species.

Perhaps most difficult of all is species equity which attempts to balance the interests of different non-human species against each other (see Stone, 1996, p. 126). We use human-centred criteria, e.g. rarity or attractiveness or possibly we apply the land ethic so as to favour the species that is most important to the ecosystem. However, as Stone points out it is difficult to respect any particular ecosystem. Nature is constantly replenishing itself so that by destroying one ecosystem we benefit its successor. How do we choose between endangered species and animal welfare? Suppose for example we clean up oil pollution on a beach in order to make life pleasant for hundreds of common seabirds but in doing so destroy rare species of seaweed.

The different ethical perspectives offer a variety of tools which sometimes converge and sometimes conflict with each other but, as we saw in Chapter 11, ethical arguments can be used to mask economic and political self-interest. Moreover the purposes of a given area of law may be subverted by introducing other concerns (see Nolkaemper, 1996). All perspectives face the problem that, when it comes to balancing interests, one way or another they seem to favour human interests without giving a clear justification for so doing. For example, non-anthropocentrists often start by denying that humans as such deserve special moral concern but then go on to rank the interests of living things in an order of priority based on characteristics that humans possess to a greater extent than other beings such as intelligence, complexity sensitivity or versatility or capacity to make moral judgements. It is said that we are not prejudiced in favour of our own species but rather that we (fortunately) happen to possess morally important features in greater abundance than other creatures (see Anderson, 1993; Van De Veer, 1979; Gillroy, 1995, chapter 4; Routley, 1995). In the same way Mill (1861, p. 260) modifies utilitarianism by asserting that some values are more worthy than others:

> 'it is better to be Socrates dissatisfied than a pig satisfied ... and if the pig (is) of a different opinion it is because (it) only knows its own side of the case'.

The line between anthropocentrism and animal rights also becomes blurred in that we may favour animals such as dolphins that appear to be intelligent and conceptualise them as honorary human beings.

There is always a place in the sun for the rulers. As Dobson (1995, p. 54) puts it, even the most radical and egalitarian theories return to home base and find reasons for favouring human interests. And as Stone says (1997, p. 237) 'a non-homocentric argument to preserve biodiversity... has even in philosophical circles, a hard time overcoming counter-arguments to develop which are rooted in urgent, even simply clear human needs. The defence of non-homocentric claims in the political fora is of course that much more formidable.'

Regan and other proponents of animal rights start from a presumption that all right holders deserve equal respect. Where rights conflict, the more important overrides the less important according to the criterion of the extent of the harm (Regan, 1983, p. 286 *et seq.*). Regan suggests that rights can be overridden on the ground of self-defence, punishment, and more controversially in order to present more serious harm to other right holders; the 'miniride' principle. Regan also endorses the 'worse-off' principle under which the rights of many innocent beings can be overridden in order to prevent worse harm to the rights of fewer innocents thus allowing us to kill creatures that threaten our lives or possibly our own health. Thus an innocent being can be sacrificed in order to save another (Regan, 1983, p. 297). This may produce the same result as utilitarianism but for different reasons.

Regan, while preferring animal rights to lesser human interests such as pleasure and non-essential medical treatment, would prefer the life of a single human being to those of any number of animals on the ground that the harm suffered by taking a human life is always greater than that suffered by taking an animal life because of the human's greater intelligence and therefore capacity for experience. The accusation of speciesism has been met by arguing that the favoured qualities of intelligence, etc. do not necessarily apply only to humans and that, if we met them in another being, that being would merit equal treatment (see Regan, 1983, p. 155). However, this argument does not overcome an allegation of *indirect* discrimination which says that we discriminate unlawfully by imposing a requirement or condition that in fact is more difficult to meet by the group discriminated against than by the favoured group. The test of closeness to ourselves has also been justified on the ground that within the human community we owe stronger duties towards our families than towards strangers (Wenz, 1988).

Passmore (1980, chapter 3 and pp. 110–18) takes an enlightened anthropocentric approach, broadly utilitarian but also influenced by virtue ethics according to which animals cannot have rights as such but we owe duties to our human community because of admiration for life and self-interest in the face of ignorance to respect life and to welcome the diversity of nature. The interests of nature can, however, be outweighed by greater goods such as self-defence. Passmore also thinks that we are entitled to prefer important aesthetic and cultural values of our own. The concept of proportionality may be helpful in this context. Proportionality requires that we can override a right only if it is necessary to do so in defence of an important interest and if we do no more harm than is absolutely necessary in order to achieve the goal in question.

Paul Taylor's method of weighing the rights of nature has been mentioned earlier (above p. 60). Taylor places *prima facie* equal value on all living things as 'centres of a life' but allows important social and economic concerns to override the interests of individual beings provided that principles of self-defence or proportionality and compensation are applied. The different ethical perspectives therefore share some common ground.

In practice, as the tuna–dolphin case perhaps reveals (see Chapter 11) the solution may be found in public acceptability backed by a pragmatic use of valid ethical argument thus embodying a virtue ethics perspective which stresses the importance of having the right intentions. Stone proposes a pluralist approach according to which different moral tests might apply in different contexts without having to reconcile them with a single overarching principle such as utilitarianism or believing that there is a 'single right answer' (Stone, 1996). Such tests might include for example pain, preferences, consent, an aesthetic sense of fitness, respect for the flourishing of another entity, and empathy.

Environmental Rights in the Law

English law has not adopted the notion of direct environmental rights nor is there a coherent ethical approach. So-called environmental rights arising for example in the law of nuisance, are not intrinsically environmental but are aspects of property which happen to be violated by way of environmental media. The indirect duty approach with utilitarian back up perhaps represents a broad area of judicial agreement.

This fits in particular the law of charity which depends upon establishing a human benefit in relation to trusts for nature (above Chapter 8). In *National Anti-Vivisection Society* v. *IRC* [1947] 2 All ER 217 Lord Wright did not balance human and animal rights along strictly utilitarian lines but regarded human interests as necessarily superior subject to an obligation to avoid unnecessary suffering. Similarly in *R.* v. *Somerset County Council ex parte Fewings* [1995] 1 All ER 513 the Court of Appeal was at most prepared to consider the moral issue of a ban on deer hunting as a matter affecting the human community. In *R.* v. *Coventry City Council ex parte Phoenix Aviation* [1995] 3 All ER 37 Simon-Brown L. J. appeared to discount altogether the legitimacy of animal rights. He held that the Council acted unlawfully in banning the transport of live animals in order to prevent disruption at its airport by animal rights protesters. His Lordship's reasoning was based upon the legal right to trade against which no other right fell to be balanced. There is a general interest in the preservation of public order and in this case the protesters whose interests were not buttressed by rights were at a disadvantage, just as in strike-breaking cases the contractual right to work outweighs any residual freedom to protest (see e.g. *Moss* v. *McLachlan* [1984] IRLR 76 – police power to protect right to work against picketers).

Possible environmental legal rights fall into three broad categories. Firstly there are public law rights. These are of three kinds; the right to institute criminal proceedings against environmental wrongdoers; the right to challenge government action in the courts – *locus standi*; and procedural rights including access to information and participation in decision-making processes by means for example of environmental impact assessment. Secondly there are private law property rights for example to sue in nuisance or to enforce a restrictive covenant. Confusion between public law and private law rights seems to have affected the debate in European law as to how far environmental interests are capable of having direct effect (below). Thirdly there is possibly a human rights argument in favour of a right to a decent environment.

Public Law Rights

Public law rights arise in three main contexts. First there is the possibility of criminal prosecution by citizens, secondly the question of *locus standi* to challenge government action, and thirdly the question of rights to participate in decision making involving access to information and environmental impact assessment. We have already discussed the latter in relation to the precautionary principle.

Prosecutions

The law of public nuisance constitutes to a certain extent a public environmental right since any person can bring a prosecution at common law. Similarly in the case of a statutory nuisance under the Environment Protection Act 1995, where the local authority fails to take action, any person can apply to the magistrates court in relation to an existing nuisance (EPA 1990 5. 82).

Any person can bring a prosecution in relation to any criminal offence unless statute provides otherwise (*R.* v. *Stewart* (1896) 1 QB 300). There are no statutory restrictions upon prosecuting the main pollution offences or the cruelty to animals offences. However, enforcement of planning legislation is limited to the local authority and the conservation provisions of the Wildlife and Countryside Act 1981 can be enforced only by the Nature Conservancy Council or with the consent of the DPP (s.28(10)). As a general principle where the law involves broad discretionary concepts or strategic concerns, it makes sense for the right to prosecute to be limited to a public agency. Conversely where there are fixed standards or standards based upon the effect of pollution upon the community, prosecution should be open to the public.

Where prosecutions can be brought only by officials there are the problems of limited measures and of shared cultural attitudes and information between regulator and regulated. Moreover it is plausible to believe that big companies wield more influence than other potential polluters and can cope better with official regulatory requirements. Pollution regulation in the UK features a relatively small number of prosecutions (less than 1% of reported offences), there being a strong tradition of regulation by voluntary methods, particularly in relation to agriculture. Until recently environmental regulating agencies were staffed mainly by technical specialists such as engineers who shared a common technocratic background with the business that produced pollution and so were required to regulate problems that, from the ecocentric perspective, they themselves created. More recently, however, the Environment Agency has recruited personnel with broader backgrounds in the biological and human sciences and with more affinity with environmental interests (see Lowe *et al.*, 1997).

Where there is a public right to prosecute, prosecutions are usually brought by voluntary bodies such as the RSPCA or Greenpeace. These have no special powers of investigation but are dependent upon provisions for public access to information. Here there is also a cultural problem of conflict of interest in this case a three-way conflict between the lobbying political role of the body, the environmental or animal right in itself and the general public interest in enforcing the law. For example, should the RSPCA operate a similar strategy to the Crown Prosecution Service in prosecuting only where there is a substantial chance of success or should it, as apparently is the practice with other pressure groups, use the power to prosecute as a political tool to advance its moral agenda?

In both cases the ability to prosecute successfully depends upon public access to information. Even where prosecutions can be brought only by the public authority, complaints by the public are an important factor since the Environment Agency, the NCC and local planning authorities are unlikely to commend sufficient resources to monitor their territories effectively. Again cultural attitudes are important. For example, do officials regard public involvement as a welcome part of the regulatory process or as an intrusion into professional territory?

Locus Standi

English law has not reached a clear view on the question of standing and has not espoused any notion of environmental rights as such. Environmental rights are often collective rights whereas the law tends to be dominated by ideas of private property (see Gerard, 1996 and Chapter 8).

The Supreme Court Act 1981 s.31(3) imposes the test of 'sufficient interest in the matter to which the application relates'. This has led to differences of opinion in environmental cases. These may reflect more general disagreement about the purpose of judicial review itself but also reflect differences between broad and narrow anthropocentric perspectives.

The speeches of the House of Lords in *IRC* v. *National Federation for the Self Employed* [1982] AC 617 established that the applicant does not have to show a right in the strict legal sense. However, their Lordships disagreed in their approach. Lords Diplock and Scarman approached the matter as one of broad discretion based on all the circumstances including the seriousness of the issues and the strength of the applicant's case. Lord Diplock in particular was prepared to recognise the possibility that, in an appropriate case, a public-spirited citizen would have the right to challenge. Lords Wilberforce, Fraser and Roskill took a narrower approach that focused upon the nature of the interests recognised by the particular statute under which the decision to be challenged was made.

The environmental cases show a reluctance to treat public environmental concerns as sufficient in themselves. Some judges have required that the applicant be personally affected by the decision (see *R.* v. *Secretary of State ex parte Rose Theatre Trust:* [1990] 1QB 504, *R* v. *North Somerset District Council ex parte Garnett* [1998] JEL 161) or possess interests recognised by the statute for example as objector at a public inquiry (*Covent Garden Community Association* v. *GLC* [1981] JPL 183.

Otton J.'s judgement in *R.* v. *Pollution Inspectorate ex parte Greenpeace (No 2)* [1994] 4 ALL ER 329 is sometimes regarded as a breakthrough for public environmental interests. Greenpeace was given standing to challenge a decision to approve certain discharges of nuclear waste from the Sellafield processing plant. However, the case is ambivalent. Otton J.'s reasoning was based upon the cumulative effect of several factors none of which appeared to suffice in itself. Greenpeace was a responsible and expert body with an established concern with the issues and was able to assist the court. Many of its supporters lived in the district: their health might therefore be at risk and they might not have any other means of bringing their concerns before the court. Greepeace had already been actively involved in the consultation process. The remedy sought, *certiorari* to quash the decision but without any mandatory order for the future, was relatively weak. The case is therefore ambivalent. Moreover it seems to disadvantage poorly funded groups and those whose ethical attitudes are outside mainstream ideas.

In *R.* v. *Somerset County Council ex parte Dixon* [1998] JEL 161 Sedley J. took a more radical approach where a local activist sought to challenge a planning permission to extend quarrying operations. Sedley J. approached the case on the basis that the applicant had no greater interest than that of the general public but nevertheless granted standing. His Lordship held that a special interest was not required and that the correct approach was to ask whether the applicant was merely a busybody with no connection with the matter at all and whether the applicant could show 'some substantial default or abuse'. The proposed quarrying operations would have a serious and possibly irreversible impact on the environment which justified a challenge by a member of the public (see also *R.* v. *Secretary of State for Foreign Affairs ex parte World Development Movement* [1995] 1 WLR 386). If Sedley J.'s decision stands a citizen's action based on public environmental values would therefore be possible.

However, these cases concern only the initial question of leave to apply for judicial review. This is merely a threshold test designed to prevent the court's time being wasted by busybodies. At the full hearing standing is looked at again and the nature of the applicant's interest will be taken into account in relation to the seriousness of the issues (see *R.* v. *Monopolies and Mergers Commission ex parte Argylle Group plc* [1986] 2 ALL ER 257 at 265–66).

Christopher Stone's notion of conferring rights directly upon natural objects may help to meet the problem of standing in that it avoids having to identify particular human interests, focusing instead upon the environmental object itself, a habitat, a river, a landscape, etc. In 1972 the Disney Corporation planned to turn an area of pristine American wilderness (Mineral King Valley) into a theme park. Appalled by this Stone wrote a provocative essay, Should Trees Have Standing? (Stone, 1972; see also Stone, 1985a) in which he argues that the concept of right is valuable because it emphasises the political and moral importance of nature's claims, helps to change our attitudes to nature and is a convenient method of holding a duty holder to account. Stone suggests that *locus standi* to challenge environmentally degrading decisions should be afforded not merely to those with affected economic interests, but to the trees, rivers and valleys affected. The essence of Stone's claim is that affording rights to nature is merely a logical extension of the natural rights tradition that, beginning with Magna Carta, has afforded rights to more and more of the population.

In order to substantiate what, on its face, appears to be a radical claim, Stone has to explain just how it would be possible for rights to be extended to trees and valleys. This involves primarily demonstrating that the concept of a 'right' can conceptually be extended to such entities. As we have seen, as a matter of legal mechanics it is possible to do so.

The unlikelihood of a valley or river expressing a preference may be overcome by the appointment of a guardian (e.g. Friends of the Earth) to conduct litigation on its behalf. There is an analogy with the position in respect of children or people who cannot express their preferences due to age or incapacity. Such guardians are in an advantageous position since unlike the state, they do not have to balance the interests of competing groups, but can focus exclusively on the represented party. This is one reason why Stone's device is preferable to the present law under which the Attorney General who is a member of the government of the day institutes legal proceedings on behalf of the public interest. The guardian's connection with the matter would not necessarily be the concern of the court provided that the proceedings were funded. On the other hand if environmental interest groups (NGOs) are to be guardians they are likely to quarrel among themselves as to who should act in any particular case.

Stone's views were supported by Douglas J. in *Sierra Club* v. *Morton* 405 US 727 (1972). However, the Supreme Court in *Lugan* v. *Defenders of Wildlife* 112 Sct 2130 (1996) stopped this development by forbidding states to create rights of action except in the case of genuine human disputes. The environmental issue is therefore sometimes trivialised by attempts to find a human interest on which to hang litigation (see e.g. *Japanese Whaling Association* v. *American Cetacean Society* 478 US 221 (1986) – whale watching).

Access to Information

Environmental rights must be supported by public access to information. It will be recalled that public participation and access to information featured in the Rio Declaration (1992). In ethical terms access to information is consistent with every perspective. However, English law is dominated by a tradition of executive and professional secrecy which excludes direct public involvement and, of course, there is no reason to assume that wide public involvement will necessarily favour environmental interests.

In recent years public rights of consultation have been strengthened albeit in a fragmented way. Section 54A of the Town and Country Planning Act 1990 by placing greater emphasis upon development plans has strengthened the position of pressure groups and individuals because of the machinery for public consultation as part of the plan-making process. The introduction of Environmental Impact Assessment for major public projects, and the strengthening of public consultation rights in relation to individual planning applications (Town and Country Planning (General Development Procedure Order) 1995, SI No. 419) are further examples.

On the other hand there is no right of appeal against an unconditional grant of planning permission or a refusal to hold an environmental impact assessment, thus limiting the public to judicial review. The applicant for planning permission has a right of appeal to the Secretary of State (Town and Country Planning Act 1990 s.78) and only the applicant and the local planning authority have a statutory right to be heard (Town and Country Planning Act 1990 s.79(2)). This might take the form of a 'hearing' which does not involve formal cross-examination or adversarial procedures. If the parties so choose the appeal can be decided on the basis of written representations. About 80 percent of appeals are decided this way.

The Secretary of State, or more usually an inspector to whom the power is delegated, has a discretion to hold a local inquiry into a planning appeal (Town and Country Planning Act 1990 s.320(1)). Where a local inquiry is held it must be in public (Town and Country Planning Act 1990 s.321(2)). In practice the inspector usually allows anyone to make representations although full rights of participation, access to documents, cross-examination and the calling of witnesses are confined to the persons entitled to appear. These are the appellant, the local planning authority, other public bodies, those who made representations at the initial application stage, and any other person who has notified the Secretary of State that he wishes to appear and the Secretary of State has required a written 'statement of case' from that person (see Town and Country Planning (Inquiries Procedure) Rules SI 1992 No. 2038; see also SI 1992 No. 2039).

There are provisions for public participation in the integration pollution control regime. These take the form of a requirement on the operator of a process to advertise for authorisations and substantial variations of authorisation in a local newspaper. Certain public bodies are entitled to be consulted (see Environmental Protection Act (Applications, Appeals and Registers Regulations) 1991 SI 1991, No. 507). There are no formal public consultation provisions in relation to water pollution and waste management, the duty to consult is limited to specified public bodies (EPA 1990, s.36). Nor is there any duty to consult the public under the contaminated land regime introduced by the Environment Act 1995, Part II although the Secretary of State has a discretion to prescribe who shall be consulted (EPA 1990, s.78).

The procedure for designating Sites of Special Scientific Interest under the Wildlife and Countryside Act 1981 requires the NCC to notify and consider representation from the relevant local authority, owners and occupiers and the Secretary of State that it proposes to designate the site (Wildlife and Countryside Act 1981 s.28(1)). The Secretary of State's power to make a nature conservation order under section 29 requires consultation only with the NCC. Designation as a National Nature Reserve under s.15 of the National Parks and Access to the Countryside Act 1949 and section 35 of the 1981 Act does not involve public consultation at all but involves voluntary arrangements between the NCC and the landowner. There are no additional consultation rights in the machinery relating to European Sites under the Habitats Directive.

Provisions for giving public access to environmental information take two main forms. Firstly, there are public registers in respect of the main pollution regulatory regimes and also the planning regime which includes SSSIs and other special zones. Secondly there are requirements imposed by European law upon public bodies.

Public registers include information about formal transactions, applications, consents, variations, exemptions, enforcement, convictions and official monitoring (see Ball and Bell, 1997, pp. 162–71). There are standard exemptions in relation to commercial confidentiality and national security. General information about prescribed standards, the state of the environment and the effectiveness of enforcement depends upon the voluntary publication of information by official agencies (e.g. the Chemical Release Inventory). There is, of course, as in any statistical system, room for interpretation. For example where the Environment Agency publishes details of 'substantiated' pollution incidents what does substantiated mean? What is the difference between an 'operational' and a 'compliance' sample? Moreover, it seems that the public have little interest in participation in environmental regulation in general and consulting the registers in particular except in furtherance of commercial concerns or by environmental groups (Ball and Bell, 1997).

European law gives particular importance to public access to environmental information. It requires national and local public bodies to disclose information although these requirements do not apply to its own institutions. The Environmental Information Regulations 1992 (SI 1992, No. 3240) which complement EC Directive 90/313 on Freedom of Access to Information on the Environment require public bodies to make environmental information in its possession available, on request, to any person as soon as possible but in any event within two months. However, a reasonable charge can be made and these are broad exceptions which allow considerable discretion (Article 4). These exceptions suggest that commercial concerns and to some extent administrative convenience outweigh any right to environmental information. However, reasons have to be given for any refusal to disclose information so that there is at least a presumption in favour of the environment.

Under the regulations, information can be treated as confidential in the following cases:

(a) it relates to international relations, defence or public security;
(b) it relates to legal or other proceedings broadly defined to include any statutory quasi-judicial proceedings;
(c) it relates to the confidential deliberations of public bodies or to the content of internal communications within companies and other organisations;
(d) information contained in uncompleted documents;
(e) commercial confidentiality.

Information *must* be treated as confidential in the following cases:

(a) where is can be treated as confidential (above) and its disclosure would otherwise be unlawful or in breach of any agreement;
(b) personal information related to an individual who has not consented to disclosure;
(c) information voluntarily supplied;
(d) where disclosure would increase the likelihood of damage to the environment.

These exceptions suggest that the duty to disclose environmental information has a low priority in relation to other human values (see Birtles, 1993). However, in contrast with other regulatory concerns, environmental information equally includes pollution and ecological matters (Reg. 2 (2)). As we have seen the law is normally more active in relation to pollution than in relation to nature conservation.

At the European level there is no general right to information held by European public bodies even though the Maastricht Conference of 1992 included Declaration no. 17 stating that the public should have greater access to such information. A Code of Conduct was subsequently produced which was adopted by a Decision of the Commission (Decision 94/90, OJ 1994 L 46, P58). *World Wide Fund For Nature* v. *Commission* [1997] JEL 328 concerned a Commission investigation into a scheme to use European money to build a visitors centre in a National Park in Ireland. WWF wished to challenge the Commission's decision in favour of the project thus pitting non-anthropocentric views against human interests. The Commission refused to disclose certain information relying upon exceptions contained in the code these being 'the public interest' (public security, international relations, monetary stability, court proceedings and investigations) and the 'confidentiality of the Commission's internal proceedings'. In this case the relevant public interest related to investigations into a possible breach of community law. The Court of First Instance held that although the obligations of the Code were assumed voluntarily, they gave rise to enforceable legal rights. Exceptions to the right of access to information must be construed restrictively and that the Commission must give reasons for refusing to disclose information which are sufficiently detailed to identify the interests involved and how they have been balanced except where this would result in destroying the purpose of the confidentiality claim.

Private Law Rights

English law confers private rights only upon human beings or corporations and regards animals as at best the subject of indirect duties to people. In the absence of negligence only a person with a property interest or, in the case of public nuisance, who has suffered special damage, has access to the courts to protect the environment (*Hunter* v. *Canary Wharf* [1997] 2 All ER 426). Private law also gives particular weight to commercial certainty. As we have seen private law property rights pull in opposite directions. On the one hand property gives an incentive to conserve at least resources of economic value thus supporting intergenerational equity. On the other hand property owners have an incentive to pollute so as to pass costs on to others.

The question of compensation for environmental damage raises problems which we referred to in relation to the polluter pays principle in Chapter 6 and in connection with civil liability in Chapter 7. Suppose that property rights were to include environmental interests how might they be compensated? More broadly if we were to move away from the anthropocentric perspective how would we compensate nature for any evil we do to it? If a habitat is destroyed by an oil spill, who gets compensation and how is it to be calculated? Is it based on restoration costs even where these are far greater than the value of the habitat to humans and if so who pays the bill? If we destroy a habitat we can compensate humans by providing another one but the habitat as such cannot be compensated. However, nature as a whole can be compensated and Christopher Stone's suggestion of a trust fund which can be credited or debited provides a possible solution.

As we saw in Chapter 8, the Habitats Directive 1992 Art. 6(4) requires compensation to be provided if a designated wildlife habitat is subsequently developed. Compensation under the Directive can apparently take the form of providing an alternative environmental benefit which need not benefit the particular species displaced. For example loss of a bird sanctuary could be compensated by creating a reptile reserve. Similarly compensation in the form of environmental amenities can be provided by developers under s.106 of the Town and Country Planning Act 1990 in return for planning permission or by landowners under management agreements in relation to SSSIs.

These forms of compensation make sense in holistic terms of interests and from a utilitarian perspective but not from a rights perspective or in terms of social justice. A business that offers to provide a town with a nature reserve in return for planning permission to build a factory is not compensating the victims of pollution created by the factory. The legal test for the validity of such compensation is a liberal one requiring only that the benefit provided bears some connection to the proposed development that is not *de minimis* (see *Tesco Stores* v. *Secretary of State* [1995] 2 All ER 637). In the USA by contrast a stricter test is available: that the benefit is a response to a need generated by the development and is proportionate to that need (see Purdue, 1992). The difference between the two approaches reflects the importance of property rights under the United States Constitution.

What is the measure of damages for loss of a species? The damages should not only reflect human loss but also loss to nature. The replacement cost of the species might be appropriate but if this exceeds the value of the land then possibly the value of the land should provide a ceiling provided that the compensation is earmarked for environmental purposes. In this way the idea of compensating nature fits in with the principles of sustainable development and intergenerational equity in as much as we are creating environmental capital in the form of the trust fund. The notion of compensating nature by replacement or by means of Stone's trust fund makes sense from the ecocentric perspective but not if we are individualists unless we argue, in virtue ethics mose, that we are doing the best we can.

Another problem with the idea of compensation is the 'plastic trees' problem (see Tribe, 1974 and above p. xxx). If nature has interests and entitlements independently of human beings, it is arguably wrong to interfere with nature for better or worse. First, is it not an abuse of nature's autonomy to presume to improve upon its natural state? Second, is it not wrong, unless we admit that we are serving human interests, to fake nature even for the best of motives such as compensating it for our previous abuses as when we landscape an exhausted mine (see Elliot, 1995, chapter iv)? A forgery, however perfect is still worth less than the real thing. Is nature compensated by restoration for being torn apart? However, this is arguably an aesthetic rather than a moral issue. As with the restoration of a vandalised work of art we are doing the best we can in the circumstances despite the slur on nature's integrity. The concept of second best is a familiar one in the law of trusts. If a charitable trust fails or is impossible to carry out, the property can be used *cy pres* for a purpose as near as possible to the original purpose without consulting any human objects of the trust (Charities Act 1993 s.13(1)).

European Law Rights

European law has not produced a vehicle for environmental rights enforceable by the European Court of Justice. One reason for this may lie in the emphasis placed by European law on the language of individual rights (McRory, 1996; Miller, 1998). Different economic and political priorities and different ideas about the place of science within the culture of the different member states may also be complicating factors.

At the European level enforcement is by the European Commission (Art. 169 EC). Individuals can invoke the European Court of Justice only in respect of a decision that is specifically addressed to them or in relation to regulations which are of direct and immediate concern to them (Art. 173). European environmental laws are usually cast as directives not regulations and the concept of 'direct and immediate concern' has been narrowly interpreted. In *Greenpeace and others* v. *Commission* [1996] JEL 139, the ECJ First Instance Court denied standing to a group of local residents, fishermen and farmers to challenge a decision of the Commission to subsidise the building of two power stations in Spain. It was held that environmental concerns could not give standing unless the applicants could show some effect peculiar to themselves. Similarly, Greenpeace had no standing because its members were not especially affected and it claimed to represent only the general interest.

EC instruments that are enforceable in domestic law include 'regulations' which under Article 189 of the European Treaty are automatically 'directly applicable' and provisions of the treaties themselves provided in both cases that the rule is sufficiently clear, precise and unconditional to be capable of enforcement (below). However, most environmental measures take the form of Directives although the rationale for choosing one method rather than another is not clear. Directives are addressed to member states. They lay down objects to be achieved and leave it to the domestic law as to the method of implementation (see Article 189 EC). Directives are sometimes enforceable under the doctrine of direct effect which is the result of creative law making by the European Court of Justice. Unlike the treaty and a regulation, a Directive has direct effect only against a public body as opposed to a private person. This is because the rationale of the direct effect doctrine appears to be that the 'state', defined for this purpose as public bodies, cannot rely on its own failure to implement a directive (see *Marshall* v. *Southampton and South West Area Health Authority* [1985] QB 401, *Faccini Dori* [1994] ECR 1-3325).

In order to have direct effect, the subject matter of the provision which it is sought to enforce must be clear and unconditional and sufficiently precise to be relied upon by an individual. The state must have failed to implement the directive in national law by the time limit prescribed or failed to implement the directive correctly. These requirements means that a provision will be less likely to have direct effect if it confers a substantial discretion upon the government as to the method of implementation. For example in *Comitato di Coordinamento per la Defesa della Cava* v. *Regione Lombardia* [1994] 1 ECR 1337, a group of individuals challenged a decision by a regional council to set up a waste tip. They claimed that Directive 75/444 as amended by Directive 91/156, the framework directive on waste, required recycling arrangements. The directive required waste to be disposed of 'without harm to man or the environment'. The ECJ held that the provision did not have direct effect because governments had discretion as to how to achieve its objective.

Many environmental directives impose duties upon governments to create pollution control machinery or to designate special areas of protection but without prescribing specific standards or enforcement methods, (see e.g. Directive 84/360 EEC 7 Air pollution from industrial plants Article 3; Directive 92/43 EEC – Habitats; Directive 85/337 – Environmental impact assessment, Annex II; discretion to designate projects having 'significant' environmental impact). These aspects of the directives in question would not have direct effect. Conversely, provisions that prohibit the discharge of definite substances or which fix concentration levels or which prohibit the destruction of habitats may have direct effect even if there is a margin of local discretion as to implementation methods since the impact on the litigant is certain (see Kramer, 1991; Directive 80/68 – groundwater; Directive 80/778 – drinking water; *Commission* v. *UK* [1992] ECR 1-6013). Public rights to information under Directive 90/313 probably have direct effect.

It is sometimes maintained that a directive must also create a 'right' thus raising the question of whether there can be purely environmental rights (see Kramer in Somsen, 1996, p. 108). If this is correct then environmental law may be at a disadvantage in that environmental Directives are often for the benefit the public at large or non-humans rather than affecting the rights of individuals. Hence governmental officials on behalf of the general interest have the job of enforcing environmental values and this has sometimes been held to exclude individual access to the courts. For example in *Cinsinello Balsamo* [1989] ECR 2491, the ECJ held that individuals had no right to enforce a provision in a directive that required local authorities to inform the Commission of certain measures concerning waste disposal because the duties created by the directive were intergovernmental and only indirectly affected citizens.

Possibly the 'rights' requirement means only that the provision in question is intended to benefit the person who seeks to rely on it (Kramer in Somsen, 1996, p. 110). The requirement might mean only that a citizen who seeks to rely upon a directive must have sufficient interest in the matter to give him standing. Thus a directive that does not confer a right may be enforceable at a public law level to require the state to perform its duties. The purpose of the direct effect doctrine appears to be to enable the court to enforce the substance of the directive without having to exceed its proper judicial function by exercising political or administrative discretion (see Jans in Somsen, 1996, p. 49). Therefore a court could intervene on behalf of a person with *locus standi* if the government exceeds or abuses its discretion in the way it implements or fails to implement a directive. Any directive can therefore have direct effect in public law to this extent (see *Kraaijeveld BV* v. *Gedeputeerde Staten van Zuid-Holland* [1996] ECR 1-5403; Boch, 1997).

In the English case of *Twyford Parish Council* v. *Secretary of State* (1990) 4 JEL 273 the applicants could not invoke the European Directive on Environmental Impact Assessment even though the provision in question had direct effect because they had not suffered detriment by reason of any failure to comply. However, since that case, the *locus standi* requirements of English law have perhaps become more liberal (above).

There is another unfortunate limitation to the direct effect doctrine. The state cannot use the direct effect doctrine against a private person because in doing so it would be relying on its own failure to implement the directive. In *Wychavon DC* v. *Secretary of State* [1994] JEL 351 Tucker J. refused to allow the Council to require the Secretary of State to enforce the requirement of an environmental impact assessment against a developer. As Fitzgerald (*ibid.* p. 364) points out, this is particularly unfortunate as in this case an environmental wrong is 'victimless' in terms of individuals who might raise the matter. Tucker J.'s judgement also seems to be flawed by his belief that the test of direct effect has to be applied to a directive as a whole rather than to its individual provisions. It is clear that a directive can have partial direct effect (see also *R.* v. *North Yorkshire County Council ex parte Brown* [1997] Env LR 391).

There are two other ways of raising European principles in domestic courts. Firstly, domestic courts must interpret the law in conformity with European Community legal principles. This 'indirect effect' doctrine certainly applies in the case of domestic laws passed to implement European Law (Art. 5 EC, *Von Colson* [1984] ECR 1891) and might apply to all domestic law. (*Marleasing SA* v. *La Comercial Internacional de Alimentacion SA* [1990] ECR1-4135). Secondly according to *Francovich* v. *Italy* [1991] ECR 1-5357, a citizen might have an action for damages against the government for failing to implement a European Directive, or perhaps for implementing a directive incorrectly, even one which is not sufficiently definite in terms of its requirements or outcome to qualify for direct effect. The *Francovich* doctrine goes further than direct effect in that it would apply to the activities of private persons. The requirements *of Francovich* are as follows:

1. the directive is intended to confer rights for the benefit of individuals of whom the plaintiff is one;
2. the content of the right can be determined from the directive;
3. there is a causal link between the breach of the directive and the damage suffered by the plaintiff.

Francovich has potential as an environmental remedy in that broad discretionary duties of a kind familiar in environmental law could fall within its scope. On the other hand if 'right' is given a strict legal meaning it would be difficult to apply the doctrine to environmental interests concerned with nature conservation or to interference with amenity caused by pollution. It is, however, possible that in this context a right means only that the directive is intended to be of benefit to the plaintiff even if in common with the rest of the public (see Somsen, 1996, chapter 7).

Human Rights

Human rights differ from ordinary legal rights in that human rights doctrine elevates certain rights to a specially high status and regards them as generally applicable across all branches of the law. Human rights also claim to be universally valid irrespective of particular nations, cultures or political organisations and attract special institutional mechanisms in international law. It may, therefore, be attractive to regard environmental concerns as generating human rights. Environmental rights are regarded as 'third generation' rights. First generation rights comprise traditional freedoms such as freedom of expression. Second, generation rights are social and economic welfare rights. Third generation rights are 'solidarity' or community rights. Solidarity rights differ from the earlier kinds of right in that they belong to groups not only to individuals. The notion of third generation rights is controversial and international instruments have been cautious in treating environmental concerns as human rights. The Stockholm Declaration (1972) used the language of rights but the Rio Declaration (1992) avoided doing so although recognising a 'right' to development in Article 3.

In *Minors Oposa* v. *Secretary of the Department of Environment and National Resources* 33 ILM (1994) 173, the Philippines Supreme Court used a human rights analysis to permit children on behalf of future generations to challenge governmental action in respect of forestry licenses. The same result could arguably have been achieved by means of ordinary public law concepts since in *Oposa* the human right was not sufficient in itself to make the decision unlawful.

Some state constitutions including those of Spain, Portugal, Austria, Greece and the Netherlands have included the notion of a right to a decent or healthy environment (see Kiss and Shelton, 1993) but significantly without enforcement machinery. Indeed in one case it was held that general environmental rights were too vague to be enforceable (*Commonwealth of Pennsylvania* v. *National Gettysberg Battlefield Tower*, 8 PA 231).

In 1994 the UN Commissioner on Human Rights published the Final Report of its Special Rapporteur on Human Rights and the Environment (Ksentini, 1994). This formulated a list of rights derived from state practice and international instruments. Examples include intergenerational equity, adequate living conditions, freedom from pollution and environmental degradation the preservation and protection of the air, soil, water, sea-ice, flora and fauna and the essential processes and areas necessary to maintain biological diversity, and the right to the highest attainable standard of health free from environmental harm.

The Ksentini report also draws attention to procedural rights. These include:

1. The right to information 'necessary to enable effective public participation in environmental decision-making'. The information shall be timely, clear, understandable and available without undue financial burden to the applicant.
2. The right to hold and express opinions and to disseminate ideas and information regarding the environment.
3. The right to environmental and human rights education.
4. The right to active, free and meaningful participation in planning and decision-making activities and processes that may have an impact on the environment and development. This includes the right to a prior assessment of the environmental, developmental and human rights consequences of proposed actions.
5. The right to associate freely and peacefully with others for purposes of protecting the environment or the rights of persons affected by environmental harm.
6. The right to effective remedies and redress in administrative or judicial proceedings for environmental harm or the threat of such harm.

According to Ksentini the listed environmental rights can be overridden only by 'restrictions provided by law which are necessary to protect public order, health and the fundamental rights and freedoms of others' although 'all persons have a right not to be evicted from their homes or land for the purpose of, or as a consequence of decisions or actions affecting the environment except in emergencies or due to a compelling purpose benefiting society as a whole and not attainable by other means'. There should be a right to 'participate effectively' in eviction decisions and to 'timely and adequate restitution, compensation and/or appropriate and sufficient accommodation or land'. In addition 'indigenous peoples have a right to control their territories and national resources and to maintain their traditional way of life. This includes the right to security in the enjoyment of their means of subsistence'.

This catalogue illustrates some of the problems inherent in the idea of environmental human rights (see Boyle and Anderson, 1996, chapters 2, 3, 8). The substantive rights listed are extremely broad, many of them being little more than policy aspirations. Against who are they enforceable and by what means? Most of the environmental human rights require positive state action and large-scale public spending. Could a court adjudicate in, for example, the proper level of public health? Who has standing to bring proceedings? Boyle (1996 at 58) points out that the implementation of environmental rights raises questions of economic justice between rich and poor nations involving the transfer of funds and technology without which the notion of rights is empty. The human rights in question cannot be strictly applied without bringing most economic activity to a halt. They, therefore, have to be balanced against other economic and social values. Is a court competent to do this?

Boyle also points out that existing methods of international law which involve international instruments filtering into domestic law and thereby becoming concrete within different political and economic contexts may work better than would human rights reasoning. At this more modest level several international instruments, notably the Law of the Sea Convention and the Convention on Trade in Endangered Species have had pragmatic success buttressed by emerging soft law concepts such as sustainable development and the precautionary principle. The major international problems notably that of climate change may require large-scale co-operation between states and perhaps new institutions in relation to which human rights doctrine is of minor significance.

Existing Human Rights Instruments

Environmental concerns play ambiguous roles in human rights law. On the one hand they may generate rights but on the other hand they may feature as overrides in the sense that they might be part of the public interest 'necessary in a democratic society' for the economic well being of the country (see *Herrick* v. *UK* 42 D and R 275 (1985); Desgagne, 1995, pp. 280–7).

There have been attempts to extend existing human rights in the European Convention on Human Rights to environmental concerns (see Desgagne, 1995). This is of particular importance now that the UK has enacted the convention as part of domestic law (Human Rights Act 1998). It must be remembered that any domestic legal remedies must be exhausted before seeking the aid of the European judicial process. The main provisions of the European Convention potentially relevant to environmental interests are Article 2 – the right to life, Article 3 – protection against torture or inhuman and degrading treatment or punishment, Article 8 – respect for private life, home and correspondence. Article 1 of the First Protocol which protects the right to property could also be used for environmental purposes but is probably limited to protection against the deprivation of property or the loss of economic property values (see *Rayner* v. *UK, 47 D and R* 5 (1986) at 14; Desgagne, 1995, pp. 277–80).

The case law of the European Court of Human Rights and the European Commission on Human Rights has taken a conspicuously restrictive approach to the recognition of environmental rights and has been willing to allow governments a considerable margin of application to apply their own social and economic policies (*Fredin* v. *Sweden ECHR* ser. A. No. 192 (1991) at 6). The European Convention is a product of the first generation of human rights which is individualistic and focuses upon the protection of traditional liberties against state interference. Outside these concerns, it is doubtful whether the convention has sufficient political legitimacy to underpin an expansionist judicial policy (see *M* v. *Austria* 39 D. and R. 85 (1984)). For example, similar *locus standi* problems arise to those experienced by domestic law where a pressure group seeks to raise an environmental right (Desgagne, 1995, p. 284).

It appears that the Article 2 'right to life' imposes a duty on the state not to take away life but does not concern the kind of quality of life problems that raise environmental concerns. It seems, however, that Article 2 might require the state to take preventive or even precautionary action against clear environmental risks that threaten life (Desgagne, 1995, pp. 267–9). Article 8 – privacy – is more promising. In *Lopes Ostra* v. *Spain* Ser. A No. 303C (1994) the court found a breach of Article 8 where the applicant suffered serious health problems caused by fumes from a waste treatment plant which the state had authorised near her home (see Churchill, 1996, p. 94). In other cases under Article 8 involving pollution, the Commission held that although environmental damage may fall within Article 8, the social interests involved (running an airport – *Powell and Rayner* v. *UK*, 47 D and R (1986) 5, nuclear power station – *S* v. *France*, 65 D and R (1990) 250) overrode the right as being necessary in a democratic society for the economic well being of the country (see also *Arrondelle* v. *UK,* 19 D and R (1980) 186, *Vearncombe* v. *UK* 65 D and R (1990) 250, *G and E* v. *Norway* 35 D and R (1984) 30). It appears that in order to qualify for protection under Article 8 the interference must threaten the enjoyment of property in a way similar to a nuisance in domestic law. Moreover, as in domestic law, the interference must be exceptional and not compatible with the normal character of the area (*Powell and Rayner* (above)). This illustrates the individualistic bias of the European Convention and raises doubts as to whether the human rights approach is a useful environmental tool.

It is often argued that procedural rights are a more effective tool for protecting environmental interests than substantive rights (see e.g. Shelton, 1991; Boyle and Anderson, 1996). Article 25 of the International Covenant on Civil and Political Rights 6 ILM 368 (1967) provides for a right to take part in the conduct of public affairs directly or through freely chosen representatives but the European Convention goes no further than provisions for free elections and rights related to a fair trial. The right to a fair trial would reinforce judicial review of government action but does not seem to relate to procedural rights such as access to information and environmental impact assessment.

Article 10 of the European Convention confers a right to receive and impart information but this has been interpreted narrowly. In *Leander* v. *Sweden*, 116 Eur Ct. H.R. (ser A) (1987) Article 10 was confined to the role of preventing the government from restricting access to information which others wished to provide. Article 10 does not, therefore, impose a duty on anyone to provide information. However, as Desgagne (1995, p. 288) points out, the court can take into account the government's attitude to democratic values such as information and participation when it assesses the claims of a state to override protected rights in the public interest (see *Powell and Rayner* v. *UK* 172 Eur Ct. H. R. (ser A) (1990), para. 44)).

The Rio Declaration (1991) and the World Charter for Nature Principle 23 ((1982) 22 ILM 445 at 456) also include procedural rights, such as participation, due process and access to remedies.

Conclusion

In conclusion it might be suggested that the case law of human rights illustrates both the strengths and weaknesses of the ethical dimension in environmental law. The main strength of the ethical approach is that it can identify underlying value judgements behind debates couched in terms of legal analysis and policy assumptions. It can help us to understand whether techniques such as legal or economic analysis which are sometimes presented as objective are based on subjective moral or factual assumptions. Ethics can also help us to understand whether our disagreements are resolvable because for example we are disagreeing about facts rather than values or because although our ethical positions may be incommensurable they are not uncombinable.

The weakness of the ethical approach, if indeed in a democracy it is a weakness, is that ethics cannot give us hard and fast answers but can at best give us a range of options to guide political choice. There is no ethical master principle that can help us choose between the different theories. We might be able to rule out some ethical perspectives by subjecting them to the test of logical consistency but no one has yet found a way to justify fundamental choices such as those between freedom and equality or individualism and communitarianism. It is doubtful whether environmental ethics has introduced any fundamentally different perspectives on to these dilemmas that seem to be inherent in the biological condition. In terms of practical decision making therefore both law and ethics are subordinate to the political process.

Summary

1. We discussed the difference between legal rights and moral rights. Legal rights are mechanisms for conferring benefits on a right holder. Moral rights are the subject of dispute and could be regarded as entitlements or claims that deserve respect for their own sake.

2. Duties and rights are not two sides of the same coin. To say that we have a moral duty not to harm X does not necessarily mean that X has a right. However, if for whatever reason we think that X has a right someone must have a duty to X to respect that right.

3. There is a distinction between indirect duties in respect of nature and direct duties to nature. Utilitarians may regard the notion of rights either as superfluous or as a weighted factor in the scale of values but animal rights proponents reject utilitarianism because it seems to deny the value of the individual and to lead to behaviour that violates widely shared moral attitudes.

4. We discussed some of the pros and cons of the 'rights' perspective. Rights focus political and legal attention and signify the importance of the interest in question. They draw upon familiar legal ideas so as to provide remedies, and make decision-makers accountable. Objections to rights include the belief that only humans can possess rights; the assertion that all rights are nonsense; the problem that rights tend to be individualistic thus threatening broader ecocentric concerns; the fear that rights give too much protection to animals; and the danger that environmental rights may be so easily outweighed by other concerns as to be discredited.

5. The problem of adjudicating between rights arises because rights may be incommensurable so that, sometimes, one cannot be protected without sacrificing the other. In environmental law this is complicated by the variety of different ethical conflicts *viz.* international equity, intranational equity, intergenerational equity, species equity and planetary equity. In practice political acceptance seems to provide the only answer rationalised by means of the virtue ethics perspective. Some conflicting interests are not incommensurable but uncombinable in the sense that for practical reasons they cannot both be fully satisfied. Uncombinable but not incommensurable interests are susceptible to utilitarian cost-benefit analysis.

6. English law seems to regard animal welfare as a matter of indirect duty and the law seems to be informed by a pragmatic mix of different ethics possible best explained from the virtue ethics perspective.

7. There are a range of public law rights that give individuals access to the courts and environmental information. However, the law relating to *locus standi* remains uncertain as to how far a personal interest is needed. Stone's proposal to give rights directly to collective natural entities such as habitats may make a valuable contribution.

8. Private law rights are dominated by property concerns and students should refer Chapter 8.

9. There are problems in relating the idea of compensation to environmental interests particularly from an individualistic perspective.

10. European law faces similar problems in relation to the enforceability of directives in domestic courts. The emphasis on individual rights does not fit with the collective and sometimes ecocentric nature of European environmental policy.

11. Environmental concerns can be related to human rights contained in international instruments or state constitutions. However, the width and uncertain nature of environmental interests raise problems. Attempts to fit environmental concerns within existing human rights law have met with only limited success. It is sometimes argued that procedural rights such as access to environmental information and environmental impact assessment meet environmental concerns more effectively than do substantive human rights.

Further Reading

Birnie, P.W. and Boyle, A.E. (1992) *International Law and the Environment* (Oxford: Clarendon Press).

Boyle, A.E. and Anderson, M.R. (eds) (1996) *Human Rights Approaches to Environmental Protection* (Oxford: Clarendon Press).

Desgagné, R. (1995) Integrating Environmental Values into the European Convention on Human Rights. *American Journal of International Law*, **89**, 263.

Elder, P.S. (1984) Do Species and Nature Have Rights? – The Wrong Answer to the Right(s) Question. *Osgoode Hall Law Journal*, **22**, 285–95.

Elliot, R. (ed.) (1995) *Environmental Ethics*, chapters 3 and 5 (Oxford: Oxford University Press).

Miller, C. (1998) *Environmental Rights, Critical Perspectives*, chapters 1 and 9 (London: Routledge).

Nash, J. (1993) The Case for Biotic Rights. *Yale Journal of International Law*, **18**, 235–51.

Shelton, D. (1991) Human Rights, Environmental Rights and the Right to Environment. *Stanford Journal of International Law*, 103–38.

Stone, C.D. (1972) Should Trees have Standing? Towards Legal Rights for Natural Objects. *Southern California Law Review*, **45**, 450–501.

Stone, C.D. (1985) Should Trees Have Standing? Revisited. How Far Will Law and Morals Reach – A Pluralist Perspective. *Southern California Law Review*, **59**(1) 1–154.

Stone C.D. (1996) *Should Trees Have Standing and Other Essays on Law, Morals, and the Environment*, chapters 2, 3, 7 and 8 (Dobb's Ferry NY: Oceana).

Van Der Veer, D. (1979) Interspecific Justice. *Inquiry*, 22, 55–79.

Workshop

1. You are the legal adviser to an environmental pressure group which promotes radical ecocentric views. The group wishes to object to a local authority proposal to build a waste disposal site in the vicinity of a beautiful lake which is host to rare species and where there is a retirement home for low income disabled people. The authority informs them that moral concerns about animal welfare are not relevant to its decision. Advise the group as to how they might challenge the decision in the UK courts and in the European Court of human rights.

2. The Rio Declaration states that human beings are 'entitled' to a healthy and productive life in harmony with nature (Article 1) and that there is a 'right to development' (Article 3). Discuss the significance of this choice of language.

3. The EC draft Directive on Civil Liability for Waste defines 'impairment of the environment' as 'any significant physical, chemical or biological deterioration of the environment insofar as this is not considered to be private property'. In the light of this discuss the problems inherent in compensation for environmental damage.

4. To what extent does English law recognise animal rights? What is the ethical basis of English law's approach to the welfare of animals?

5. Does Stone's concept of 'rights of nature' make a useful contribution to the problem of access to environmental justice? How can we provide compensation for damage to nature?

6. 'Animals cannot have rights since they are not members of human society. This is one of the many points at which I am troubled by the apparent dogmatism of my observations.... I am only too conscious of the fact that many would wish to challenge my assumption that the proper starting point for a theory of rights is the use of the word in legal contexts' (Passmore). Discuss.

7. Do you agree with Miller (1998, chapter 9) that the law protects the 'interests' of animals and plants in a way similar to the way it protects children and that this amounts to a right'?

Bibliography

Agora (1990) What Does Our Generation Owe to the Next? *American Journal of International Law*, **84**, 190.

Ackerman, B.A and Stewart, R.B. (1983) Reforming Environmental Law, The Democratic Case for Market Incentives, *Columbia Journal of Environmental Law*, **13**, 171.

Ackerman, B.A. (1975) *Economic Foundations of Property Law* (Boston: Little, Brown).

Aguiler, A.F. and Popovic, N.A.F. (1994) Lawmaking in the UN: The UN Study on Human Rights and the Environment, *RECIEL*, **3**(4), 197.

Allen, D.W. (1983) The Rights of Non-human Animals and World Public Order: A Global Assessment, *New York Law School Law Review*, 377–429.

Anderson, J.C. (1993) Species Equality and the Foundations of Moral Theory. *Environmental Values*, **2**(4) 347–365.

Atkinson, A. (1991) *The Principles of Political Ecology* (London: Bellhaven Press).

Attfield, R. (1983) *The Ethics of Environmental Concern* (Oxford: Blackwell).

Attfield, R. (1987) *A Theory of Value and Obligation* (London: Croom Helm).

Attfield, R. and Belsay, A. (eds) (1994) *Philosophy and the Natural Environment* (Cambridge: Cambridge University Press).

Attfield, R. and Wilkins, B. (1994) Sustainability, *Environmental Values*, **3**, 155–158

Austin, R.C. (1985) Beauty: A Foundation for Environmental Ethics. *Environmental Ethics*, **7**, 197.

Auxter, T. (1979) The Right not to be Eaten. *Inquiry*, **22**, 221–230

Ayer, A.J. (1946) *Language, Truth and Logic* (New York: Dover Publications).

Baier, A. (1984) For the Sake of Future Generations. In T. Regan (ed.) *Earthbound: New Introductory Essays in Environmental Essays* (New York: Random House).

Baker, K. (1995) Consorting With Forests: Rethinking Our Relationship to Natural Resources and How We Should Value Their Loss, *Ecology Law Quarterly*, **22**, 677.

Bales, J.S. (1996) Transnational Responsibility and Recourse for Ozone Depletion, *Boston College International and Comparative Law Review*, **49**(2), 259–295.

Ball, S. and Bell, S. (1997) *Environmental Law: The Law and Policy Relating to the Protection of the Environment*, 4th edn (London: Blackstone Press).

Bambrough, R. (ed.) (1979) *Moral Scepticism and Moral Knowledge* (London, Routledge & Kegan Paul).

Barry, J. (1993) Deep Ecology and the Undermining of Green Politics. In J. Holder et al. (eds) *Perspectives on the Environment: Interdisciplinary Research in Action* (Aldershot: Avebury).

Barry, J. and Sikora, R.I. (eds) (1978) *Obligations to Future Generations* (Philadelphia: Temple University Press).

Beckerman, W. (1994) Sustainable Development: Is It a Useful Concept? *Environmental Values*, **3**(3) 191–209.

Been, V. (1994) What's Fairness Got to Do With it? Environmental Justice and the Siting of Locally Undesirable Land Uses, *Cornell Law Review*, **78**, 1001.

Bentham, J. (1789) Introduction to the Principles of Morals and Legislation. In J.H. Burns and H.L.A. Hart (eds) 1970 edn (London: Athlone Press).

Benton, T. (1993). In A. Dobson and P. Lucardie (eds) *The Politics of Nature* (London: Routledge).

Berat, L. (1993) Defending the Right to a Healthy Environment: Towards a Crime of Genocide in International Law, *Boston University International Law Journal*, **11**, 327.

Berlin, I. (1968) *Two Concepts of Liberty* (Oxford: Oxford University Press).

Berlin, I. (1990) *The Crooked Timber of Humanity: Chapters in the History of Ideas* (London: John Murray).

Biekart, J.W. (1995) Environmental Covenants: Between Government and Industry: A Dutch NGO's Experience, *Review of European Community and International Environmental Law*, **4**(2), 141–149.

Beckerman, W. (1993) The Environmental Limits to Growth: A Fresh Look. In H. Giersch (ed.) *Economic Progress and Environmental Concerns* (Berlin: Springer-Verlag).

Biden, J.R., Jr. (1997) Keep the Current Dolphin-Safe Label. Remarks in the Senate. *Congressional Record* [daily ed.] v.143, January 29, 1997: S792-S793.

Bilbray, B.P. (1996) The International Dolphin Conservation Program Act. Remarks in the House. *Congressional Record* [daily ed.] v.142, July 31, 1996: H9437-H9438.

Birch, T.H. (1990) The Incarceration of Wilderness: Wilderness Areas as Prisons, *Environmental Ethics*, 12.

Birnie, P.W. and Boyle, A.E. (1992) *International Law and the Environment* (Oxford: Clarendon Press).

Birnie, P.W. and Boyle, A.E. (1995) *Basic Documents on International Law and the Environment* (Oxford: Oxford University Press).

Birtles, W. (1993) A Right to Know: The Environmental Information Regulations 1992, *Journal of Planning and Environmental Law*, 615.

Blackman, D.E., Humphreys, P.N. and Todd, P. (eds) (1989) *Animal Welfare and the Law* (Cambridge: Cambridge University Press).

Blackstone, W.T. (1982) Ethics and Ecology. In W.T. Blackstone (ed.) *Philosophy and Environmental Crisis* (Athens, GA: University of Georgia Press).

Blackstone, W.T. (ed.) (1982) *Philosophy and Environmental Ethics* (Athens, GA: University of Georgia Press).

Blomquist, R.F. Symposium of Waste Managements & Law Policy: Developing a Long-term Waste Management Strategy: Beyond the EPA & OTA Reports: Towards a Comprehensive Theory & Approach to Hazardous Waste Reduction in America, *Environmental Law*, **18**, 817.

Boardman, R. (1981) *International Organization and the Conservation of Nature* (London: Macmillan).

Boch, C. (1997) The Enforcement of the Environmental Assessment Directive in the National Courts: A Breach in the Dyke, *Journal of Environmental Law*, **9**, 137.

Bodansky D. (1991) Scientific Uncertainty and the Precautionary Principle, *Environment*, September, 4–5 and 43–44.

Bodansky, D. (1994) The Precautionary Principle in US Environmental Law. In T. ORiordan and J. Cameron, *Interpreting the Precautionary Principle* (London: Earthscan).

Boehlert, S.L. (1996) The International Dolphin Conservation Program Act. Remarks in the House. *Congressional Record* [daily ed.] v.142, July 31, 1996: H9433-H9434.

Boehmer-Christiansen, S. (1994) The Precautionary Principle in Germany – enabling Government. In T. ORiordan and J. Cameron, *Interpreting the Precautionary Principle* (London: Earthscan).

Bonteaux, L. and Leone, F, (1997) *The Legal Definition of Waste and its Impact on Waste Management in Europe* (Seville: Institute for Prospective Technological Studies).

Bookchin, M. (1989) *Remaking Society* (Montreal: Black Rose).

Bookchin, M. (1990) in S. Chase (ed.) *Defending the Earth: A Dialogue Between Murray Bookchin and Dave Foreman* (Boston: South End Press).

Bookchin, M. (1995) *The Philosophy of Social Ecology: Essays on Dialectical Naturalism*, 2nd edn (London: Black Rose Books).

Boulding, K.E and Jarret H. (eds) (1966) *Environmental Quality in a Growing Economy* (Baltimore: John Hopkins Press).

Bowers, J.K. (1997) *Sustainability and Environmental Economics: An Alternative Text* (Harlow, Essex: Longman).

Bowers, J. (1995) An Alternative View of Sustainable Development, Memorandum to the Select Committee on Sustainable Development, Session 1993–94, HL Paper 72–I (21 June 1995) 36.

Bowett, D.W. (1982) *The Law of International Institutions*, 4th edn (London: Stevens & Sons).

Bowman, M. and Redgewell, C. (eds) (1995) *International Law and the Conservation of Biological Diversity* (Deventer: Kluwer Law & Taxation).

Bowman, M.J. (1989) The Protection of Animals under International Law, *Connecticut Journal of International Law*, **4**, 487–499.

Boxer, B. (1996) The International Dolphin Conservation Program Act. Remarks in the Senate. *Congressional Record* [daily ed.] v.142, September 28, 1996: S11700–S11701.

Boxer, B. (1997) Tuna–Dolphin Bill. Remarks in the Senate.*Congressional Record* [daily ed.] v.143, January 29, 1997: S789–S790.

Boyle, A.E. (1991) Saving the World? Implementation and Enforcement of International Environmental Law through International Institutions, *Journal of Environmental Law*, **3**(2) 229–245 .

Boyle, A.E. and Anderson, M.R. (eds) (1996) *Human Rights Approaches to Environmental Protection* (Oxford: Clarendon Press).

Brennan, A. (1984) The Moral Standing of Natural Objects, *Environmental Ethics*, **6**(1) 35–56.

Brennan, A. (1988) *Thinking About Nature* (London: Routledge).

Brennan, A (1995) Ecological Theory and Value in Nature. In Elliot, R. (ed.) *Environmental Ethics* (Oxford: Oxford University Press).

Brenner J.F. (1974) Nuisance Law and the Industrial Revolution, *Journal of Legal Studies*, **3**, 403.

Broonman, S. and Legge, D. (1997)*Animal Law: Text, Cases and Materials* (London: Cavendish).

Brophy, B. (1989) *The Rights of Animals* (London: Sphere).

Brundtland, G. (1987) *Our Common Future: Report of the World Commission on Environment and Development* (Oxford: Oxford University Press).

Buck, E.H. (1997) Dolphin Protection and Tuna Seining, CRS Issue Brief for Congress, No. 96011, available at http: //www.cnie.org/nle/crs_main.html.

Buente, D.T. (1991) A Review of Major Provisions: Citizen Suits and the Clean Air Act Amendments of 1990: Closing the Enforcement Loop, *Environmental Law*, **21**, 2233.

Burgess, J. (1993) Representing Nature: Conservation and the Mass Media. In F.B. Goldsmith, and A. Warren (eds) *Conservation in Progress* (Chichester: Wiley).

Calabresi, G. and Melamed, A.D. (1972) Property Rules, Liability Rules and Inalienability. One View of the Cathedral, *Harvard Law Review*, **85**, 1089–1128.

Caldwell, L.K. (1990) *International Environmental Policy*, 2nd edn (Durham: Duke University Press).

Caldwell, L.K. (1992) *Between Two Worlds, Science, the Environmental Movement and Policy Choice* (Cambridge: Cambridge University Press).

Callicott, J.B. (ed.) (1987) *Companion to a Sand County Almanac: Interpretive and Critical Essays* (Madison: University of Wisconsin Press).

Callicott, J.B. (1989) *In Defense of the Land Ethic* (Albany: State University of New York Press).

Callicott, J.B. (1995) Animal Liberation: A Triangular Affair. In R. Elliot (ed.) *Environmental Ethics* (Oxford: Oxford University Press).

Cameron, J. and Aboucher, J. (1991) The Precautionary Principle: a Fundamental Principle of Law and Policy, *Boston College International and Comparative Law Review*, **xiv**(1) 1–27.

Cameron, J. and Mackenzie, R. (1996) Access to Environmental Justice and Procedural Rights in International Institutions. In A.E. Boyle and M.R. Anderson (eds) (1996) *Human Rights Approaches to Environmental Protection* (Oxford: Clarendon Press).

Cane, Standing, Representation and the Environment. In I. Loveland (ed.) *A Special Relationship: American Influences on Public Law in the UK* (Oxford: Clarendon Press).

Capra, F. (1997) *The Web of Life: A New Synthesis of Mind and Matter* (London: HarperCollins).

Carr, I.M. (1992) Saving the Environment – Does Utilitarianism Provide a Justification? *Legal Studies*, **12**, 92–102.

Carruthers (1992) *The Animals Issue: Moral Theory in Practice* (Cambridge: Cambridge University Press).

Carson, R. (1992) *Silent Spring* (Boston: Houghton Miflin).

Cheyne, I. and Purdue, M. (1995) Fitting Definition to Purpose: The Search for a Satisfactory Definition of Waste, *Journal of Environmental Law*, **7**, 149–67.

Chinkin, C.M. (1989) The Challenge of Soft Law: Development and Change in International Law, *International and Comparative Law Quarterly*, **38**, 850–66.

Churchill, R., Gibson J. and Warren, L. (eds) (1991) *Law, Policy and the Environment* (Cambridge, MA: Blackwell).

Clark, S.R.L. (1979) The Rights of Wild Things, *Inquiry*, **22**, 171–87.

Clark, S.R.L. (1997) *Animals and their Moral Standing* (London: Routledge).

Clements, C.D. (1995) Stasis: the Unnatural Value. In Elliot, R. (ed.) *Environmental Ethics* (Oxford: Oxford University Press).

Coleman, J. *Markets, Morals and the Law* (Cambridge: Cambridge University Press).

Commission of the European Communities (1993) Communication from the Commission to the Council and the European Parliament on the Protection of Animals: COM(93) 384 final.

Commission of the European Communities (1993) Towards Sustainability, Fifth Action Plan, Document COM(92) 23 final, 3 (Brussels: Commission of the European Communities) OJ C138. 17.5.1993.

Commission of the European Communities (1997) Communication from the Commission to the Council and the European Parliament concerning the application of Directives 75/439/EEC, 75/442/EEC, 78/319/EEC and 86/278/EEC on waste management COM(97) 23 final.

Commission on Global Governance (1995) *Our Global Neighbourhood: the Report of the Commission on Global Governance* (Oxford: Oxford University Press).

Commoner, B. (1972) *The Closing Circle: Confronting the Environmental Crisis* (London: Cape).

Commoner, B. (1985) Economic Growth and Environmental Quality: How to Have Both, *Social Policy*, **16**, 18–25.

Cooper, D.E. and Palmer, J.A. (eds) (1992) *The Environment in Question: Ethics and Global Issues* (London: Routledge).

Cooper, M.E. (1987) *An Introduction to Animal Law* (London: Academic Press).

Coquillette, D. (1979) Mosses from an Old Manse: Another Look at Some Historic Cases About the Environment, *Cornell Law Review*, **64**, 761.

Council of Europe (1993) Convention on Civil Liability for Damage Resulting from Activities Dangerous to the Environment, Lugano, 21 June 1993, European Treaty Series 150 (Strasbourg: Council of Europe).

Cross, F.B. (1996) Paradoxical Perils of the Precautionary Principle, *Washington and Lee Law Review*, **53**(3) 851–925.

Cunningham, R. (1996) The International Dolphin Conservation Program Act. Remarks in the House. *Congressional Record* [daily ed.] v.142, July 31, 1996: H9435.

Cunningham, R. (1997) The International Dolphin Conservation Program Act. Remarks in the House. *Congressional Record* [daily ed.] v.143, May 21, 1997: H3114.

Daly, H.E. (1991) *Steady-State Economics* (Washington, D.C.: Island Press).

D'Amato, A. (1990) Do We Owe a Duty to Future Generations to Preserve the Global Environment?, *American Journal of International Law*, **84**(1) 190–98.

D'Amato, A. and Chopra, S.K. (1991) Whales: Their Emerging Right to Life, *American Journal of International Law*, **85**, 21–62.

Dawkins, R. (1989) *The Selfish Gene*, revised edn (Oxford: Oxford University Press).

Dawkins, R. (1993) in Cavalieri and Singer (eds) *The Great Ape Project: Equality Beyond Humanity* (New York: St Martins Press).

Dennett, D.C. (1995) *Darwin's Dangerous Idea: Eution and the Meanings of Life* (London: Allen Lane).

Department of the Environment (1997) Economic Instruments for Water Pollution (consultation paper).

Department of the Environment (1995) *Guide to Risk Assessment and Risk Management for Environmental Protection* (London: HMSO).

Department of the Environment (1995a) The Environment Agency and Sustainable Development, Draft Guidance.

Department of the Environment (1995b) The Environment Agency Management Statement, Draft Guidance.

Department of the Environment (1994) *Sustainable Forestry: The UK Programme*, (cm 2429) (London: HMSO).

Department of the Environment (1994a) *Biodiversity: The UK Action Plan* (London: HMSO).

Department of the Environment (1994b) *Sustainable Development – the UK Strategy* (London: HMSO).

Department of the Environment (1993) *Making Markets Work for the Environment* (London, HMSO).

Department of the Environment (1993a) *Integrated Pollution Control: A Practical Guide* (London: HMSO).

Department of the Environment (1992) *Fit for the Future: A Statement by the Government on Policies for the National Parks* (London: HMSO).

Department of the Environment (1989) *Sustaining Our Common Future: A Progress Report by the United Kingdom on Implementing Sustainable Development* (London: Department of the Environment).

Des Jardins, J.R. (1997) *Environmental Ethics: An Introduction to Environmental Philosophy*, 2nd edn (Belmont, CA: Wadsworth).

Desgagné, R. (1995) Integrating Environmental Values into the European Convention on Human Rights, *American Journal of International Law*, **89**, 263.

Devlin (1965) *The Enforcement of Morals* (Oxford: Oxford University Press).

Dobson, A. (1995) *Green Political Thought*, 2nd edn, (London: Routledge).

Dobson, A. and Lucardie (eds) (1993) *The Politics of Nature: Explorations in Green Political Theory* (London: Routledge).

Dockray, M. (1985) Why do we need Adverse Possession? *Conveyancer and Property Lawyer*, 272.

Doran (1996) The UN Commission on Sustainable Development 1995, *Environmental Politics*, **5**(1) 100–107.

Dovers, S.R. and Handmer, J.W. (1993) Contradictions in Sustainability, *Environmental Conservation*, **20**, 217.

Du Bey, R.A., Tano, M.T., Parker, G.D. and Dudeck, D.J. (1995) Institutional Guidelines for Designing Successful Transferable Rights, *Yale Journal on Regulation*, **6**, 369.

Dworkin, R.M. (1977) *Taking Rights Seriously* (London: Duckworth).

Dworkin, R.M. (1984) Rights as Trumps. In J. Waldron (ed.) *Theories of Rights* (Oxford: Oxford University Press).

Eckersley, R. (1992) *Environmentalism and Political Theory: Toward an Ecocentric Approach* (London: UCL Press).

Economic Commission for Europe (1990) *The ECE and Sustainable Development* (New York).

Edwards, R.W. (1991) Fit for the Future: Report of the National Parks Review Panel , CCP 334 (Cheltenham: Countryside Commission).

Ehrenfeld, D. (1976) The Conservation of Non–Resources, *American Scientist*, 64.

Ehrlich, R. (1971) *The Population Bomb* (New York: Ballantine Books).

Ehrlich, R. (1974) *The End of Affluence* (New York: Ballantine Books).

Elder, S. (1984) Do Species and Nature Have Rights? – The Wrong Answer to the Right(s) Question, *Osgoode Hall Law Journal*, **22**, 285–95.

Elliot, R. (1993) Environmental Ethics. In Singer (ed.) *A Companion to Ethics* (London: Blackwell).

Elliot, R. (ed.) (1995) *Environmental Ethics* (Oxford: Oxford University Press).

Elliot, R. and Gare, A. (eds) (1983) *Environmental Philosophy* (Milton Keynes: Open University Press).

Elworthy, S. (1998) Finding the Causes of Events or Preventing a State of Affairs: The Designation of Nitrate Vulnerable Zones, *Journal of Environmental Law*, **10**, 93.

Elworthy, S. and Holder, J. (1997) *Environmental Protection, Text and Materials* (London: Butterworths).

Emmenegger, S. and Tschentscher, A. (1994) Taking Nature's Rights Seriously: The Long Way to Biocentricism in Environmental Law, *Georgetown International Environmental Law Review*, **6**, 545–92.

Esty, D.C. (1994) *Greening the GATT* (Washington D.C.: Institute for International Economics).

Expert Committee on Compensation and Betterment (Uthwatt Committee) (1942) Final Report, Cmnd. 6386 (London: HMSO).

Faber, M., Manstetten, R. and Proops, J.L.R. (1992) Humankind and the Environment: An Anatomy of Surprise and Ignorance, *Environmental Values*, 1, 217–42.

Fairman, D. (1996) The Global Environment Facility: Haunted by the Shadow of the Future. In R.O. Keohane and M.A. Levy (eds) *Institutions for Environmental Aid: Pitfalls and Promise* (Cambridge, MA: MIT Press).

Faleomavaega, E.F.H. (1996a) The International Dolphin Conservation Program Act. Remarks in the House. *Congressional Record* [daily ed.] v.142, July 31, 1996: H9430–H9431.

Faleomavaega, E.F.H. (1996b) The International Dolphin Conservation Program Act. Remarks in the House. *Congressional Record* [daily ed.] v.142, July 31, 1996: H9428–H9429.

Favre, D.S. (1979) Wildlife Rights: the Ever Widening Circle, *Environmental Law*, 9, 241–81.

Feinberg, J. (1991) The Rights of Animals and Unborn Generations. In J.E. White (ed.) *Contemporary Moral Problems*, 3rd edn (St. Paul: West Publishing Co).

Feinberg, J. (1982) The Rights of Animals and Unborn Generations. In W.T. Blackstone (ed.) *Philosophy and the Environmental Crisis* (Athens, GA: University of Georgia Press).

Finnis, J. (1983) *Fundamentals of Ethics* (Washington D.C.: Georgetown University Press).

Fitcthorn, N.W. (1991) A Review of the Major Provisions: Command & Control vs. The Market: The Potential Effects of other Clean Air Act Requirements on Acid Rain Compliance, *Environmental Law*, 21, 2069.

Fitzpatrick, D. (1996) The United Nations General Assembly and the Security Council. In J. Werksman (ed.) *Greening International Institutions* (London: Earthscan).

Fox, W. (1990) *Towards a Transpersonal Ecology: Developing New Foundations for Environmentalism* (Boston: New Science Library).

Fox, W. (1984) Deep Ecology: A New Philosophy For Our Time?, *The Ecologist*, 14, 194–200.

Francione, G.L. (1995) *Animals, Property, and the Law* (Philadelphia: Temple University).

Francis, J.M (1996) *Nature Conservation and the Precautionary Principle*, *Environmental Values*, 5(3), 257–64.

Francis, L. and Norman, R. (1978) Some Animals are more Equal than Others, *Philosophy*, 53, 507–27.

Freestone, D. (1991) The Precautionary Principle. In R.R. Churchill and D. Freestone (eds) *International Law and Global Climate Change*.

Freestone, D. and Hey, E. (eds) (1996) *The Precautionary Principle and International Law: The Challenge of Implementation* (The Hague: Kluer).

French, H.F., Peterson, J.A. and Chege, N. (1995) Partnership for the Planet: An Environmental Agenda for the United Nations, World Watch Paper 126 (Washington, D.C.: Worldwatch Institute).

Frey, R.G. (1980) *Interests and Rights: The Case Against Animals* (Oxford: Clarendon Press).

Frey, R.G. (1983) *Rights, Killing and Suffering* (Oxford, Basil Blackwell).

Frey, R.G. (1987) Autonomy and the Value of Animal Life, *The Monist*, 70(1) 50–63.

Fry, M. (1995) *A Manual of Nature Conservation Law* (Oxford, Oxford University Press).

Fullem, G.D. (1995) The Precautionary Principle: Environmental Protection in the Face of Scientific Uncertainty, *Willamette Law Review*, **31**(2) 495.

Furuseth, R and Cocklin, C. (1995) An Institutional Framework for Resource Management – The New Zealand Model, *Natural Resources Journal*, **35**, 243–73.

Gandy, M (1994) *Recycling and the Politics of Urban Waste* (London: Earthscan).

Garner, R. (1993) *Animals, Politics and Morality* (Manchester: Manchester University Press).

Garner, R. (1994) Wildlife Conservation and the Moral Status of Animals, *Environmental Politics*, **3**, 114–29.

Garner, R. (1996) *Animal Rights: The Changing Debate* (Basingstoke: Macmillan).

GATT Panel Report. 1991. United States – Restrictions on Import of Tuna Panel Report, GATT BISD 39S/155, 30 I.L.M. 1594.

GATT Panel Report. 1994. United States – Restrictions on Imports of Tuna Panel Report, 33 I.L.M. 839.

GATT (1994) Symposium on Trade, Environment and Sustainable Development, Geneva, 10–11 June 1994, Trade and Environment, 28 July 1994.

Georgescu-Roegen, N. (1971) *The Entropy Law and the Economic Process* (Cambridge, MA: Harvard University Press).

Gerard, N. (1996) Access to Justice on Environmental Matters: A Case of Double Standards, *Journal of Environmental Law*, **8**, 140.

Giagnocavo, C. and Goldstein, H. (1990) Law Reform or World Re-form: The Problem of Environmental Rights, *McGill Law Journal*, **35**, 345–86.

Gibbons, J. (1996) The International Dolphin Conservation Program Act. Remarks in the House. *Congressional Record* [daily ed.] v.142, July 31, 1996: H9434–H9435.

Gilchrest, W.T. (1997) The International Dolphin Conservation Program Act. Remarks in the House. *Congressional Record* [daily ed.] v.143, May 21, 1997: H3132–H3133.

Gillespie, A (1997) *International Environment Law Policy and Ethics* (Oxford: Clarendon Press).

Gillroy J.M. (ed.) (1993) *Environmental Risk, Fundamental Values and Political Choices* (Boulder, CO: Westview Press).

Gilpin, R. (1987) *The Political Economy of International Relations* (Princeton University Press, Princeton).

Ginther, K and Denters, E. (1995) *Sustainable Development and Good Governance* (Amsterdam: Kluwer).

Glacken, C.J. (1967) *Traces on the Rhodian Shore: Nature and Culture in Western Thought from Ancient Times to the End of the Eighteenth Century* (Berkeley: University of California Press).

Glennon, M.J. (1990) Has International Law Failed the Elephant? *American Journal of International Law*, **84**, 1–43.

Gold, M. (1995) *Animal Rights: Extending the Circle of Compassion* (John Carpenter/Envirobook) HV4708.

Golding, M. (1972) Obligations to Future Generations, *The Monist*, **56**, 85–99.

Goldsmith, E. (1972) *A Blueprint for Survival* (London: Tom Stacey Ltd).

Goldsmith, F.B. and Warren, A. (eds) (1993) *Conservation in Progress* (Chichester: Wiley).

Goodkin (1986) The Rights of Animals, *Columbia Human Rights Review*, **18**, 259.

Goodpaster, K.E. (1978) On Being Morally Considerable, *Journal of Philosophy*, **78**, 308.

Goodpaster, K.E. and Sayre, K.M. (eds) (1974) *Ethics and Problems of the 21st Century* (Notre Dame, Ind.: University of Notre Dame).

Goss, P.J. (1996) The International Dolphin Conservation Program Act. Remarks in the House. *Congressional Record* [daily ed.] v.142, July 31, 1996: H9425.

Grabitz, E. and Zacker, C. (1989) Scope for Action by the EC Member States for the Improvement of Environmental Protection under EEC Law – The example of Environmental Taxes and Subsidies, *Common Market Law Review*, **26**(3), 423–47.

Gray, J.(1993) *Post-Liberalism* (London: Routledge).

Gray, J. (1997) *Endgames: Questions in Late Modern Political Thought* (Oxford: Blackwell).

Gray, J.S. (1990) Statistics and the Precautionary Principle, *Marine Pollution Bulletin*, **21**, 174.

Gray, K. (1994) Equitable Property, *Current Legal Problems*, **47**(2) 157–214.

Grieder, T. and Garkovich, L. (1994) Landscapes, the Social Construction of Nature and the Environment, *Rural Sociology*, **59**, 1.

Gullet, W. (1997) Environmental Protection and the Precautionary Principal: A Response to Scientific Uncertainty in Environmental Management. *Environmental and Planning Law Journal*, **14**(1), 52–69.

Gullet, W. (1997) Environmental Protection and the Precautionary Principle. *Environmental and Planning Law Journal*, **14**(1), 52.

Gundling, L. (1990) The Status in International Law of the Principle of Precautionary Action, *International Journal of Estuarine and Coastal Law*, **5**, 23–30.

Gundling, L. (1990a) What Obligation Does One Generation Owe To The Next? *American Journal of International Law*, **84**, 190.

Gundling, L. (1990b) Our Responsibility to Future Generations, *American Journal of International Law*, **84**, 207–12.

Gupta, J. (1995) The Global Environment Facility in its North–South Context, *Environmental Politics*, **4**(1) 19–43.

Gurr, T.R. (1985) On the Political Consequences of Scarcity and Economic Decline, *International Studies Quarterly*, **29**(1) 51–75.

Haas, M., Keohane, R.O. and Levy, M.A. (eds) (1993) *Institutions for the Earth: Sources of Effective International Environmental Protection* (Cambridge, MA: MIT Press).

Hahn, R.W. and Hester, G.L. (1989) Where Did All the Markets Go? An Analysis of EPA's Emissions Trading Programme, *Yale Journal on Regulation*, 6, 109–53.

Hardin, G. (1974) Living in a Lifeboat, *Bioscience*, **24**, 561.

Hardin, G. (1968) The Tragedy of the Commons, Science. Reprinted in A. Markandya and J. Richardson (eds) (1992) *The Earthscan Reader in Environmental Economics* (London: Earthscan).

Hargrove, E.C. (1987) Foundation of Wildlife Protection Attitudes, *Inquiry*, **30**, 3.

Hargrove, E.C. (1989) *Foundations of Environmental Ethics* (Englewood Cliffs, NJ: Prentice-Hall).

Harrison, C.M. (1993) Nature Conservation, Science and Popular Values. In F.B. Goldsmith and A. Warren (eds) *Conservation in Progress* (Chichester: Wiley).

Harrison, J. (1997) Environmental Mediation: The Ethical and Constitutional Dimension, *Journal of Environmental Law*, **9**, 79.

Harrop, S.R. (1997) The Dynamics of Wild Animal Welfare Law, *Journal of Environmental Law*, **9**, 287–302.

Hart, H.L.A. (1961) *The Concept of Law* (Oxford: Clarendon Press).

Hart, H.L.A. (1968) *Law, Liberty and Morality* (Oxford: Oxford University Press).

Hayward, T. (1994) Kant and the Moral Considerability of Nonrational Beings. In R. Attfield and A. Belsey (eds) *Philosophy and the Natural Environment* (Cambridge: Cambridge University Press).

Healey, P. and Shaw, T. (1994) Changing Meanings of Environment in the Planning System, *Transactions of the Institute of British Geographers*, 19.

Helm, D. and Pearce, D. (eds) Economic Policy towards the Environment, *Oxford Review of Economic Policy*, **6**(1), 1–16.

Helm, D. and Pearce, D. (1991) Economic Policy towards the Environment: An Overview. In D. Helm (eds.) *Economic Policy Towards the Environment* (Oxford: Blackwell).

Hey, E. (1992) The Precautionary Concept in Environmental Law and Policy: Institutionalizing Caution, *The Georgetown International Environmental Law Review*, **4**, 303–18.

High North Alliance, Marine Mammal Management Debate at http:/www.highnorth.no/.

Hill, T.E., Jr. (1983) Ideals of Human Excellence and Preserving Natural Environment, *Environmental Ethics*, 5, 211–24.

HMSO (1995) Making Waste Work, Cmnd 9675 (London: HMSO) .

HMSO (1994) Sustainable Development: the UK Strategy, Cmnd 2426 (London HMSO).

HMSO (1990) This Common Inheritance: Britain's Environmental Strategy, Cmnd 1200 (London: HMSO).

Hobhouse, A. (1947) Report of the National Parks Committee, Cmnd 7121, (London: HMSO).

Holder, J. (ed.) (1997) *The Impact of EC Law on the United Kingdom* (Chichester: John Wiley and Sons).

Horta, K. (1996a) The World Bank and the International Monetary Fund. In J. Werksman (ed.) *Greening International Institutions* (London: Earthscan).

Horta, K. (1996b) Environmental Policies of the World Bank, *Journal of Environmental Law and Practice*, **3**(6), 36.

Houck, O.A. (1995) Why Do We Protect Endangered Species, and What Does That Say About Whether Restrictions on Private Property to Protect Them Constitute 'Takings?', *Iowa Law Review*, **80**, 297–332.

House of Lords Environment Select Committee (1993–4 Session) 3rd Report, Remedying Environmental Damage.

House of Lords Select Committee on the European Communities (1996–7 Session) 1st Report, Freedom of Access to Information on the Environment (London: HMSO).

Howarth, R. (1995) Sustainability under Uncertainty – A Deontological Approach, *Land Economics*, **71**, 417–27.

Howarth, W. (1997) Self-Policing, Self-Incrimination and Pollution Law, *Modern Law Review*, **60**, 200–29.

Howarth, W. and Rodgers, C. (eds) (1992) *Agriculture, Conservation and Land Use* (Cardiff: University of Wales Press).

Huffmann, J.L. (1992) Do Species and Nature Have Rights?, *Public Land Law Review*, **13**, 51–76.

Hughes, D. (1996) *Environmental Law*, 3rd edn (London: Butterworths).

Hume, D. (1975) *An Enquiry Concerning the Principles of Morals in Enquiries*, 2nd edn, (Oxford: Oxford University Press).

Huxley (1947) Conservation of Nature in England and Wales: Report of the Wildlife Conservation Special Committee, Cmnd 7122 (London: HMSO).

International Union for the Conservation of Nature (1980) World Conservation Strategy: Living Resource Conservation for Sustainable Development (Gland, Switzerland: International Union for the Conservation of Nature).

International Union for the Conservation of Nature (1991) Caring for the Earth: A Strategy for Sustainable Living ICUN/UNEP/WWF.

Irvine, S. and Ponton, A. (1988) *A Green Manifesto: Policies for a Green Future* (London: Optima).

Jacobs, M. (1989) *The Green Economy: Environment, Sustainable Development and the Politics of the Future* (London: Pluto Press).

Jestin, K. (1995) International Efforts to Abate the Depletion of the Ozone Layer, *Georgetown International Environmental Law Review*, 7(3), 829.

Jewell, T. and Steele, J. (1996) UK Regulatory Reform and the Pursuit of Sustainable Development. *Journal of Environmental Law*, **8**, 283.

Johnson, L.E. (1991) *A Morally Deep World: An Essay on Moral Significance and Environmental Ethics* (Cambridge: Cambridge University Press).

Jung, H.Y. (1983) Marxism, Ecology and Technology, *Environmental Ethics*, **5**(2) 169–71.

Kant, I. (1887) in Hastie, W. (trans.) (1974) *The Philosophy of Law: An Exposition of the Fundamental Principles of Jurisprudence as the Science of Right* (Edinburgh: T&T Clark).

Kant, I. (1963) in Infield L. (trans.) *Lectures on Ethics* (New York: Harper and Row).

Keat, R. (1994) Citizens, Consumers and the Environment: Reflections on the Economy of the Earth, *Environmental Values*, 3(4) 333–49.

Kenyon ,W. and Edwards-Jones, G. (1998) What Level of Information Enables the Public to Act Like Experts when Evaluating Ecological Goods, *Journal of Environmental Planning and Management*, 41, 463.

Khan, H. and Bruce-Biggs, B. (1972) *Things to Come: Thinking about the Seventies and Eighties* (New York: Macmillan).

Kheel, M. (1985) The Liberation of Nature: A Circular Affair, *Environmental Ethics*, 7(2) 135–49.

Kimball, L.A. (1992) Towards Global Environmental Management: The Institutional Setting, *Yearbook of International Environmental Law*, **3**, 18–42.

Kimball, L.A. and Boyd, W.C. (1992) International Institutional Arrangements for Environment and Development: A Post Rio Assessment, *Review of European Community and International Environmental Law*, 1(3) 295–306.

Kirkby et al. (eds) (1995) *The Earthscan Reader in Sustainable Development* (London: Earthscan).

Kiss, A. and Shelton, D. (1993) *Manual of European Environmental Law* (Cambridge: Grotius Publications).

Kittichaisaree, K. (1993) Using Trade Sanctions and Subsidies to Achieve Environmental Objectives in the Pacific Rim. *Colorado Journal of Environmental Law and Policy*, **4**, 296.

Klinowska, M. (1994) Brains, Behaviour and Intelligence in Cetaceans (Whales, Dolphins and Porpoises). In *11 Essays on Whales and Man*, 2nd edn (High North). Available at http://www.highnorth.no/br-be-an.htm.

Kolbe, J. (1997) The International Dolphin Conservation Program Act. Remarks in the House. *Congressional Record* [daily ed.] v.143, May 21, 1997: H3125.

Kramer, L. (1991) The Implementation of Community Directives Within Member States: Some Implications of the Direct Effect Doctrine, *Journal of Environmental Law*, **3**, 915.

Kramer, L. (1992) *Focus on European Environmental Law* (London: Sweet & Maxwell).

Ksentini (1994) UN Commission on Human Rights, Final Report of the Special Rappoteur (UN Doc. E/CN. 4/Sub. 2/1994/9).

Kuhlman, W. (1997) Can the Precautionary Principle Protect Us From Imperial Ecology, *Wild Earth*, **7**, 67.

Kunich, C. Species and Habitat Conservation, The Fallacy of Deathbed Conservation under the Endangered Species Act 1973, *Environmental Law*, **24**, 40.

Kupferberg, I.M. (1994) Fixing a Hole: Recent Attempts by the European Community to Preserve the Ozone Layer, *Boston College International and Comparative Law Review*, **27**(1), 165–76.

Lahey, W.L. (1984) Economic Charges for Environmental Protection – Ocean Dumping Fees, *Ecology Law Quarterly*, **11**(3), 305–42.

Latin, H. (1991) Overview and Critique: Regulatory Failure, Administrative Incentives and the New Clean Air Act, *Environmental Law*, **21**, 1647.

Layard, A. (1997) The 1994 Directive on the Incineration of Hazardous Waste, Substitute Fuels and Trans-Scientific Choices, *European Environmental Law Review*, 16.

Leahy, M. (1994) *Against Liberation: Putting Animals in Perspective* (London: Routledge).

Lee, D.C. (1980) On the Marxian View of the Relationship Between Man and Nature, *Environmental Ethics*, **2**, 3–16.

Leeson, J.D. (1995) *Environmental Law* (London: Pitman).

Leopold, A. (1949) *A Sand County Almanac; and Sketches Here and There*, (New York: Oxford University Press).

Lieberman, B.C. (1994) Stratospheric Ozone Depletion And The Montreal Protocol: A Critical Analysis, *Buffalo Environmental Law Journal*, **2**(1), 1.

Lomas, O. (ed.) (1991) *Frontiers of Environmental Law* (London: Chancery Law Publishing).

Lovelock, J.E. (1979) *Gaia: A New Look at Life on Earth* (Oxford: Oxford University Press).

Lovelock, J.E. (1989) *The Ages of Gaia: A Biography of Our Living Earth* (Oxford: Oxford University Press).

Lovelock, J.E. (1994) Taking Care. In T. O'Riordan and J. Cameron (eds) *Interpreting the Precautionary Principle* (London: Earthscan).

Lowe, P., Clark, J., Seymour, S. and Ward, N. (1997) *Moralising the Environment* (London: UCL Press).

Lowe et al. (1986) Countryside Conflicts, *The Politics of Farming, Forestry and Conservation* (Aldershot, Hampshire: Gower).

Lucy, W.N.R. (1997) The Common Law According to Hegel, *Oxford Journal of Legal Studies*, **4**, 685.

Lucy, W.N.R. and Mitchell, C. (1996) Replacing Private Property: The Case for Stewardship, *Cambridge Law Journal*, **55**, 566–600.

Lyster, S. (1985) *International Wildlife Law: An Analysis of International Treaties Concerned With The Conservation of Wildlife* (Cambridge: Grotius Press).

MacDonald, M. (1984) Natural Rights. In J. Waldron (ed.) *Theories of Rights* (Oxford: Oxford University Press).

MacIntyre, A.C. (1985) *After Virtue: a Study in Moral Theory* (London: Duckworth).

Mackie, J.L. (1977) *Ethics: Inventing Right and Wrong* (Harmondsworth: Penguin).

Maddox, J.R. (1972) *The Doomsday Syndrome* (London: Macmillan).

Magel, C.R. (1989) *Keyguide to Information Sources in Animal Rights* (London: Mansell).

Malcolm, R. (1994) *A Guidebook to Environmental Law* (London: Sweet and Maxwell).

Mannion A.M. and Bowlby S.R. (1990) *Environmental Issues in the 1990s* (Chichester: Wiley).

Marchant, G. (1992) Global Warming: Freezing Carbon Dioxide Emissions: an offset policy for slowing global warming, *Environmental Law*, **22**, 623.

Marietta, D.E. (1988) Environmental Holism and Individuals, *Environmental Ethics*, **10**(3) 251–58.

Markandya, A. and Richardson, J. (eds) (1992) *The Earthscan Reader in Environmental Economics* (London: Earthscan).

Marshall, G. (1997) Letter presented to the House by Mr Faleomavaega. *Congressional record* [daily ed.] v.143, May 21, 1997: H3127.

Masters, R.D. (1961) A Multi-bloc Model of the International System, *American Political Science Review*, **55**(4) 780–98.

Mathews, F. (1991) *The Ecological Self* (London: Routledge).

May, R.M. (1973) *Stability and Complexity in Modern Ecosystems* (Princeton, NJ: Princeton University Press).

Mayr, E. (1969) The Biological Meaning of Species, *Biological Journal of the Linnean Society*, **1**, 311.

Mazmaian, D.A. and Morell, D.L. (1991) EPA: Coping With the New Political Economic Order, *Environmental Law*, **21**, 1477.

McPherson, C.B. (1964) *The Political Theory of Possessive Individualism: From Hobbes to Locke* (Oxford: Oxford University Press).

McCarthy, V. (1982) The Changing Concept of Animals as Property, *Journal of International Studies of Animal Problems*, **3**, 295–300.

McDermott, J. (1996) The International Dolphin Conservation Program Act. Remarks in the House. *Congressional Record* [daily ed.] v.142, July 31, 1996: H9436.

McDonald, J.M. (1995) Appreciating the Precautionary Principle as an Ethical Eution in Ocean Management, *Ocean Development and International Law*, **26**(3), 255–86.

McEldowney, J.F. and McEldowney, S. (1997) *Environment and the Law: An Introduction for Environmental Scientists and Lawyers* (Harlow, Essex: Longman).

McIntosh, R. (1985) *The Background of Ecology: Concept and Theory* (Cambridge: Cambride University Press).

McGarity, T.O. (1990) Implementing NEPA: Some Specific Issues: Article: Judicial Enforcement of NEPA–Inspired Promises, *Environmental Law*, **20**, 569.

McIntyre, O. and Mosedale, T. (1997) The Precautionary Principle as a Norm of Customary International Law, *Journal of Environmental Law*, **9**(2), 221–41.

McKay, S., Pearson, M. and Meadows, D.H. (eds) (1974) *Limits to Growth: A Report for the Club of Rome's Project on the Predicament of Mankind* (New York: Universe Books).

McRory, R. (1992) The Enforcement of Community Environmental law, Some Critical Issues, *Common Market Law Review*, 29, 347.

McRory, R. (1996) Environmental Citizenship and the Law: Repairing the European Road, *Journal of Environmental Law*, **8**, 219.

Meadows, D.H. et al. (1974) *The Limits to Growth* (London: Pan Books).

Meadows, D.H., Meadows, D.L. and Randers, J. (1992) *Beyond the Limits: Global Collapse or a Sustainable Future* (London: Earthscan).

Mehta, A. and Hawkins, D. (1998) Integrated Pollution Control and its Impact: Perspectives From Industry, *Journal of Environmental Law*, **10**, 61.

Mensah, C. (1996) The UN Commission on Sustainable Development. In j. Werksman (ed.) *Greening International Institutions* (London: Earthscan).

Merchant, C. (1992) *Radical Ecology: The Search for a Liveable World* (New York: Routledge).

Midgely, M. (1983) *Animals and Why They Matter* (Athens, GA: University of Georgia Press).

Mill, J.S. (1962). In M. Warnock (ed.) *Utilitarianism* (London: Collins/Fontana).

Miller, C. (1998) *Environmental Rights, Critical Perspectives* (London: Routledge).

Miller, G. (1997a) The International Dolphin Conservation Program Act. Remarks in the House. *Congressional record* [daily ed.] v.143, May 21, 1997: H3129.

Miller, G. (1997b) The International Dolphin Conservation Program Act. Remarks in the House. *Congressional record* [daily ed.] v.143, May 21, 1997: H3131.

Millichap, D. (1993) Sustainability: A long Established Concern of Planning Law, *Journal of Planning and Environmental Law*, 110.

Mintz, J.A. (1988) Symposium on Waste Management Law & Policy: Failure of the Current Waste Managements Policy: Agencies Congress & Regulatory Enforcement: A Review of EPA's Hazardous Waste Enforcement Effort 1970–1987, *Environmental Law*, **18**(988), 683.

Moffet, J. (1997) Legislative Options for Implementing the Precautionary Principle, *Journal of Environmental Law and Practice*, **7**(2), 157.

Momtaz, D. (1996) The United Nations and the Protection of the Environment: From Stockholm to Rio de Janiero, *Political Geography*, **15**(3/4) 261–71.

More, J.D. (1991) A Review of Major Provisions: Clean Air Act Allowance Trading, *Environmental Law*, **21**, 2021.

Mullinder, R. (1998) Privacy, Paedophilia and the European Convention on Human Rights: A Deontological Approach, *Public Law*, 384.

Murphy, E.F. (1971) Has Nature Any Right to Life?, *Hastings Law Journal*, **22**, 467–84.

Myrick, A.C., Jr. (1996) Statement on Physiological Effects on Dolphins Due to Chase and Capture by the Tuna Industry. Submitted to the House Resources Committee and Senate Commerce Committee, June 1996. Available at http://www.earthisland.org/ei/immp/myrick.html.

Naess, A. (1973) The Shallow and the Deep, Long–Range Ecology Movement. A Summary, *Inquiry*, **16**, 95–100.

Naess, A. (1989) *Ecology, Community and Lifestyle: Outline of an Ecosophy* (Cambridge: Cambridge University Press).

Nanda (1995) Environment. In O. Schacter and C.C. Joyner (eds) *United Nations Legal Order* (Cambridge: Grotius Publications).

Narveson, J. (1977) Animal Rights, *The Canadian Journal of Philosophy*, **7**, 177.

Narveson, J. (1983) On the Survival of Human Kind. In R. Elliot and A. Gare (eds) *Environmental Philosophy* (Milton Keynes: Open University Press).

Nash, J. (1993) The Case for Biotic Rights, *Yale Journal of International Law*, **18**, 235–51.

Nash, R. (1977) Do Rocks Have Rights? *Centre Magazine*, **10**, 32–43.

Nash, R. (1989) *The Rights of Nature: A History of Environmental Ethics* (Madison: University of Wisconsin Press).

Nature Conservancy Council (1989) *Guidelines for Selection of Biological Sites of SSSIs* (Peterborough: Nature Conservancy Council Publications).

Nolkaemper, A. (1991) The Precautionary Principle in International Environmental Law: What's new under the sun?, *Marine Pollution Bulletin*, 22(3), 107.

Nollkaemper, A. (1996) An Analysis of the EC Ban on Furs from Animals taken by Leghold Traps, *Journal of Environmental Law*, 8(2), 237–56.

Nolkaemper, A. (1996a) The Legality of Moral Crusades Disguised in Trade Laws, *Journal of Environmental Law*, 8, 237–56.

Nolkaemper, A. (1997) Habitat Protection in European Community Law: Eving Conceptions of a Balance of Interests. *Journal of Environmental Law*, 9(2).

Nordhaus, W.D. (1993) Reflections on the Economics of Climate Change, *Journal of Economic Pespectives*, 7, 11–25.

Northcote, M.S. (1996) *The Environment and Christian Ethics* (Cambridge: Cambridge University Press).

Norton, B.G. (1982) Environmental Ethics and Non-Human Rights, *Environmental Ethics*, 4, 35–49.

Norton, B.G. (ed.) (1986a) *The Preservation of Species: The Value of Biological Diversity* (Princeton, NJ: Princeton University Press).

Norton, B.G. (1986b) Conservation and Preservation: A Conceptual Rehabilitation, *Environmental Ethics*, 8, 195–211.

Norton, B.G. (1987) *Why Preserve Natural Variety?* (Princeton, NJ: Princeton University Press).

Norton, B.G. (1991) *Towards Unity Among Environmentalists* (Oxford: Oxford University Press).

Nozick, R. (1974) *Anarchy, State and Utopea* (Oxford: Blackwell).

Nye, J.S. (1973) Regional Institutions. In R.A. Falk and S.H. Mendlovitz (eds) *Regional Politics and World Order* (San Francisco: W.H. Freeman).

Oates, W.E. (1985) Marketable Permits for the Prevention of Environmental Deterioration, *Journal of Environmental Economics & Managements*, 12, 207.

O'Connor, M. (1994) Valuing Fish in Aotearoa: The Treaty, the Model and the Intrinsic Value of the Trout, *Environmental Values*, 3(3) 245–65.

O'Keefe D.M. and Twomey, P. (eds) (1994) *Legal Issues of the Maastricht Treaty* (London: Chancery Law Publishing).

OECD (1994) *The Environmental Effects of Trade* (Paris: OECD).

Onimode, B. (ed.) (1989) *The IMF, The World Bank and the African Debt – the Social and Political Impact* (London: ZED Books with the Institute for African Alternatives).

Ophuls, W. (1977) *Ecology and the Politics of Society* (San Francisco: W.H. Freeman).

O'Riorden, T. and Jordon, A.(1995) The Precautionary Principle in Contemporary Environmental Poliyics, *Environmental Values*, 4, 191.

O'Riordan, T. and Cameron, J. (1994) *Interpreting the Precautionary Principle* (London: Earthscan).

O'Riordan, T. (1981) *Environmentalism*, 2nd edn, (London: Pion)

Osborn, D. (1997) Some Reflections on UK Environmental Policy 1970–1995, *Journal of Environmental Law*, 9, 3–22.

Paddock, L.C. (1991) Environmental Enforcement at the Turn of the Century, *Environmental Law*, 21, 1509.

Paddock, W. and Paddock, L.C. (1967) *Famine 1975! America's Decision: Who Will Survive?* (Boston: Little Brown).

Paehlke, R. (1989) *Environmentalism and the Future of Progressive Politics* (New Haven, Conn: Yale University Press).

Palmer, G. (1992) New Ways to Make International Environmental Law, *American Journal of International Law*, **86**, 259–83.

Palmisano, J. (1988) Emissions Trading: Why is this Thoroughbred Hobbled? *Columbia Journal of Environmental Law*, **13**, 217–56.

Parfit, D. (1976) On Doing the Best for Our Children. In M. Bayles(ed.) *Ethics and Population* (Cambridge, MA: Schenkman Publishing Co.).

Parfit, D. (1984) *Reasons and Persons* (Oxford: Clarendon Press).

Partridge, E. (ed.) (1982) Responsibilities to Future Generations, *Environmental Ethics*, **4**(1) 75–83.

Passmore, J. (1980) *Man's Responsibility for Nature: Ecological Problems and Western Tradition*, 2nd edn, (London: Duckworth).

Pearce, D. (1992) Green Economics, *Environmental Values*, **1**, 3–13.

Pearce, D.and Warford, J. *World Without End: Economics, Environment and Sustainable Development* (Washington: World Bank).

Pearce, D. (ed.) (1991) *Blueprint 2, Greening the World Economy* (London: Earthscan).

Pearce, D. and Turner, R.K. (1990) *Economics of Natural Resources and the Environment* (Hempstead: Harvester, Wheatsheaf).

Pearce, D., Markandya, A. and Barbier, E.B. (1989) *Blueprint for a Green Economy* (London: Earthscan).

Pennock, J. and Chapman, J. (eds) (1982) *Ethics, Economics and the Law* (New York: Nomos).

Pepper, D. (1984) *The Roots of Modern Environmentalism* (London: Croom Helm).

Peters, R.S. (ed.) (1975) *Nature and Conduct, Royal Institute of Philosophy Lectures*, 8 (London: Macmillan).

Piddington, K. (1992) The Role of the World Bank. In A. Hurrell and B. Kingsbury (eds) *The International Politics of the Environment: Actors, Interests and Institutions* (Oxford: Clarendon Press).

Pimm, S.L. (1991) *The Balance of Nature* (Chicago: University of Chicago Press).

Pinchot, G. (1910) *The Fight for Conservation* (Washington, DC:University of Washington Press).

Pinchot, G. (1914) *The Training of a Forester* (New York: Lippincot).

Pirages. D. (ed.) (1977) *The Sustainable Society* (New York: Praeger).

Pluhar, E.B. (1983) The Justification of an Environmental Ethic, *Environmental Ethics*, **5**(1) 47–61.

Pluhar, E.B. (1995) *Beyond Prejudice: The Moral Significance of Human and Nonhuman Animals* (Durham: Duke University Press).

Plumwood, V. (1986) Ecofeminism: An Overview and Discussions of Positions and Arguments. In Women and Philosophy, supplement to the *Australian Journal of Philosophy*, 64.

Plumwood, V. (1993) *Feminism and the Mastery of Nature* (London: Routledge).

Ponting, C. (1991) *A Green History of the World* (London: Sinclair-Stevenson).

Porrit, J. (1984) *Seeing Green: the Politics of Ecology Explained* (Oxford: Blackwell).

Portney, R. (1988) Reforming Environmental Regulation: Three Modest Proposals, *Journal of Columbian Environmental Law*, **13**, 201–15.

Portney, P.R. (1991) The EPA 'Thirtysomething', *Environmental PR Law*, **21**, 1461.

Posner, R.A. (1981) *The Economics of Justice* (Cambridge, MA: Harvard University Press).

Posner, R.A. (1986) *Economic Analysis of Law* (Boston: Little Brown and Co).

Post, S.G. (1993) The Emergence of Species Impartiality: A Medical Critique of Biocentrism, *Perspectives in Biology and Medicine*, **36**(2) 289–300.

Purdue, M. (1991) Integrated Pollution Control in the Environmental Protection Act 1990: A Coming of Age of Environmental Law, *Modern Law Review*, **51**, 534.

Purdue, M. (1995) When a Regulation of Land Becomes a Taking: A Look at Two Recent Decisions of the United States Supreme Court, *Journal of Planning and Environment Law*, 279.

Purdue, M. and Healey, E.F. (1992) Planning Gain and the Grant of Planning Permission: Is the United States Test of Rational Nexus the Appropriate Solution? *Journal of Planning and Environmental Law*, 1012.

Rand, A. (1964) *The Virtue of Selfishness: a New Concept of Egoism* (New York: New American Library).

Rawls, J. (1972) *A Theory of Justice* (Oxford: Clarendon Press).

Raz, J. (1984) Rights-Based Moralities. In J. Waldron (ed.) *Theories of Rights* (Oxford: Oxford University Press).

Raz, J. (1986) *The Morality of Freedom* (Oxford: Clarendon Press).

Redclift, M. (1987) *Sustainable Development* (London: Methuen).

Redclift, M. (1992) *Sustainable Development: Exploring the Contradictions* (London: Methuen).

Regan, T. (1981) The Nature and Possibility of an Environmental Ethic, *Environmental Ethics*, **3**, 19–34.

Regan, T. (1983) *The Case for Animal Rights* (London: Routledge & Kegan Paul).

Regan, T. and Singer, H.W. (eds) (1989) *Animal Rights and Human Obligations*, 2nd edn (Englewood Cliffs, NJ: Prentice-Hall).

Reid, C. (1996) Environmental Regulation through Economic Instruments: the Example of Forestry, *Environental Law and Management*, 59.

Reid, C. (1994) *Nature Conservation Law* (Edinburgh: Green).

Reid, D. (1995) *Sustainable Development: An Introductory Guide* (London: Earthscan).

Reitze, Jr., A.W. (1991) Overview and Critique: a century of air pollution control law: what's worked; what's failed; what might work, *Environmental Law*, **21**, 1549.

Revesezs, R.L. (1984) Incentives for Environmental Protection, *Ecology Law Quarterly*, **11**(3), 451–69.

Rich, B. (1990) The Emperor's New Clothes: The World Bank and Environmental Reform, *World Policy Journal*, **7**(2), 305–29.

Richardson, B. (1998) Economic Instruments and Sustainable Management in New Zealand, *Journal of Environmental Law*, 10, 29–39.

Rio (1992) see UNCED.

Ritchie, D.G. (1985) *Natural Rights* (New York: Allen & Unwin).

Robinson, D. and Dunckley, J. (eds) (1995) *Public Interest Perspectives in Environmental Law* (Chichester: Chancery Law Publications).

Roddick, J. (1994) Second Session of the Commission on Sustainable Development, *Environmental Politics*, **3**(3) 503–11.

Rodgers, C. (1992). In M.R. Grossman and W. Brussaard (eds) *Agrarian Land Law in the Western World* (Wallingford: A.B. International).

Rodgers, C. (ed.) (1996) *Nature Conservation and Countryside Law* (Cardiff: University of Wales Press).

Rodman, J. (1977) The Liberation of Nature? *Inquiry*, **20**, 83–145.

Rodman, J. (1983) Four Forms of Ecological Consciousness Reconsidered. In D. Scherer and T. Attig (eds) *Ethics and the Environment* (Englewood Cliffs, NJ; Prentice-Hall).

Rolston, H. (III) (1986) *Philosophy gone Wild: Essays in Environmental Ethics* (Buffalo NY: Prometheus Books).

Rolston, H. (III) (1994) Value in Nature and the Nature of Value. In R. Attfield and A. Belsey (eds) *Philosophy and the Natural Environment* (Cambridge: Cambridge University Press).

Rose, C. (1985) Possession as the Origin of Property, *University of Chicago Law Review*, **52**, 73.

Rose, C. (1985a) Environmental Faust Succumbs to Temptations of Economic Mephistopholes, Or Value by Any Other Name is Preference, *Michigan Law Review*, **87**, 1361.

Rose, C. (1991) Rethinking Environmental Controls: Management Strategies for Common Resources, *Duke Law Journal*, 1.

Rose, C. (1996) The Comedy of the Commons: Custom, Commerce and Inherently Public Property, *University of Chicago Law Review*, **51**, 711.

Rose-Ackerman S. (1977) Market Models for Water Pollution Control: Their Strengths & Weaknesses, *Public Policy,*, **25**(3), 383–406.

Routley, R. and Routley, V. (1978) Nuclear Energy and Obligations to the Future, *Inquiry*, **21**, 133–79.

Routley, V. (1981) On Karl Marx as an Environmental Hero, *Environmental Ethics*, **3**, 237–44.

Rowan-Robinson J. and Ross, A. (1993) Compensation for Environmental Protection in Britain: A Legislative Lottery, *Journal of Environmental Law*, **5**, 245.

Royal Commission on Environmental Pollution (1989) 13th Report, Genetic Engineering, cmnd 720 (London: HMSO).

Royal Commission on Environmental Pollution(1993) 17th report, Incineration of Waste, cmnd 2181 (London: HMSO).

Royal Commission on Environmental Pollution (1995) Managing Waste: The Duty of Care, cmnd 9675.

Royal Commission on Environmental Pollution (1998) 21st Report, Setting Environmental Standards http://www.rœorg.uk/studies/standardss-chap9.html.

Ryder, R.D. (1989)*Animal Reution: Changing Attitudes Towards Speciesism* (Oxford: Basil Blackwell).

Sagoff, M. (1974) On Preserving the Natural Environment, *Yale Law Review*, **84**, 205–67.

Sagoff, M. (1980) On the Preservation of Species, *Columbia Journal of International Law*, **7**, 33 .

Sagoff, M. (1988) *The Economy of the Earth: Philosophy, Law and Economics* (Cambridge University Press, Cambridge).

Sagoff, M. (1991) Economic Theory and Environmental Law, *Michigan Law Review*, **79**, 1393–419.

Sagoff, M. (1994) Four Dogmas of Environmental Economics, *Environmental Values*, **3**(4) 285–310.

Sale, K. (1994) Mother of All; An Introduction to Bio-Regionalism. In S. Kumar (ed.) *The Schumacher Lectures* (London: Bland and Briggs).

Sands, H. (1988) *Marine Environment in the United Nations Environment Programme* (London: Cassell).

Sands, H. (ed.) (1993) *Greening International Law* (London: Earthscan).

Sands, H. (1996) The European Court of Justice: An Environmental Tribunal Tribunal. In H. Somsen (ed.) *Protecting the European Environment, Enforcing EC Environmental Law* (London: Blackstone Press).

Sandys-Winsch, G. (1984) *Animal Law* (London: Shaw & Sons).

Sax, J. (1993) Property Rights and the Economy of Nature: Understanding Lucas v South Carolina Coastal Council, *Stanford Law Review*, **45**, 1433–455.

Sax, J. (1970) The Public Trust Doctrine in Natural Resources Law: Effective Judicial Implementation, *Michigan Law Review*, **68**, 471.

Schacter, O. and Joyner, C.C. (eds) (1995) *United Nations Legal Order* (Cambridge: Grotius Publications).

Schermers, H.G. and Blokker, N.M. (1995) *International Institutional Law: Unity Within Diversity*, 3rd edn (Dordrecht: M. Nijhoff).

Schmidt, K. (1997) Five Years After Rio: Too Little, Too Slow, *World Watch*, **10**(2) 37–8.

Schnapf D. (1982) State Hazardous Waste Programs under the Federal Resource Conservation & Recovery Act, *Environmental Law*, **12**, 679.

Schoenbaum, T.J. (1992) Agora: Trade and Environment, *American Journal of International Law*, **86**, 700–27.

Schoenbaum, T.J. (1997) International Trade and Protection of the Environment: The Continuing Search for Reconciliation, *American Journal of International Law*, **91**, 268–308.

Schwartzman, S. (1986) *Bankrolling Disasters: International Development Banks and the Global Environment* (San Francisco: Sierra Club).

Schweitzer, A. (1923) in Naish, J. (trans.) *Civilization and Ethics* (London: A&C Black Ltd).

Scott-Henderson, (1951) Cruelty to Wild Animals, Cmnd 8266 (London: HMSO).

Shannuganthan and Warren, L.M (1997) Status of Sustainable Development as a Norm of International Law, *Journal of Environmental Law*, **9**, 221.

Shelton, D. (1991) Human Rights, Environmental Rights and the Right to Environment, *Stanford Journal of International Law*, **28**, 103–38.

Shere, M.E. (1995) The Myth of Meaningful Environmental Risk Assessment, *Harvard Environmental Law Review*, 19(2), 409–92.

Shrader-Frechette, K.S. Ethics and Energy. In T. Regan (ed.) *Earthbound, Introductory Essays in Environmental Ethics* (Illinois: Waveland Press).

Shrader-Frechette, K.S. and McCoy, E.D. (1994) How the Tail Wags the Dog: How Value Judgments Determine Ecological Science, *Environmental Values*, **3**(2) 107–20.

Sikora, R.I. and Barry, B. (eds) (1978) *Obligations to Future Generations* (Philadelphia: Temple University Press).

Simmonds, N.E. (1986) *Central Issues in Jurisprudence: Justice, Laws and Rights* (London: Sweet and Maxwell).

Simmons, I.G. (1991) *Earth, Air and Water: Resources and Environment in the Late 20th Century* (New York: Edward Arnold).

Simmons, I.G. (1993) *Interpreting Nature: Cultural Constructions of the Environment* (London: Routledge).

Simon, J.L. (1996) *The Ultimate Resource*, 2nd edn (Princeton: Princeton University Press).

Simpson A.W.B. (1995) *Leading Cases in the Common Law* (Oxford, Clarendon Press).

Singer, H.W. (1995) An Historical Perspective. In ul Haq, M. et al. (eds) *The UN and the Bretton Woods Institutions: New Challenges for the Twenty-First Century* (Basingstoke: Macmillan).

Singer, H.W. (1995a) *Rethinking Life and Death: the Collapse of our Traditional Ethics* (Oxford: Oxford University Press).

Singer, H.W. (1995b) *Animal Liberation*, 2nd edn (London: Cape).

Sjöberg, H. (1996) The Global Environmental Facility. In J. Werksman (ed.) *Greening International Institutions* (London: Earthscan).

Smart, J.J.C. and Williams, B. (1973) *Utilitarianism For and Against* (Cambridge: Cambridge University Press).

Smith, S. Fiscal Instruments in Environmental Policy, *Fiscal Studies*, 1–20.

Sober, E. (1995) Philosophical Problems for Environmentalism. In R. Elliot *Environmental Ethics* (Oxford: Oxford University Press).

Sohn, L.B. (1973) The Stockholm Declaration on the Human Environment, *Harvard International Law Journal*, **14**, 423.

Somsen, H. (ed.) (1996) *Protecting the European Environment, Enforcing EC Environmental Law* (London: Blackstone Press).

Soper, K. (1995) *What is Nature?* (Oxford: Blackwell).

Spash, C.L. and Simpson, I.A. (1994) Utilitarian and Rights-Based Alternatives for Protecting Sites of Special Scientific Interest, *Journal of Agricultural Economics*, **45**(1) 15–26.

Stark, F.P. (1996) In Extensions of Remarks of Fortney Pete Stark. *Congressional record* [daily ed.] v.142, August 1, 1996: E1452.

Start, R.B. (1995) Economics, Environment & the Limits of Legal Control, *Harvard Environmental Law Review*, 9(1), 1–22.

Steer, A. and Mason, J. (1995) The Role of Multilateral Finance and the Environment: A View From the World Bank, *Indiana Journal of Global Legal Studies*, **3**(1) 35–45.

Sterba, J. (1994) Recreating Anthropocentric and Non-Anthropocentric Environmental Ethics, *Environmental Values*, **3**(3) 229–244.

Sterling, R.W. (1974) *Macropolitics: International Relations in a Global Society* (New York: Alfred A. Knopf).

Stern, Alissa (1992) Control of Toxic Substances: A Proposal to Improve Corporate Compliance with RCRA, *Environmental Law*, **22**, 539.

Stevenson, C.L. (1944) *Ethics and Language* (Oxford: Oxford University Press).

Stewart, R.B. (1983) Controlling Environmental Risks through Economic Incentives, *Columbia Journal of Environmental Law*, **13**, 153.

Stone, C.D. (1972) Should Trees have Standing? Towards Legal Rights for Natural Objects, *Southern California Law Review*, **45**, 450–501.

Stone, C.D. (1985) Should Trees Have Standing? Revisited. How Far Will Law and Morals Reach – A Pluralist Perspective, *Southern California Law Review*, **59**(1) 1–154.

Stone, C.D. (1988) *Earth and Other Ethics* (New York: Harper and Row).

Stone C.D. (1996) *Should Trees Have Standing and Other Essays on Law, Morals, and the Environment* (Dobbs Ferry, NY: Oceana).

Stone, C.D. (1997) Slowing the Loss of Biological Diversity, the Institutional and Ethical Constraints, *Review of European Community and International Environmental Law*, 231–38.

Strohl (1990) Radioactive Waste Management: Ethics, Law and Policy, *Nuclear Law Bulletin*, 10.

Sullivan, G.R. (1997) Ministering Death, *Oxford Journal of Legal Studies*, **17**(1) 123–26.

Sunkin, M., Ong, D. and Wight, R. (1998) *Sourcebook on Environmental Law* (London: Cavendish).

Sylvan, R. (1985) A Critique of Deep Ecology: Part II, *Radical Philosophy*, **41**, 10–23.

Tansley, A.G. (1935) The Use and Abuse of Vegetational Concepts and Terms, *Ecology*, **16**, 284–307.

Tarlock, A.D. (1996) The Futile Search for Environmental Laws Based on Good Science, *International Journal of Biosciences and the Law*, **1**, 9.

Taylor, A.(1992) *Choosing Our Future: A Practical Politics of the Environment* (London: Routledge).

Taylor, G. (1993) *International Organization in the Modern World: the Regional and the Global Process* (London: Pinter).

Taylor, W. (1986) *Respect for Nature: A Theory of Environmental Ethics* (Princeton, NJ: Princeton University Press).

Teubner, G., Farmer, L. and Murphy, D. (eds) (1994) *Environmental Law and Ecological Responsibility* (Chichester: John Wiley).

Thacher, S. (1992) The Role of the United Nations. In A. Hurrell and B. Kingsbury (eds) *The International Politics of the Environment: Actors, Interests and Institutions* (Oxford: Clarendon Press).

Theron, C.L. (1996) What Does the Right to a Decent Environment Mean: A Jurisprudential Overview, LLM thesis, Aberdeen University.

Thompson, H. (1996) Population in Asia/Mainstreaming the Environment: The World Bank Group and the Environment Since the Rio Earth Summit, *Journal of Contemporary Asia*, **26**(4) 547.

Thornton, R.D. (1991) The Endangered Species Act: Searching for Consensus and Predictability: Habitat Conservation Planning under the Endangered Species Act 1973, *Environmental Law*, **21**, 605.

Tietenberg, T.H. (1992) *Environmental and Natural Resource Economics*, 3rd edn (New York: HarperCollins).

Timoshenko, A. and Berman, M. (1996) The United Nations Environment Programme and the United Nations Development Programme. In J. Werksman (ed.) *Greening International Institutions* (London: Earthscan).

Tischler (1977) Rights for Nonhuman Animals, *San Diego Law Review*, **14**, 484–506.

Tolman, C. (1981) Karl Marx, Alienation and the Mastery of Nature, *Environmental Ethics*, **3**, 63–74.

Toynbee, P. (1995) A Spasm Masquerading as a Movement, *The Independent*, 25 January.

Tribe, L.H. (1974) Ways Not to Think About Plastic Trees: New Foundations for Environmental Law, *Yale Law Journal*, **83**, 1315–348.

Tromans, S. (1991) The Difficulties of Enforcing Waste Disposal Licencing Conditions, *Journal of Environmental Law*, 281.

Tromans, S. (1996) Environmental Risk and the Planning System, *Journal of Environmental Law*, **8**(2), 354–68.

Tromans, S. (1996a) High Talk and Low Cunning: Putting Environmental Principles into Legal Practice, *Journal of Planning and Environment Law*, September, 779–96.

Tromans, S. (1997) Companies and the Environment, *New Law Journal*, 147, 1540.

Tuan, Y.-F. (1968) Discrepancies Between Environmental Attitude and Behaviour: Examples from Europe and China, *The Canadian Geographer*, **12**, 176–91.

Tuan, Y.-F. (1974) Topophilia: *A Study of Environmental Perception, Attitudes and Values* (Englewood Cliffs, NJ: Prentice-Hall).

Turner, E.S. (1992) *All Heaven in a Rage*, 2nd edn (Fontwell, Sussex: Centaur Press).

United Nations (1996) Commission on Sustainable Development, Report on the Fourth Session (18 April–3 May 1996) Economic and Social Council Official Records, 1996 Supplement No.8, gopher: //gopher.un.org: 70/00/esc/cn17/1996/96–38.EN.

United Nations (1997a) Earth Summit +5: Special Session of the United Nations General Assembly to Review and Appraise the Implementation of Agenda 21, http://www.un.org/dpcsd/earthsummit/.

United Nations (1997b) The High Level Advisory Board on Sustainable Development, http: //www.un.org/dpcsd/dsd/hlabref.htm.

UNCED (1991) , Poverty and Environmental Degradation. A/Conf 151/PC/45. Geneva.

UNCED (1992) UN Doc. A/CONF 151/26/Rev.1 s. I–III (Rio).

United Nations Conference on the Human Environment, Stockholm (1972) UN Doc. A/CONF 48/14/Rev.1.

Upton, W. and Harwood, R. (1996) The Stunning Powers of Environmental Inspectors, *Journal of Planning and Environmental Law*, 623.

Van Der Veer, D. (1979) Interspecific Justice, *Inquiry*, **22**, 55.

Vincent, A. (1992) *Modern Political Ideologies* (Oxford: Blackwell).

Waldron, J. (1988) *The Right to Private Property* (Oxford: Oxford University Press).

Waldron, J. (ed.) (1984) *Theories of Rights* (Oxford: Oxford University Press).

Walton, W., Ross-Robertson, A. and Rowan-Robinson, J. (1995) The Precautionary Principle and the UK Planning System, *Environmental Law and Management*, Feb, 35–40.

Wapenhans, W. et al. (1992) Report of the Portfolio Management Task Force (internal World Bank document, 1 July 1992) cited by Williams, M. (1995).

Ward, B. and Dubos, R. (1972) Only One Earth: The Care and Maintenance of a Small Planet: an Unofficial Report Commissioned by the Secretary-General of the United Nations Conference on the Human Environment (London: Deutsch).

Warren, K.J. (1990) The Power and Promise of Ecological Feminism, *Environmental Ethics*, **12**(2) 125–46.

Warren, L. (1991) Conservation, a Secondary Environmental Consideration, *Journal of Law and Society*, **18**, 64.

Warren, M.A. (1991) The Rights of the Nonhuman World. In J.E. White (ed.) *Contemporary Moral Problems*, 3rd edn (St. Paul: West Publishing Co.).

Warren, M.A. (1998) *Moral Status* (Oxford: Clarendon Press).

Watson, Paul. (1995) The Cult of Animal Celebrity, *Animal People*, June 1995. Available at http: //envirolink.org/arrs/essays/celebrity_cult.html.

Watson, R.A. (1979) Self-Consciousness and the Rights of Nonhuman Animals and Nature, *Environmental Ethics*, **1**, 99–129.

Weiss, E. (1992) Agora: Environment and Trade as Partners in Sustainable Development, *American Journal of International Law*, **86**, 728.

Weiss, E. (1993) International Environmental Law: Contemporary Issues and the Emergence of a New World Order, *Georgetown Law Journal*, **81**, 675.

Weiss, E. (ed.) (1993) *Environmental Change and International Law: New Challenges and Dimensions* (Tokyo: UN University Press).

Weiss, E. (1990) International Environmental Law, *American Journal of International Law*, **84**(1), 330–31.

Weiss, E. (1984) The Planetary Trust: Conservation and Intergenerational Equity, *Ecology Law Quarterly*, **11**, 495–581.

Weiss, E. (1989) *In Fairness to Future Generations: International Law, Common Patrimony and Future Generations* (Dobbs Ferry NY: Transnational Publishers).

Weiss, E. (1990) Our Rights and Obligations to Future Generations for the Environment, *American Journal of International Law*, **84**, 198–207.

Wenz, S. (1988) *Environmental Justice* (New York: State University of New York Press).

Werksman, J.D. (1996) *Greening Environmental Institutions* (London: Earthscan).

Westra, L. and Lemons, J. (eds) (1995) *Perspectives on Ecological* (Dordreht: Kluwer).

White, L., Jr. (1967) The Historical Roots of our Ecologic Crisis, *Science*, **155**, 1203–207.

Willetts (ed.) (1982) *Pressure Groups in the Global System: the Transnational Relations of Issue-Orientated Non-Governmental Organizations* (London: Frances Pinter).

Williams, B. (1972) *Morality: An Introduction to Ethics* (Cambridge: Cambridge University Press).

Williams, M. (1995) Role of the Multilateral Agencies after the Earth Summit. In ul Haq, M. et al. (eds) *The UN and the Bretton Woods Institutions: New Challenges for the 21st Century* (Basingstoke: Macmillan).

Wilson, E.O. (1975) *Sociobiology: the New Synthesis* (London: Harvard University Press).

Wilson, E.O. (1992) *The Diversity of Life* (London/New York: Penguin).

Winpenny, J.T. (1991) *Values for the Environment: A Guide to Economic Appraisal* (London: HMSO).

Winter (1989) Perspectives on Environmental Law: Entering the Fourth Phase, *Journal of Environmental Law*, **1**, 38.

Wolf, S. and White, A. (1997) *Environmental Law*, 2nd edn (London: Cavendish Publishing).

Wong, D.B. (1984) *Moral Relativity* (Berkeley: University of California Press).

Wong, D.B. (1993) Relativism. In Singer (ed.) *A Companion to Ethics* (Oxford: Blackwell).

Wood, A. (1993) Marx against Morality. In Singer (ed.) *A Companion to Ethics* (Oxford: Blackwell).

Woolf, Sir H. (1992) Are the Judiciary Environmentally Myopic? *Journal of Environmental Law*, **4**, 1.

Worster, D. (1994) *Nature's Economy: A History of Ecological Ideas*, 2nd edn (Cambridge: Cambridge University Press).

Young, D. (1997) The International Dolphin Conservation Program Act. Remarks in the House. *Congressional Record* [daily ed.] v.143, May 21, 1997: H3121.

Young, J. (1990) *Post Environmentalism* (London: Belhaven Press).

Index